# Chapter 7



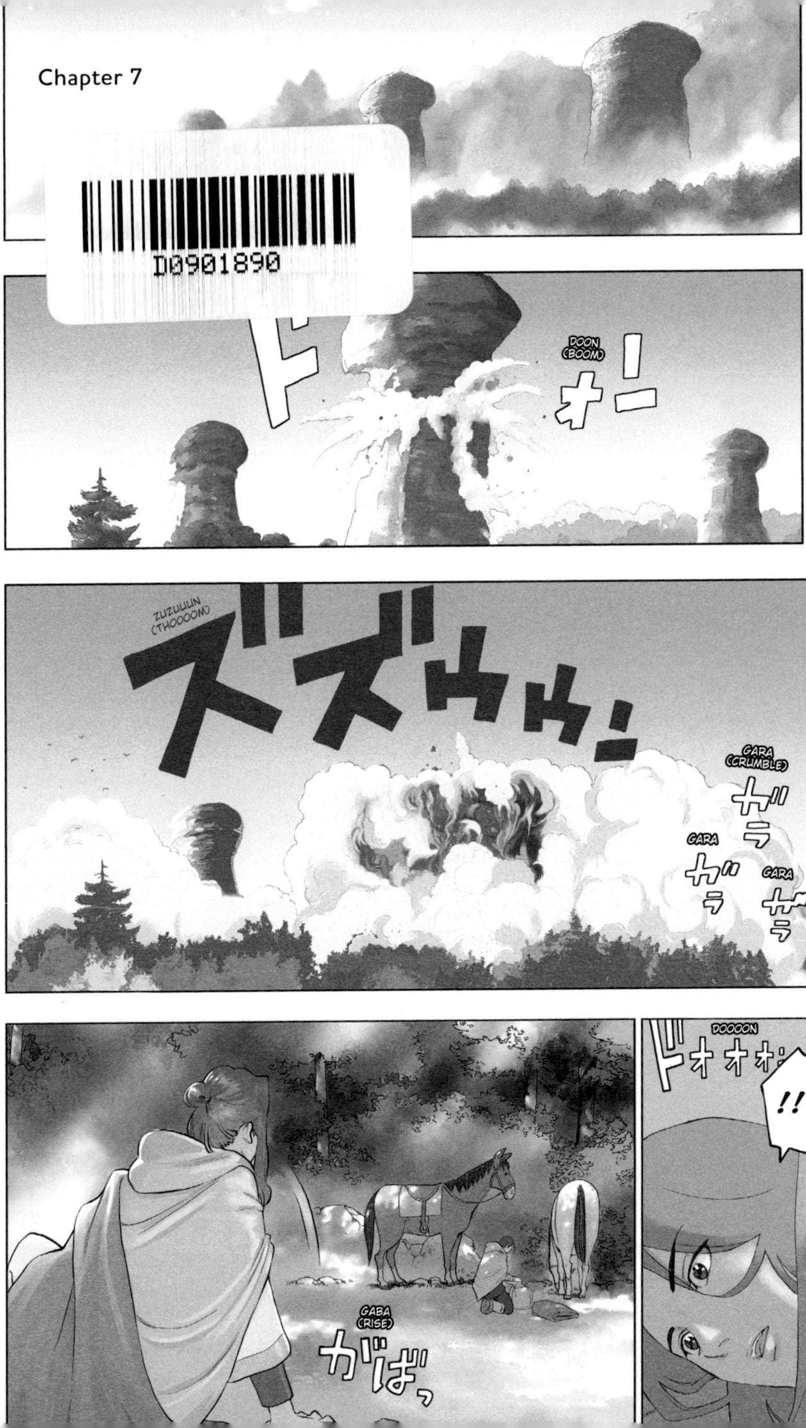
DOON (BOOM)
ドォーン
ZUZUUUN (THOOOOM)
ズズゥゥン
GARA (CRUMBLE)
ガラ
GARA
ガラ
GARA
ガラ
DOOOON
ドォオオォン
!!?
GABA (RISE)
がばっ

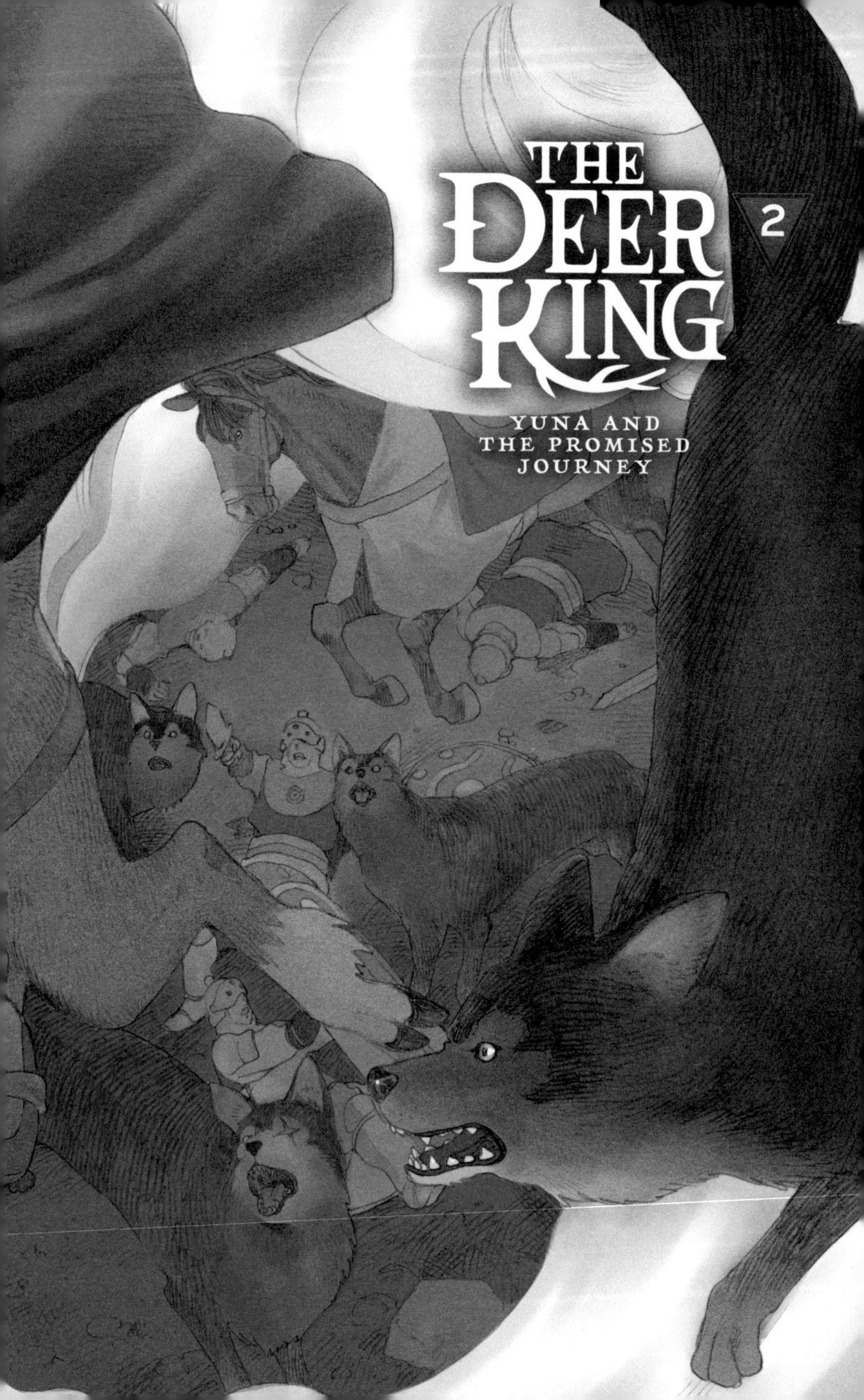
THE DEER KING
2
YUNA AND THE PROMISED JOURNEY

Art: **Taro Sekiguchi**

Original Story: **Nahoko Uehashi**

Adaptation: *The Deer King* Production Committee

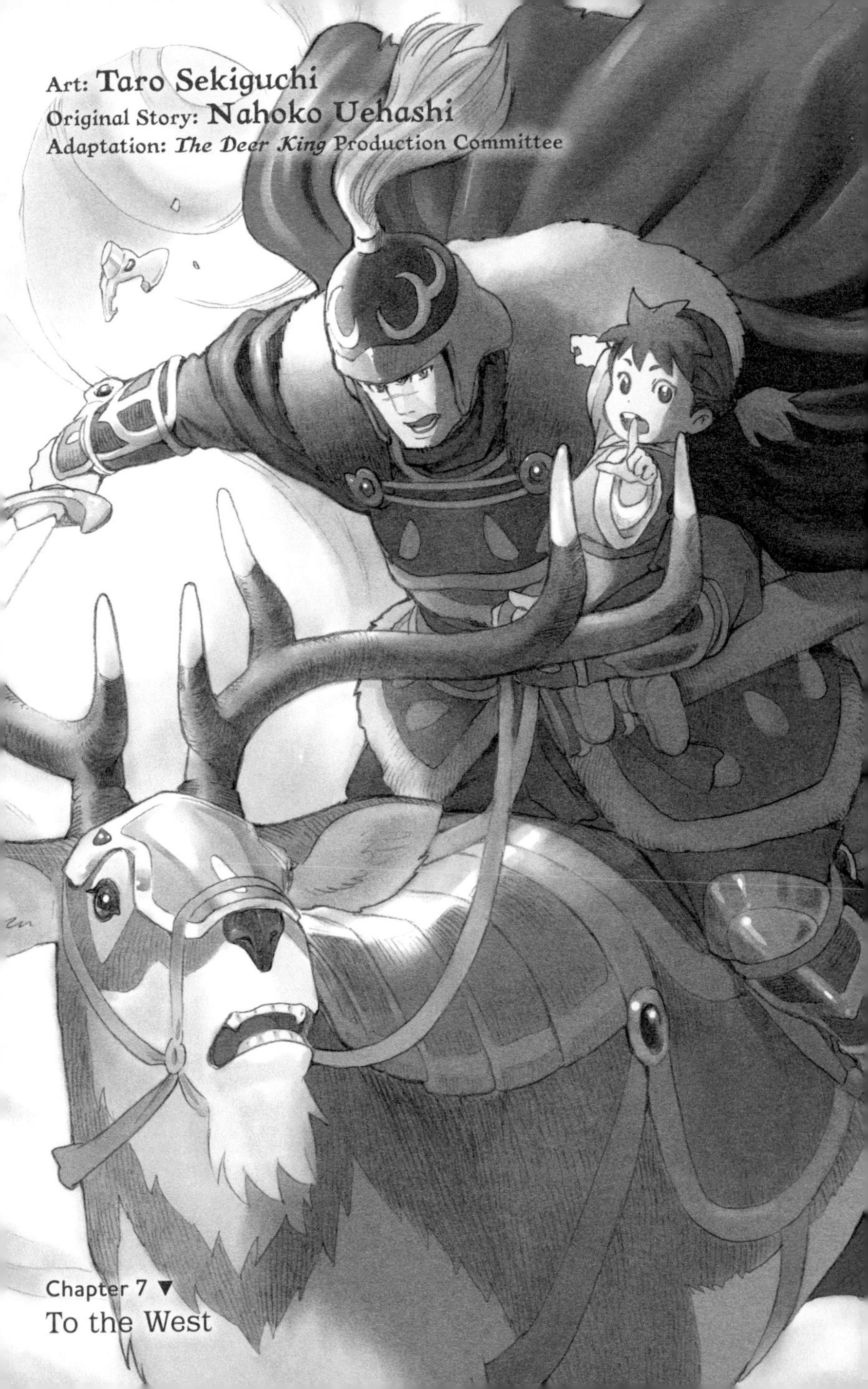

## Chapter 7 ▼ To the West

# THE DEER KING

YUNA AND THE PROMISED JOURNEY

## Table of Contents

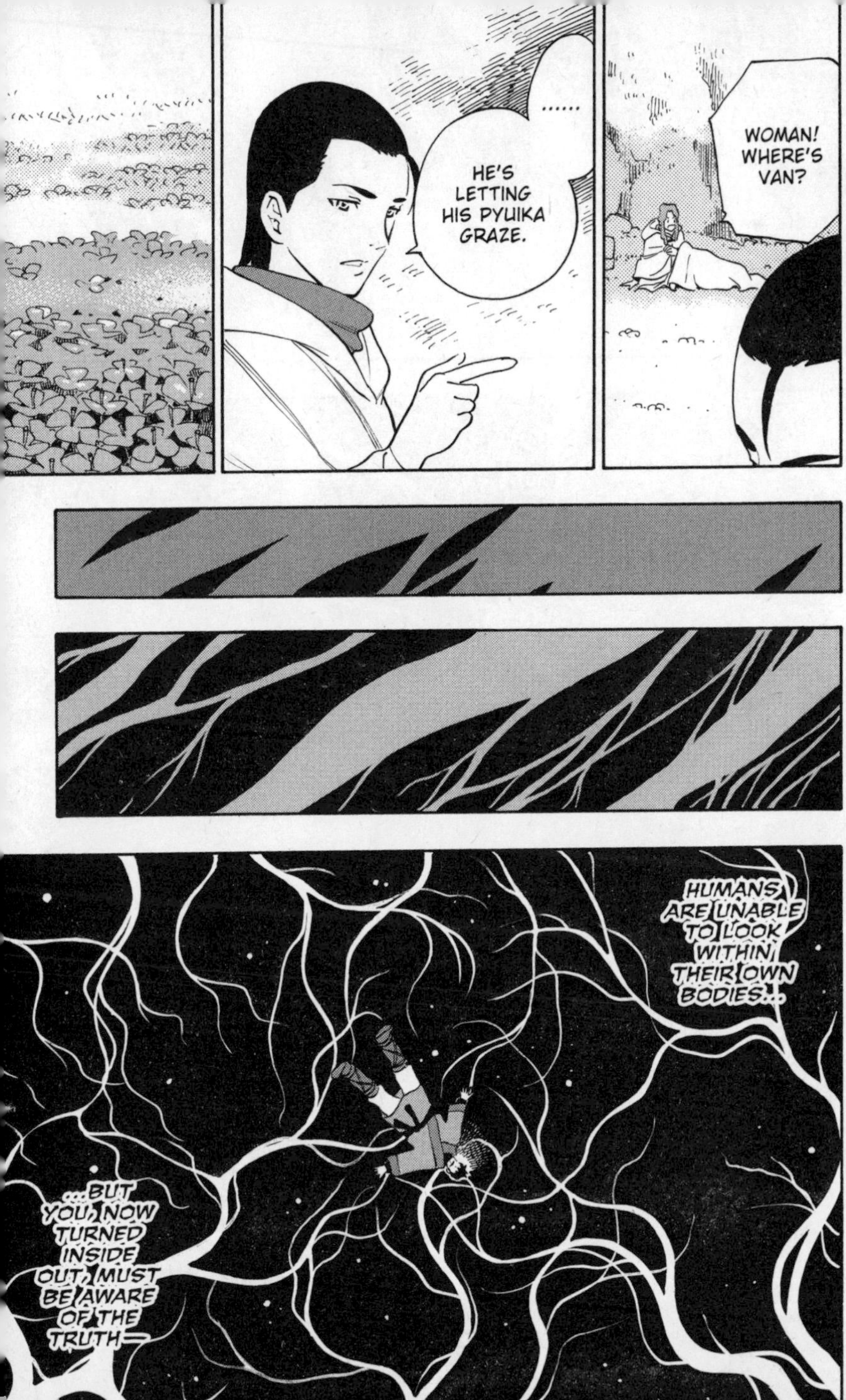
WOMAN! WHERE'S VAN?
......
HE'S LETTING HIS PYUIKA GRAZE.
HUMANS ARE UNABLE TO LOOK WITHIN THEIR OWN BODIES...
...BUT YOU, NOW TURNED INSIDE OUT, MUST BE AWARE OF THE TRUTH—

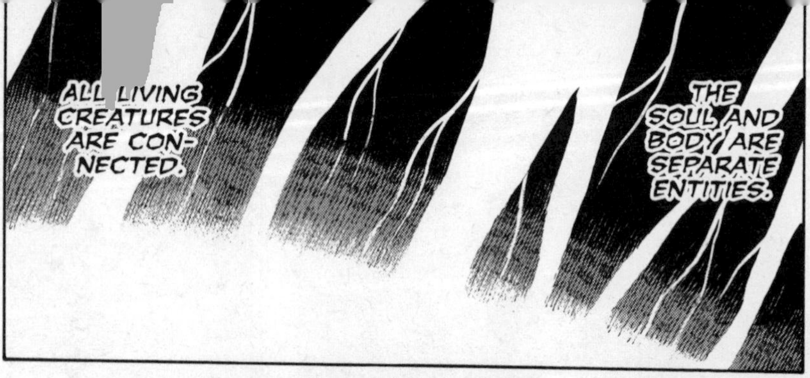
THE SOUL AND BODY ARE SEPARATE ENTITIES.
ALL LIVING CREATURES ARE CON-NECTED.
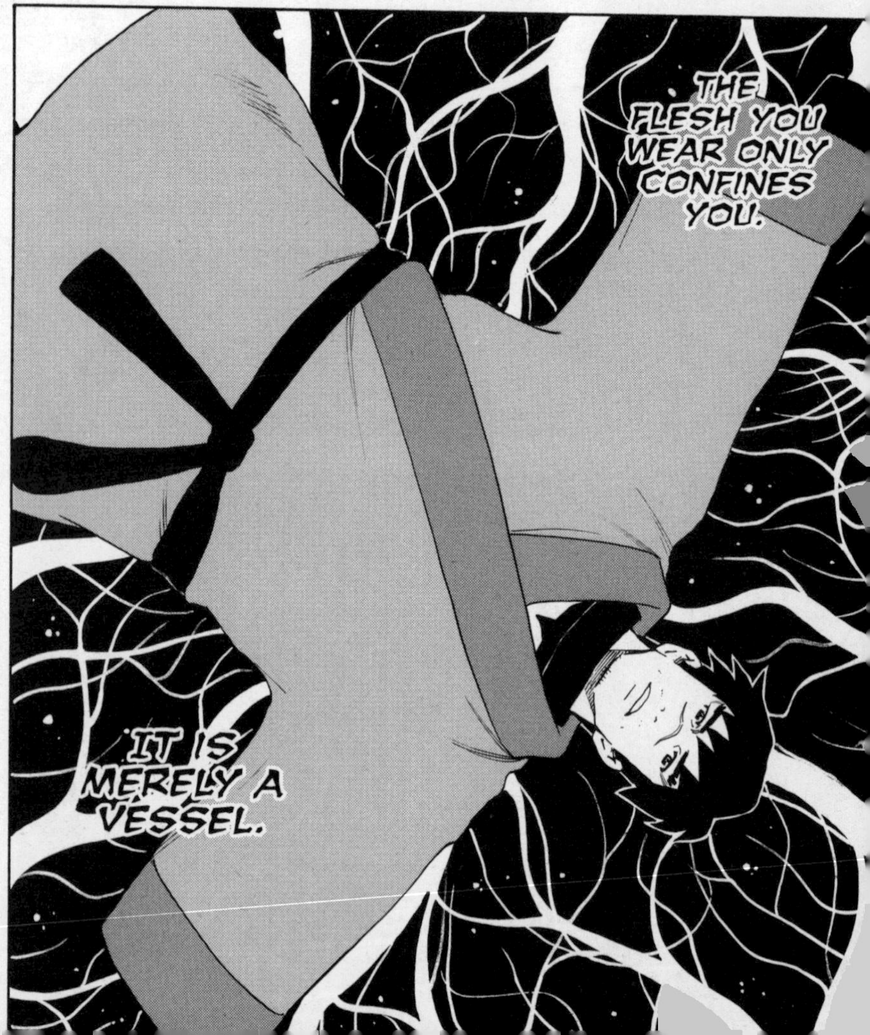
THE FLESH YOU WEAR ONLY CONFINES YOU.
IT IS MERELY A VESSEL.

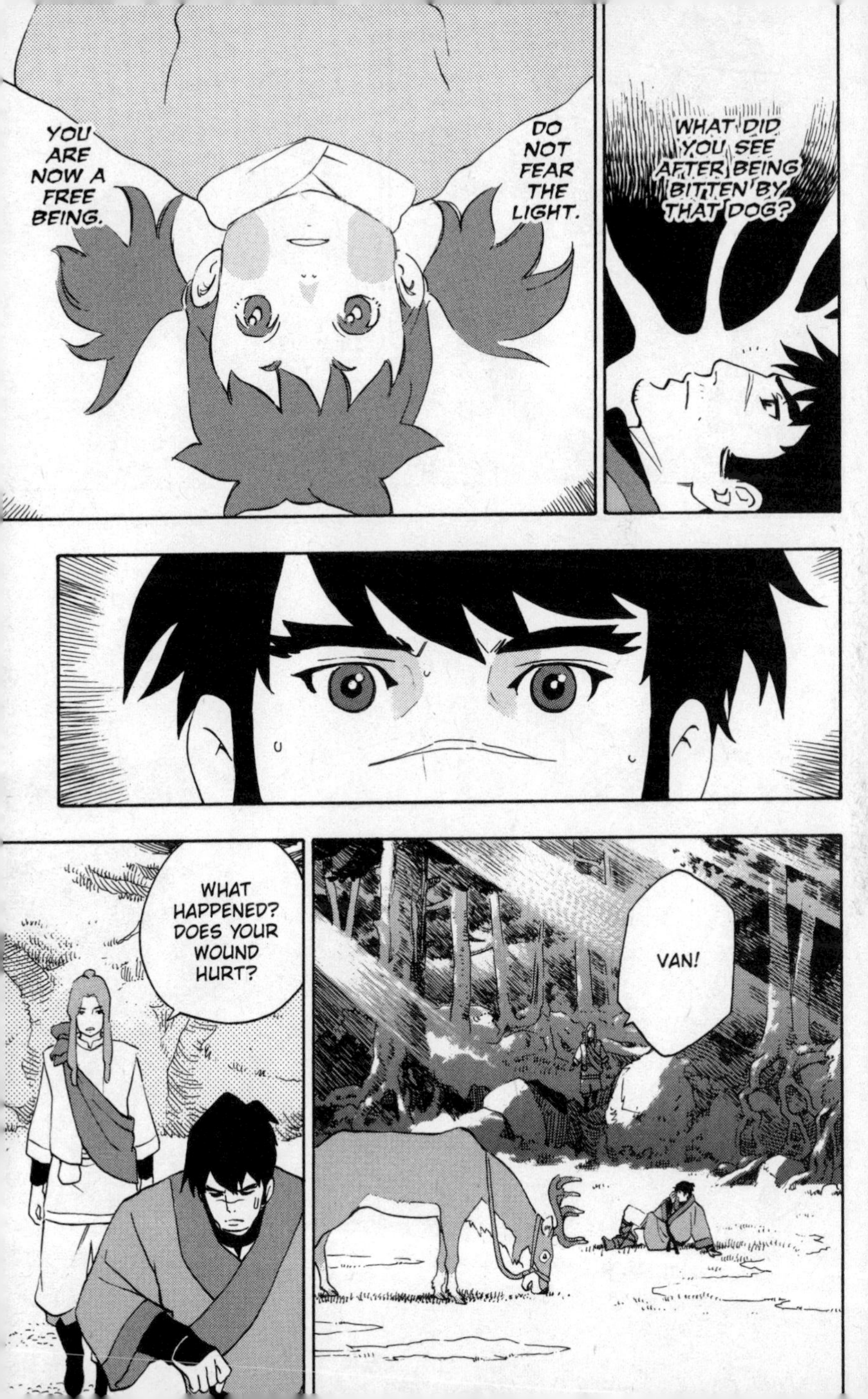
WHAT DID YOU SEE AFTER BEING BITTEN BY THAT DOG?
DO NOT FEAR THE LIGHT.
YOU ARE NOW A FREE BEING.
VAN!
WHAT HAPPENED? DOES YOUR WOUND HURT?

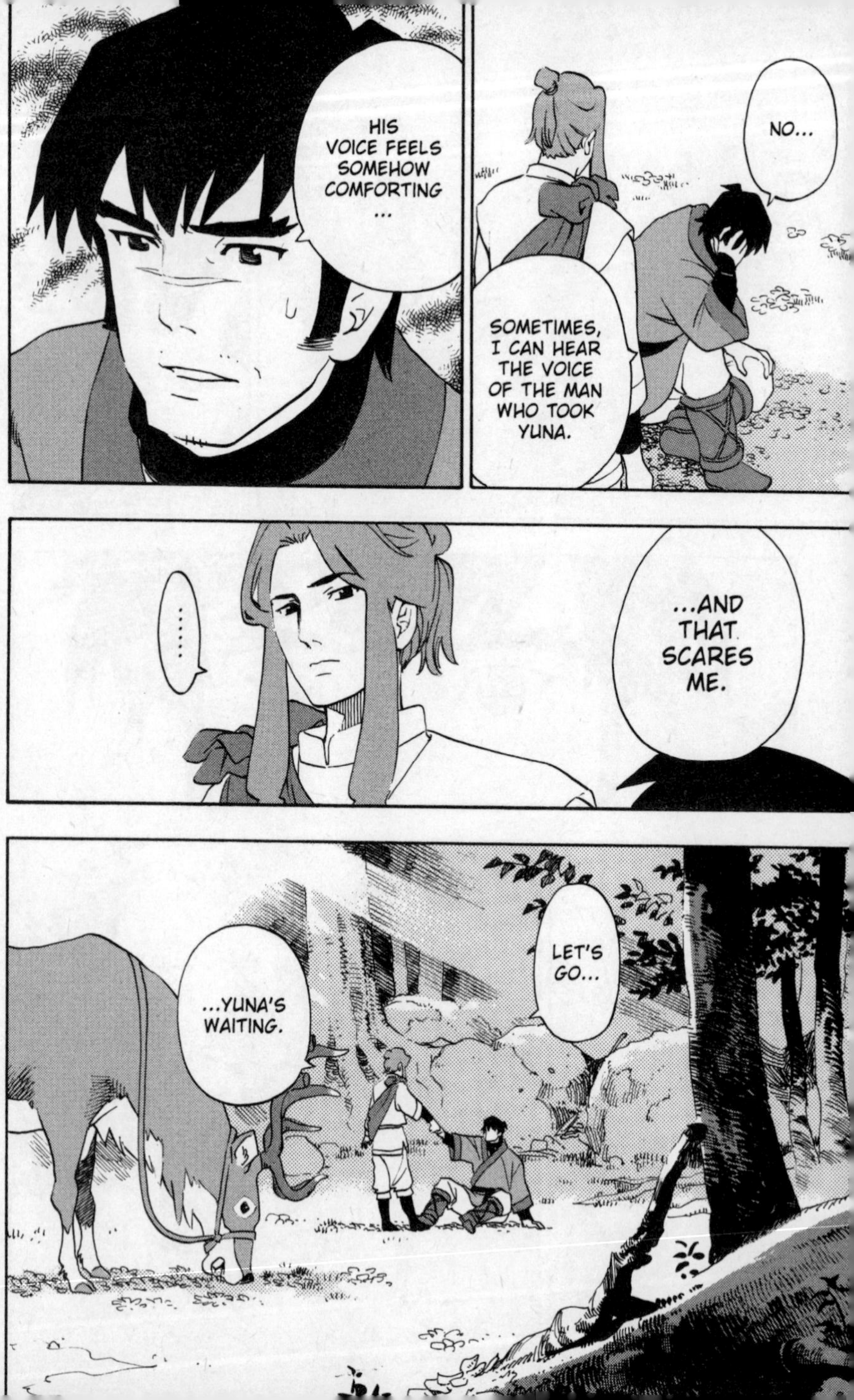
NO...
SOMETIMES, I CAN HEAR THE VOICE OF THE MAN WHO TOOK YUNA.
HIS VOICE FEELS SOMEHOW COMFORTING ...
...AND THAT SCARES ME.
......
LET'S GO...
...YUNA'S WAITING.

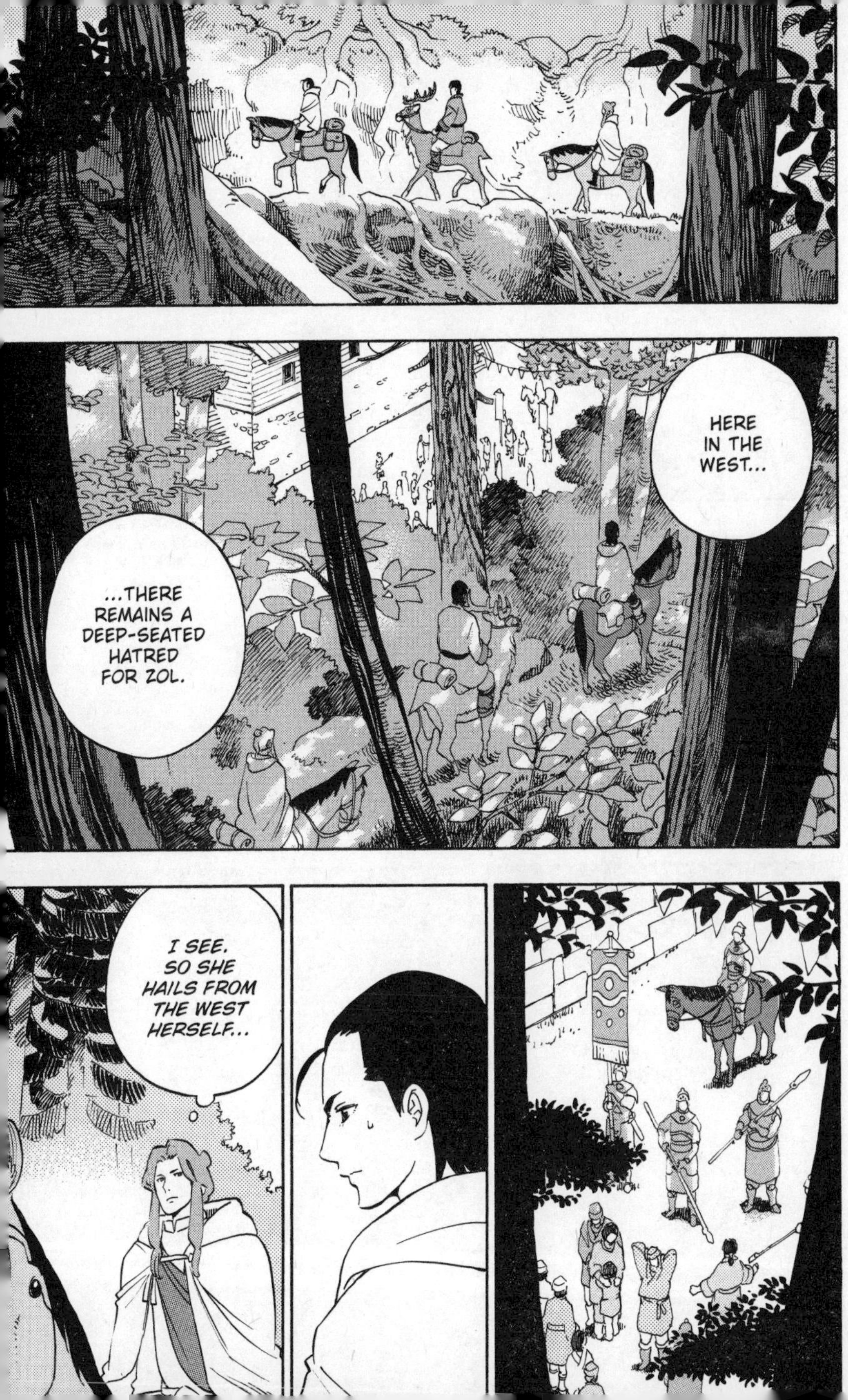
HERE IN THE WEST...
...THERE REMAINS A DEEP-SEATED HATRED FOR ZOL.
I SEE. SO SHE HAILS FROM THE WEST HERSELF...

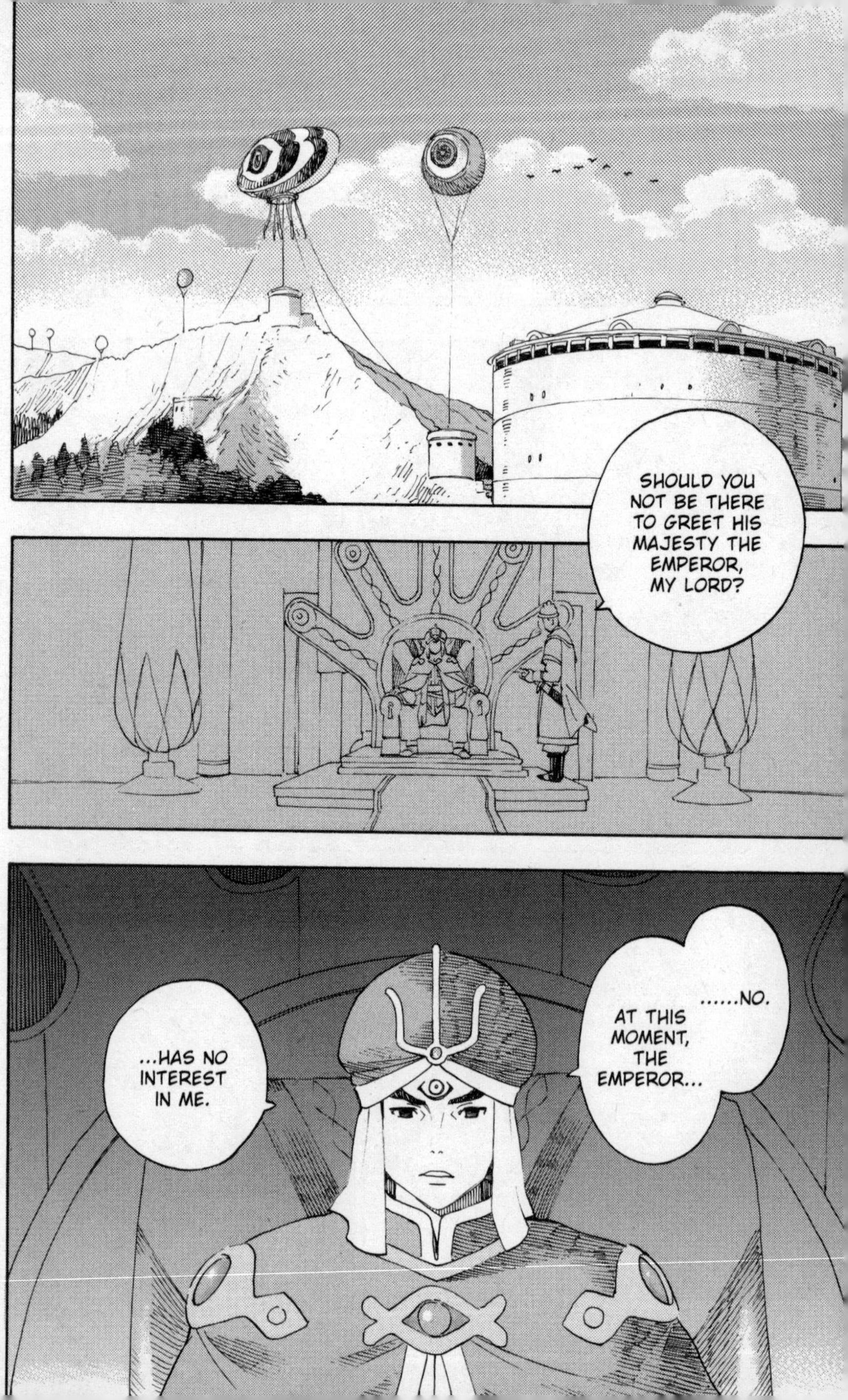
SHOULD YOU NOT BE THERE TO GREET HIS MAJESTY THE EMPEROR, MY LORD?
......NO.
AT THIS MOMENT, THE EMPEROR...
...HAS NO INTEREST IN ME.

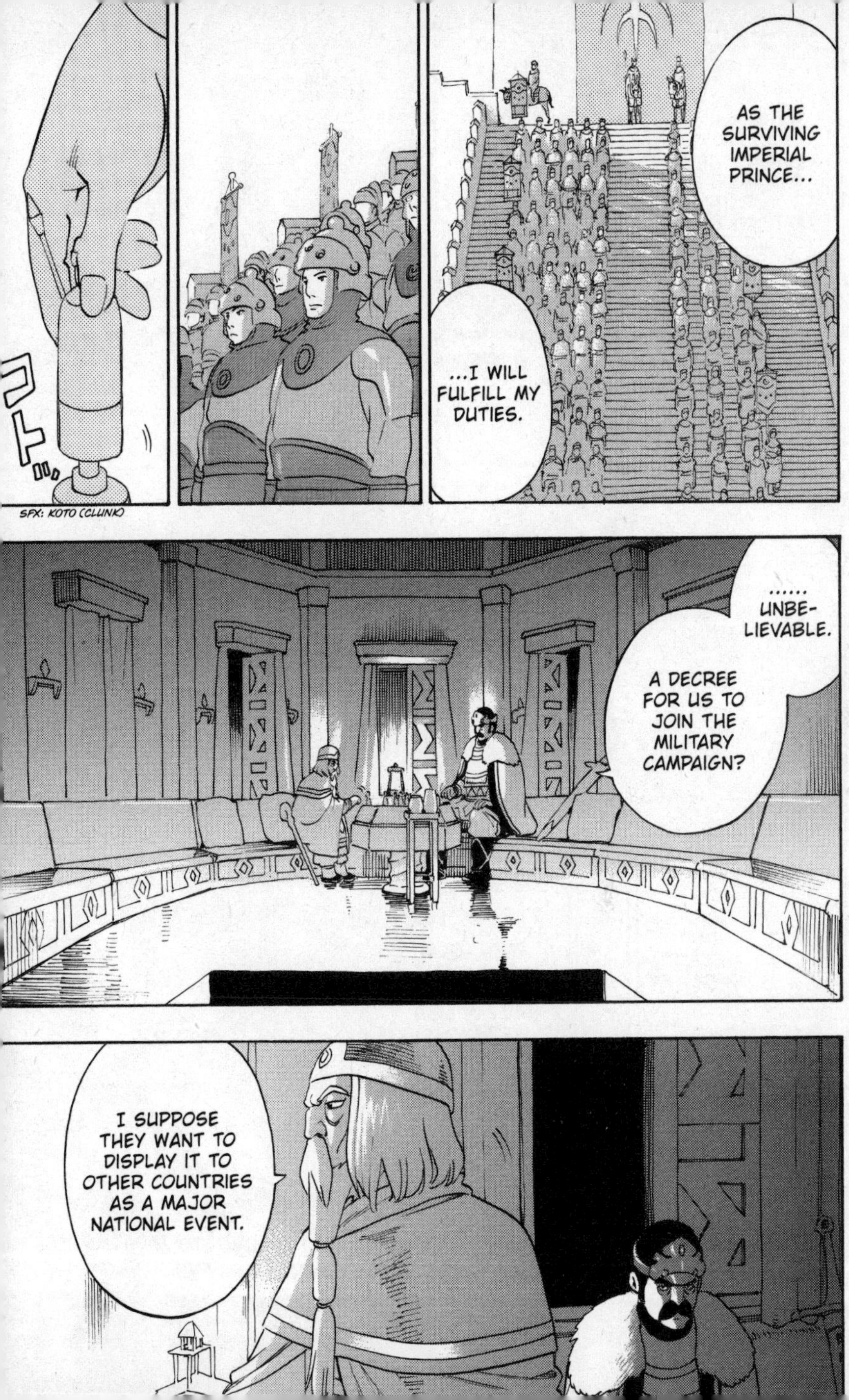
AS THE SURVIVING IMPERIAL PRINCE...
...I WILL FULFILL MY DUTIES.
SFX: KOTO (CLUNK)
...... UNBE-LIEVABLE.
A DECREE FOR US TO JOIN THE MILITARY CAMPAIGN?
I SUPPOSE THEY WANT TO DISPLAY IT TO OTHER COUNTRIES AS A MAJOR NATIONAL EVENT.

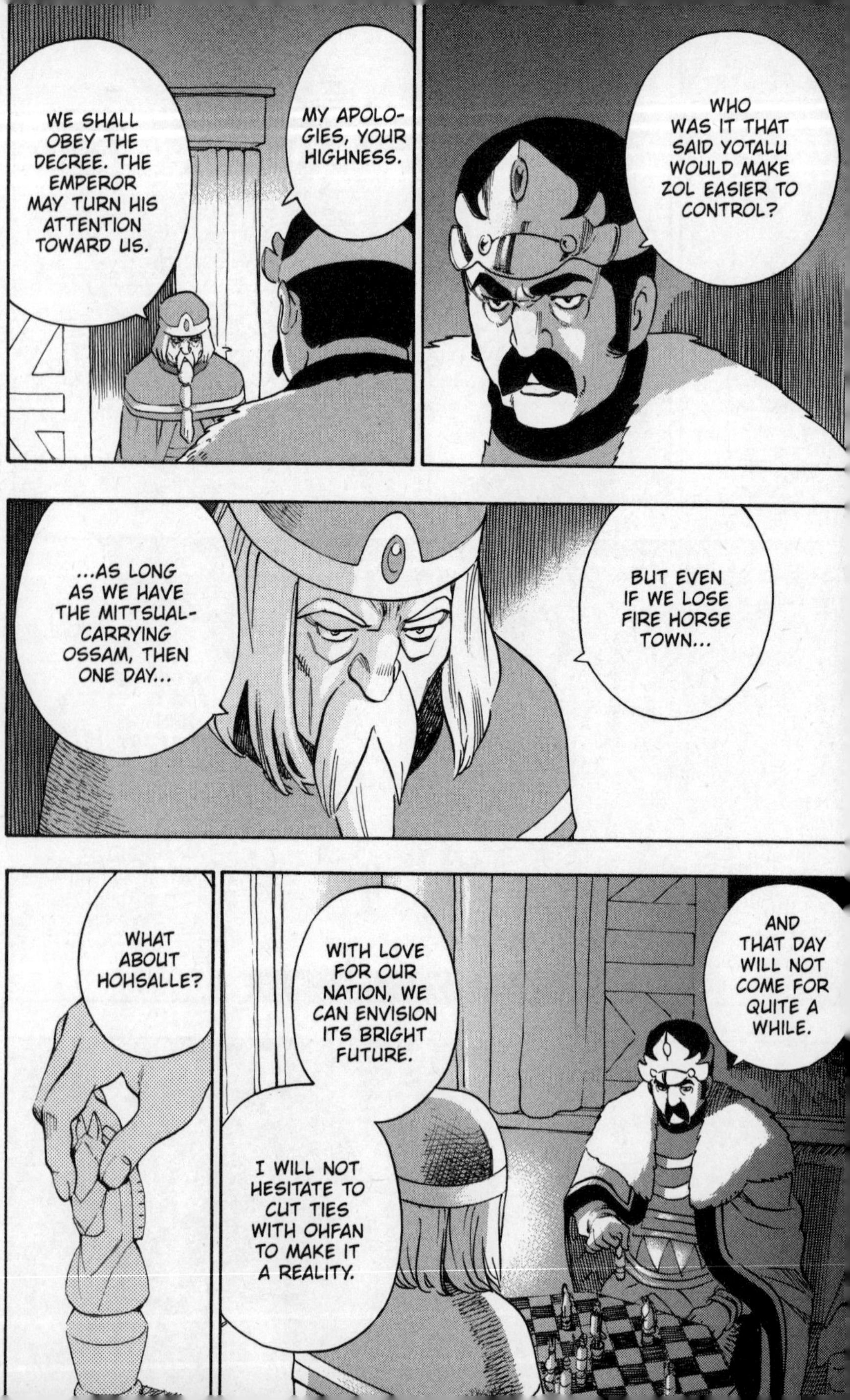
WHO WAS IT THAT SAID YOTALU WOULD MAKE ZOL EASIER TO CONTROL?
MY APOLO-GIES, YOUR HIGHNESS.
WE SHALL OBEY THE DECREE. THE EMPEROR MAY TURN HIS ATTENTION TOWARD US.
BUT EVEN IF WE LOSE FIRE HORSE TOWN...
...AS LONG AS WE HAVE THE MITTSUAL-CARRYING OSSAM, THEN ONE DAY...
AND THAT DAY WILL NOT COME FOR QUITE A WHILE.
WITH LOVE FOR OUR NATION, WE CAN ENVISION ITS BRIGHT FUTURE.
I WILL NOT HESITATE TO CUT TIES WITH OHFAN TO MAKE IT A REALITY.
WHAT ABOUT HOHSALLE?

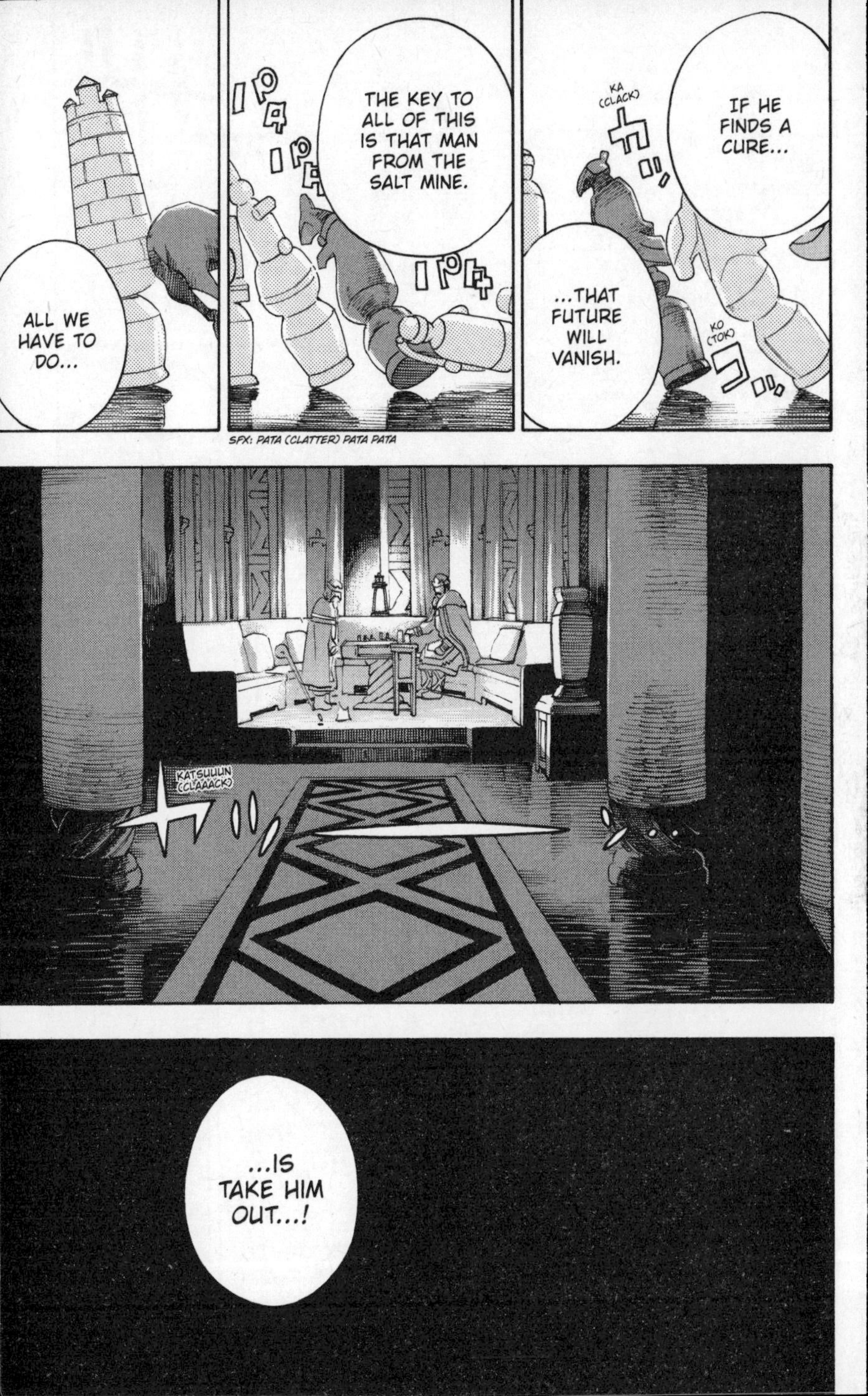
IF HE FINDS A CURE...
KA (CLACK)
...THAT FUTURE WILL VANISH.
KO (TOK)
THE KEY TO ALL OF THIS IS THAT MAN FROM THE SALT MINE.
ALL WE HAVE TO DO...
SFX: PATA (CLATTER) PATA PATA
KATSUUUN (CLAAACK)
...IS TAKE HIM OUT...!

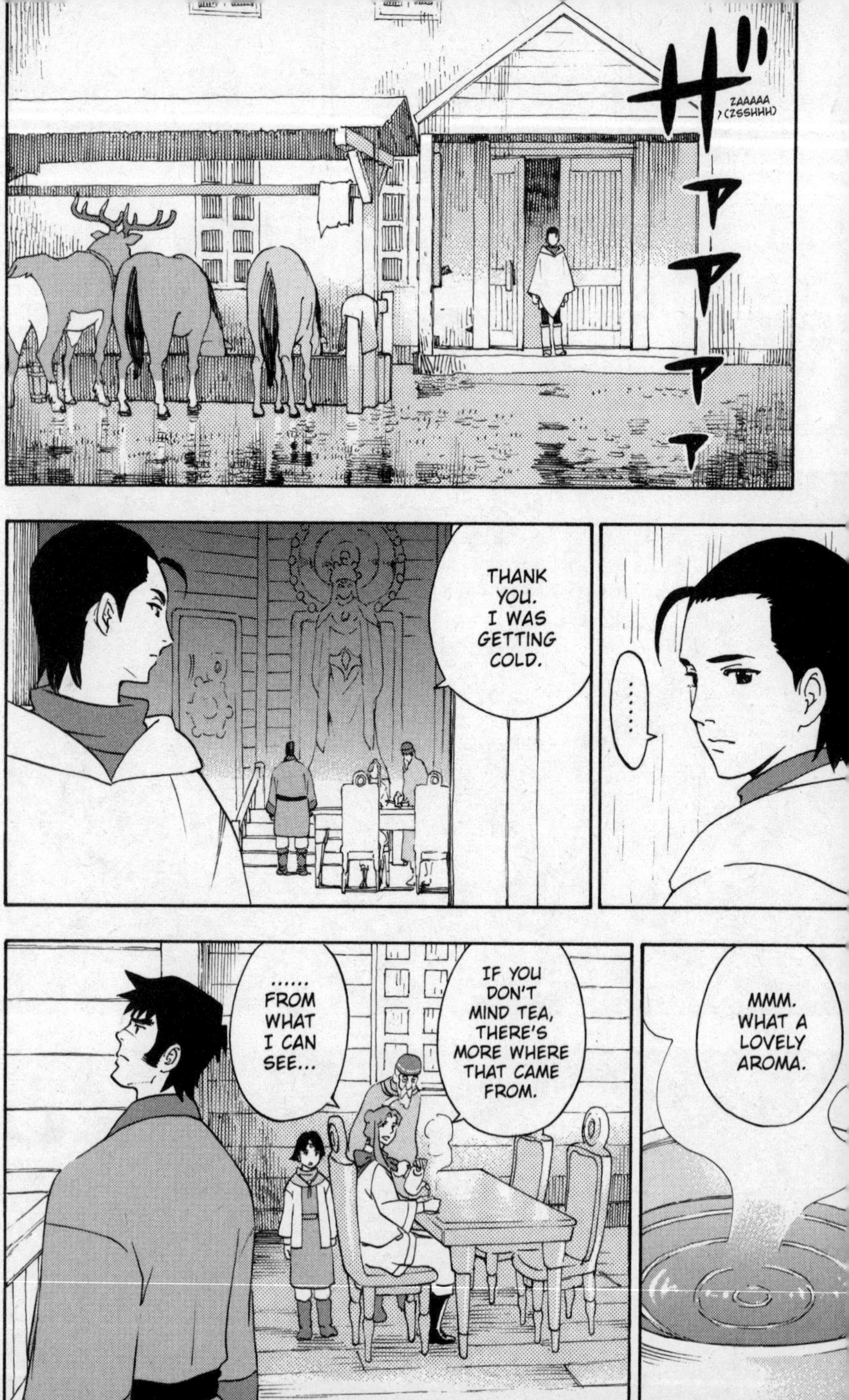
ザァァァァ
ZAAAAA (ZSSHHH)
……
THANK YOU. I WAS GETTING COLD.
MMM. WHAT A LOVELY AROMA.
IF YOU DON'T MIND TEA, THERE'S MORE WHERE THAT CAME FROM.
...... FROM WHAT I CAN SEE...

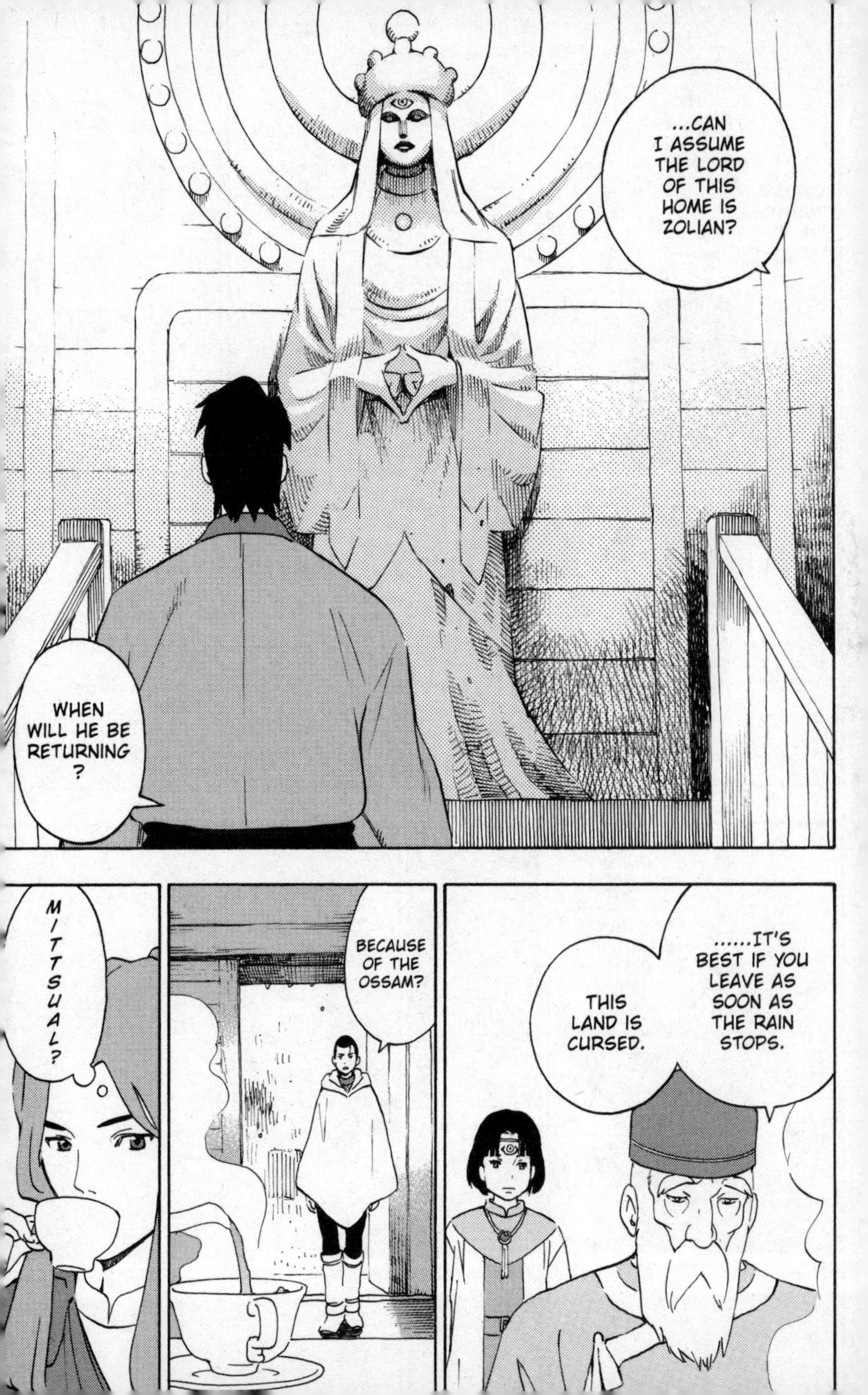
...CAN I ASSUME THE LORD OF THIS HOME IS ZOLIAN?
WHEN WILL HE BE RETURNING ?
......IT'S BEST IF YOU LEAVE AS SOON AS THE RAIN STOPS.
THIS LAND IS CURSED.
BECAUSE OF THE OSSAM?
MITTSUAL?

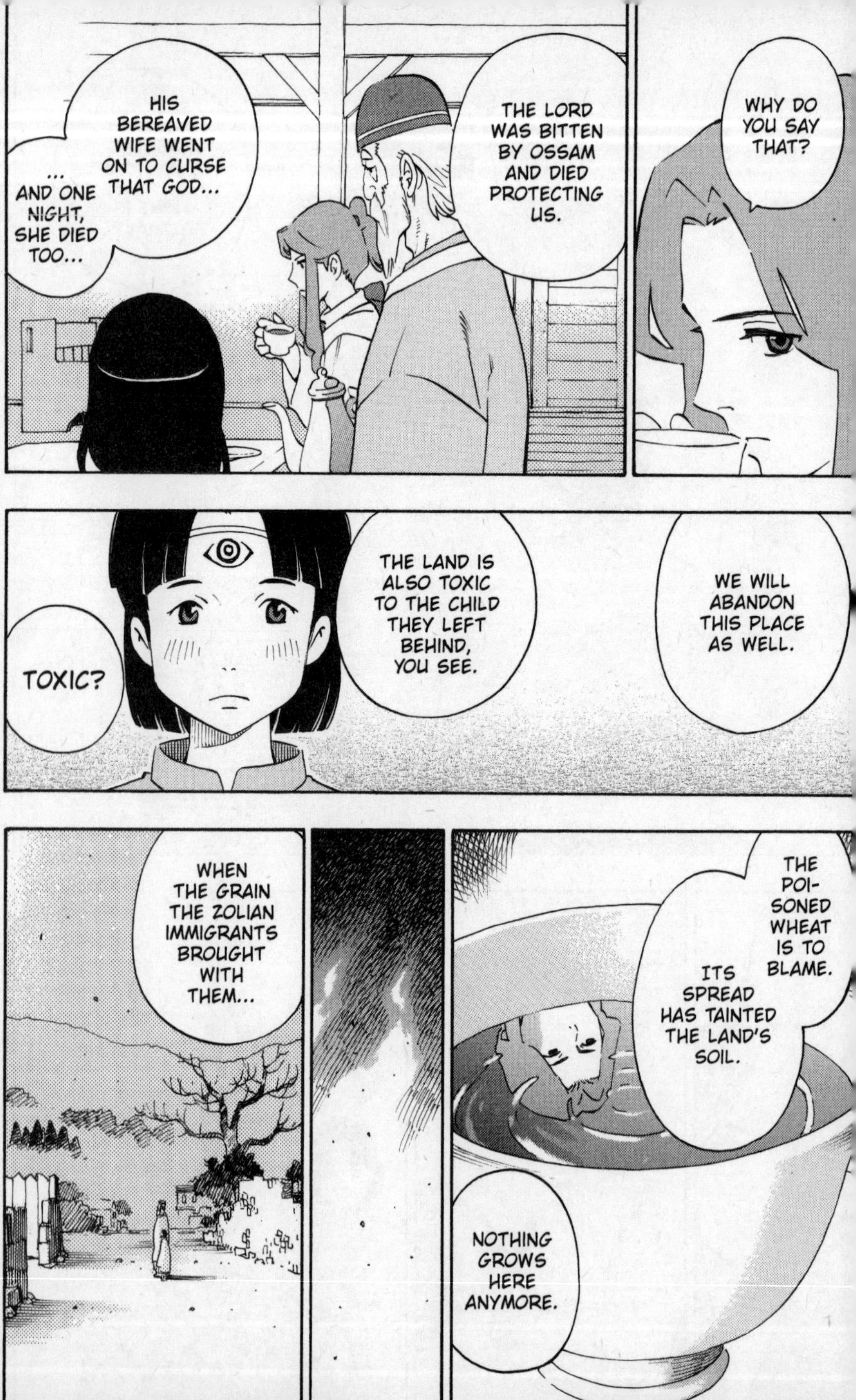
WHY DO YOU SAY THAT?
THE LORD WAS BITTEN BY OSSAM AND DIED PROTECTING US.
HIS BEREAVED WIFE WENT ON TO CURSE THAT GOD...
... AND ONE NIGHT, SHE DIED TOO...
WE WILL ABANDON THIS PLACE AS WELL.
THE LAND IS ALSO TOXIC TO THE CHILD THEY LEFT BEHIND, YOU SEE.
TOXIC?
THE POI-SONED WHEAT IS TO BLAME.
ITS SPREAD HAS TAINTED THE LAND'S SOIL.
NOTHING GROWS HERE ANYMORE.
WHEN THE GRAIN THE ZOLIAN IMMIGRANTS BROUGHT WITH THEM...

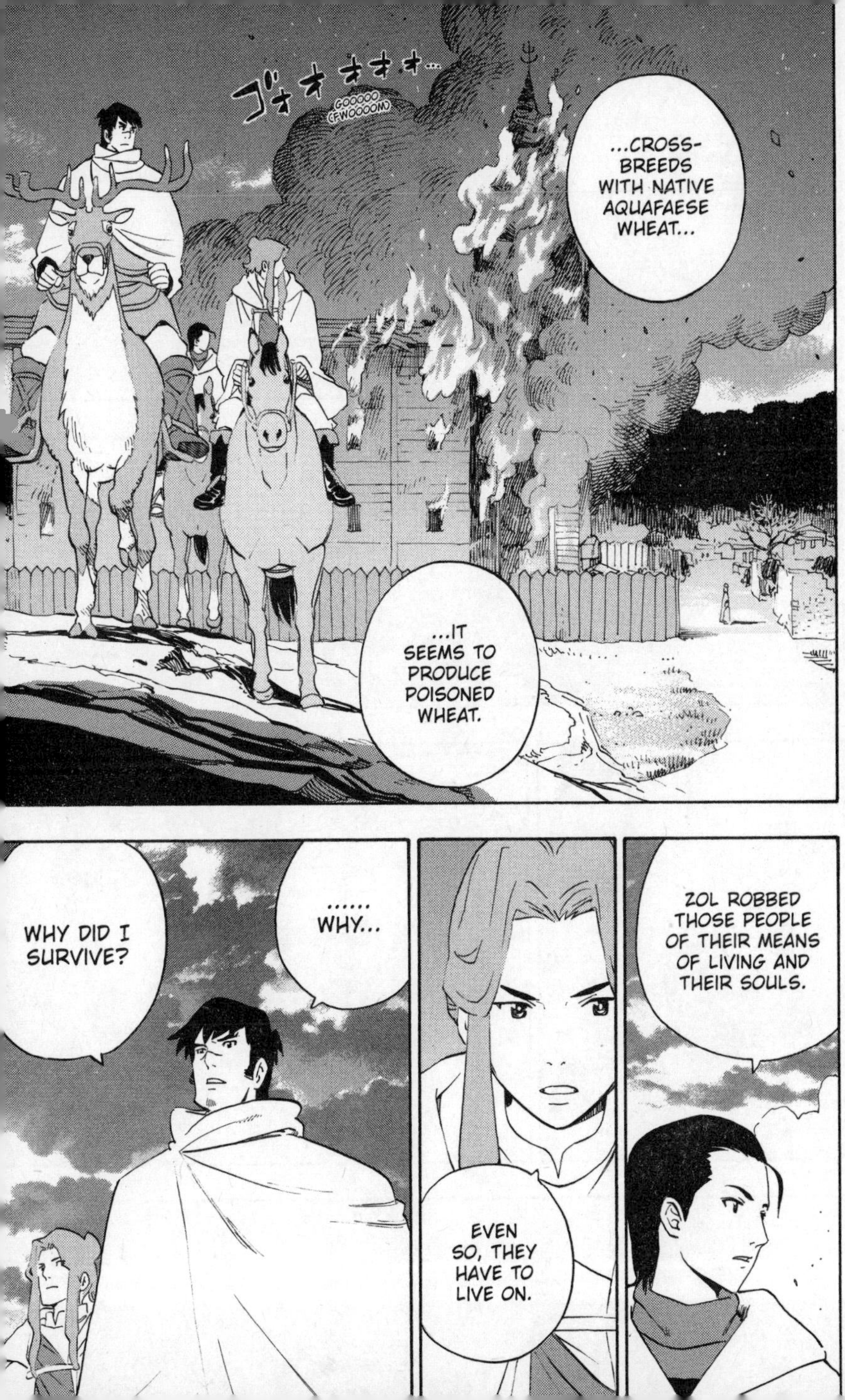
ゴォオオオ…
GOOOOO (FWOOOOM)
...CROSS-BREEDS WITH NATIVE AQUAFAESE WHEAT...
...IT SEEMS TO PRODUCE POISONED WHEAT.
ZOL ROBBED THOSE PEOPLE OF THEIR MEANS OF LIVING AND THEIR SOULS.
EVEN SO, THEY HAVE TO LIVE ON.
...... WHY...
WHY DID I SURVIVE?

...KILLS ZOLIANS, BUT NOT AQUAFAESE.

MITTSUAL...

......

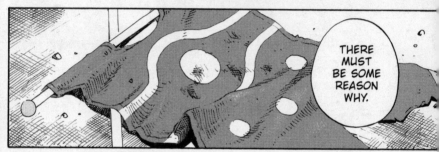

THERE MUST BE SOME REASON WHY.

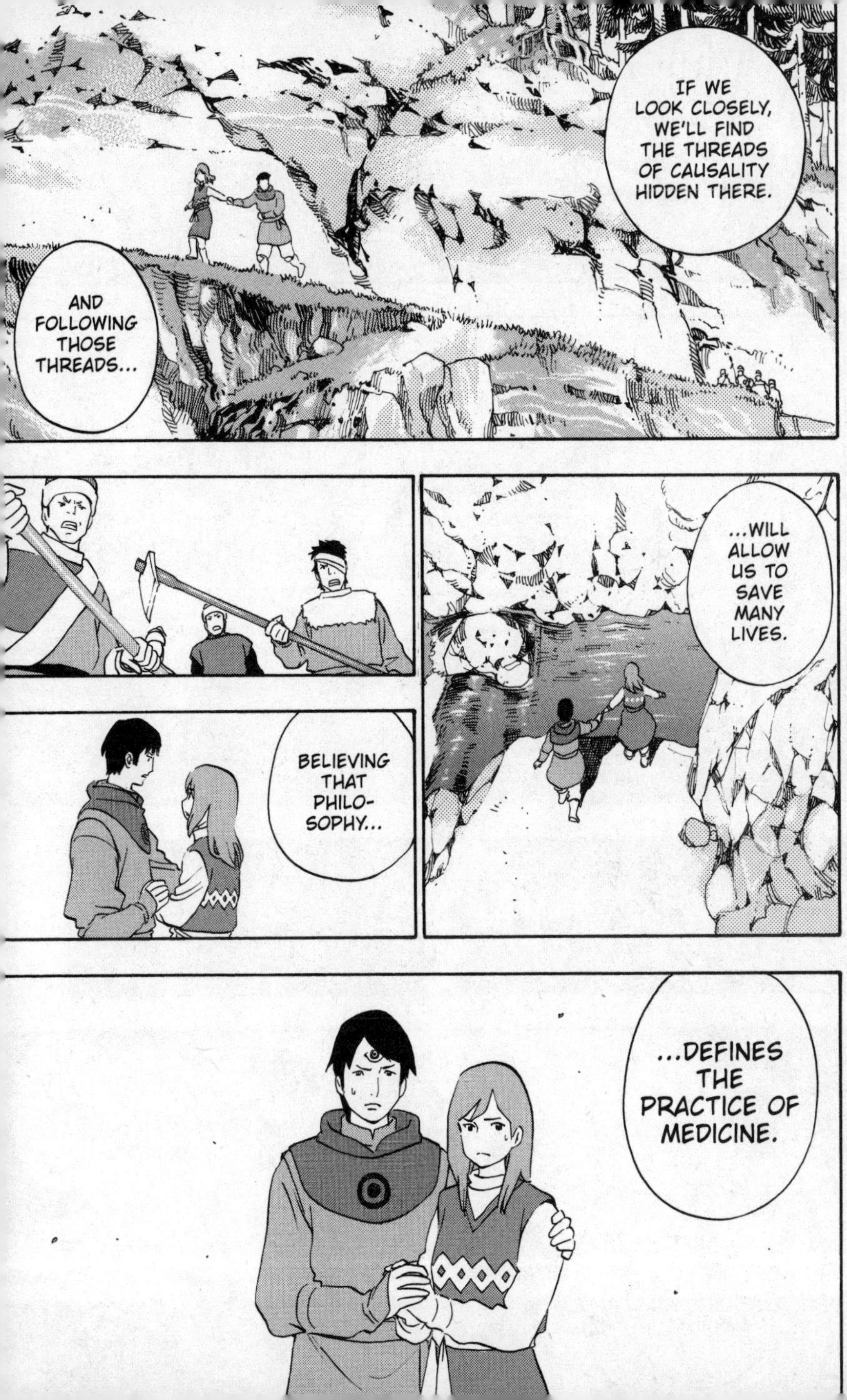
IF WE LOOK CLOSELY, WE'LL FIND THE THREADS OF CAUSALITY HIDDEN THERE.
AND FOLLOWING THOSE THREADS...
...WILL ALLOW US TO SAVE MANY LIVES.
BELIEVING THAT PHILO-SOPHY...
...DEFINES THE PRACTICE OF MEDICINE.

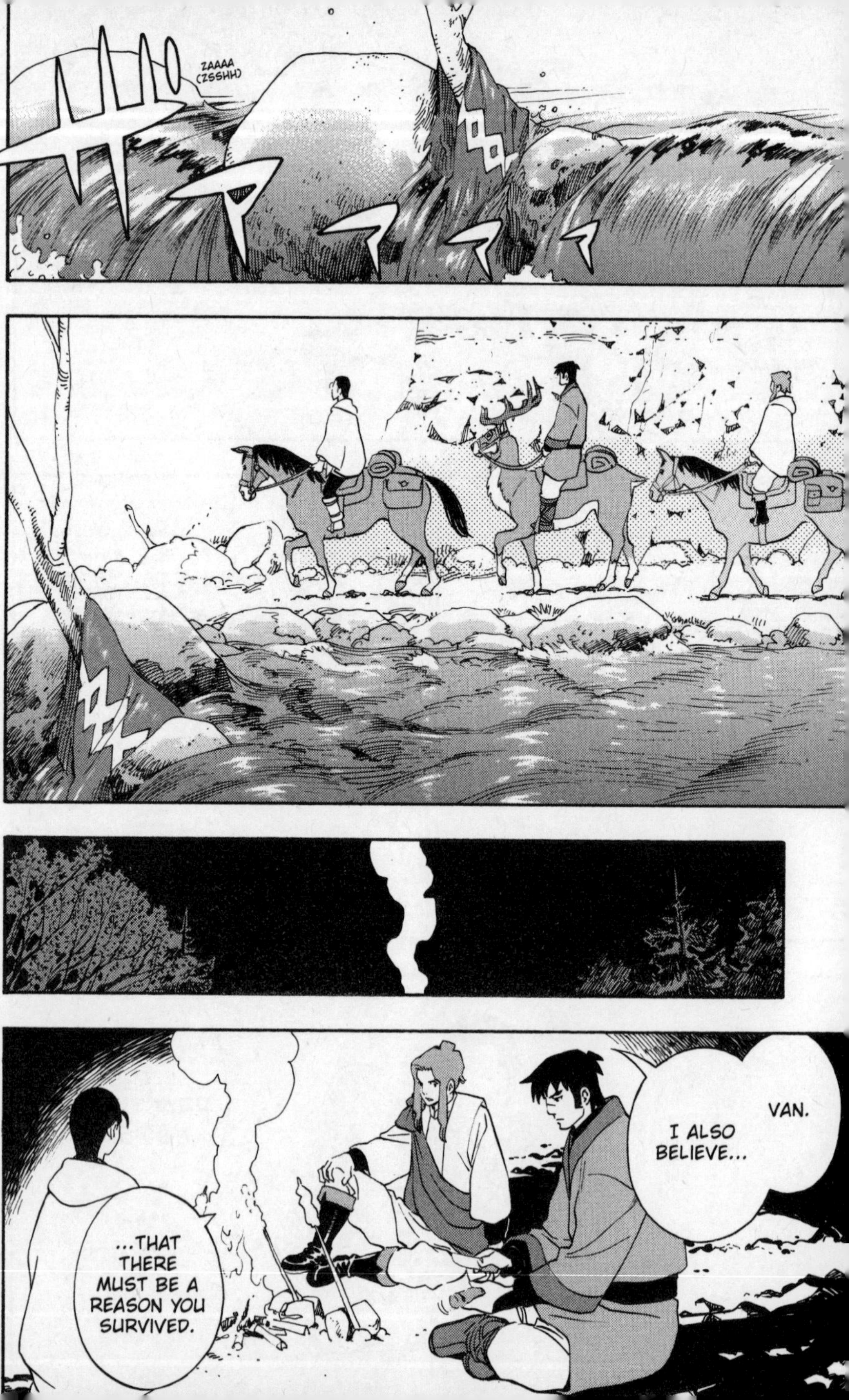
ZAAAA (ZSSHH)
VAN. I ALSO BELIEVE...
...THAT THERE MUST BE A REASON YOU SURVIVED.

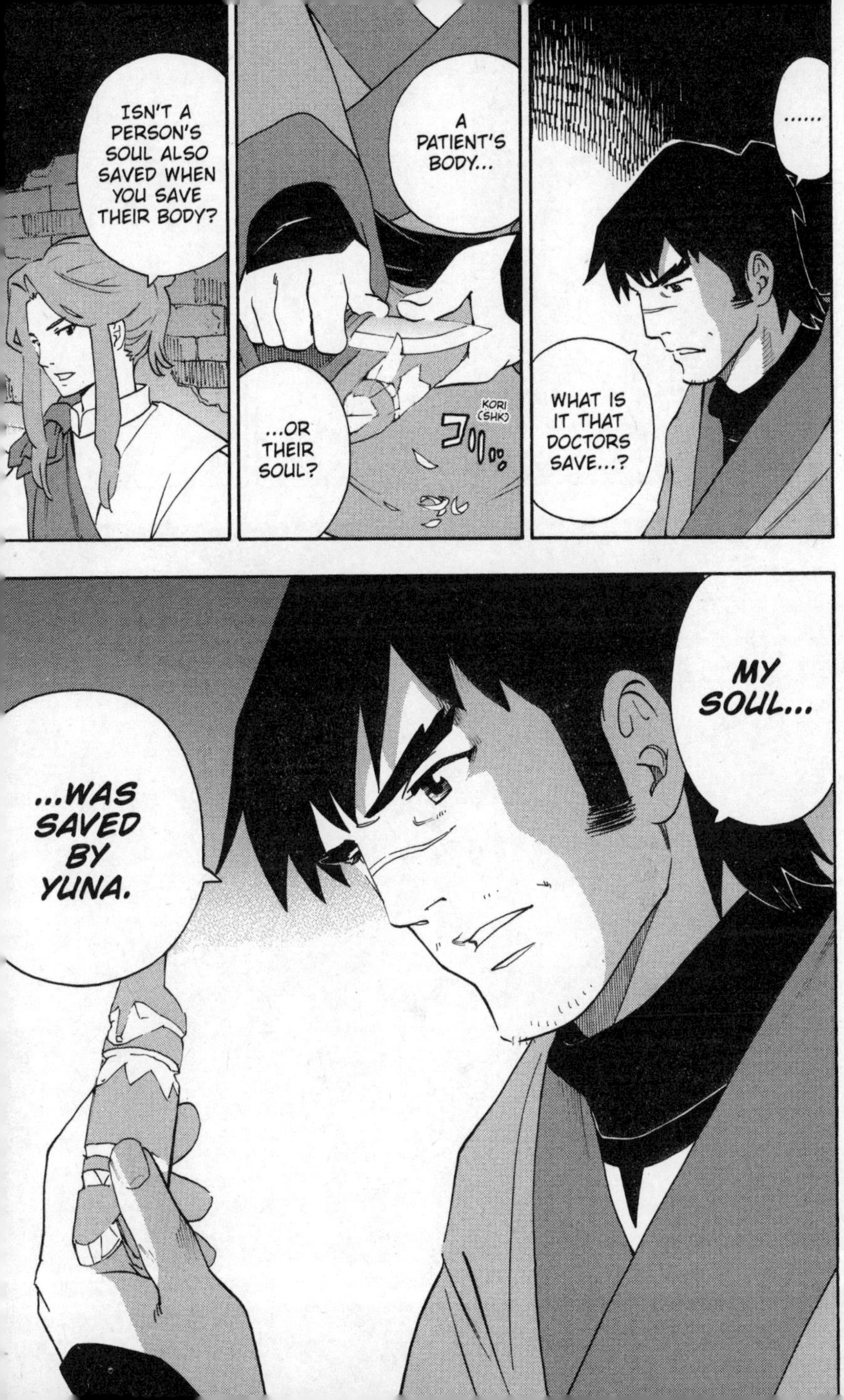
......
WHAT IS IT THAT DOCTORS SAVE...?
A PATIENT'S BODY...
KORI (SHK)
...OR THEIR SOUL?
ISN'T A PERSON'S SOUL ALSO SAVED WHEN YOU SAVE THEIR BODY?
MY SOUL...
...WAS SAVED BY YUNA.

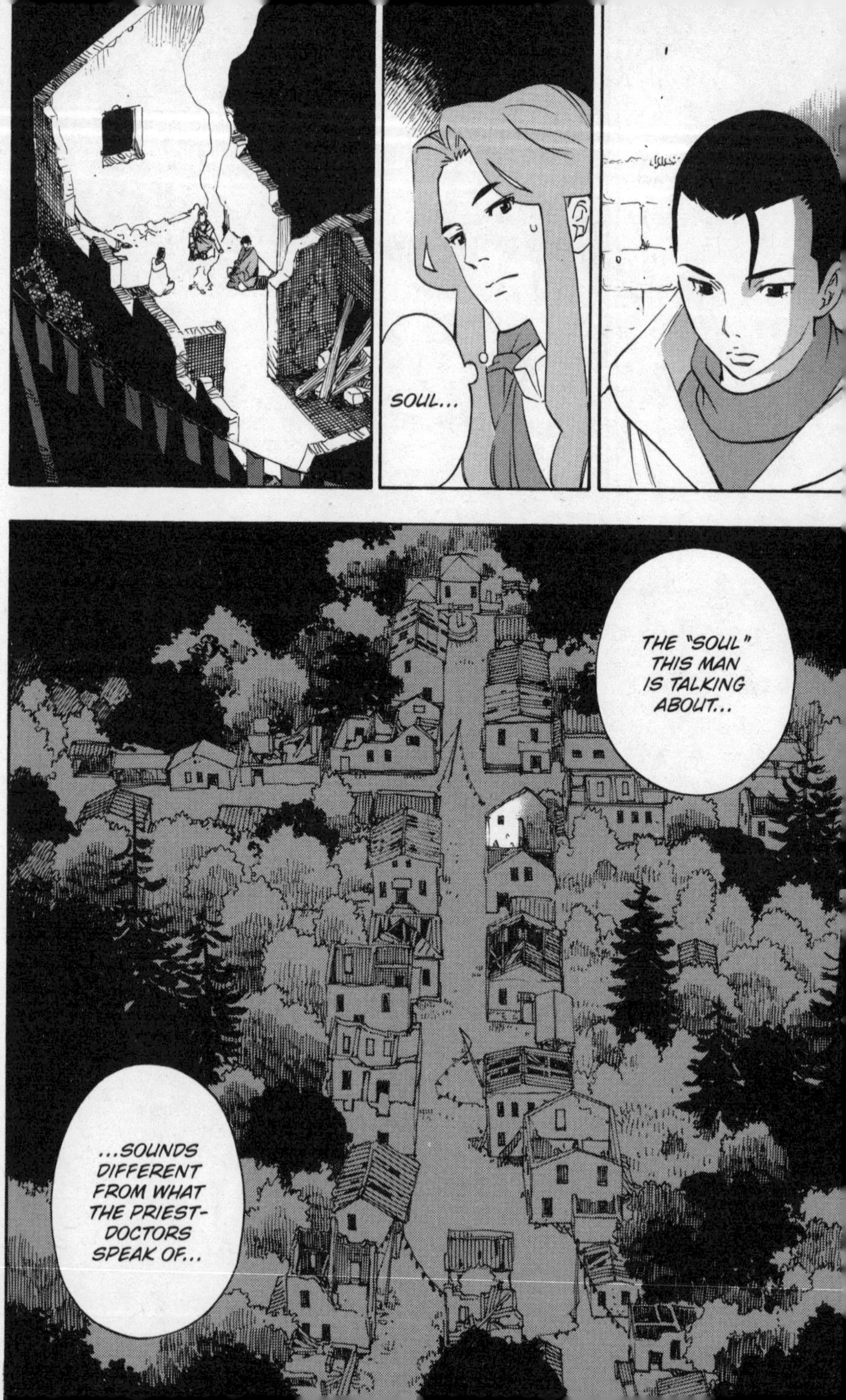
SOUL...
THE "SOUL" THIS MAN IS TALKING ABOUT...
...SOUNDS DIFFERENT FROM WHAT THE PRIEST-DOCTORS SPEAK OF...

BO (BOFF)
ボ
BUWA (BWOOSH)
ブワ
!?

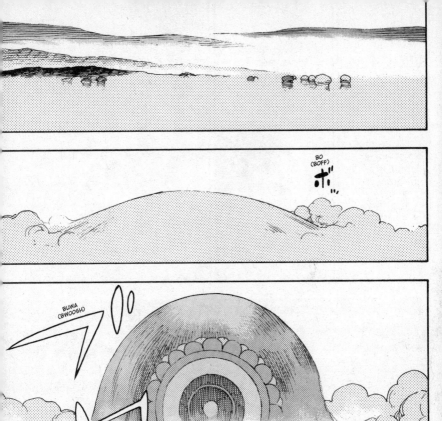

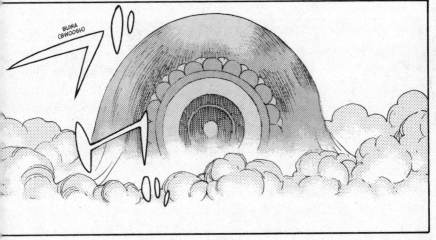

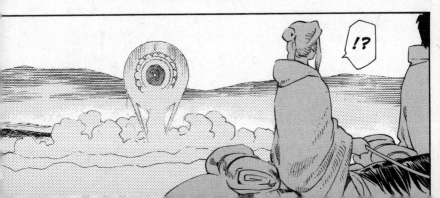

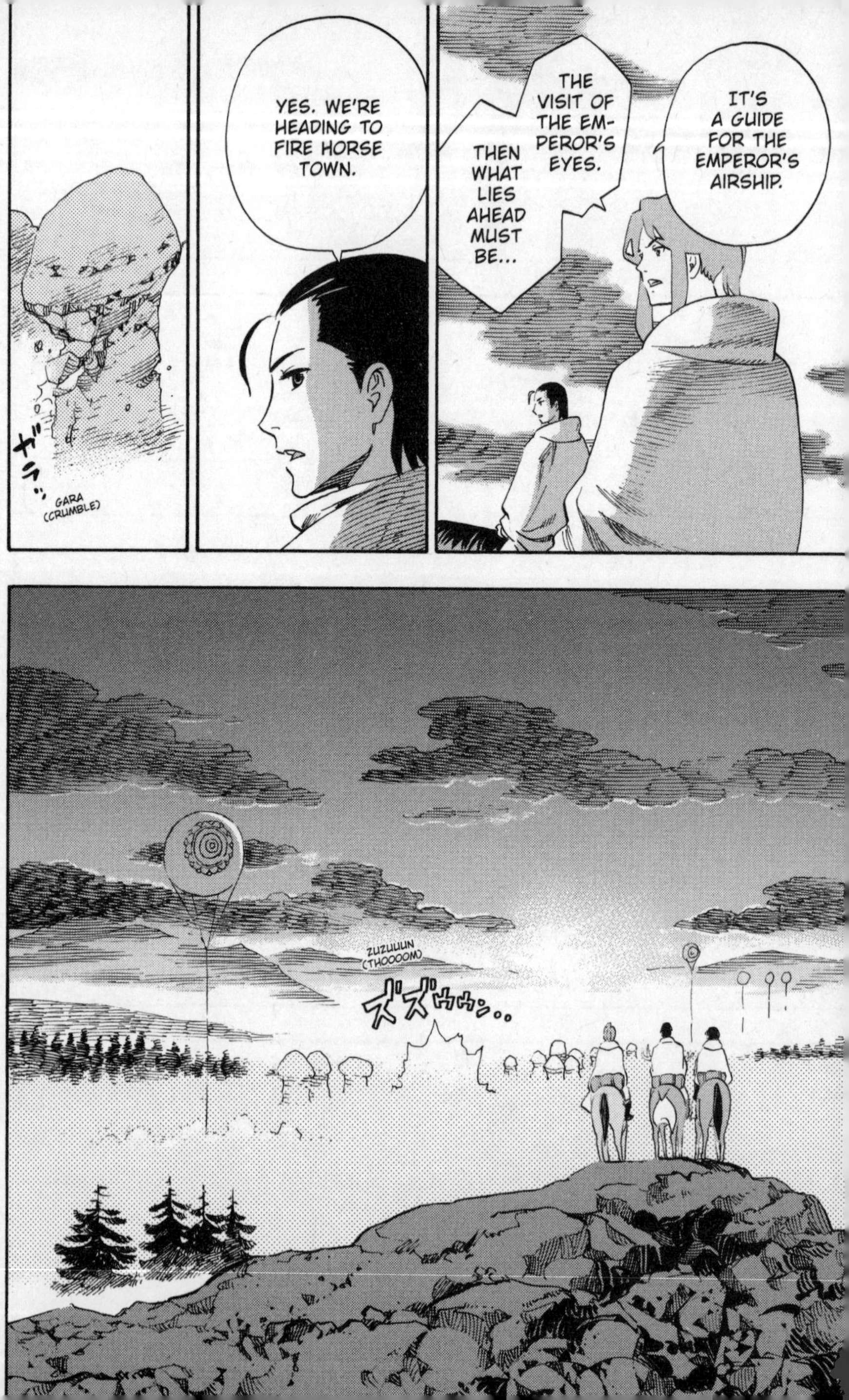
IT'S A GUIDE FOR THE EMPEROR'S AIRSHIP.
THEN WHAT LIES AHEAD MUST BE...
THE VISIT OF THE EM-PEROR'S EYES.
YES. WE'RE HEADING TO FIRE HORSE TOWN.
ガラッ
GARA (CRUMBLE)
ズズゥゥン..
ZUZUUUN (THOOOOM)

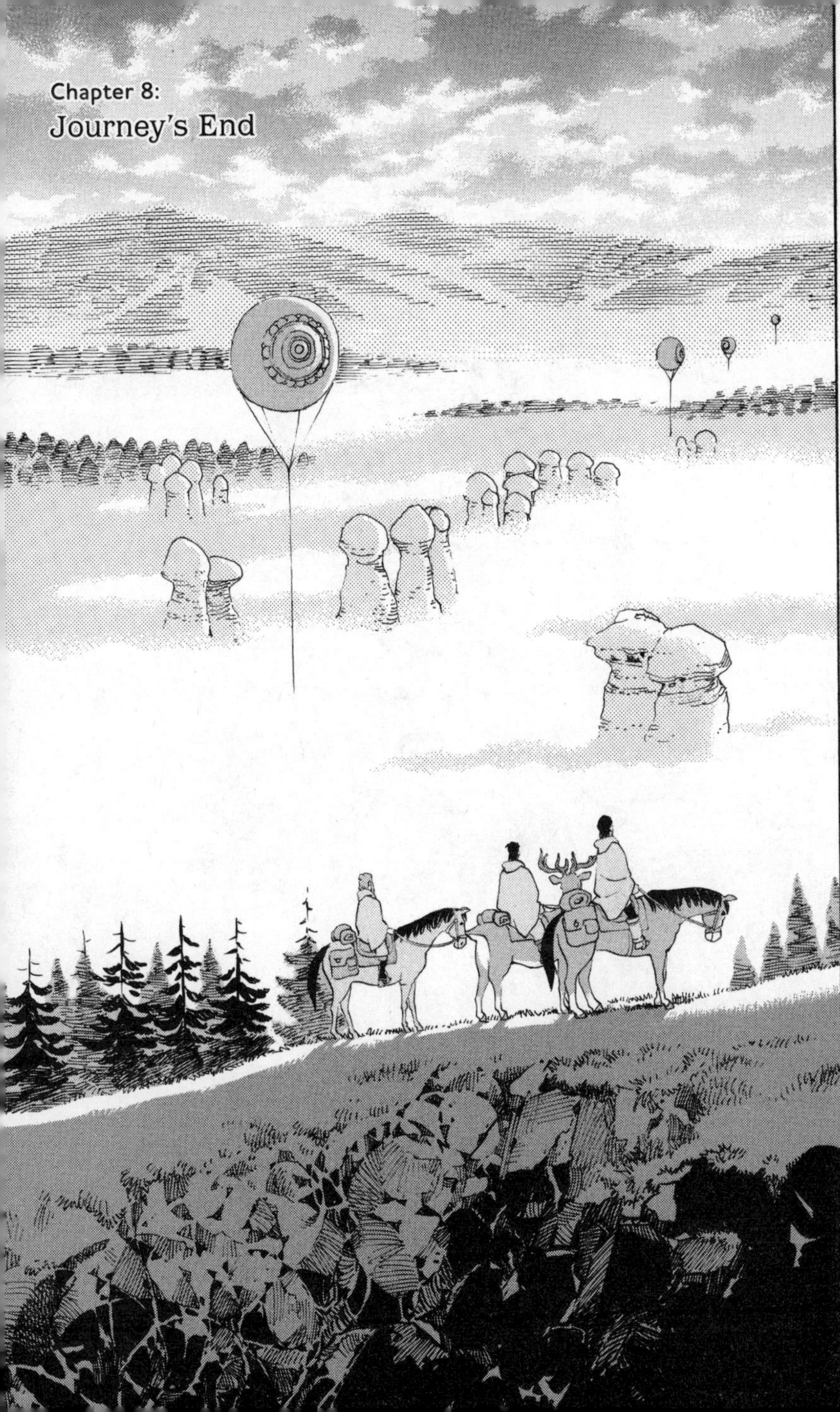
Chapter 8:
Journey's End

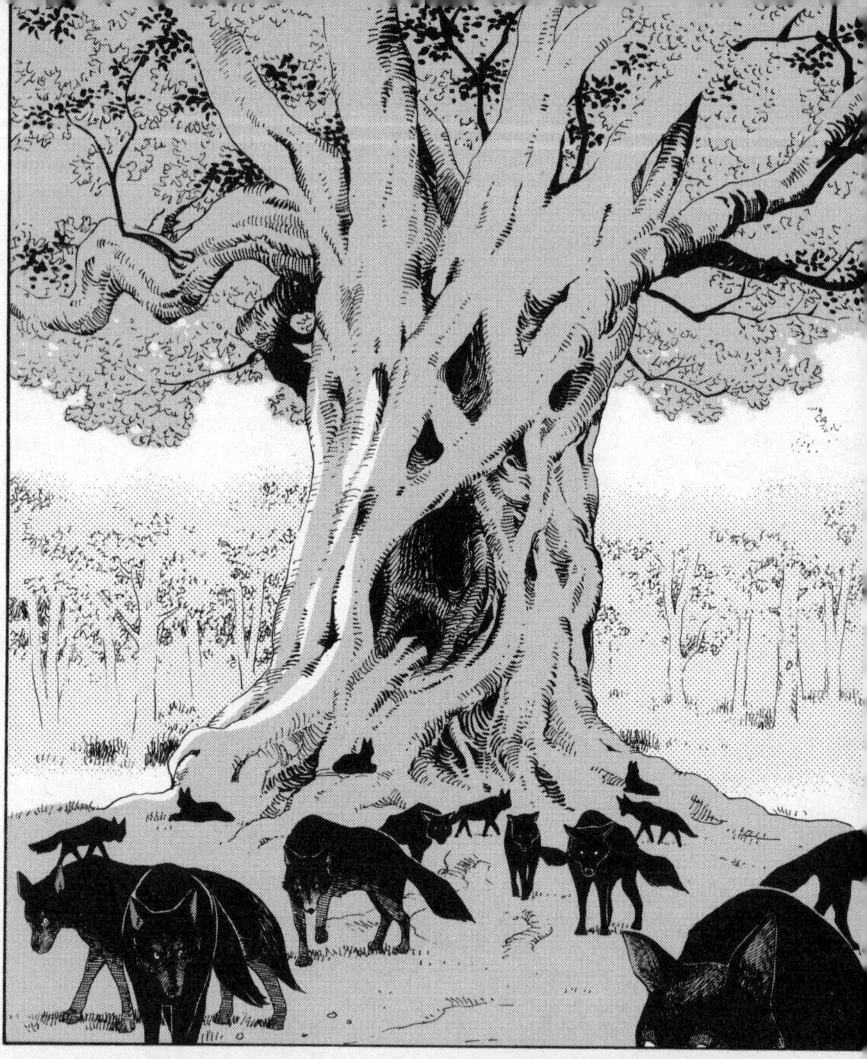

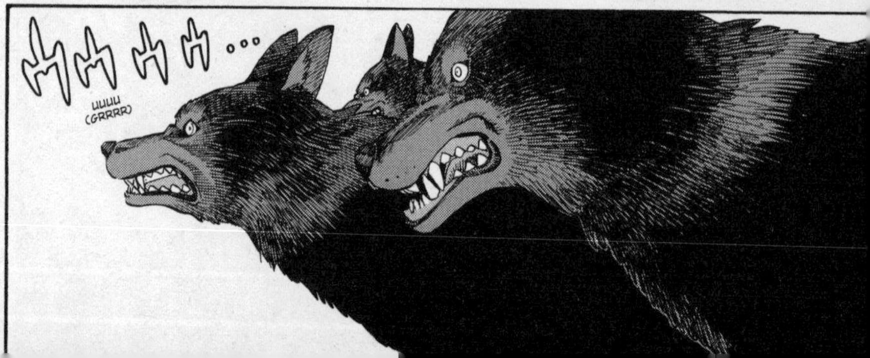
ウウウウ…
UUUU
(GRRRR)

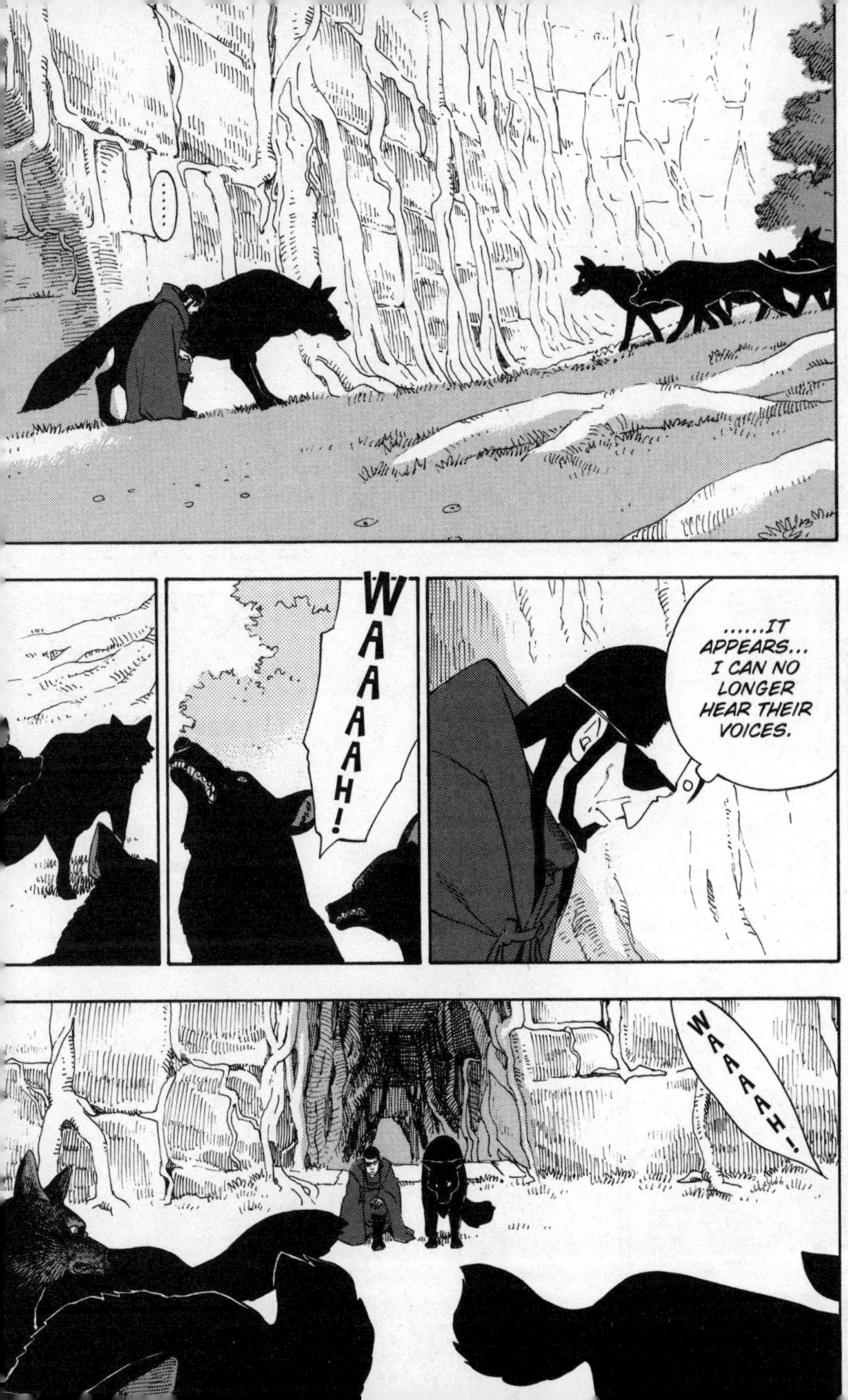
......
......IT APPEARS... I CAN NO LONGER HEAR THEIR VOICES.
WAAAAH!
WAAAAH!

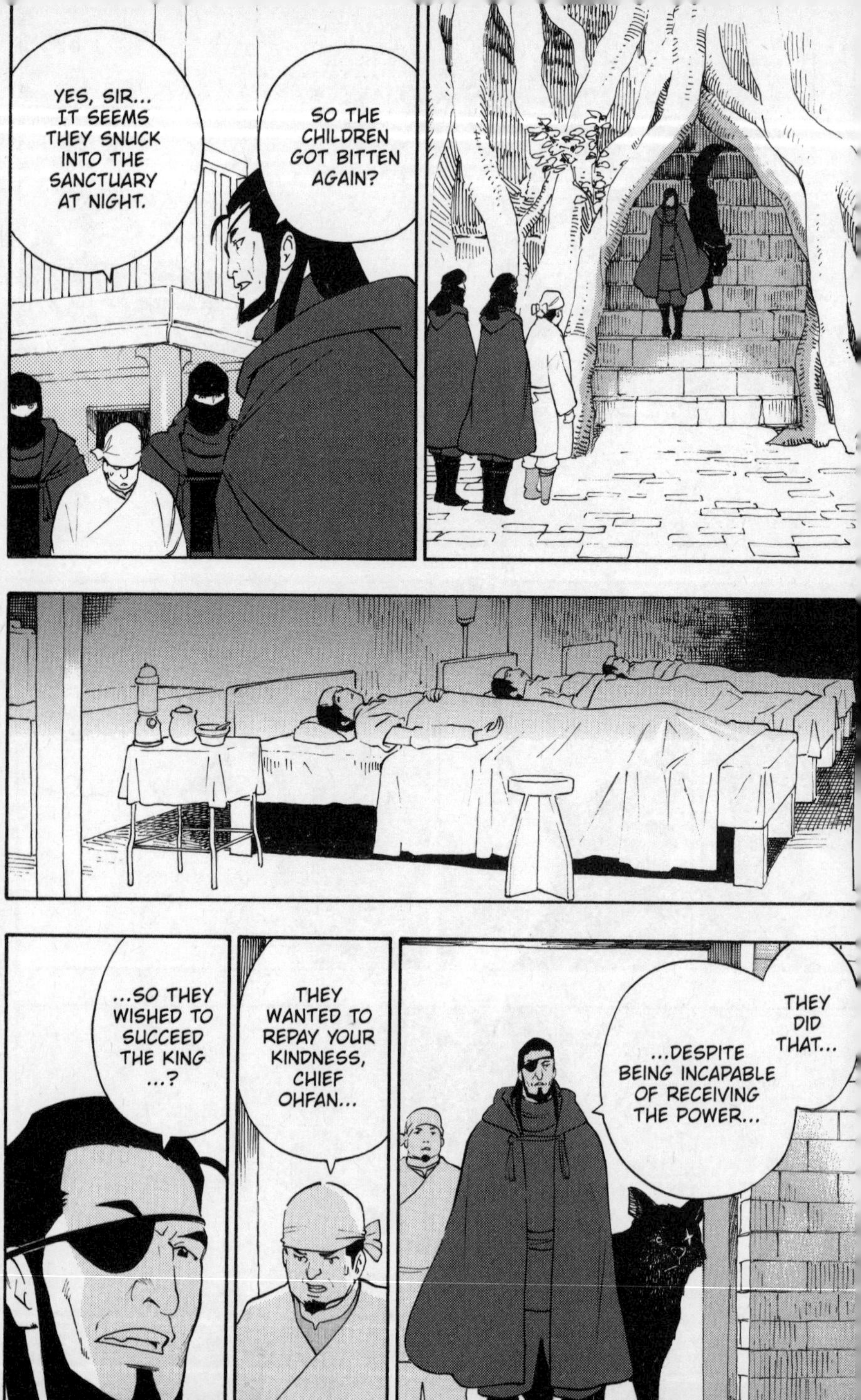
SO THE CHILDREN GOT BITTEN AGAIN?
YES, SIR... IT SEEMS THEY SNUCK INTO THE SANCTUARY AT NIGHT.
THEY DID THAT...
...DESPITE BEING INCAPABLE OF RECEIVING THE POWER...
THEY WANTED TO REPAY YOUR KINDNESS, CHIEF OHFAN...
...SO THEY WISHED TO SUCCEED THE KING ...?

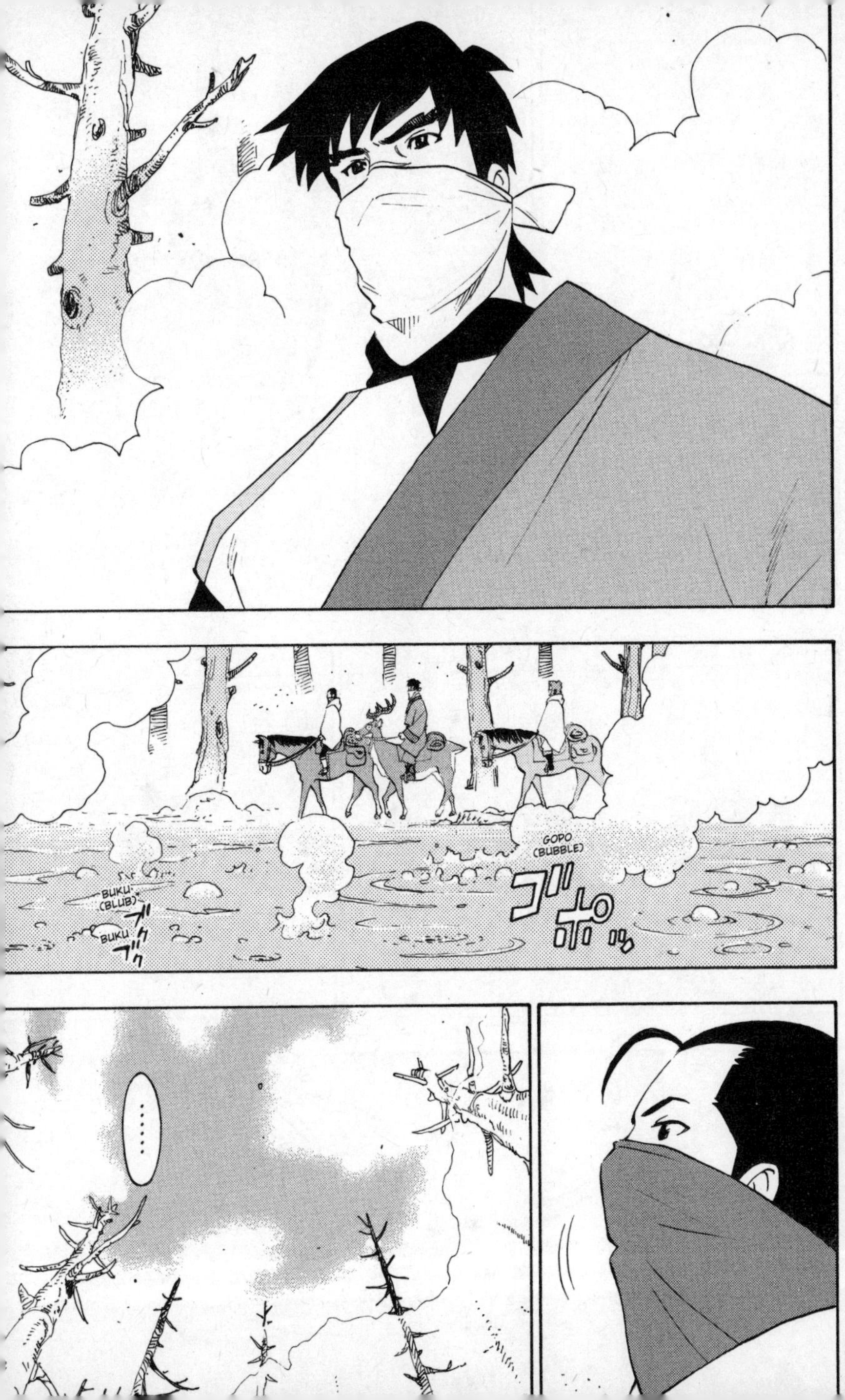
GOPO (BUBBLE)
ゴポッ
BUKU (BLUB)
ブク
BUKU
ブク
......

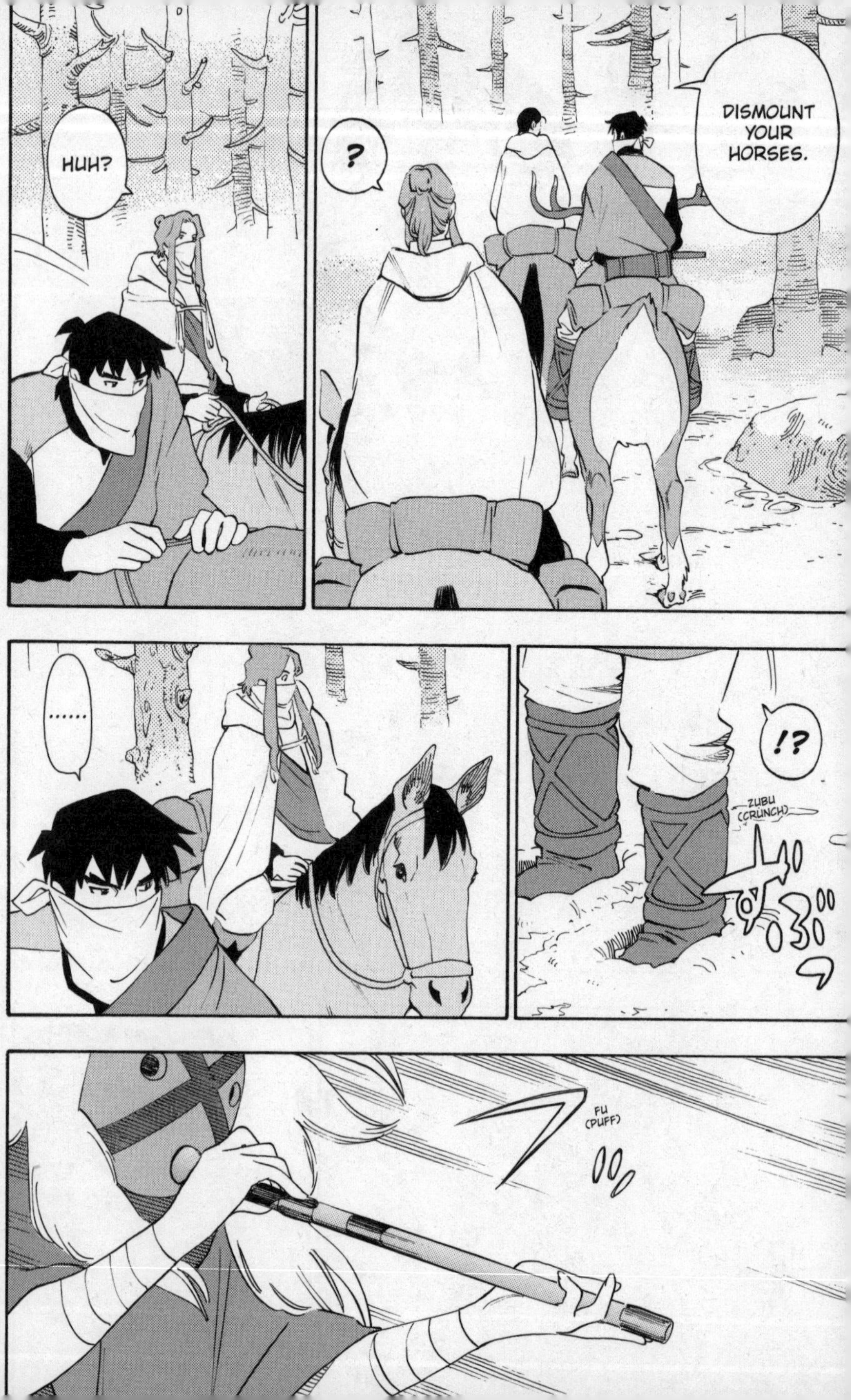
DISMOUNT YOUR HORSES.
?
HUH?
!?
ZUBU (CRUNCH)
......
FU (PUFF)

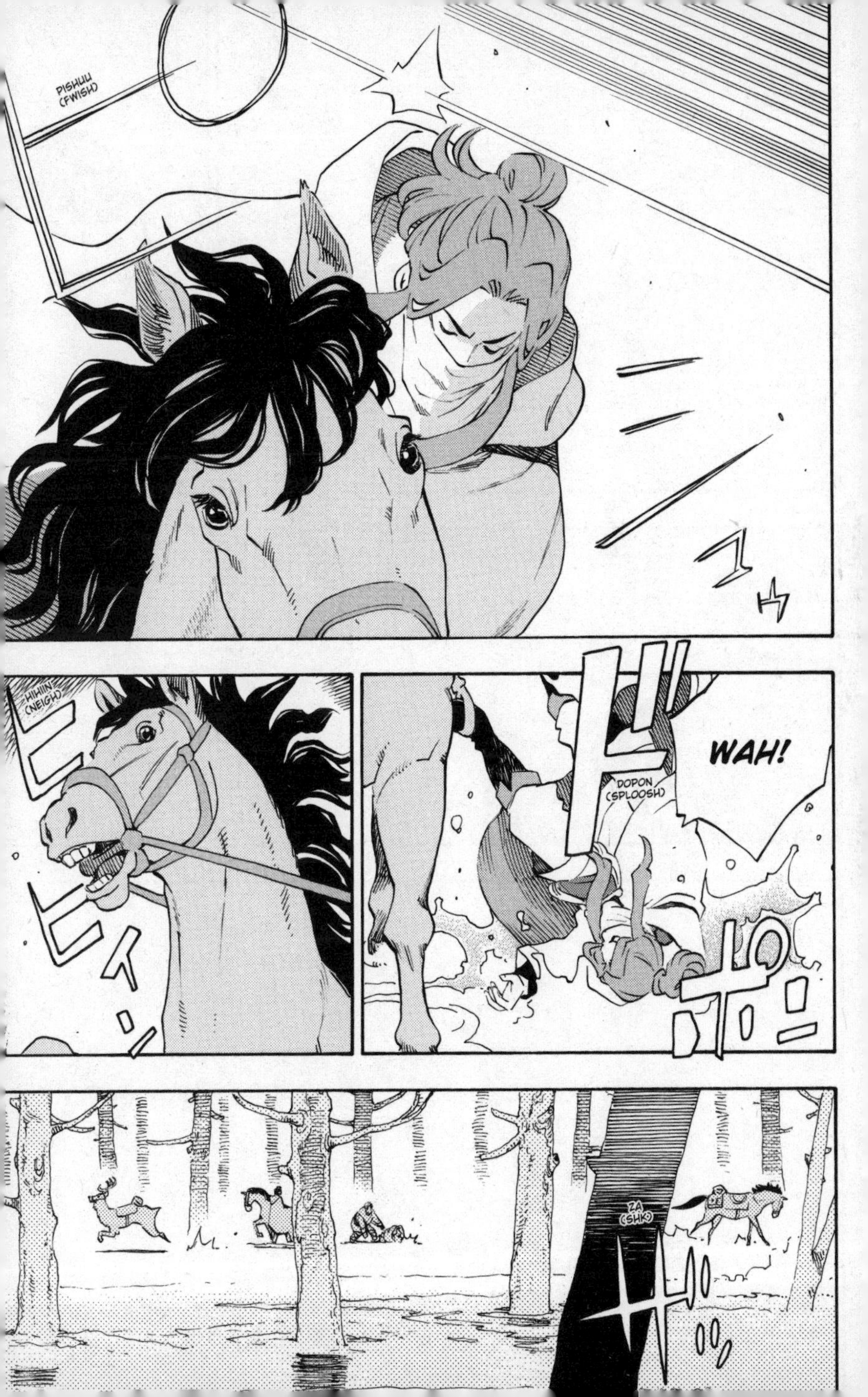
PISHUU
(FWISH)
WAH!
DOPON
(SPLOOSH)
HIHIIN
(NEIGH)
ZA
(SHK)

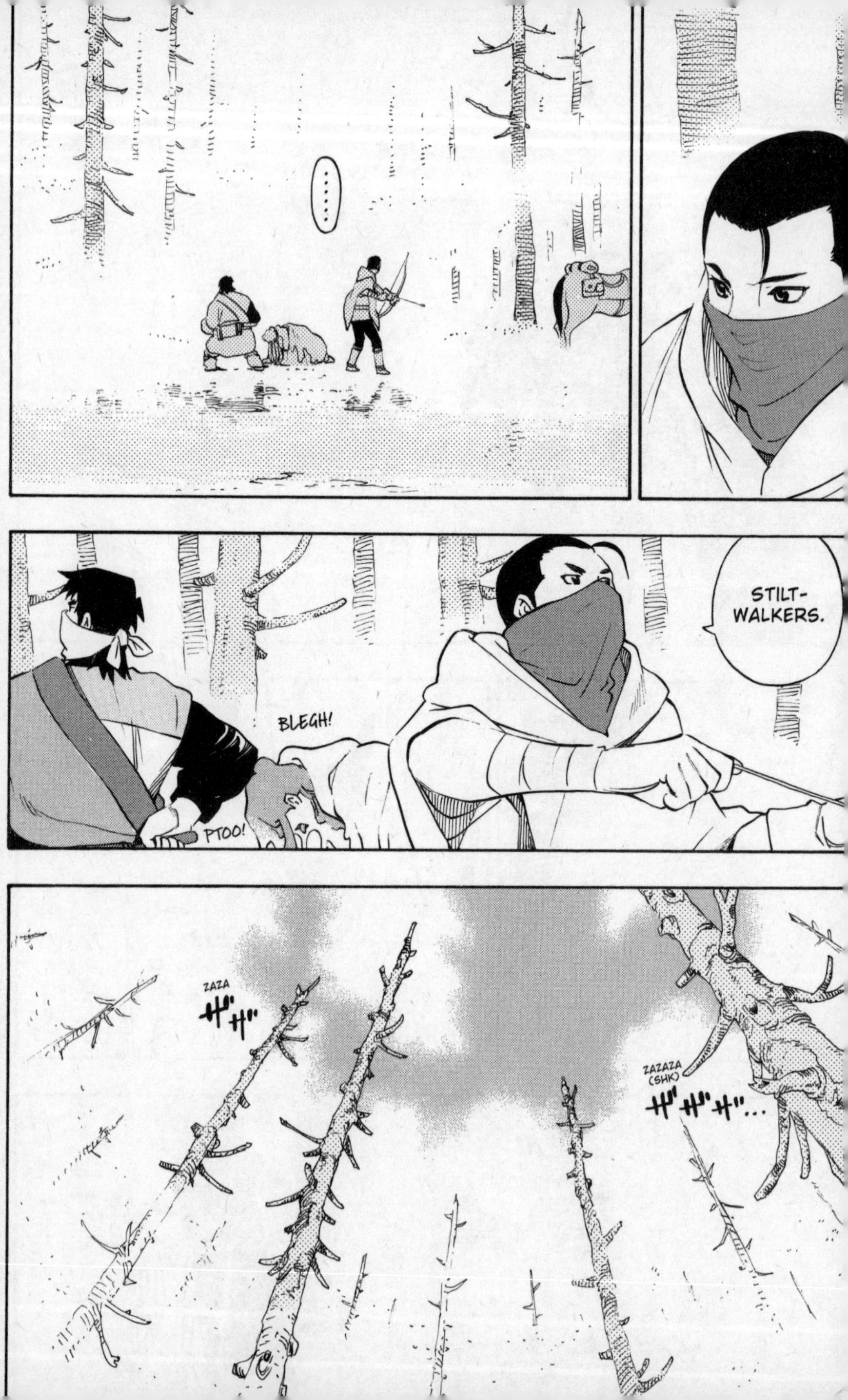
......
STILT-WALKERS.
BLEGH!
PTOO!
ZAZAZA (SHK)
ZAZA

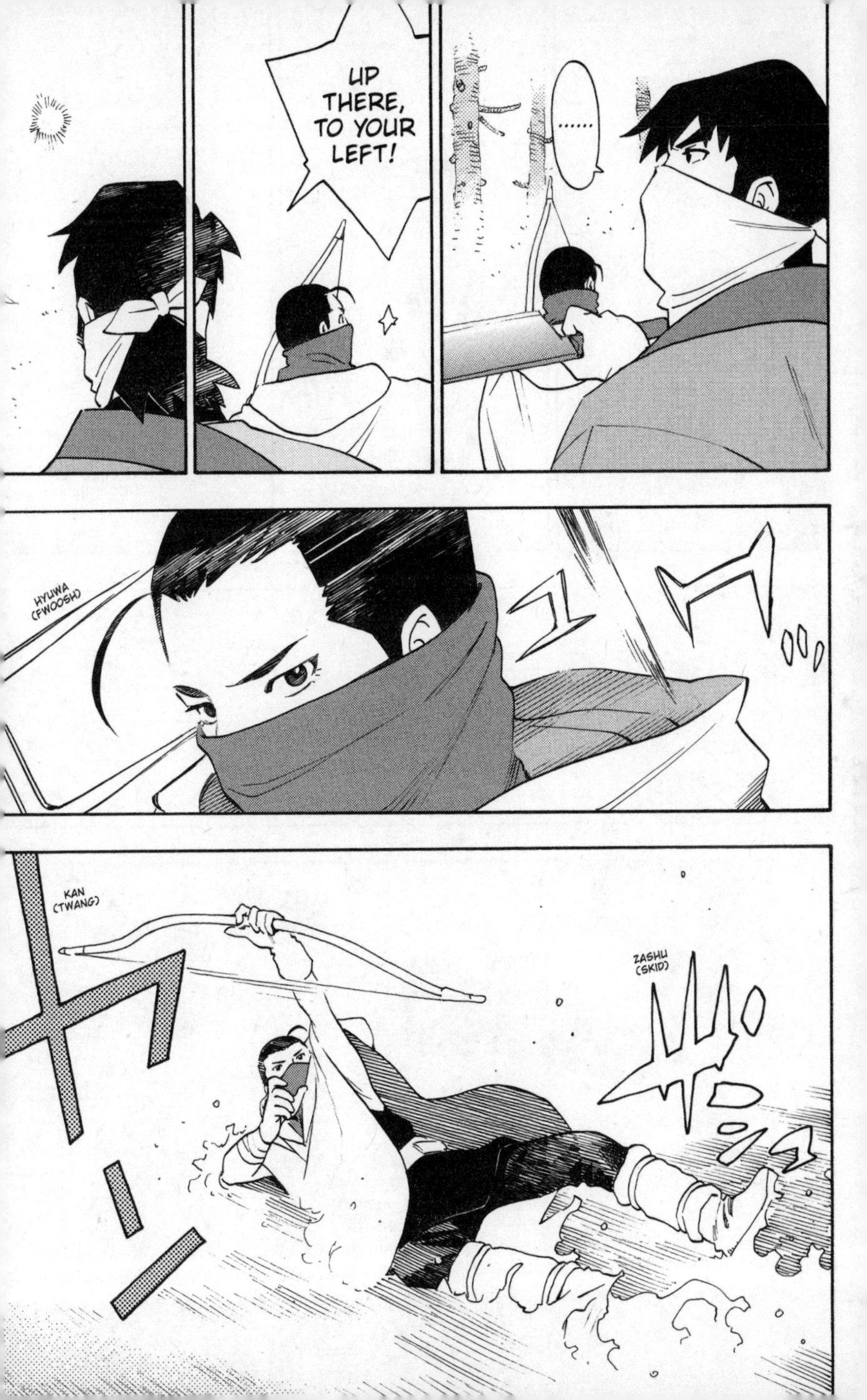
……
UP THERE, TO YOUR LEFT!
HYUWA (FWOOSH)
ZASHU (SKID)
KAN (TWANG)

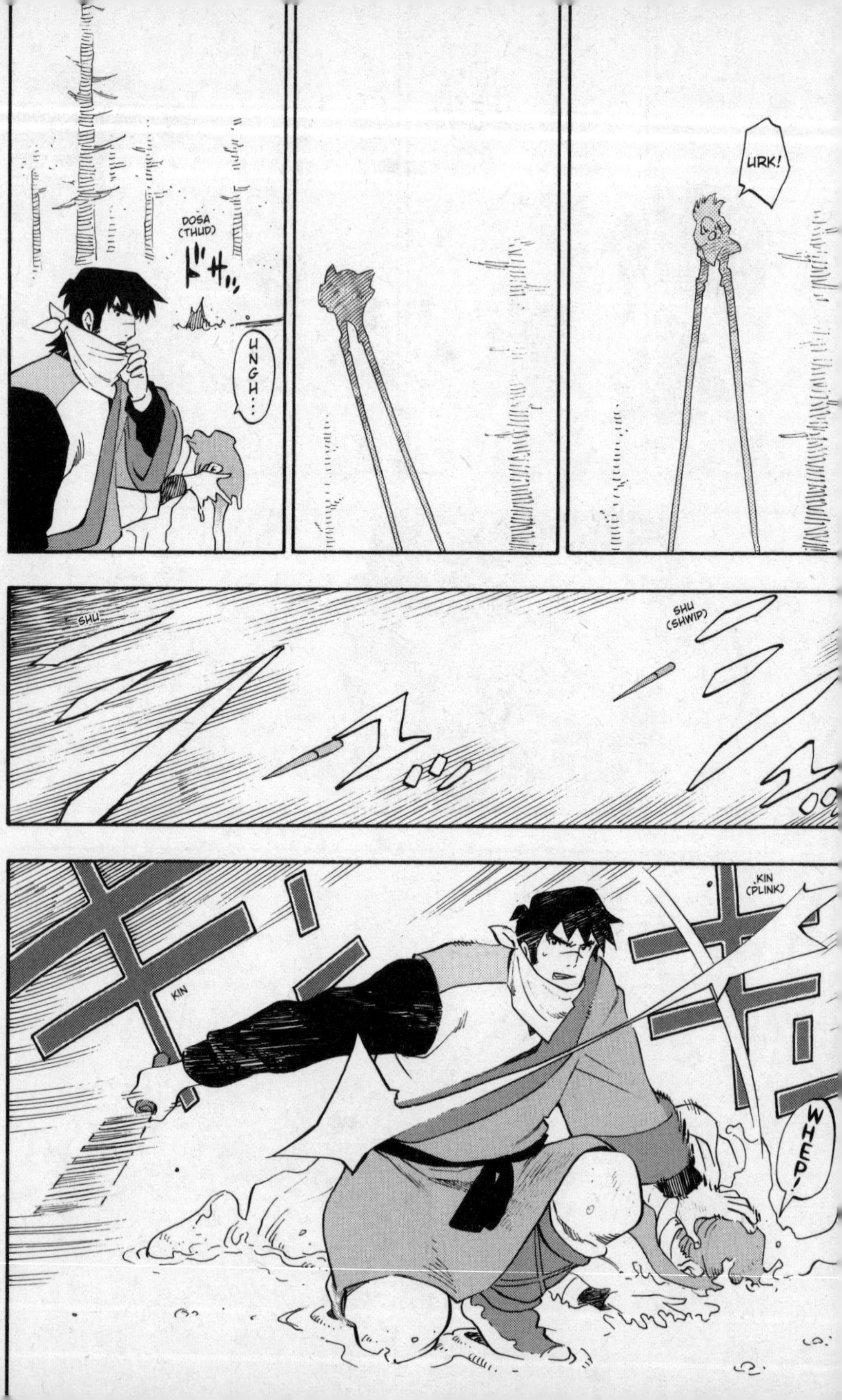
URK!
DOSA (THUD)
ドサッ
UNGH...
SHU (SHWIP)
SHU
KIN (PLINK)
WHEP!
KIN

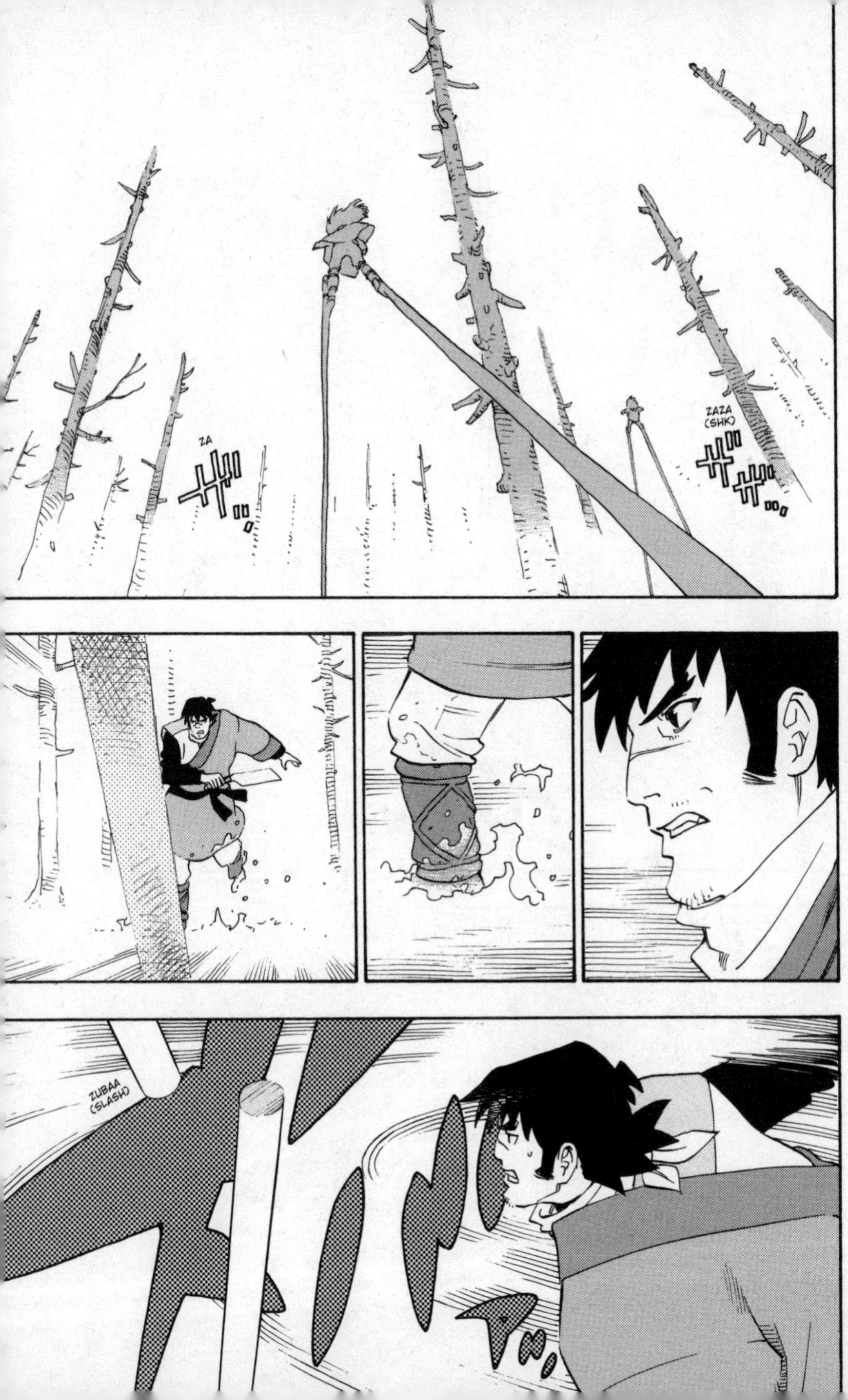
ZAZA
(SHK)
ZA
ZUBAA
(SLASH)

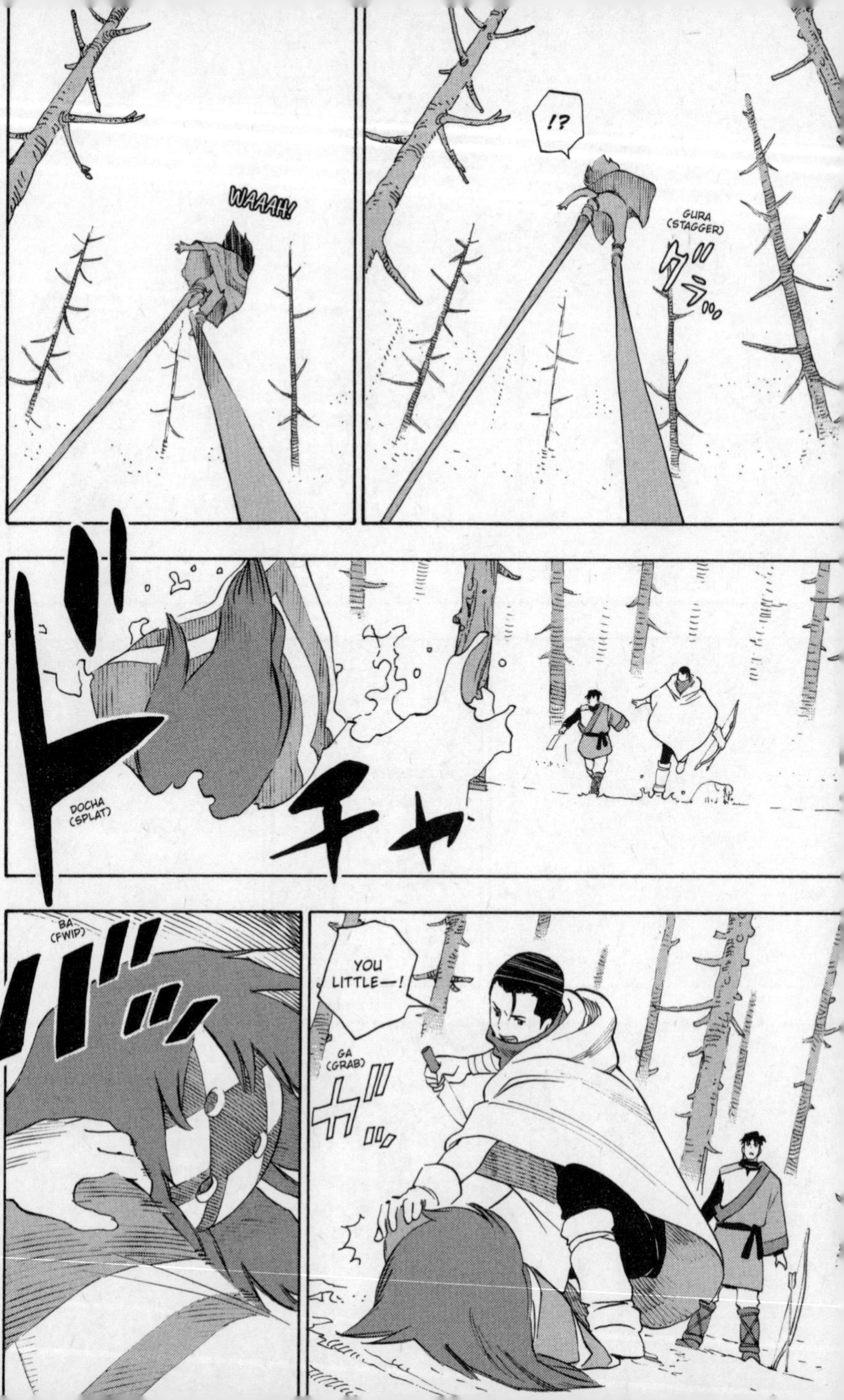
!?
GURA (STAGGER)
WAAAH!
DOCHA (SPLAT)
YOU LITTLE—!
GA (GRAB)
BA (FWIP)

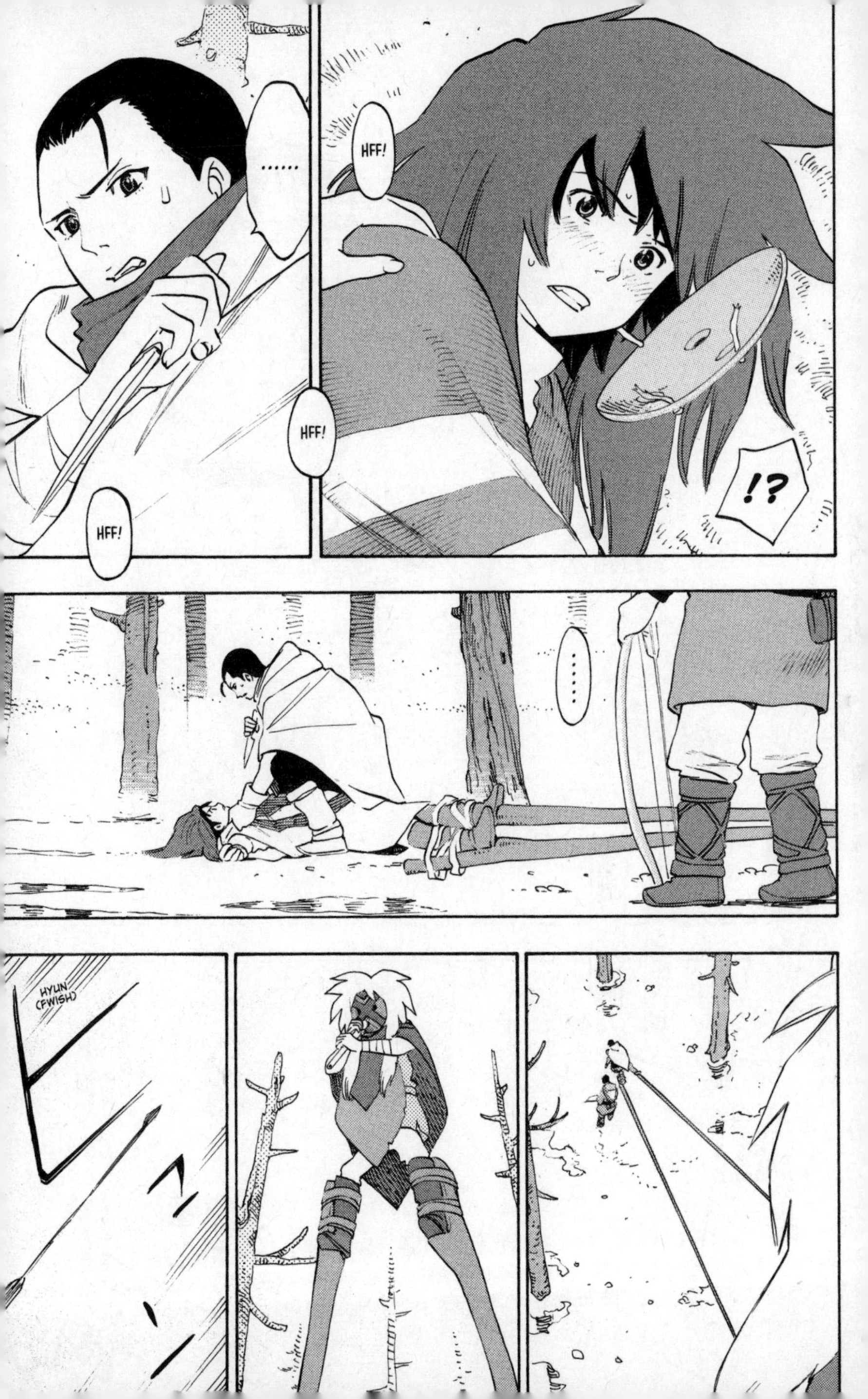
HFF!
!?
HFF!
......
HFF!
......
HYUN (FWISH)

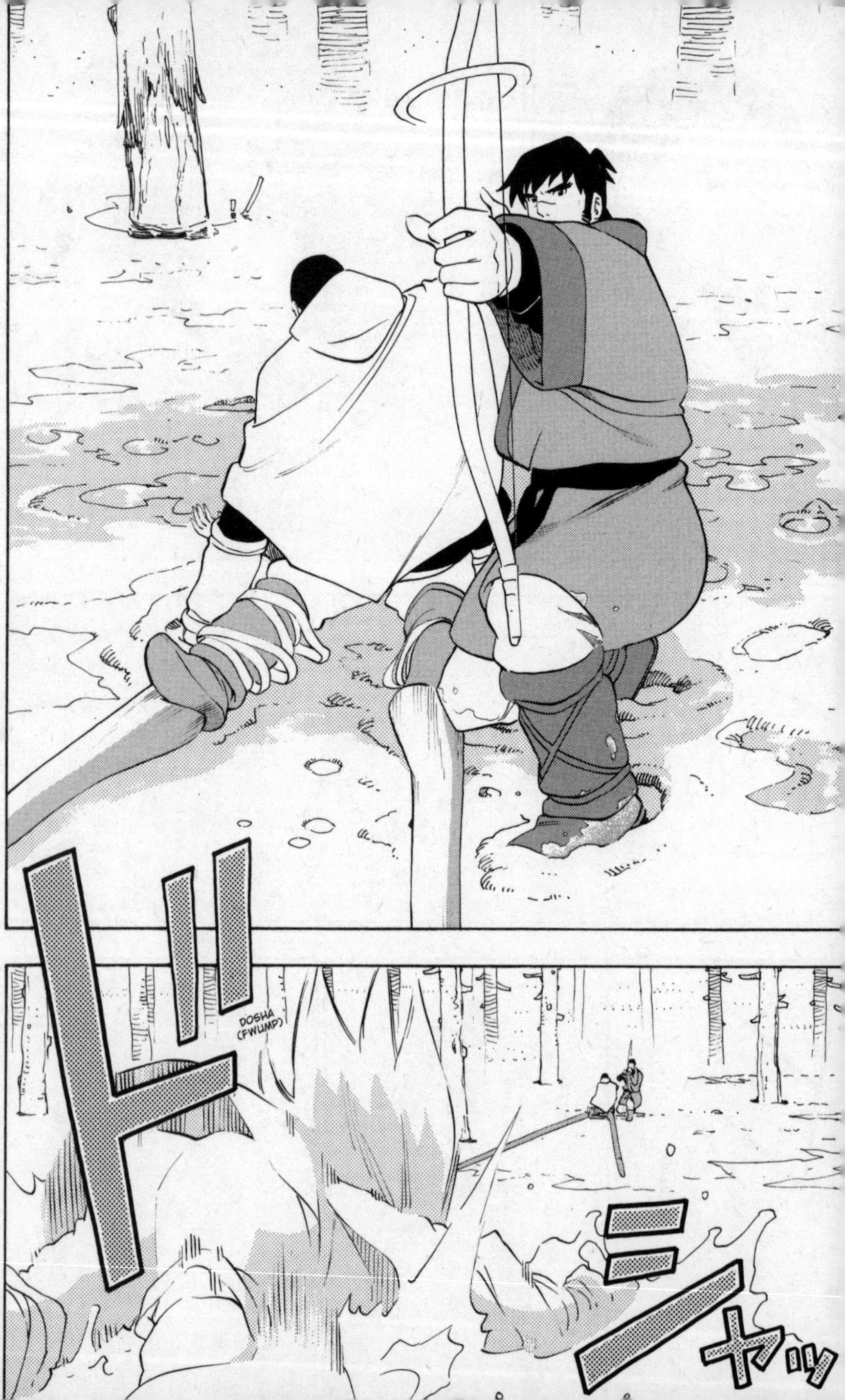
ドッ
DOSHA
(FWUMP)
シャッ

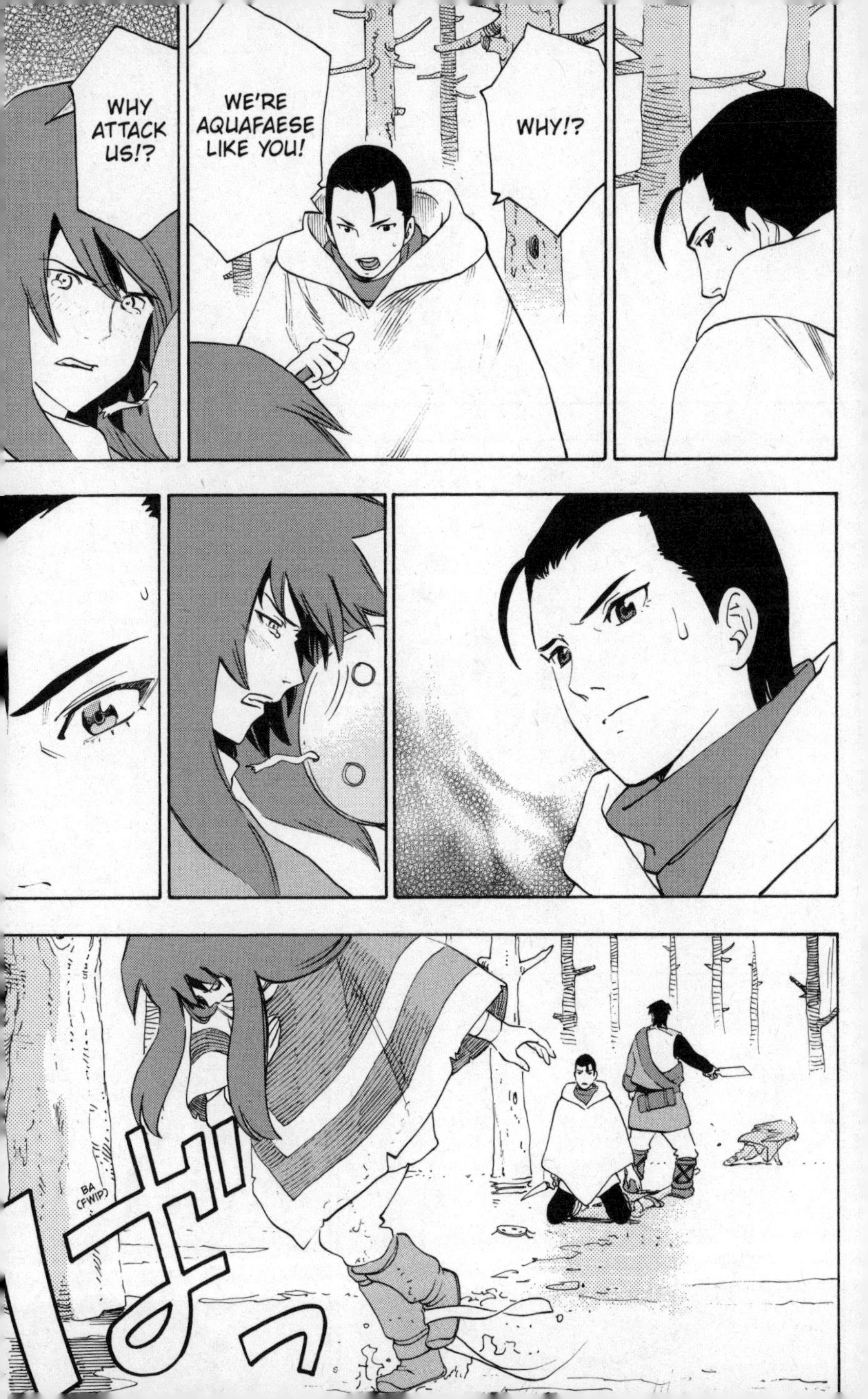
WHY!?
WE'RE AQUAFAESE LIKE YOU!
WHY ATTACK US!?
BA (FWIP)

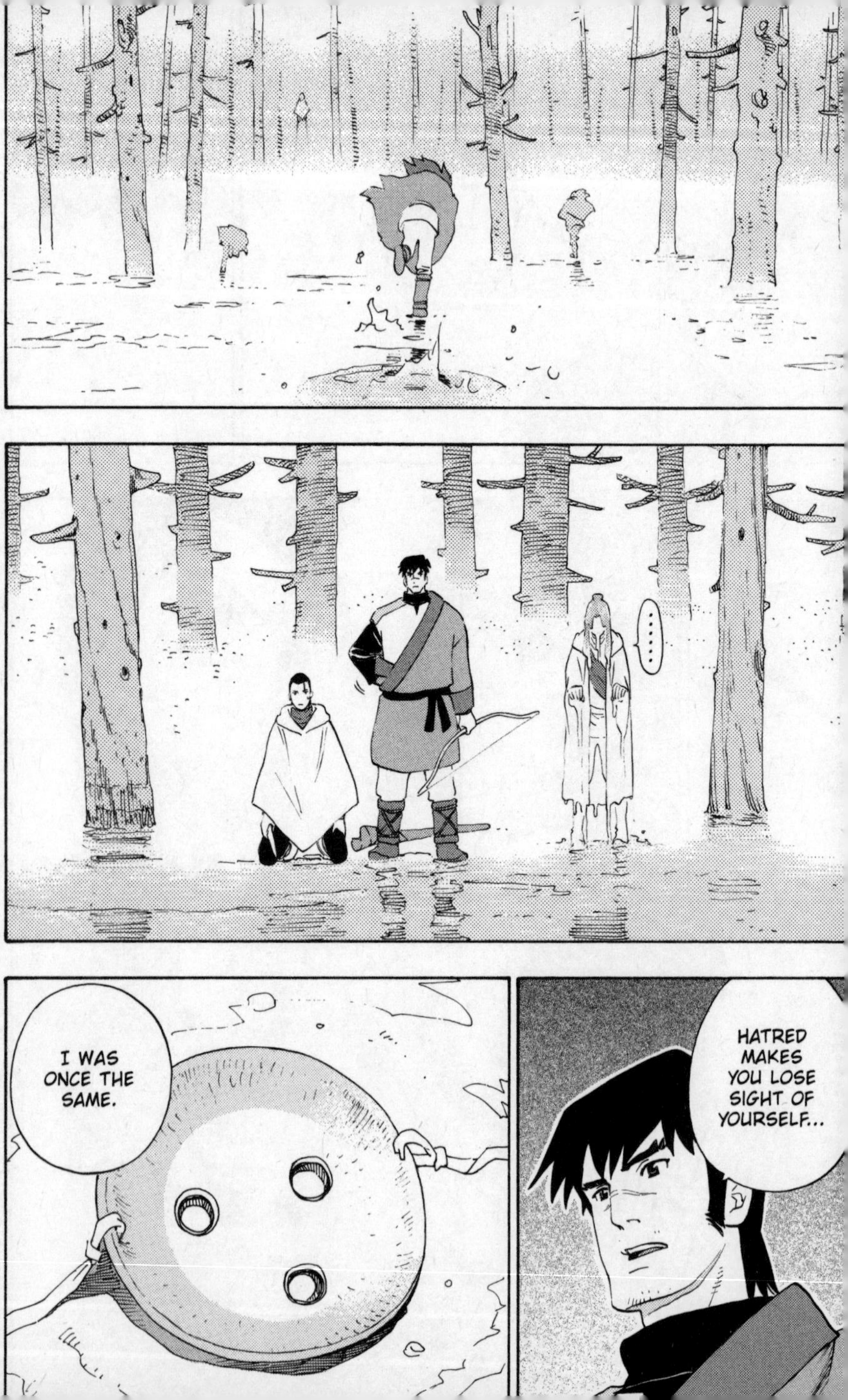
...
HATRED MAKES YOU LOSE SIGHT OF YOURSELF...
I WAS ONCE THE SAME.

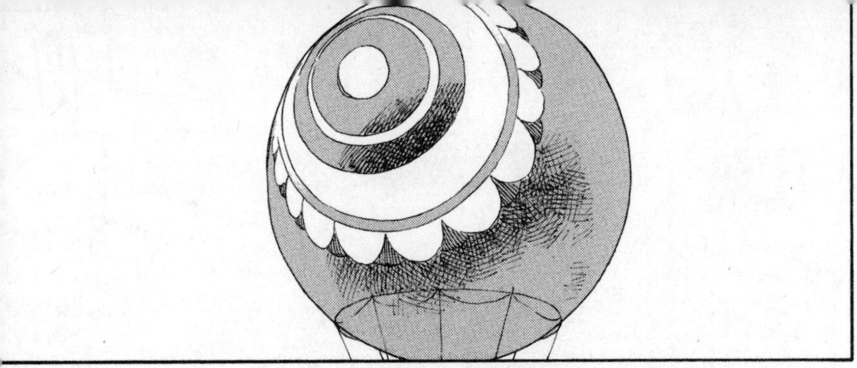

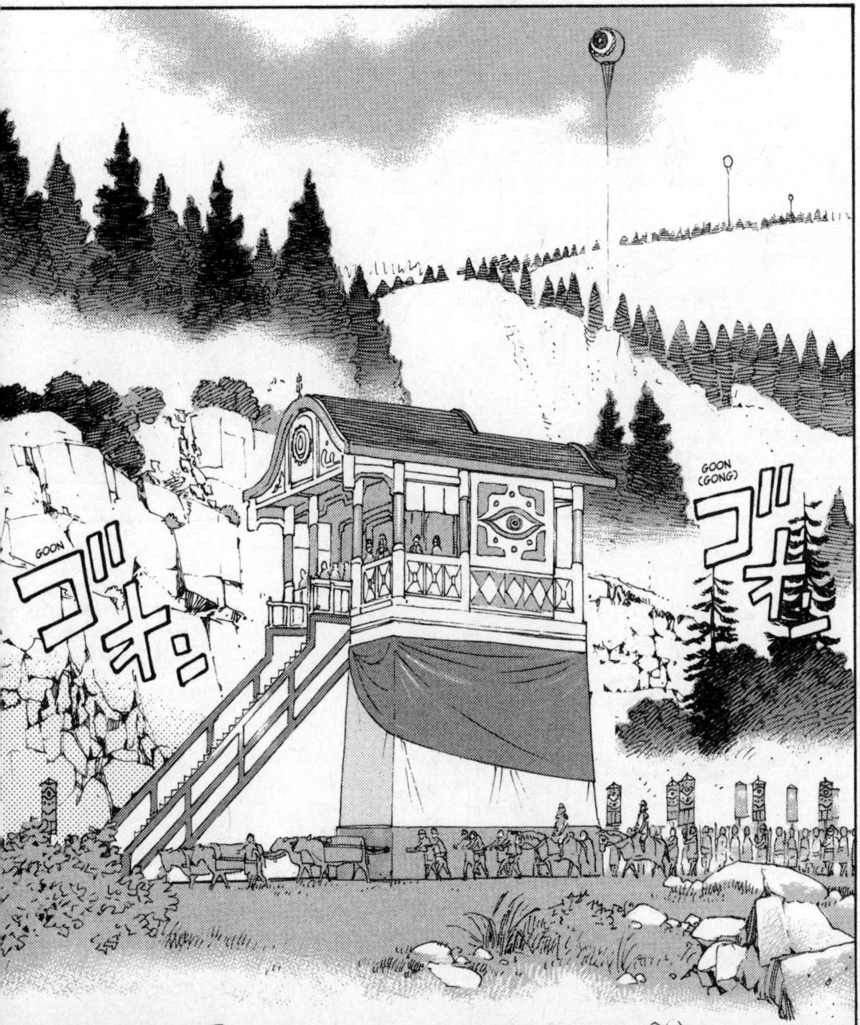
GOON (GONG)
ゴォーン
GOON
ゴォン

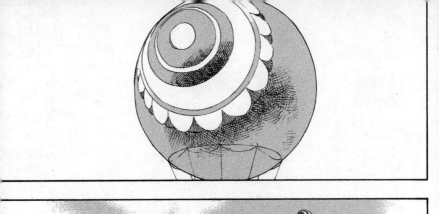

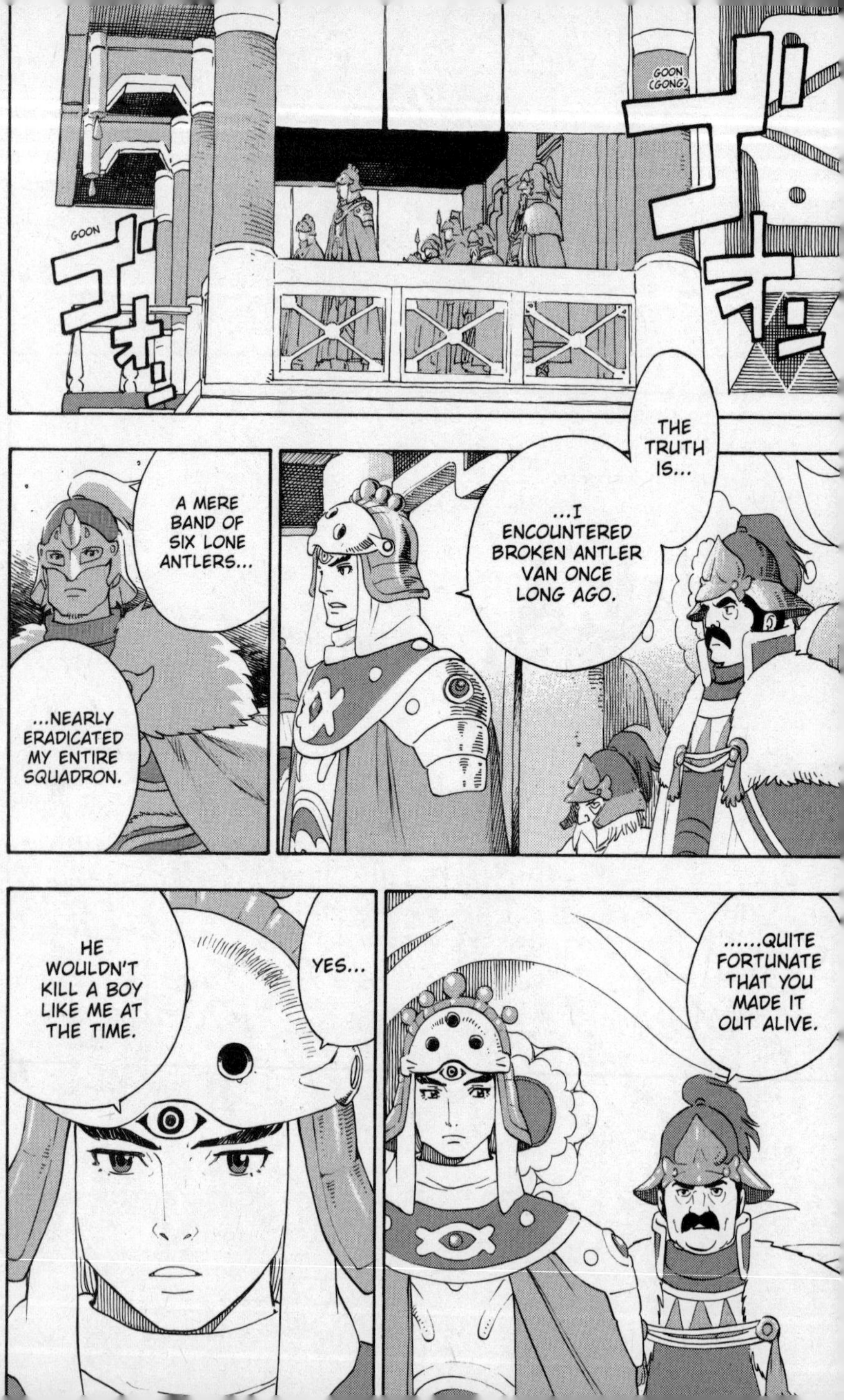
GOON (GONG)
GOON
THE TRUTH IS...
...I ENCOUNTERED BROKEN ANTLER VAN ONCE LONG AGO.
A MERE BAND OF SIX LONE ANTLERS...
...NEARLY ERADICATED MY ENTIRE SQUADRON.
......QUITE FORTUNATE THAT YOU MADE IT OUT ALIVE.
YES...
HE WOULDN'T KILL A BOY LIKE ME AT THE TIME.

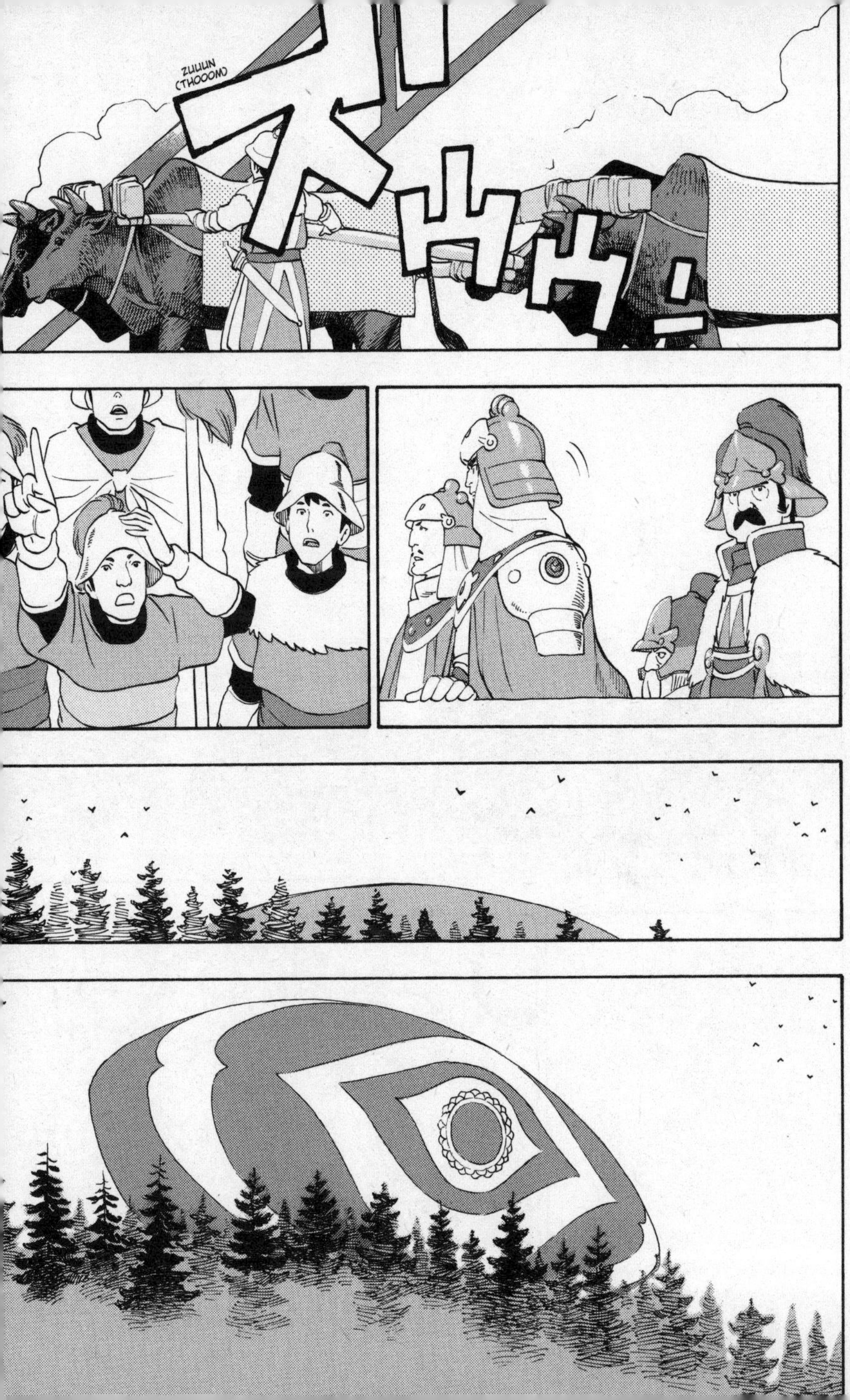
ZUUUN
(THOOOM)

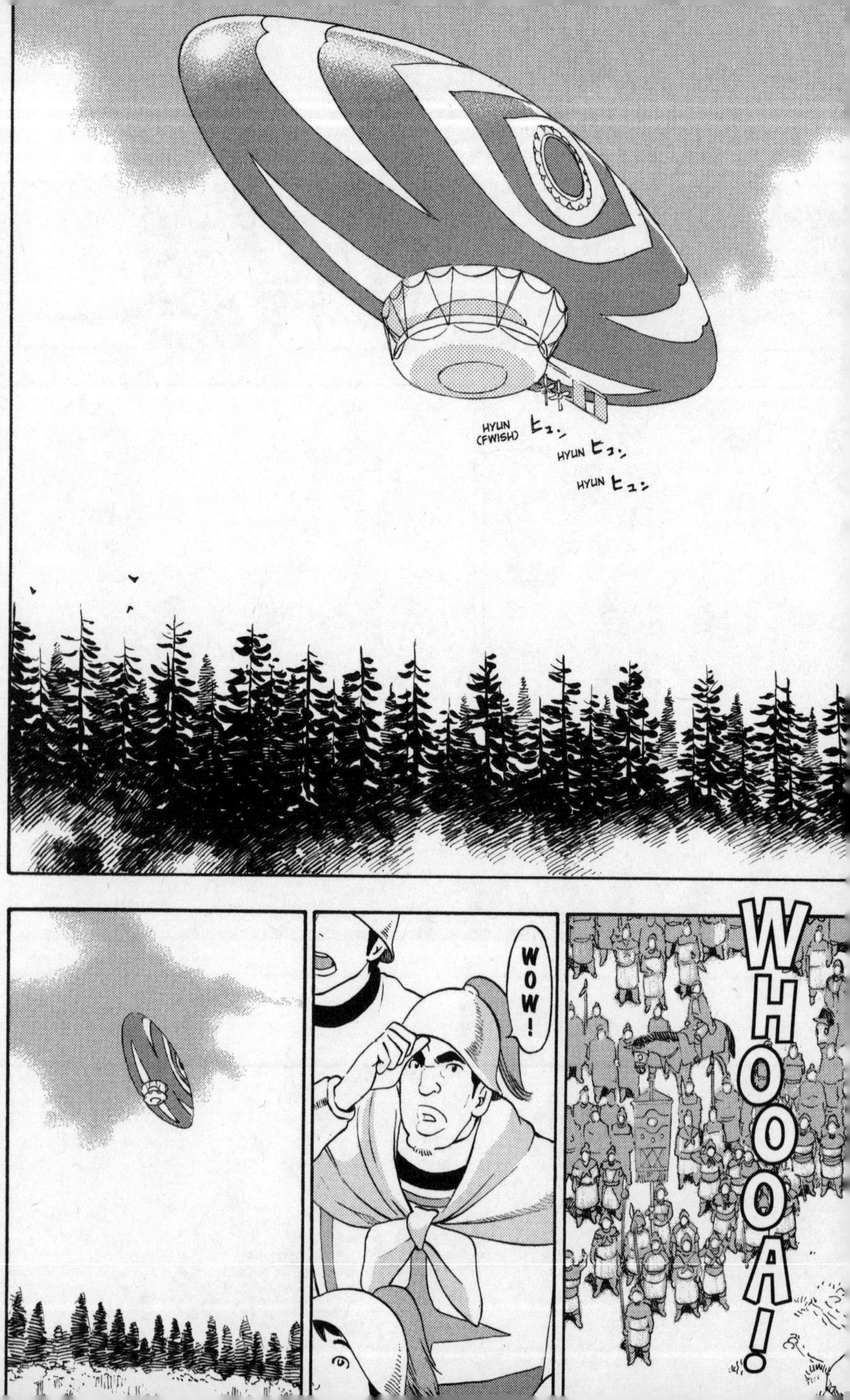

HYUN (FWISH) ヒュン
HYUN ヒュン
HYUN ヒュン
WHOOOOA!
WOW!

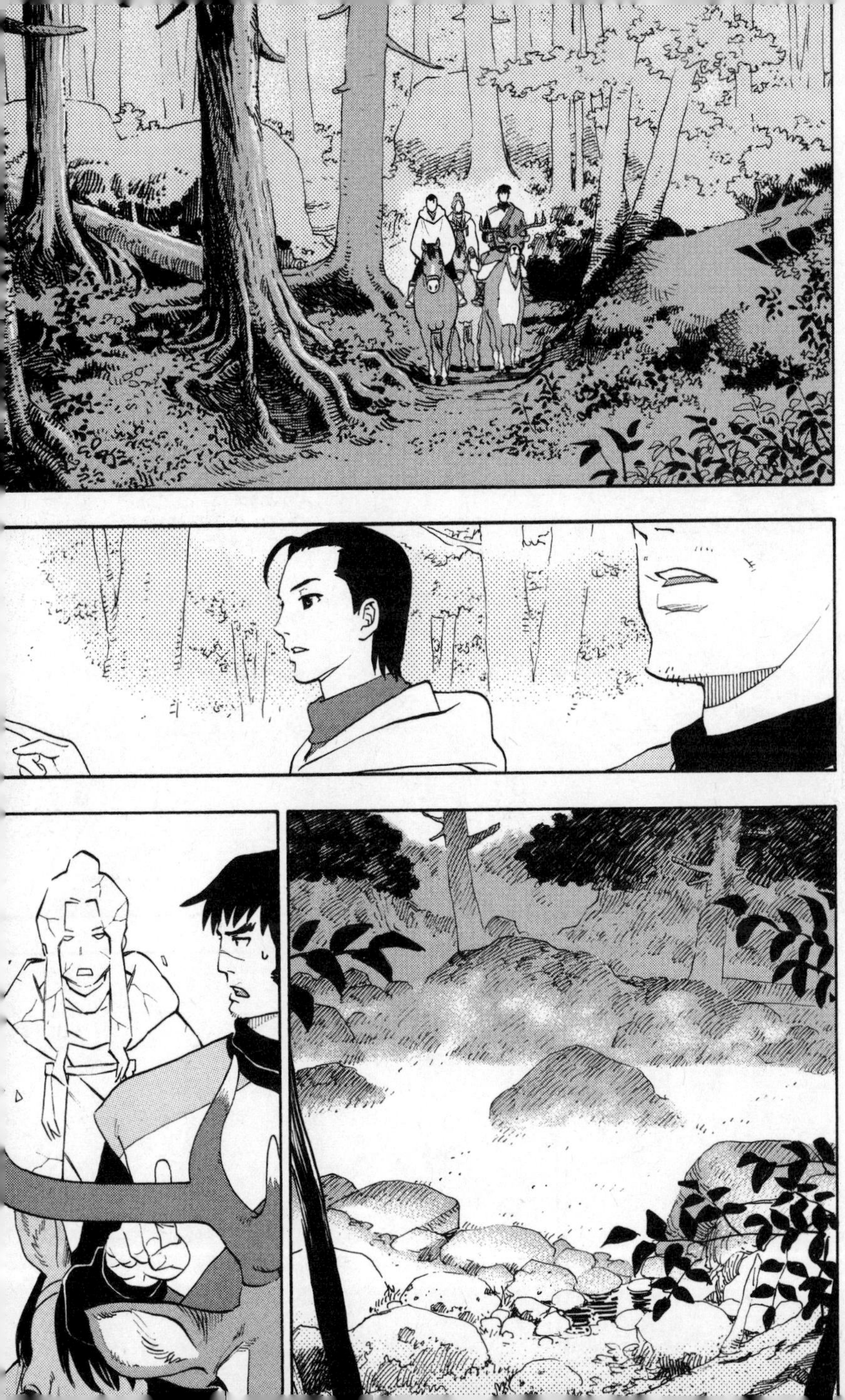

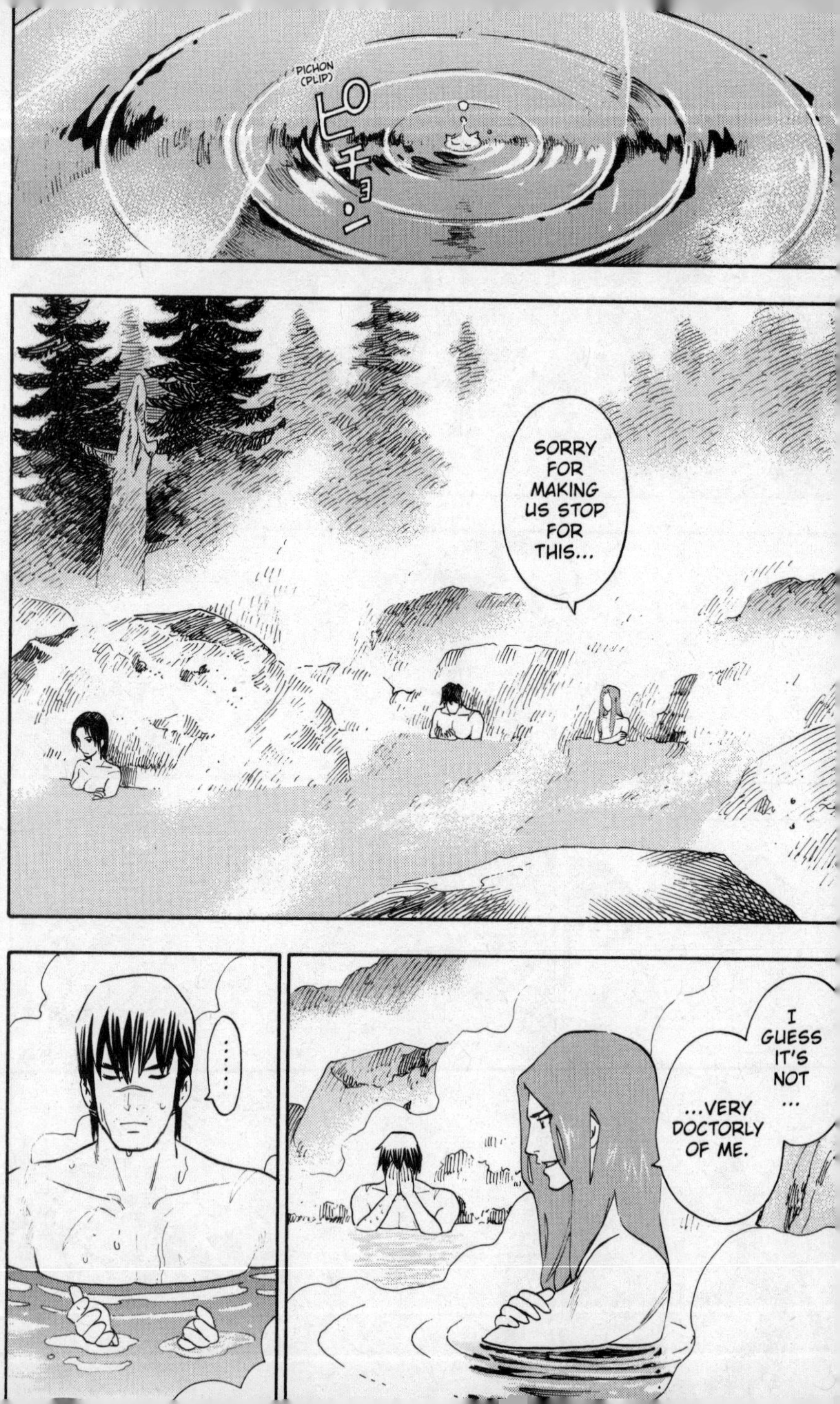
PICHON (PLIP)
SORRY FOR MAKING US STOP FOR THIS...
I GUESS IT'S NOT ...
...VERY DOCTORLY OF ME.
......

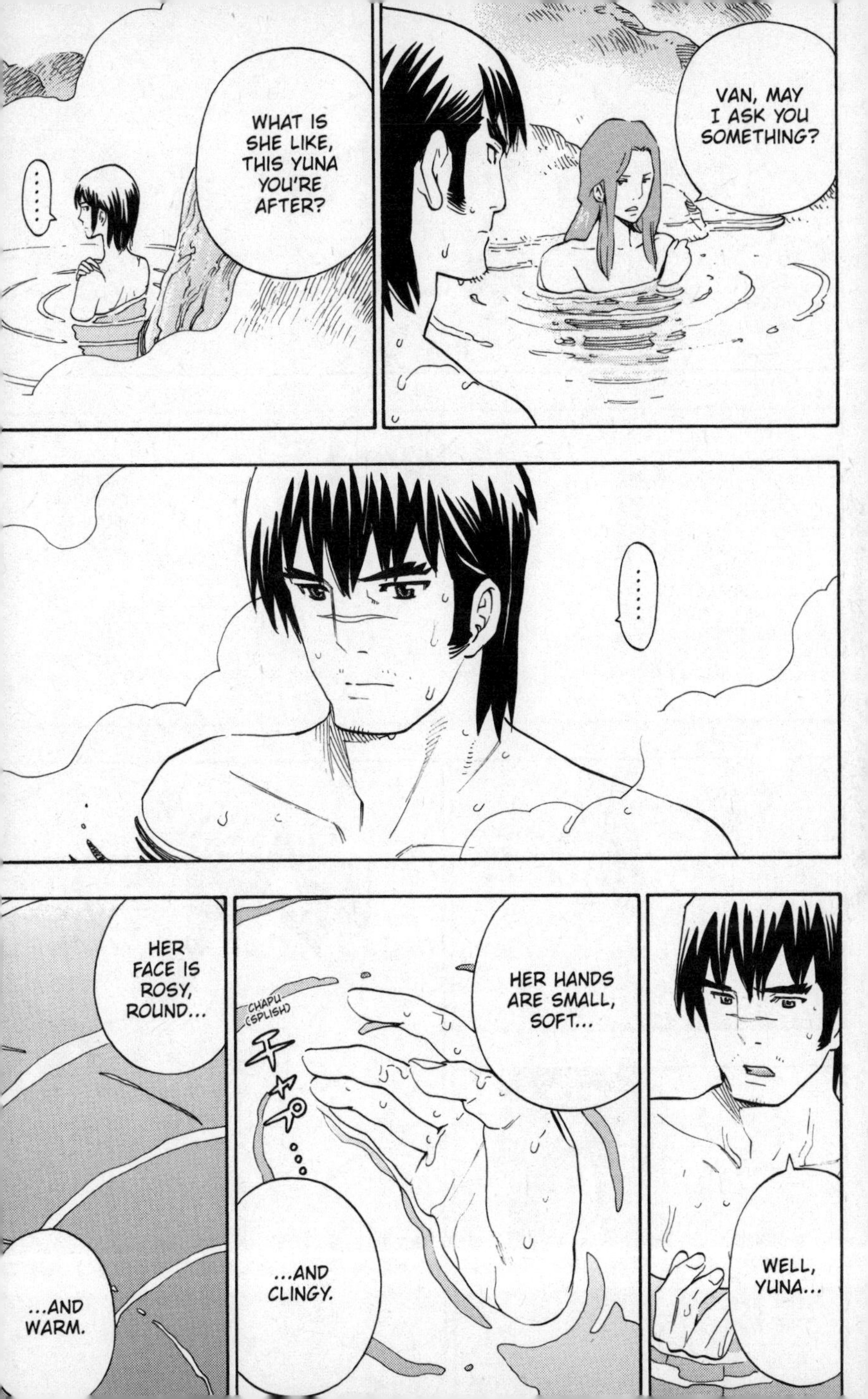
VAN, MAY I ASK YOU SOMETHING?
WHAT IS SHE LIKE, THIS YUNA YOU'RE AFTER?
......
......
WELL, YUNA...
HER HANDS ARE SMALL, SOFT...
CHAPU (SPLISH)
...AND CLINGY.
HER FACE IS ROSY, ROUND...
...AND WARM.

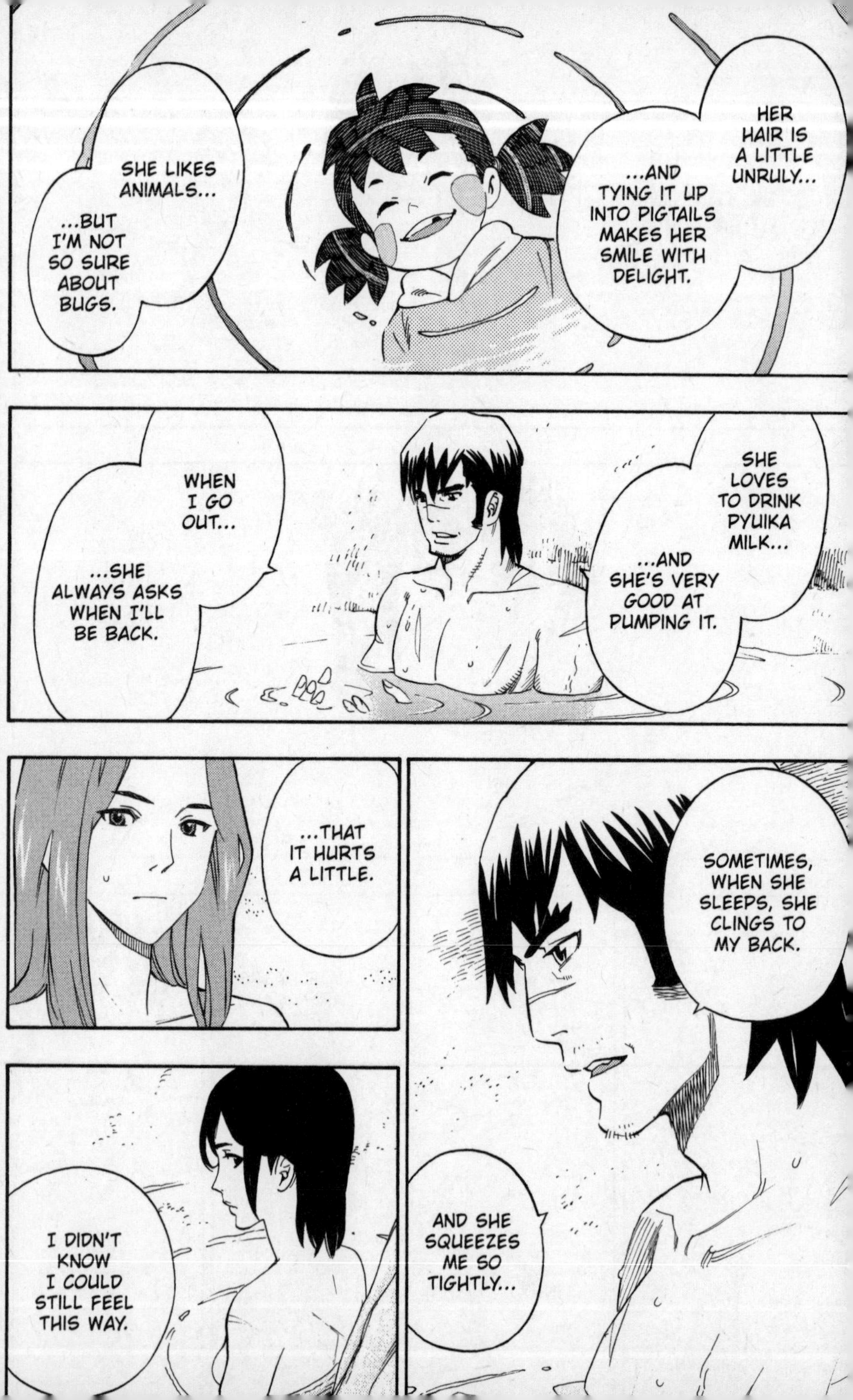
HER HAIR IS A LITTLE UNRULY...
...AND TYING IT UP INTO PIGTAILS MAKES HER SMILE WITH DELIGHT.
SHE LIKES ANIMALS...
...BUT I'M NOT SO SURE ABOUT BUGS.
SHE LOVES TO DRINK PYUIKA MILK...
...AND SHE'S VERY GOOD AT PUMPING IT.
WHEN I GO OUT...
...SHE ALWAYS ASKS WHEN I'LL BE BACK.
SOMETIMES, WHEN SHE SLEEPS, SHE CLINGS TO MY BACK.
AND SHE SQUEEZES ME SO TIGHTLY...
...THAT IT HURTS A LITTLE.
I DIDN'T KNOW I COULD STILL FEEL THIS WAY.

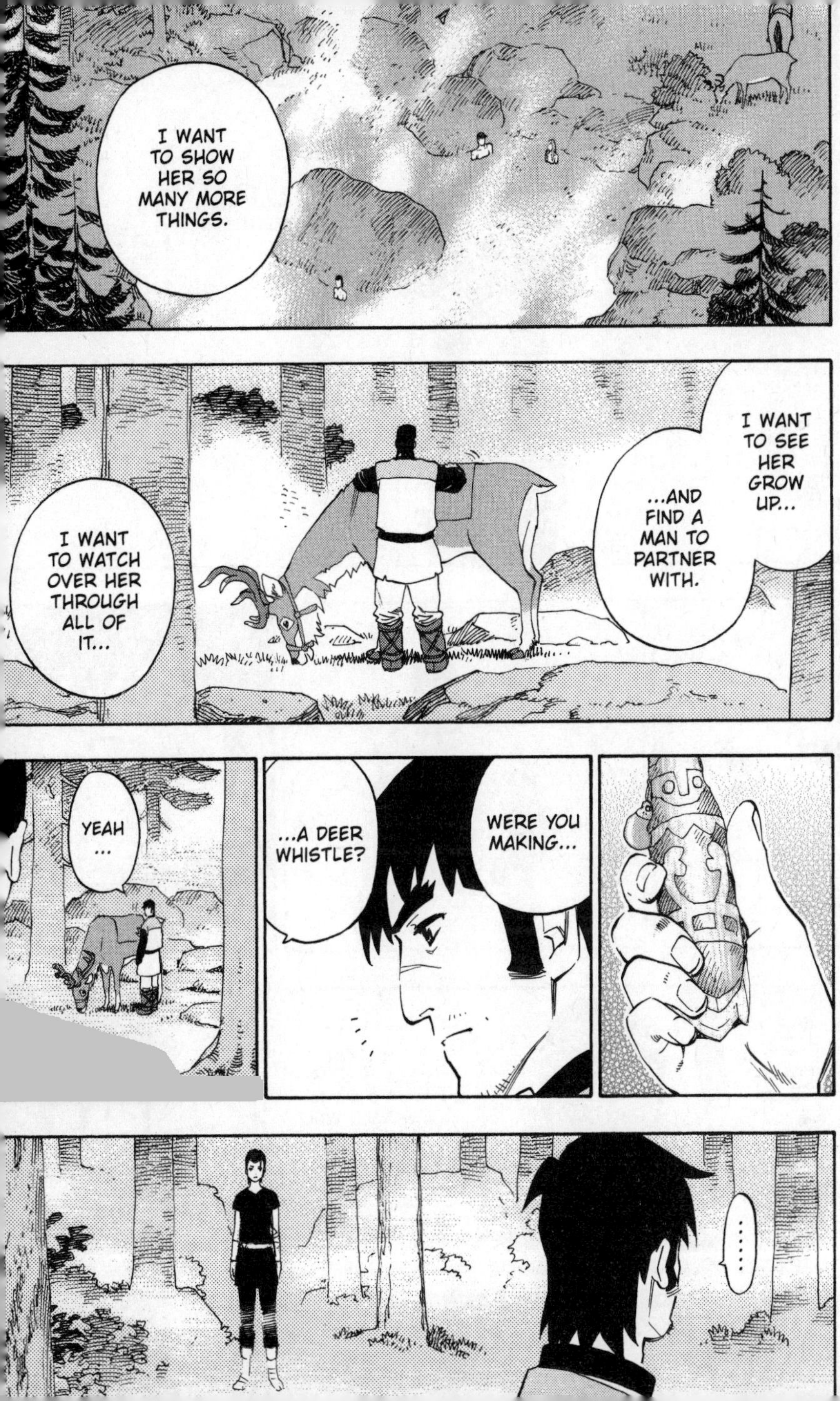
I WANT TO SHOW HER SO MANY MORE THINGS.
I WANT TO SEE HER GROW UP...
...AND FIND A MAN TO PARTNER WITH.
I WANT TO WATCH OVER HER THROUGH ALL OF IT...
WERE YOU MAKING...
...A DEER WHISTLE?
YEAH ...
......

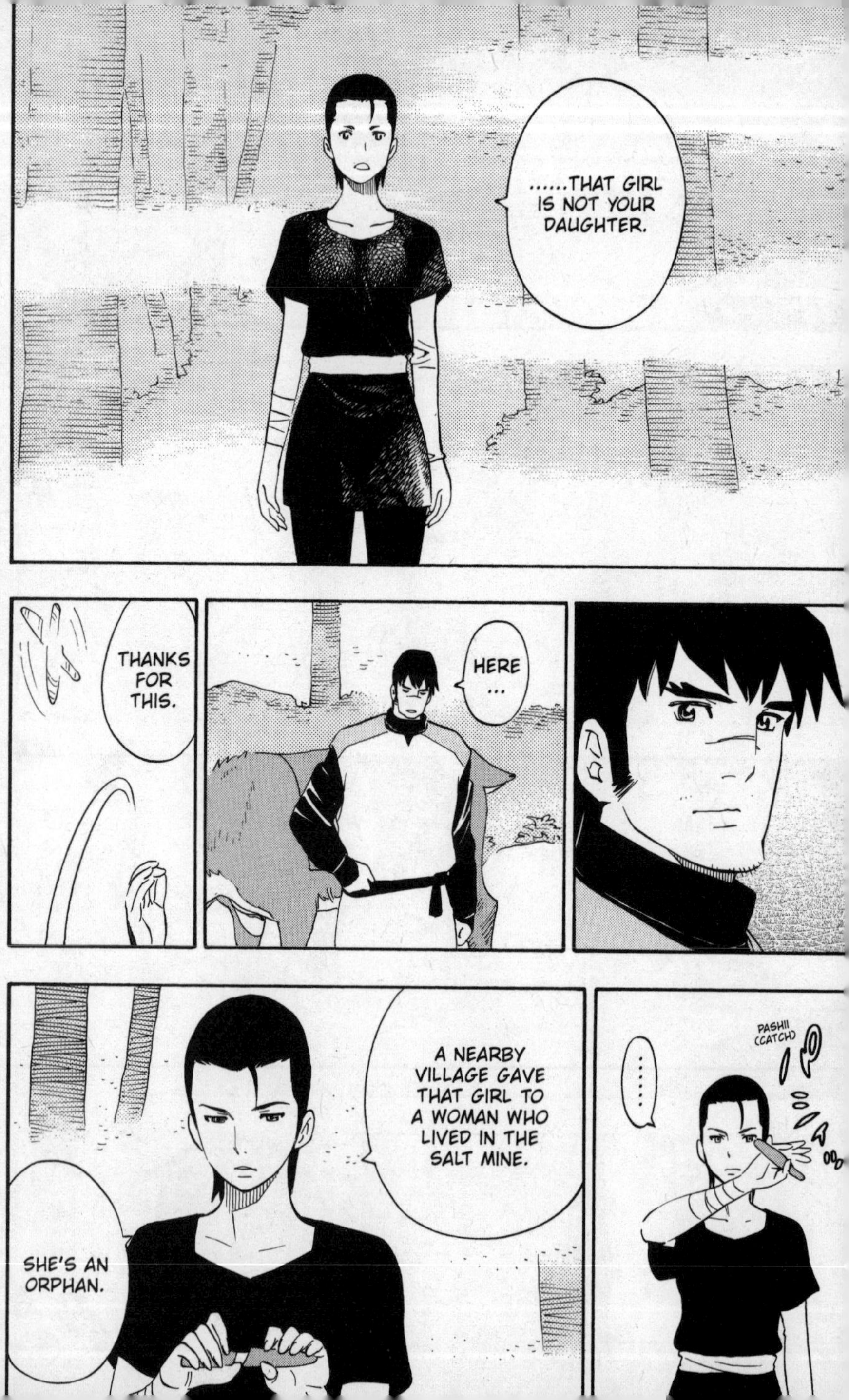
......THAT GIRL IS NOT YOUR DAUGHTER.
HERE ...
THANKS FOR THIS.
PASHII (CATCH)
......
A NEARBY VILLAGE GAVE THAT GIRL TO A WOMAN WHO LIVED IN THE SALT MINE.
SHE'S AN ORPHAN.

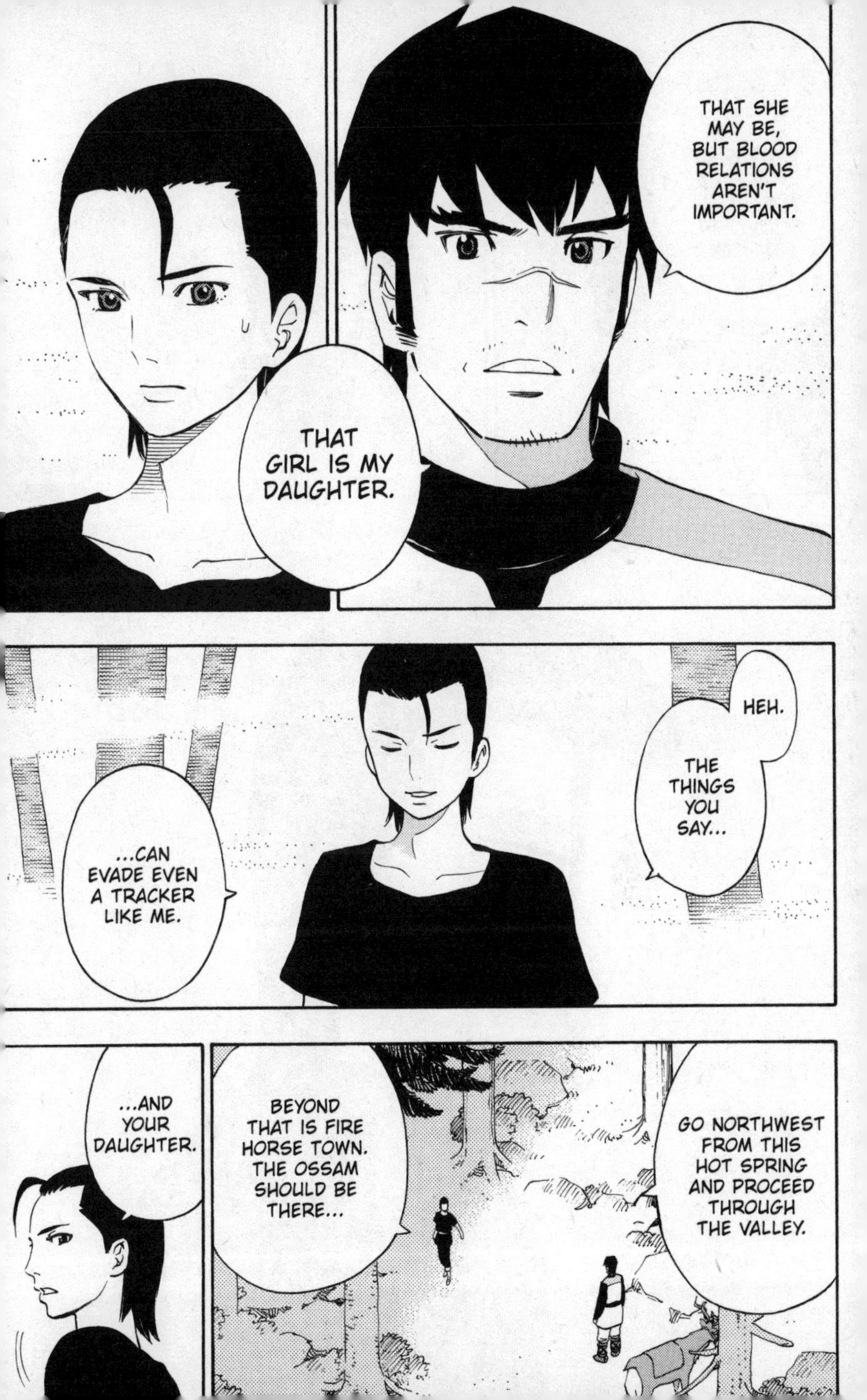
THAT SHE MAY BE, BUT BLOOD RELATIONS AREN'T IMPORTANT.
THAT GIRL IS MY DAUGHTER.
...
HEH.
THE THINGS YOU SAY...
...CAN EVADE EVEN A TRACKER LIKE ME.
GO NORTHWEST FROM THIS HOT SPRING AND PROCEED THROUGH THE VALLEY.
BEYOND THAT IS FIRE HORSE TOWN. THE OSSAM SHOULD BE THERE...
...AND YOUR DAUGHTER.

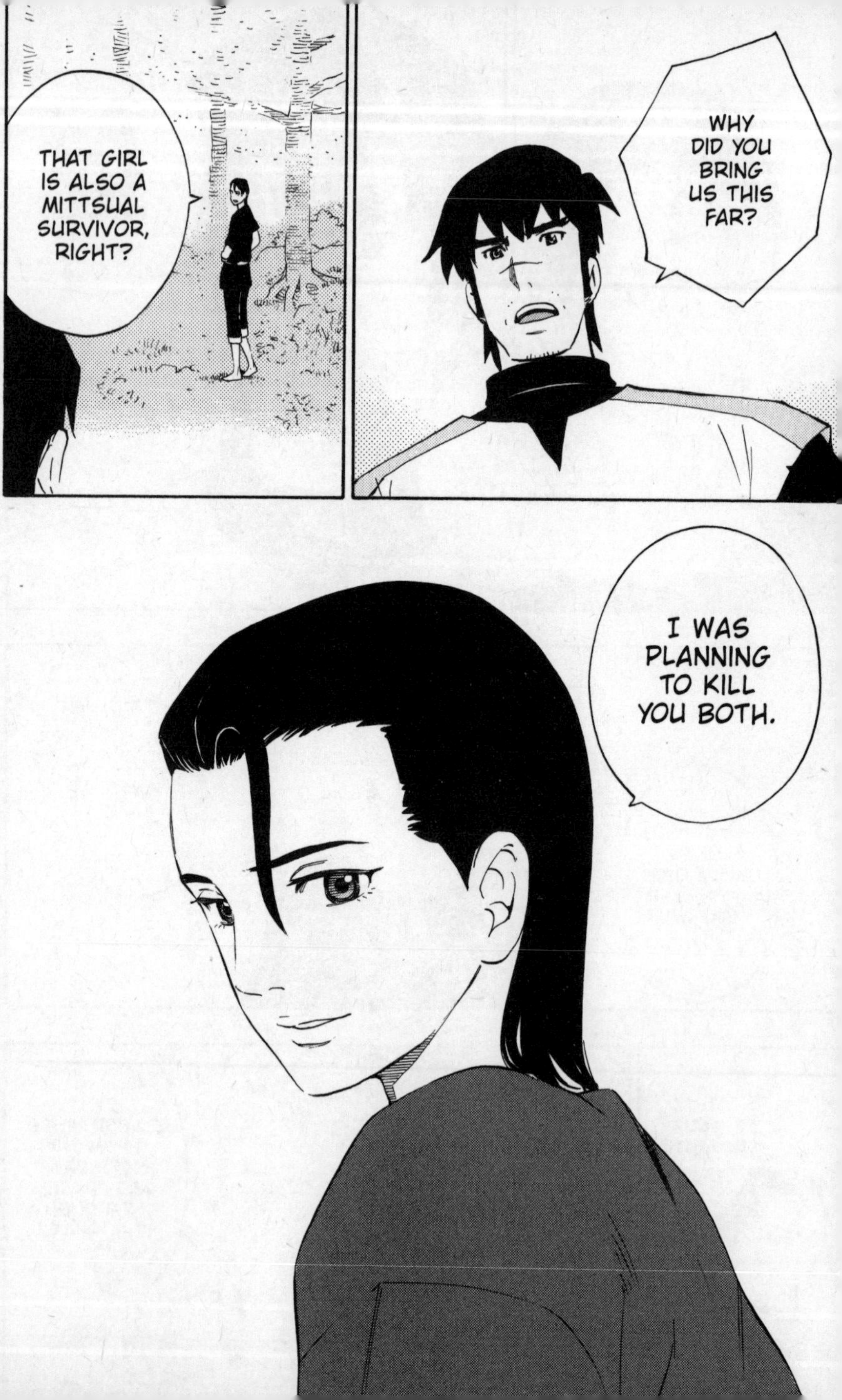
WHY DID YOU BRING US THIS FAR?
THAT GIRL IS ALSO A MITTSUAL SURVIVOR, RIGHT?
I WAS PLANNING TO KILL YOU BOTH.

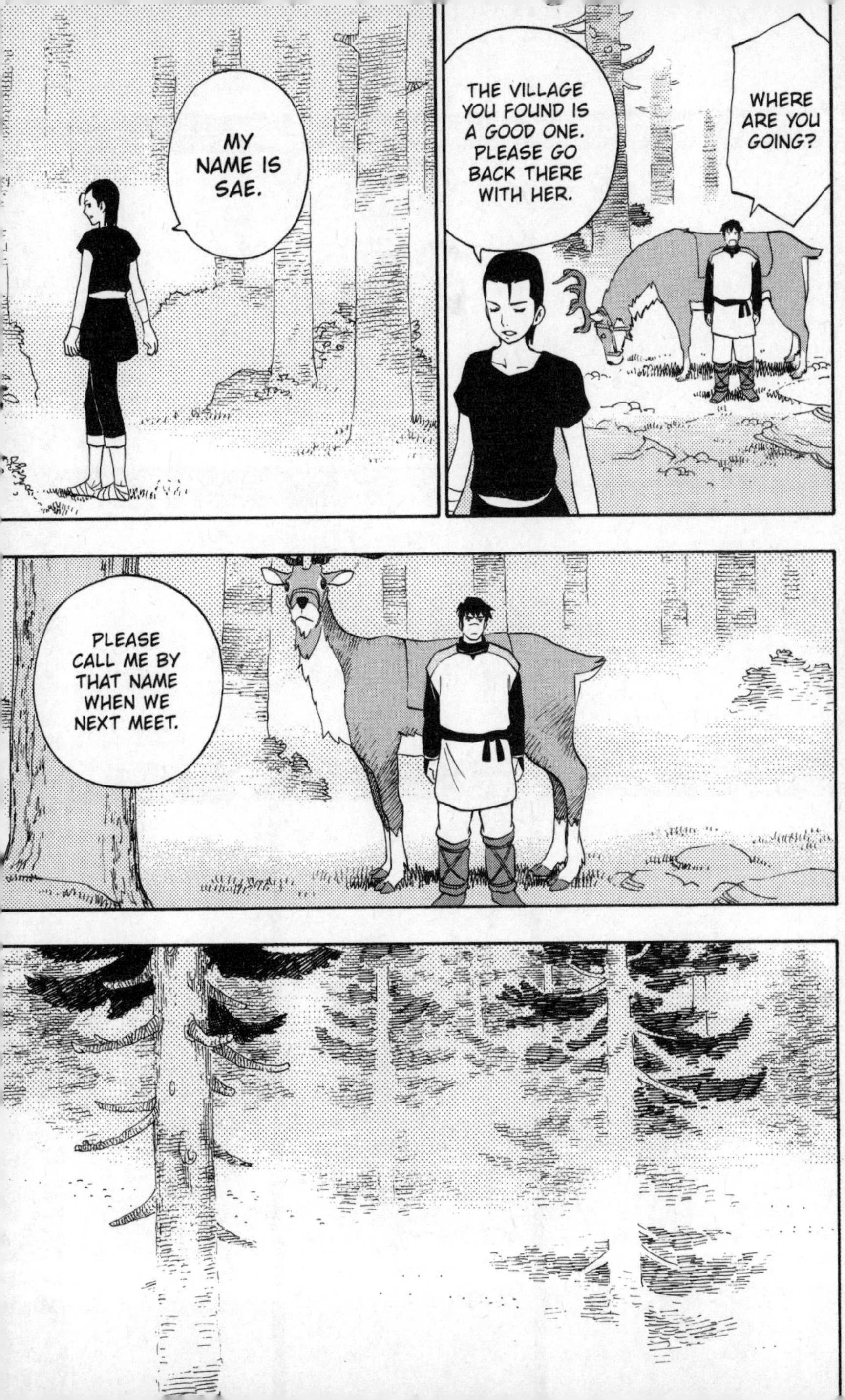
WHERE ARE YOU GOING?
THE VILLAGE YOU FOUND IS A GOOD ONE. PLEASE GO BACK THERE WITH HER.
MY NAME IS SAE.
PLEASE CALL ME BY THAT NAME WHEN WE NEXT MEET.

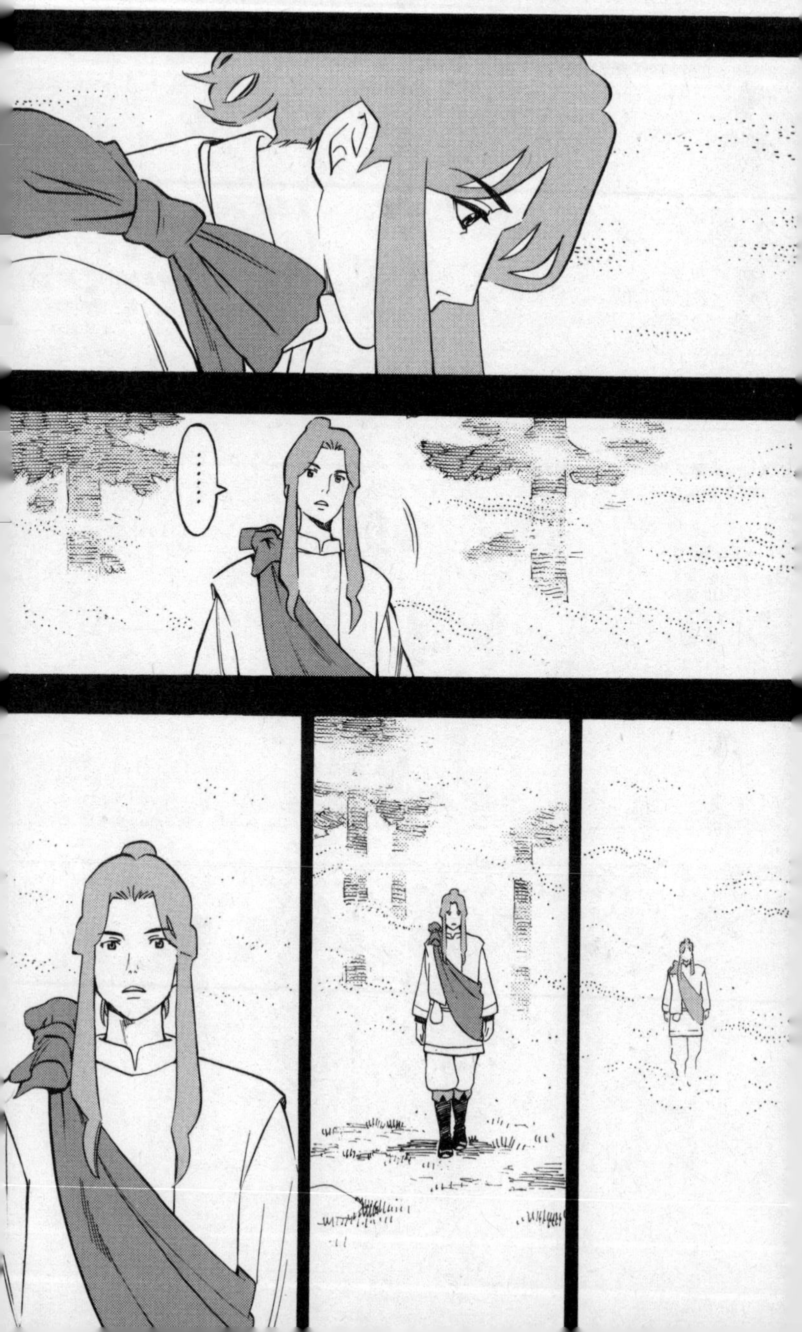
......

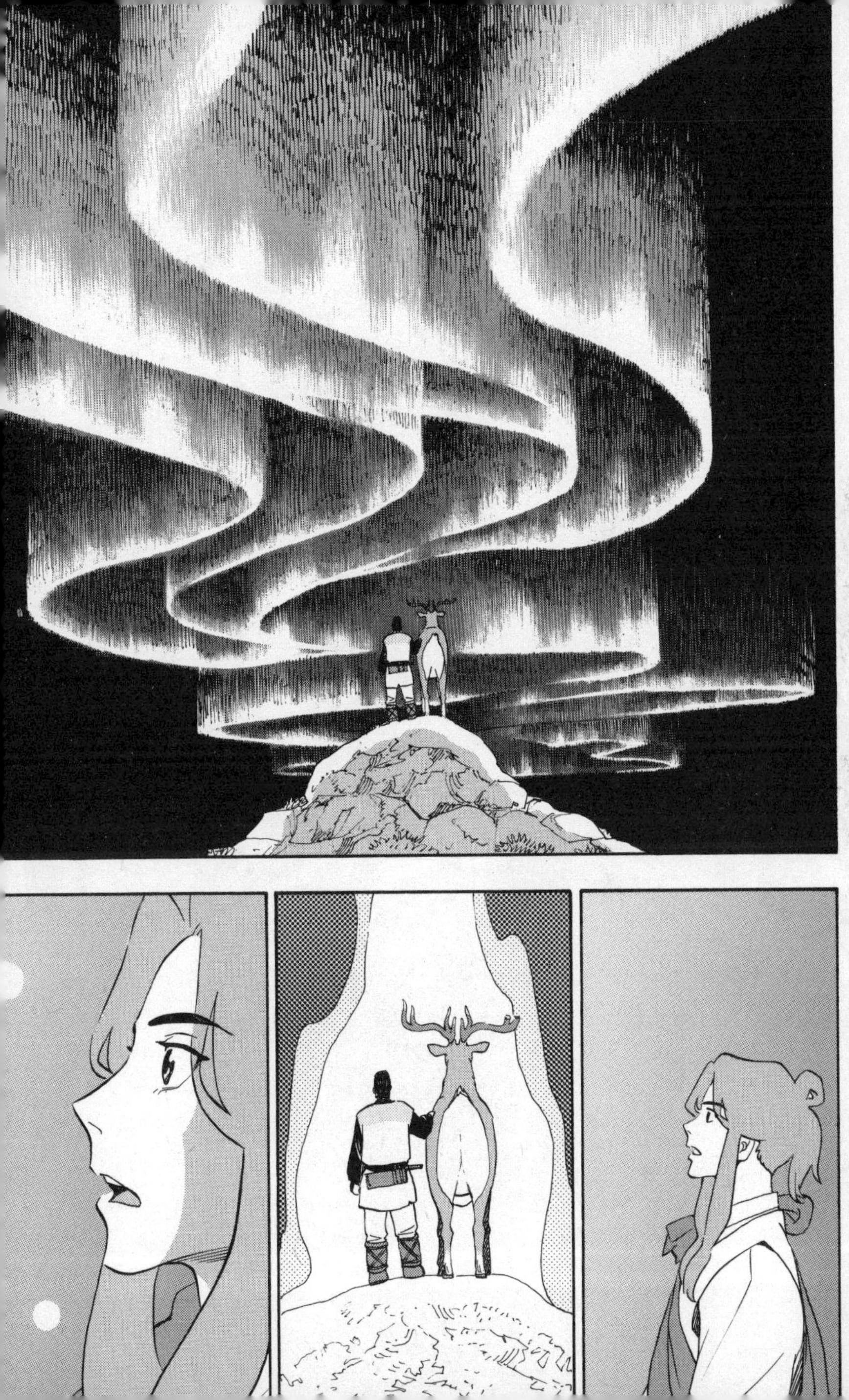

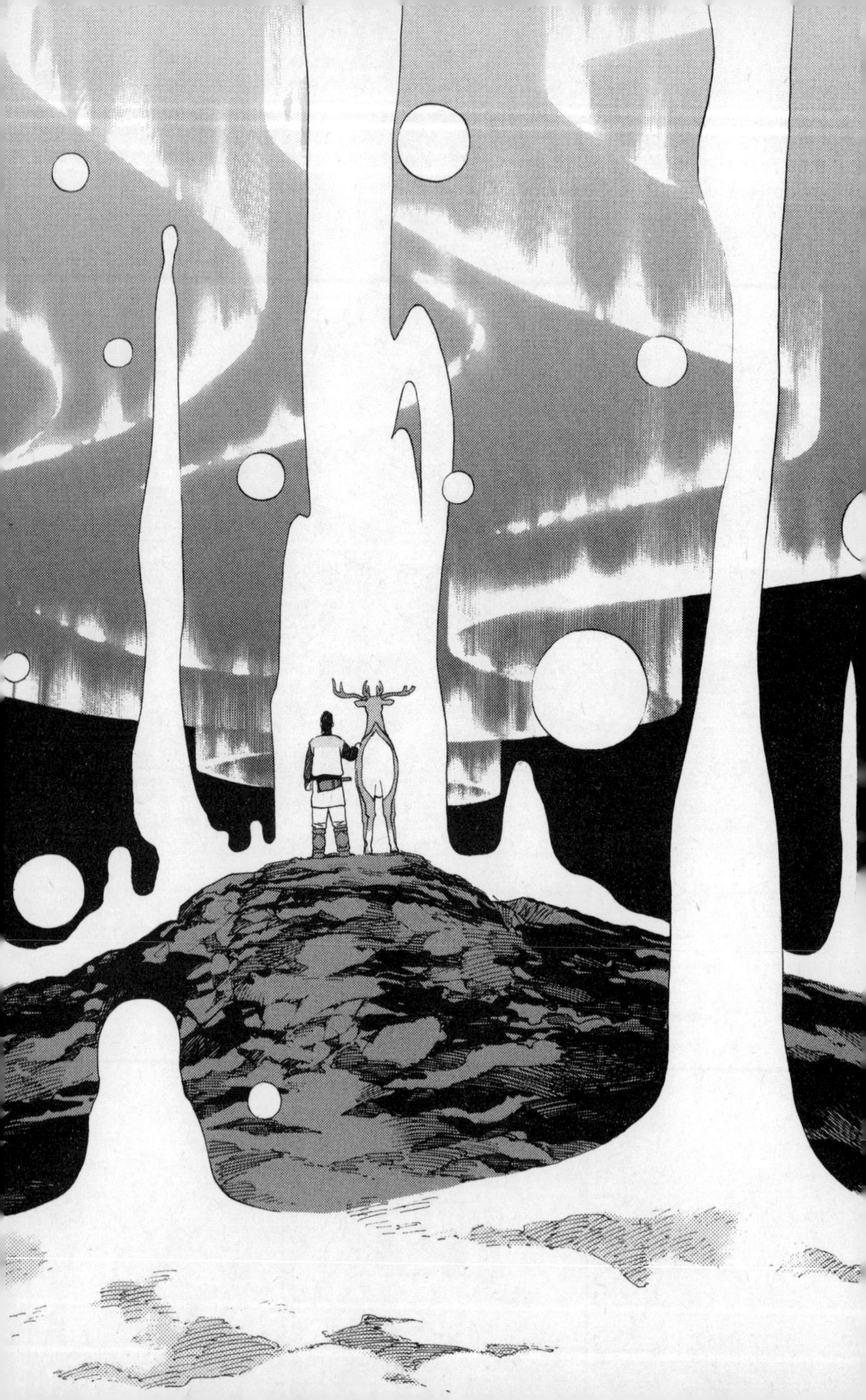

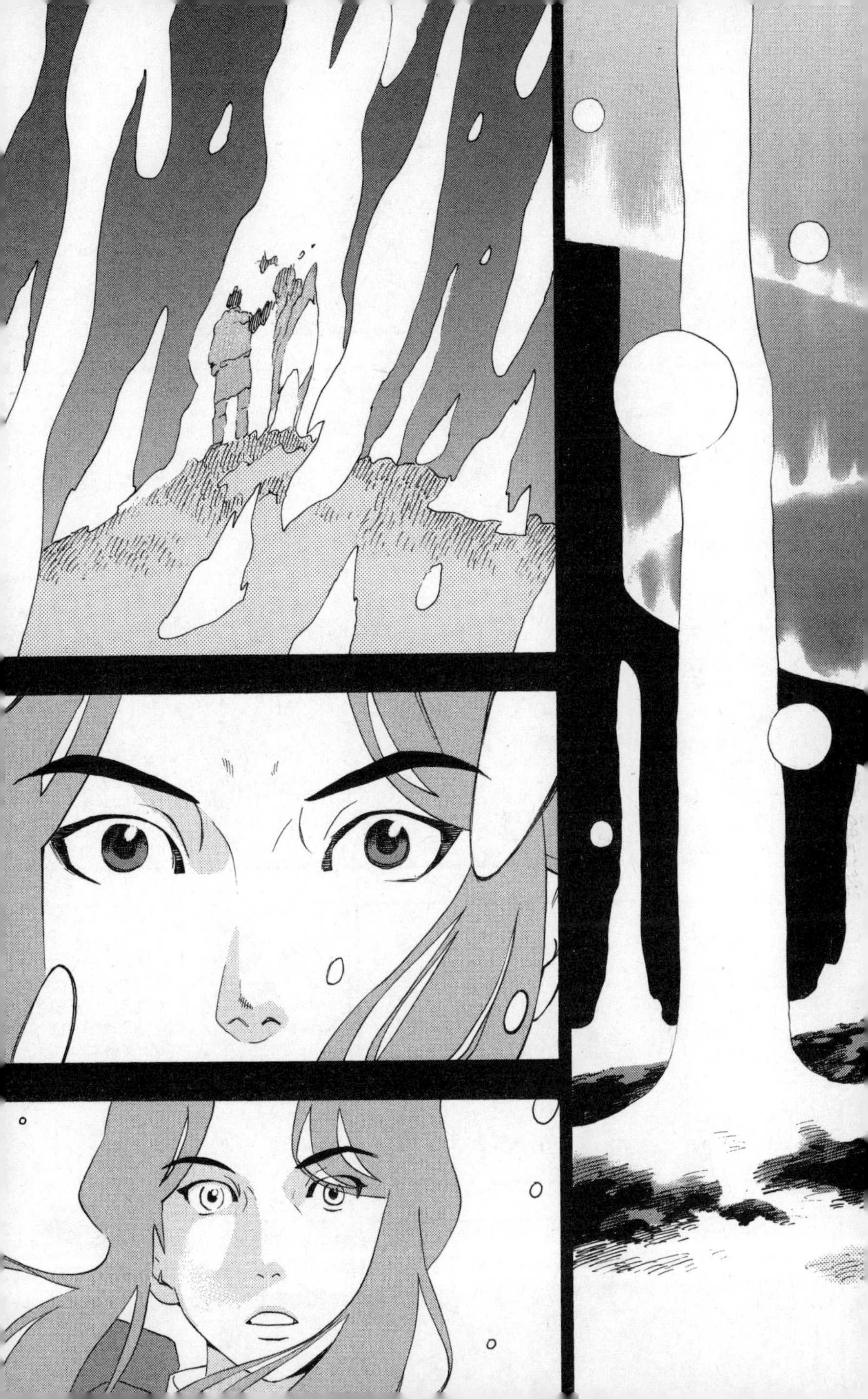

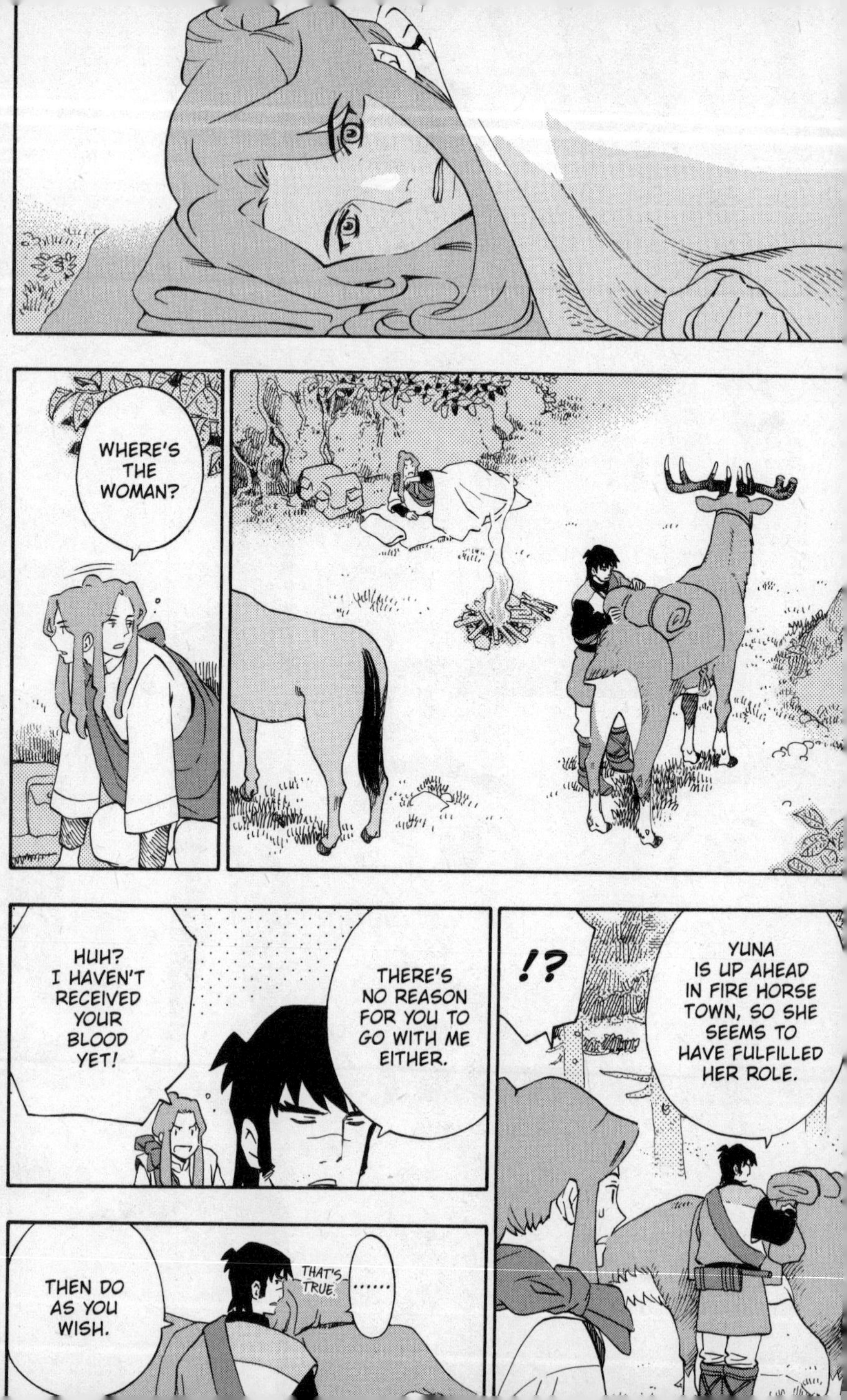
WHERE'S THE WOMAN?
YUNA IS UP AHEAD IN FIRE HORSE TOWN, SO SHE SEEMS TO HAVE FULFILLED HER ROLE.
!?
THERE'S NO REASON FOR YOU TO GO WITH ME EITHER.
HUH? I HAVEN'T RECEIVED YOUR BLOOD YET!
......
THAT'S TRUE.
THEN DO AS YOU WISH.

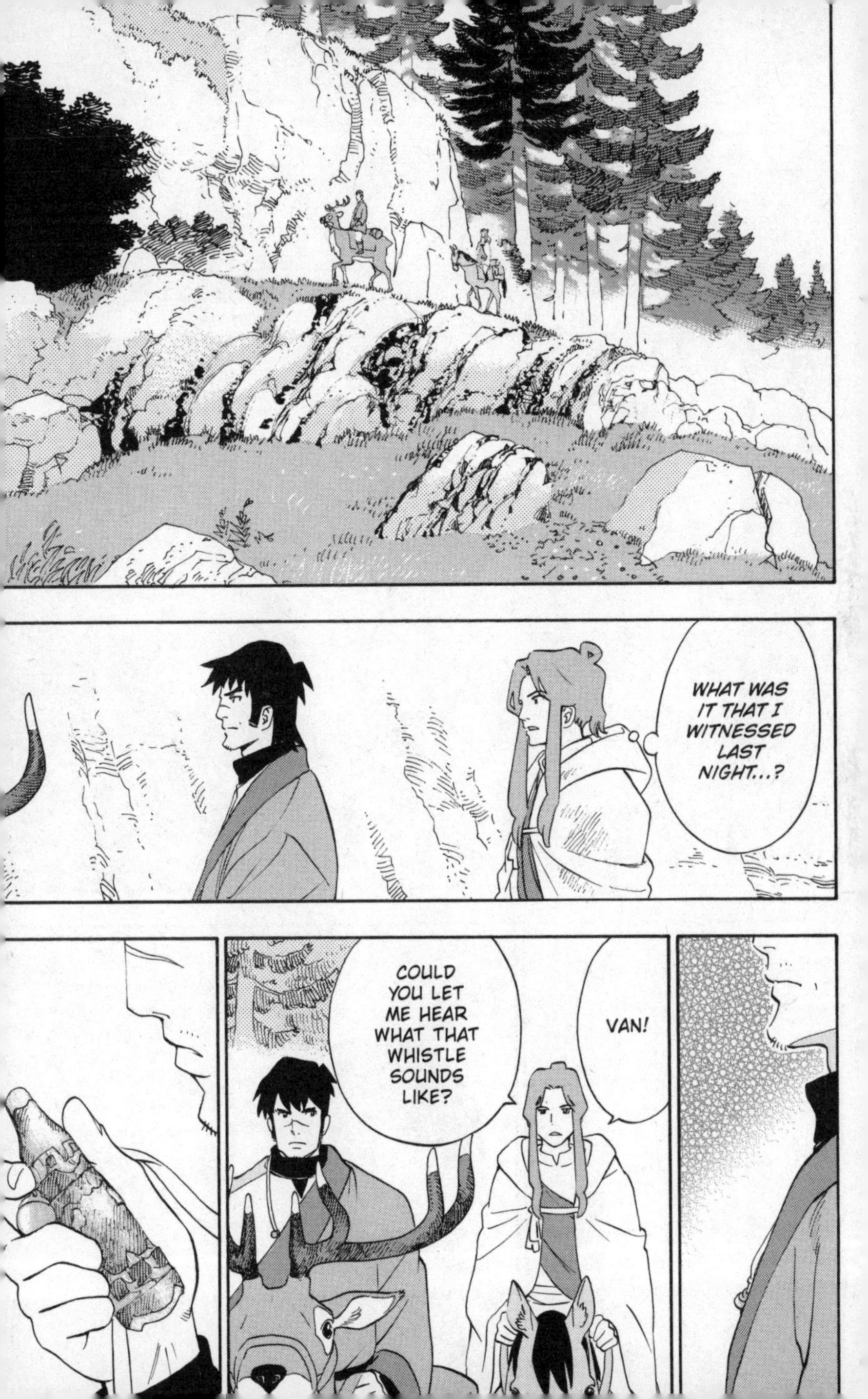
WHAT WAS IT THAT I WITNESSED LAST NIGHT...?
VAN!
COULD YOU LET ME HEAR WHAT THAT WHISTLE SOUNDS LIKE?

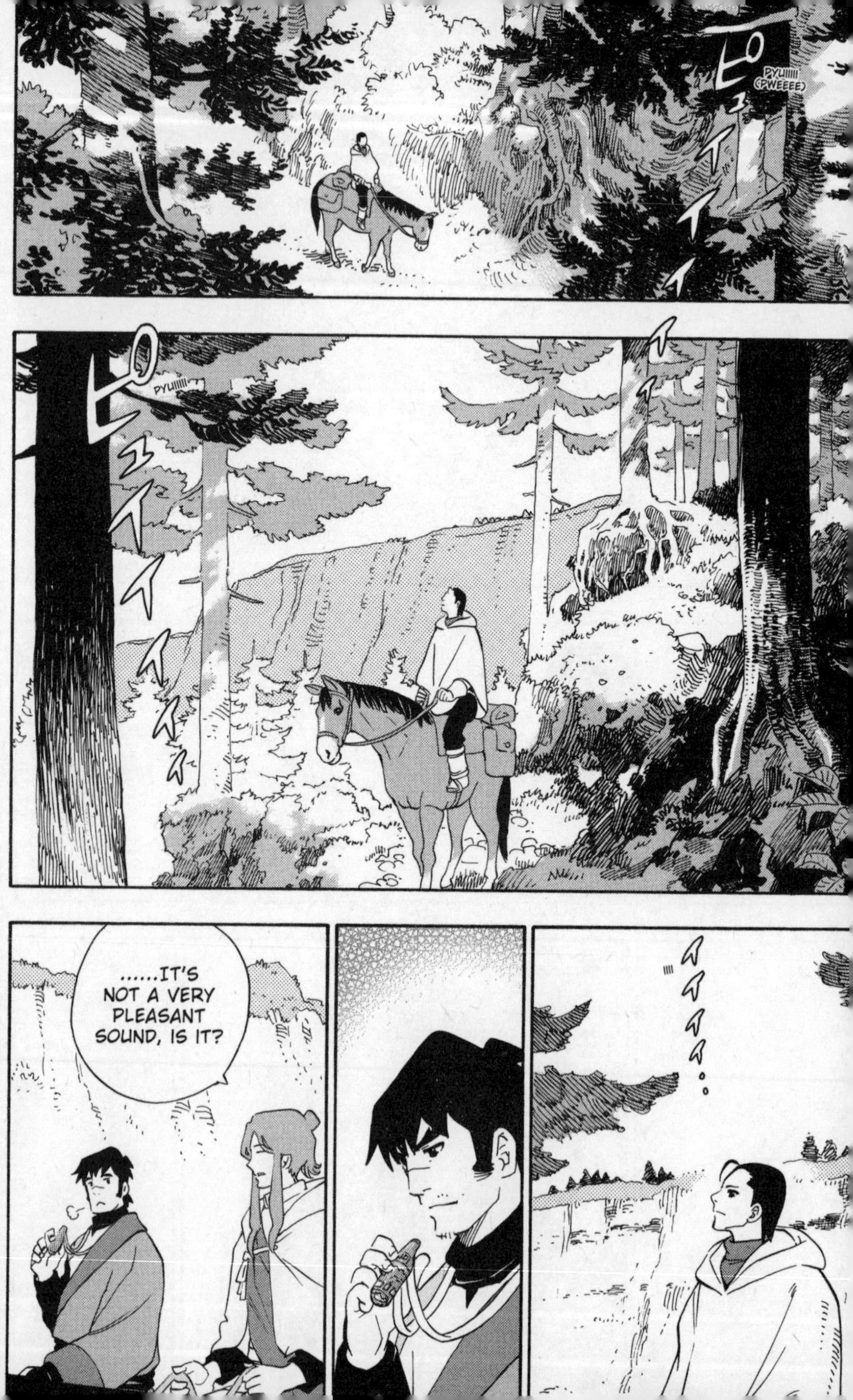
ピュイイイイ
PYUIIIIII
(PWEEEEE)
ピュイイイイイイイ
PYUIIIIII
イイイイ。。
IIII
......IT'S NOT A VERY PLEASANT SOUND, IS IT?

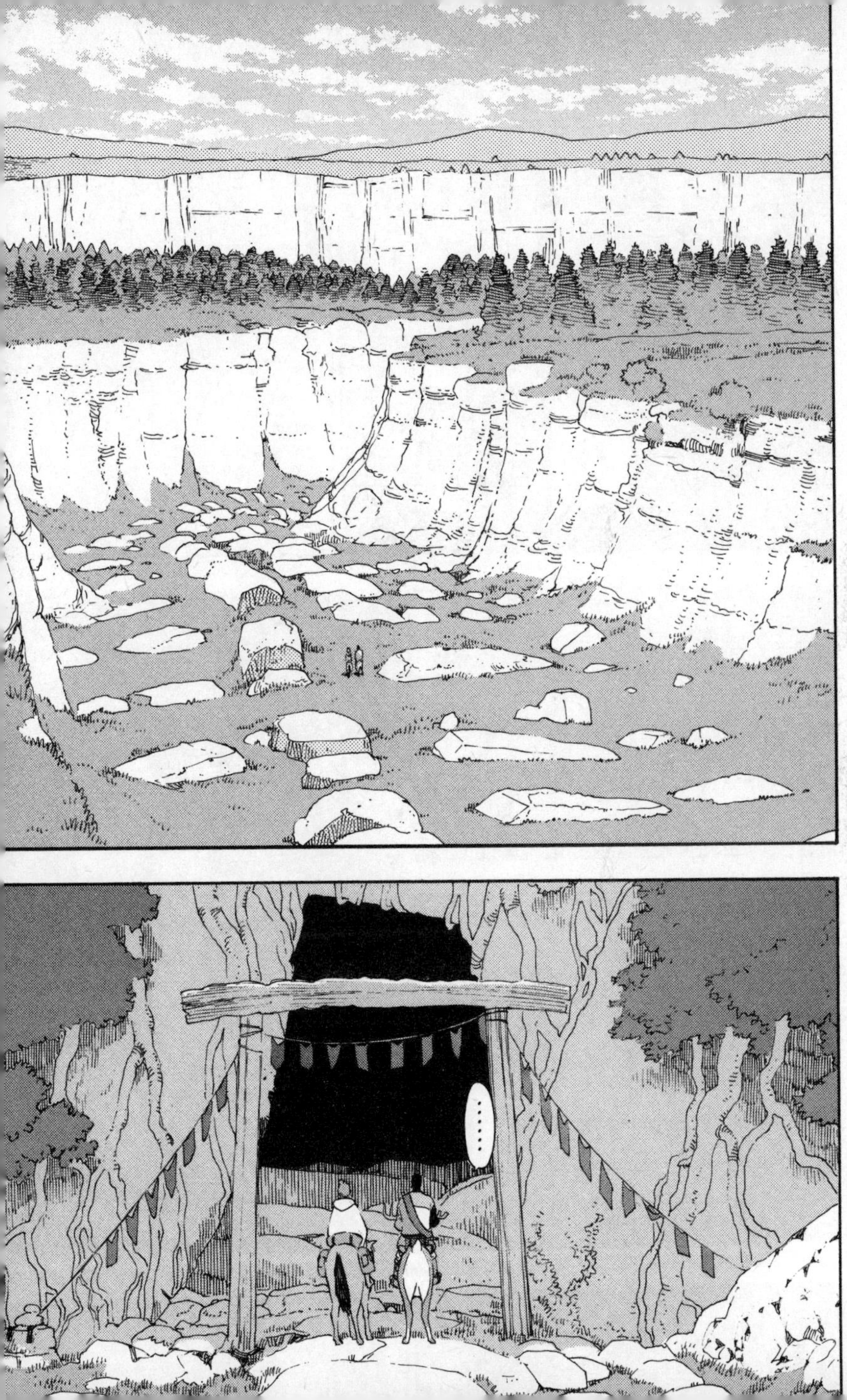
……

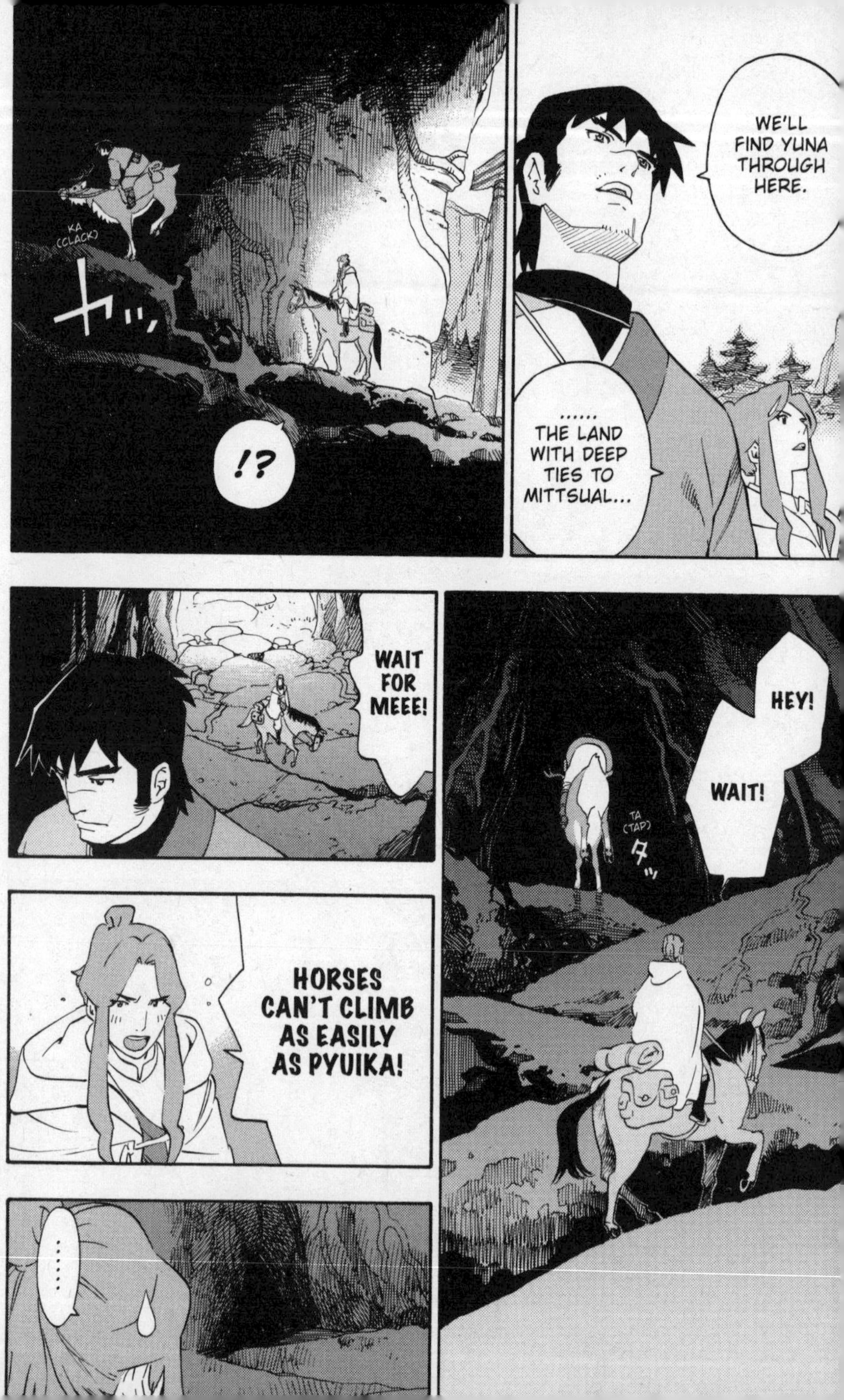
WE'LL FIND YUNA THROUGH HERE.
...... THE LAND WITH DEEP TIES TO MITTSUAL...
KA (CLACK)
!?
HEY!
WAIT!
TA (TAP)
WAIT FOR MEEE!
HORSES CAN'T CLIMB AS EASILY AS PYUIKA!
......

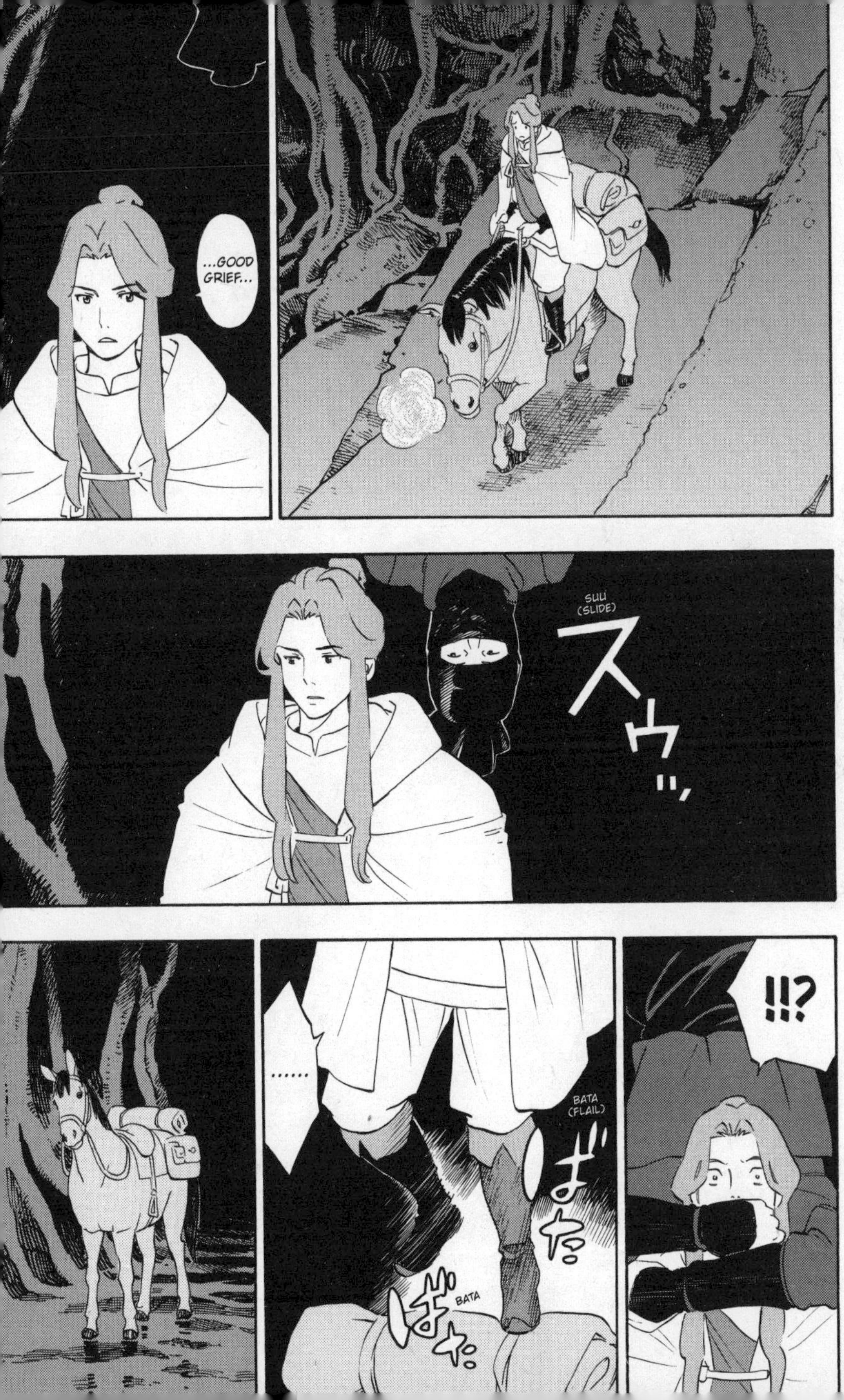
...GOOD GRIEF...
SUU (SLIDE)
スウッ
!!?
......
BATA (FLAIL)
ばた
BATA
ばた

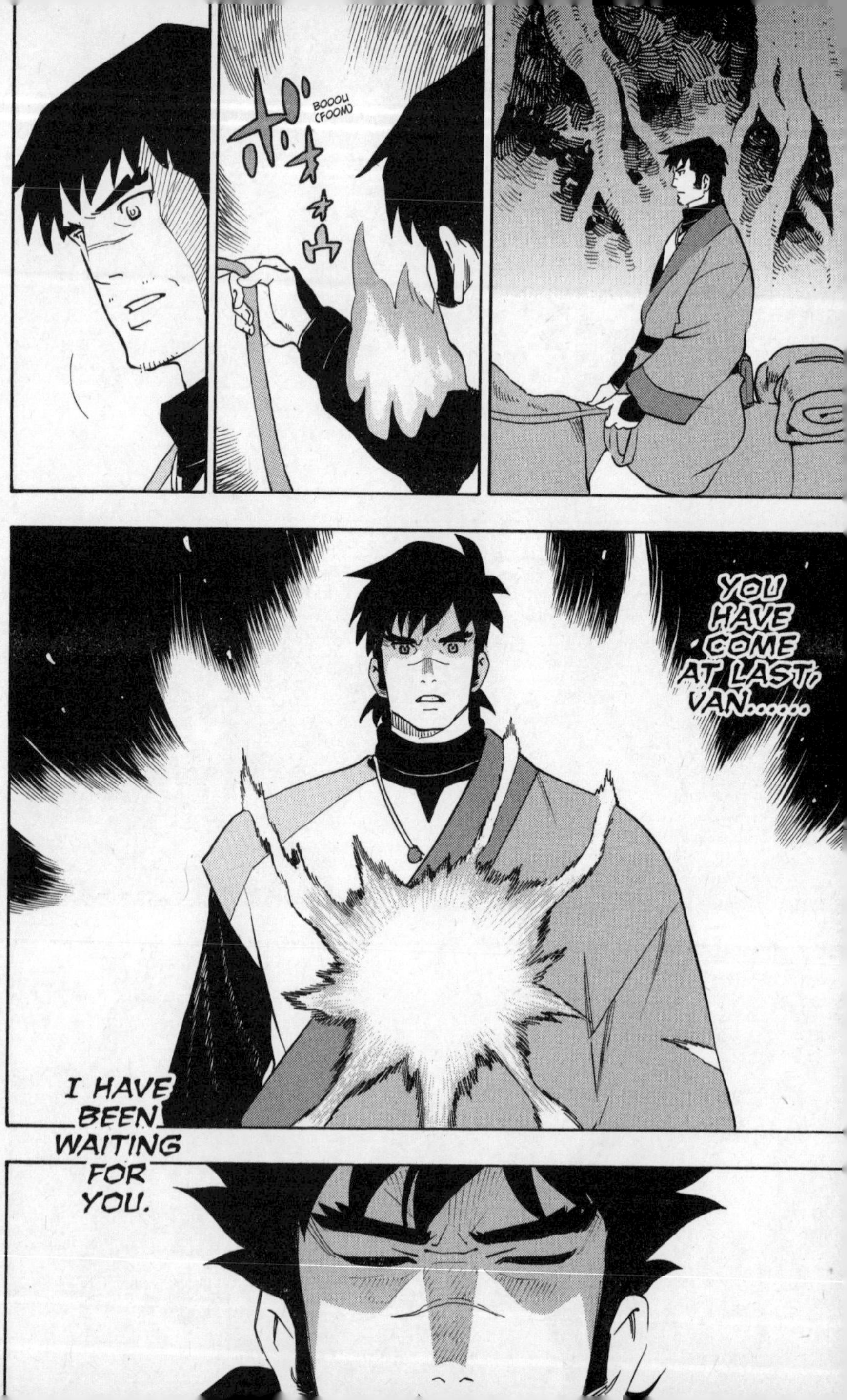
ボォォォ
BOOOU (FOOM)
YOU HAVE COME AT LAST, VAN......
I HAVE BEEN WAITING FOR YOU.

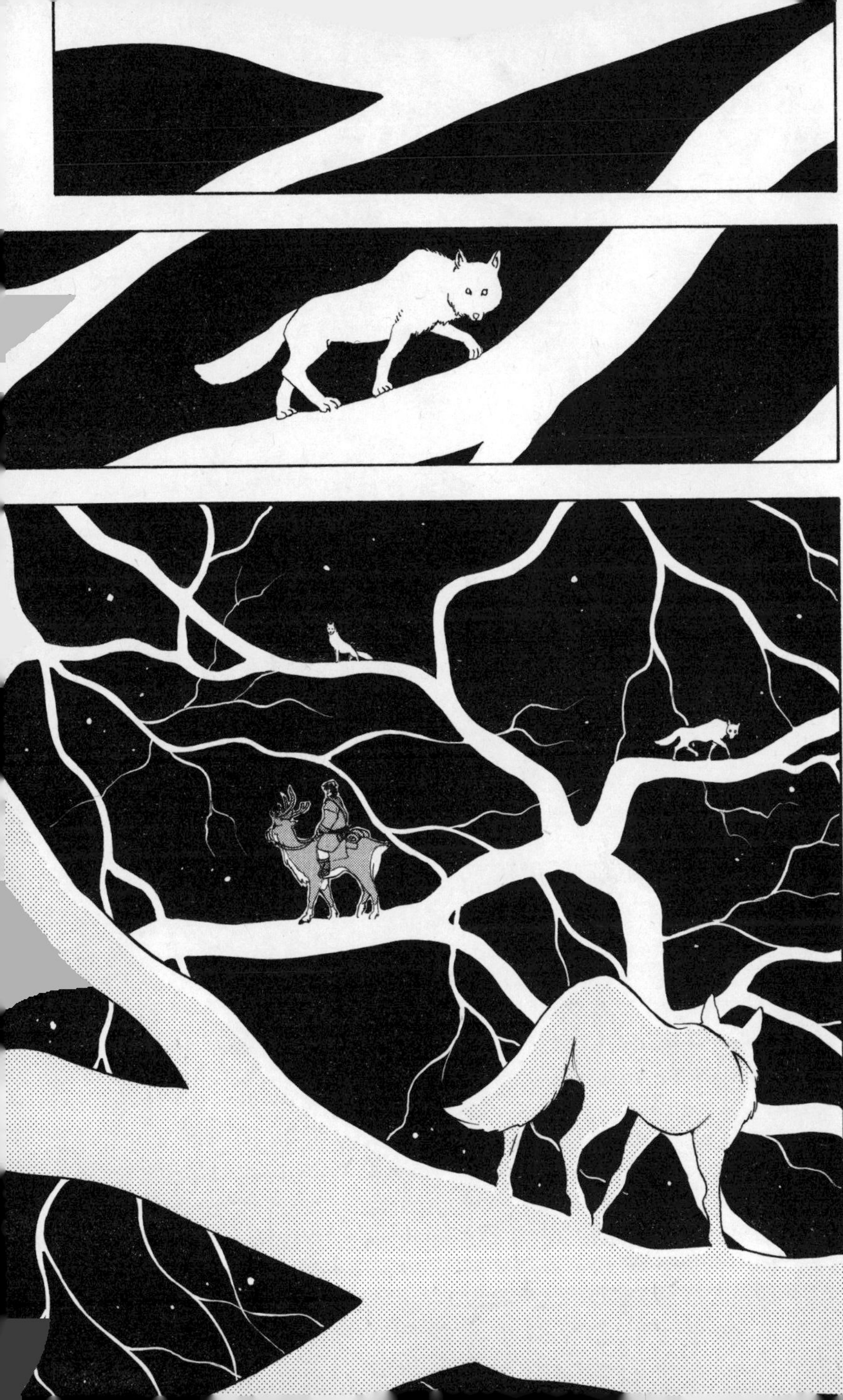

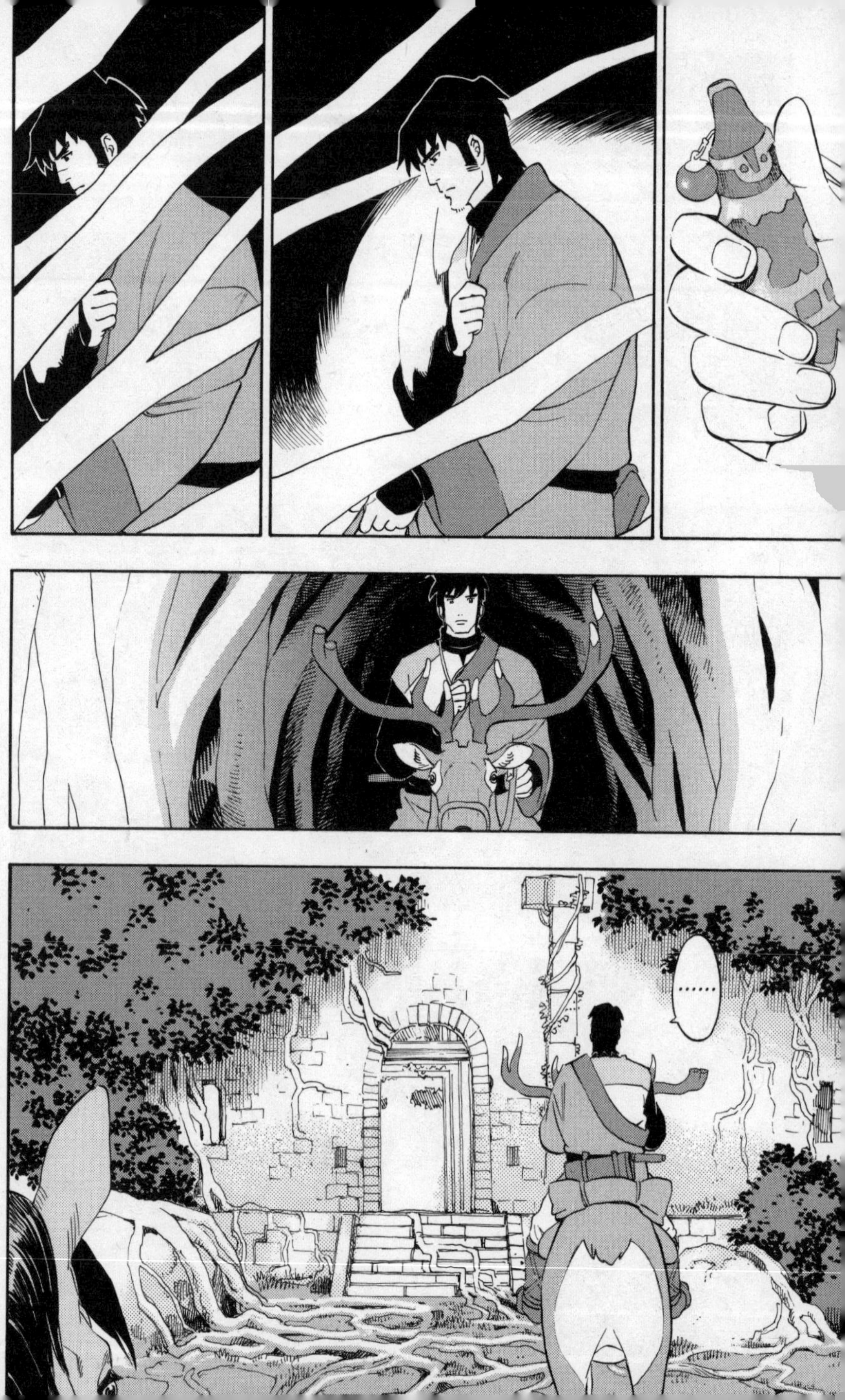
……

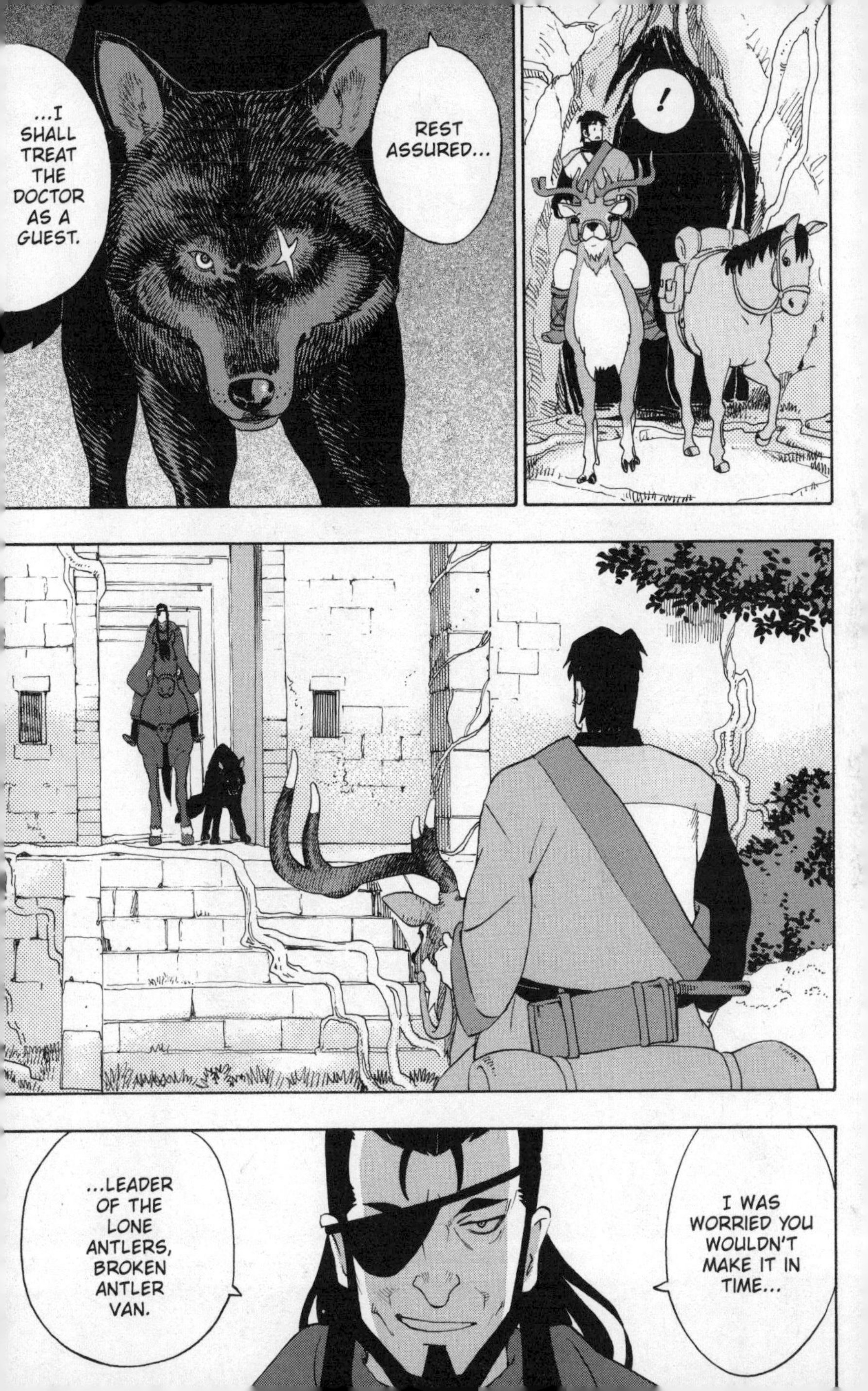
!
REST ASSURED...
...I SHALL TREAT THE DOCTOR AS A GUEST.
I WAS WORRIED YOU WOULDN'T MAKE IT IN TIME...
...LEADER OF THE LONE ANTLERS, BROKEN ANTLER VAN.

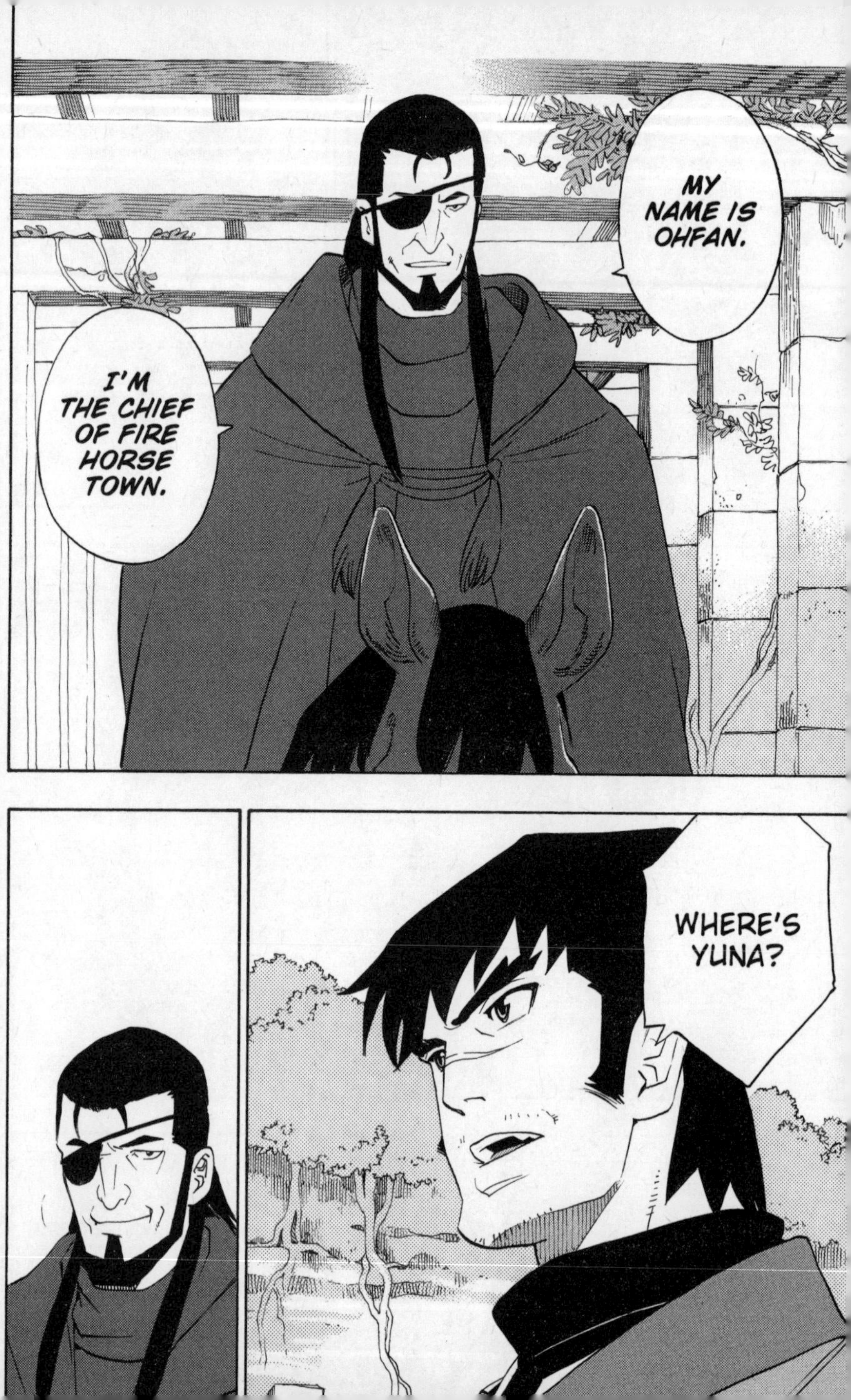
MY NAME IS OHFAN.
I'M THE CHIEF OF FIRE HORSE TOWN.
WHERE'S YUNA?

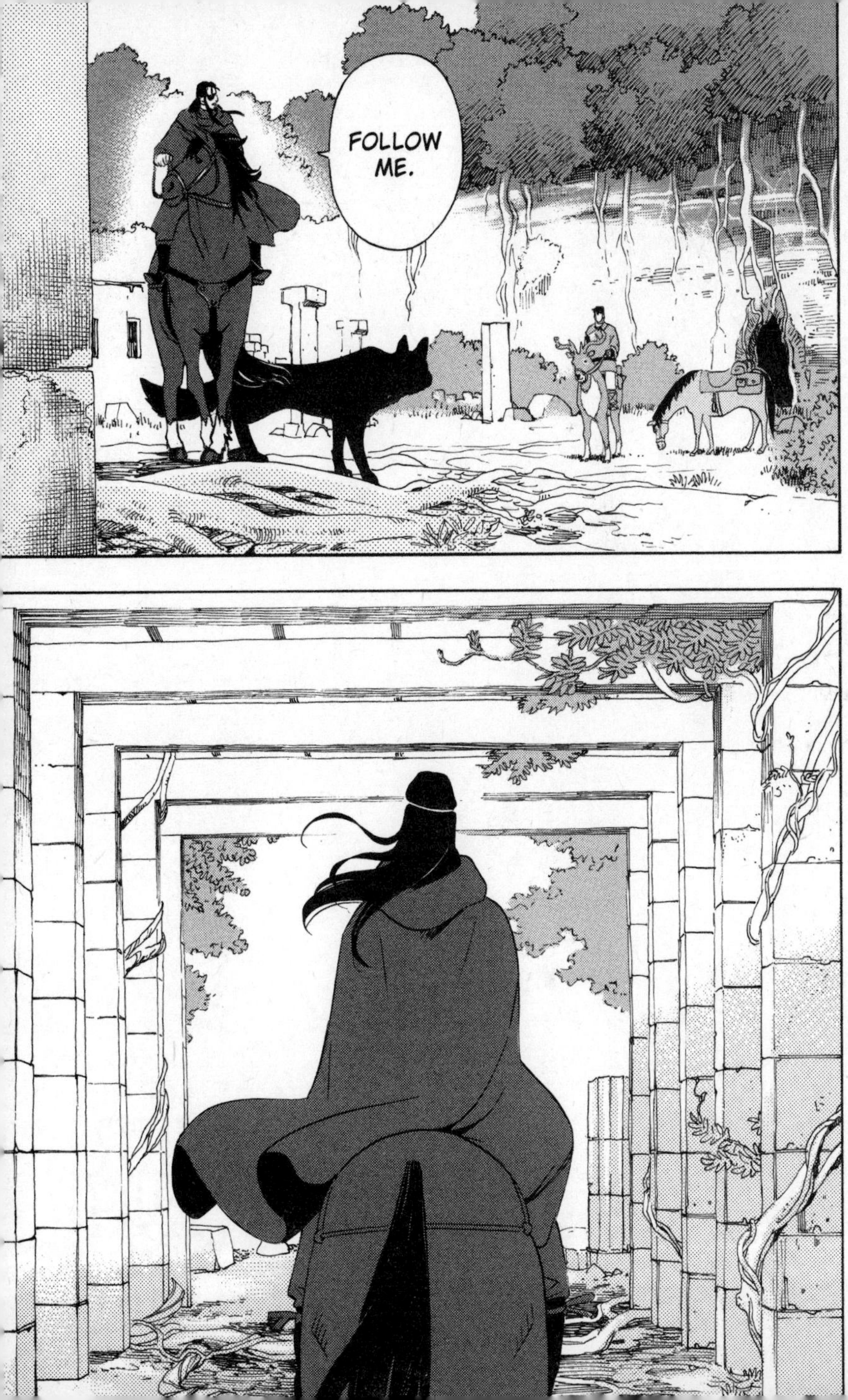
FOLLOW ME.

THE
DEER
KING

YUNA AND THE
PROMISED JOURNEY

## Chapter 9

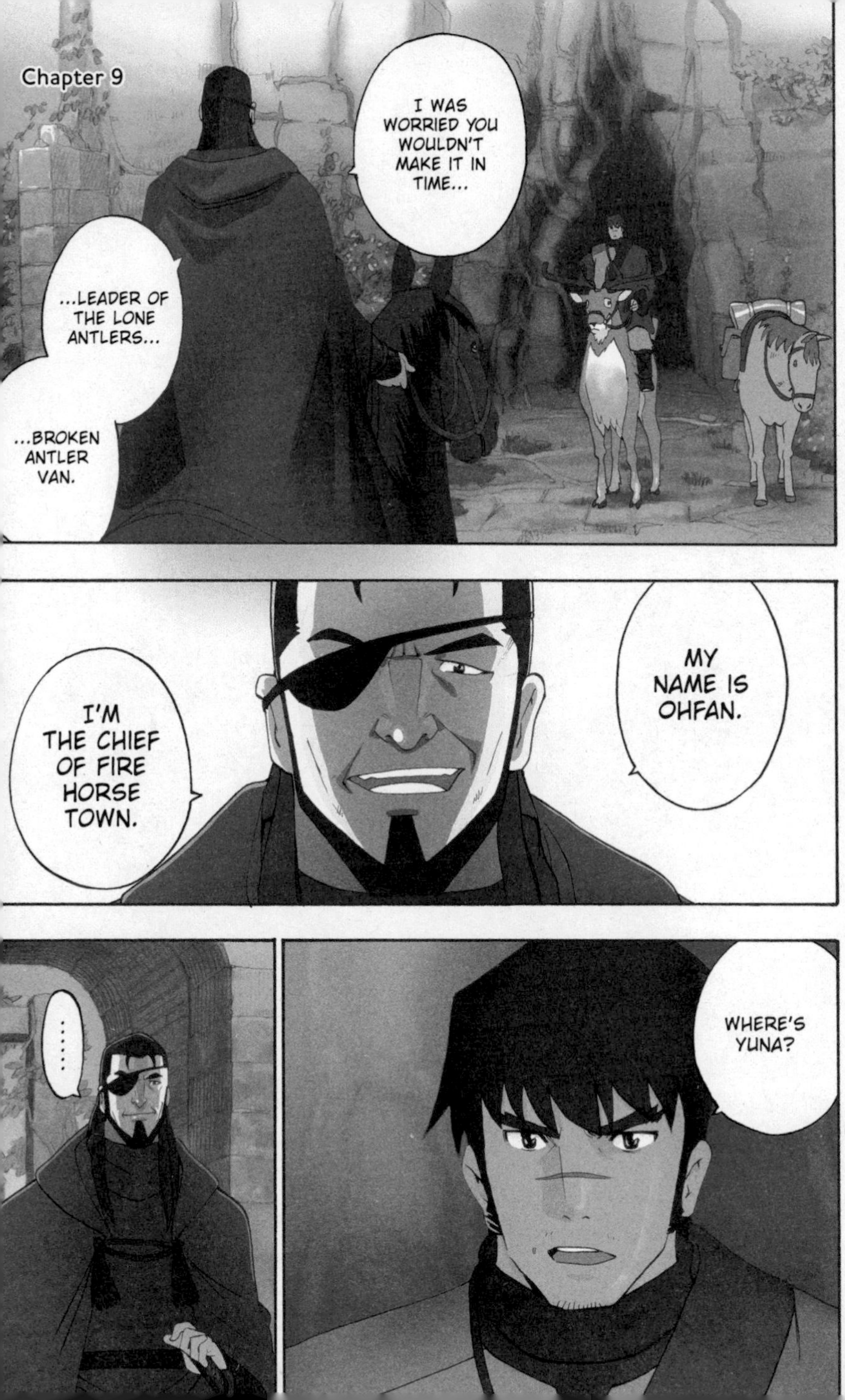
I WAS WORRIED YOU WOULDN'T MAKE IT IN TIME...
...LEADER OF THE LONE ANTLERS...
...BROKEN ANTLER VAN.
MY NAME IS OHFAN.
I'M THE CHIEF OF FIRE HORSE TOWN.
WHERE'S YUNA?
......

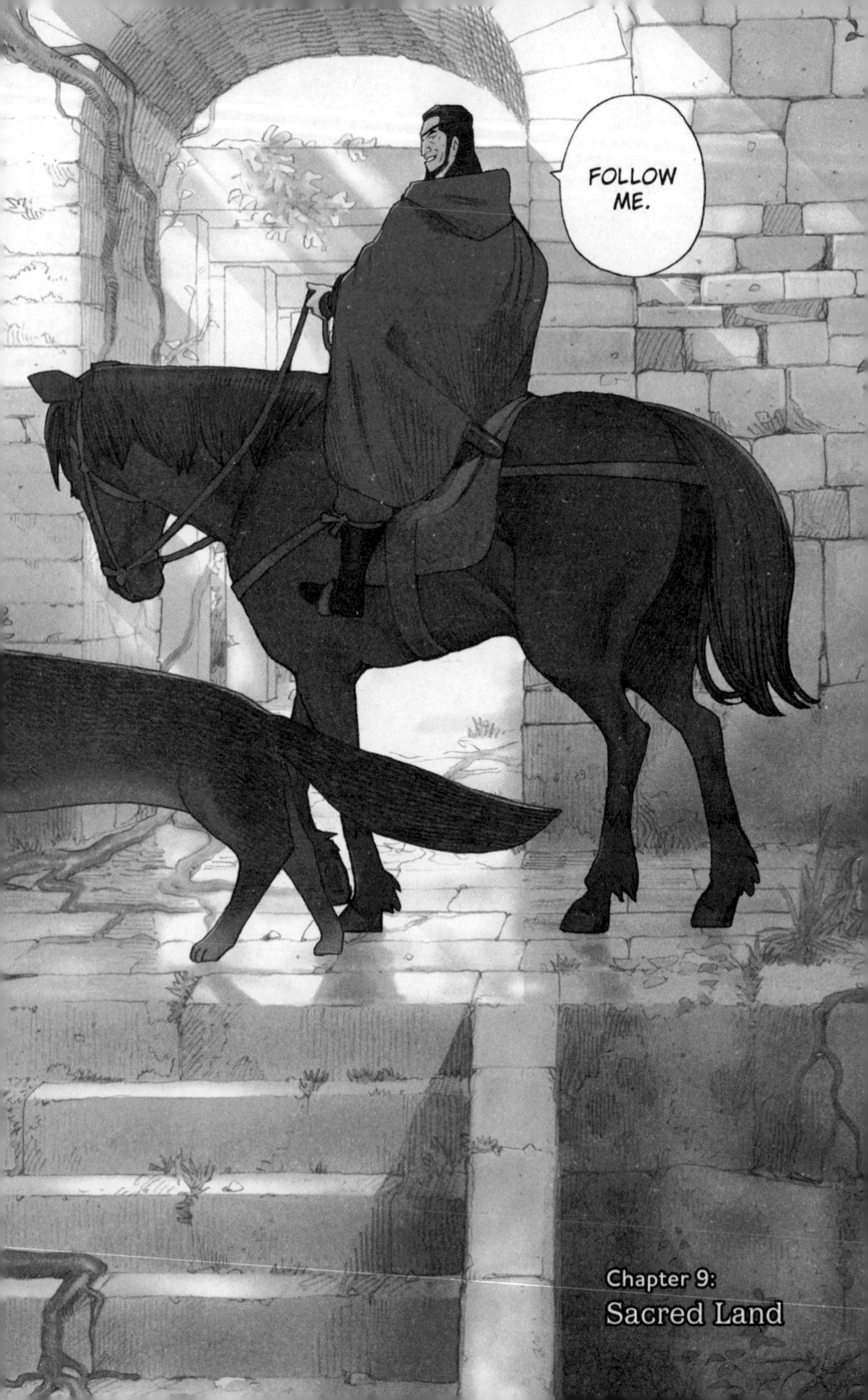
FOLLOW ME.

# Chapter 9: Sacred Land

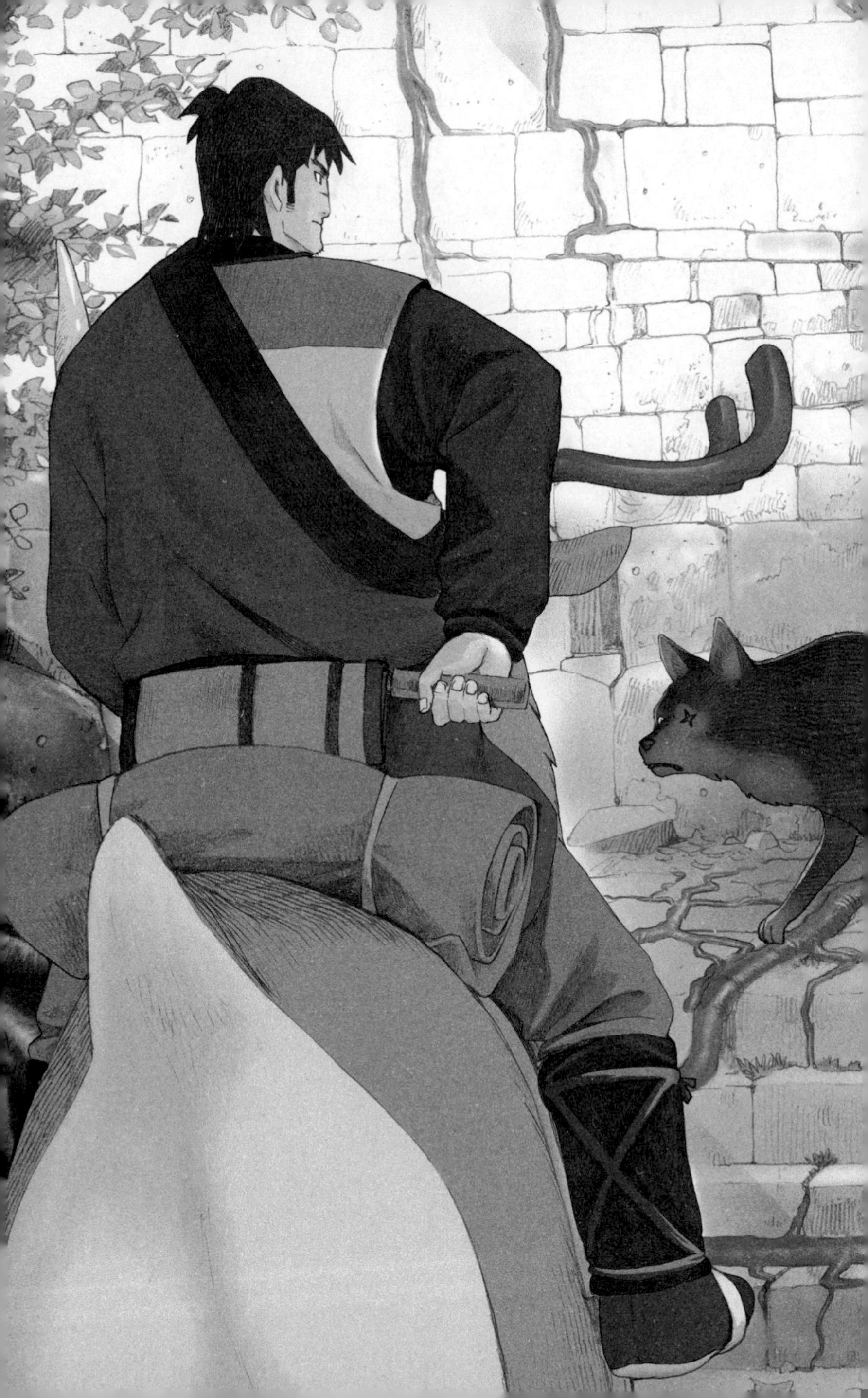

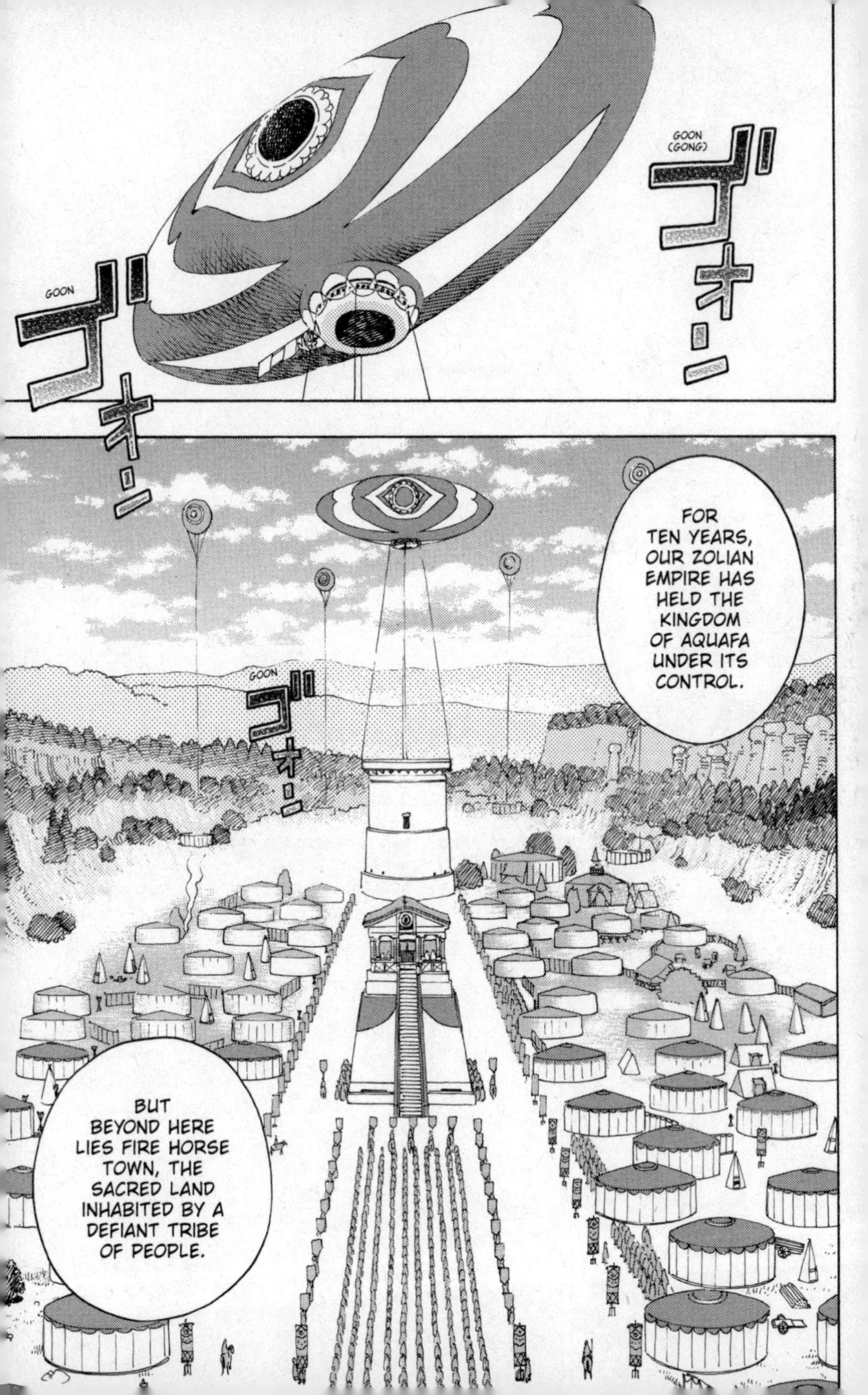
GOON (GONG)
GOON
GOON
FOR TEN YEARS, OUR ZOLIAN EMPIRE HAS HELD THE KINGDOM OF AQUAFA UNDER ITS CONTROL.
BUT BEYOND HERE LIES FIRE HORSE TOWN, THE SACRED LAND INHABITED BY A DEFIANT TRIBE OF PEOPLE.

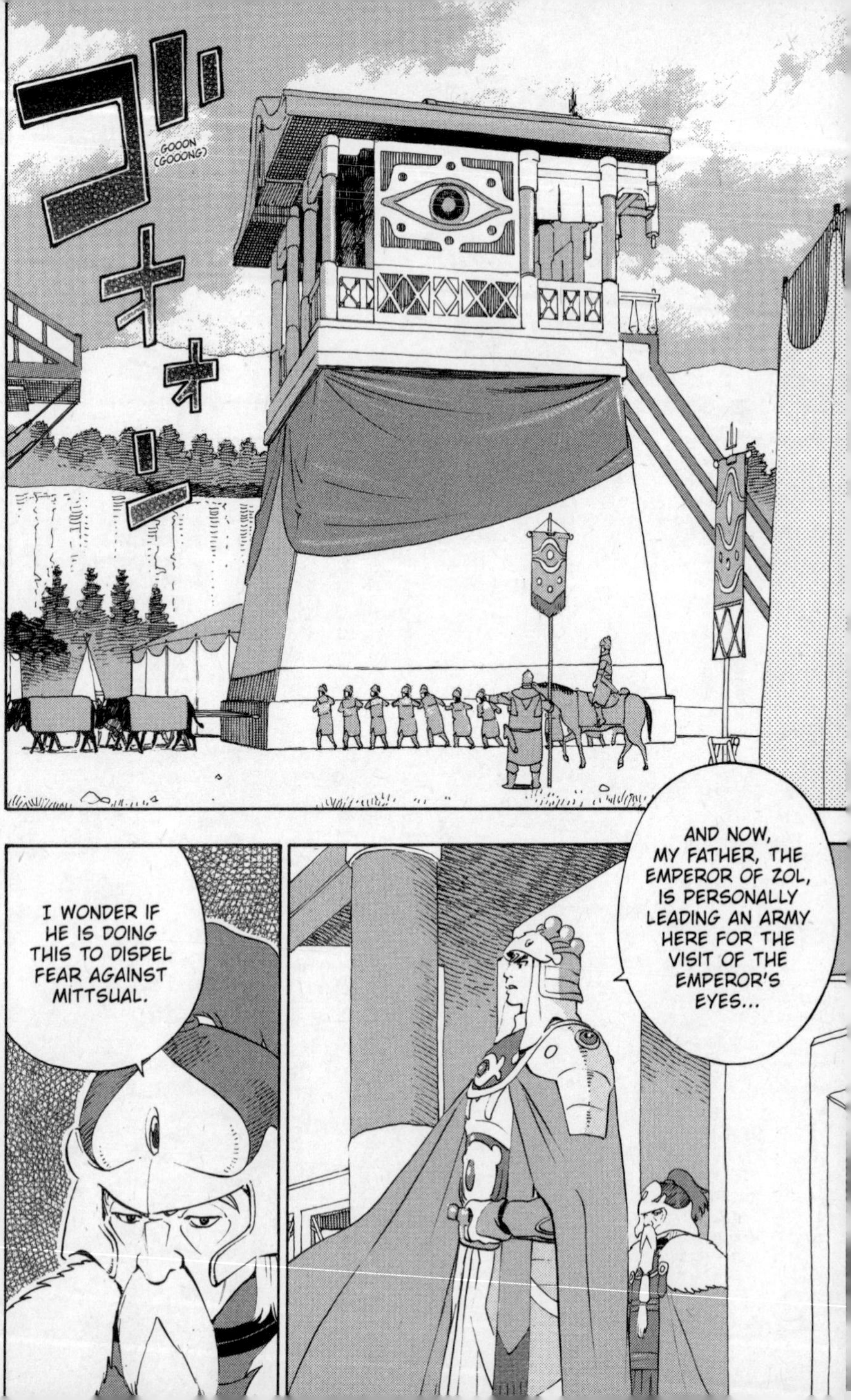
GOOON (GOOONG)
AND NOW, MY FATHER, THE EMPEROR OF ZOL, IS PERSONALLY LEADING AN ARMY HERE FOR THE VISIT OF THE EMPEROR'S EYES...
I WONDER IF HE IS DOING THIS TO DISPEL FEAR AGAINST MITTSUAL.

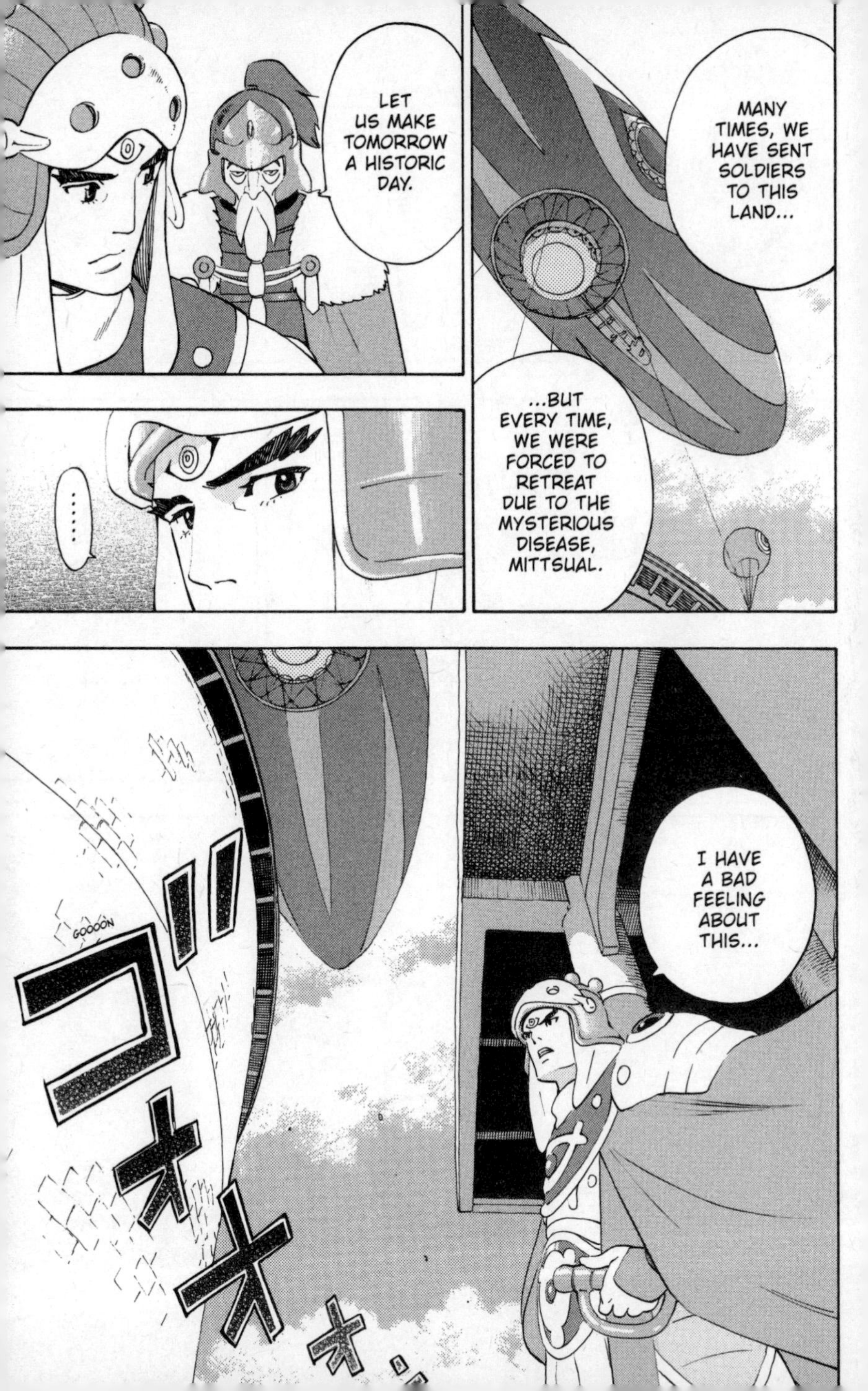
MANY TIMES, WE HAVE SENT SOLDIERS TO THIS LAND...
...BUT EVERY TIME, WE WERE FORCED TO RETREAT DUE TO THE MYSTERIOUS DISEASE, MITTSUAL.
LET US MAKE TOMORROW A HISTORIC DAY.
......
I HAVE A BAD FEELING ABOUT THIS...
GOOOON

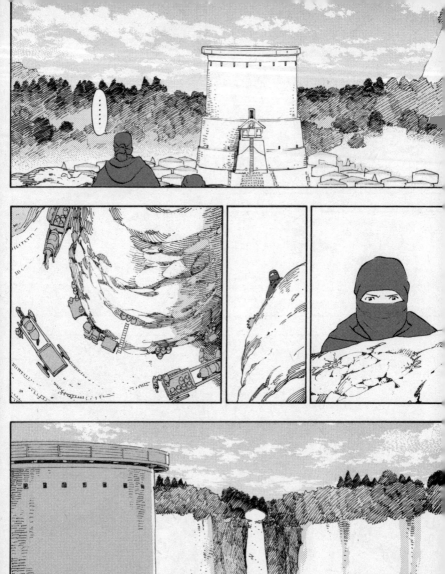

……

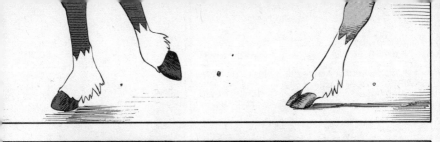

CHIEF OHFAN!

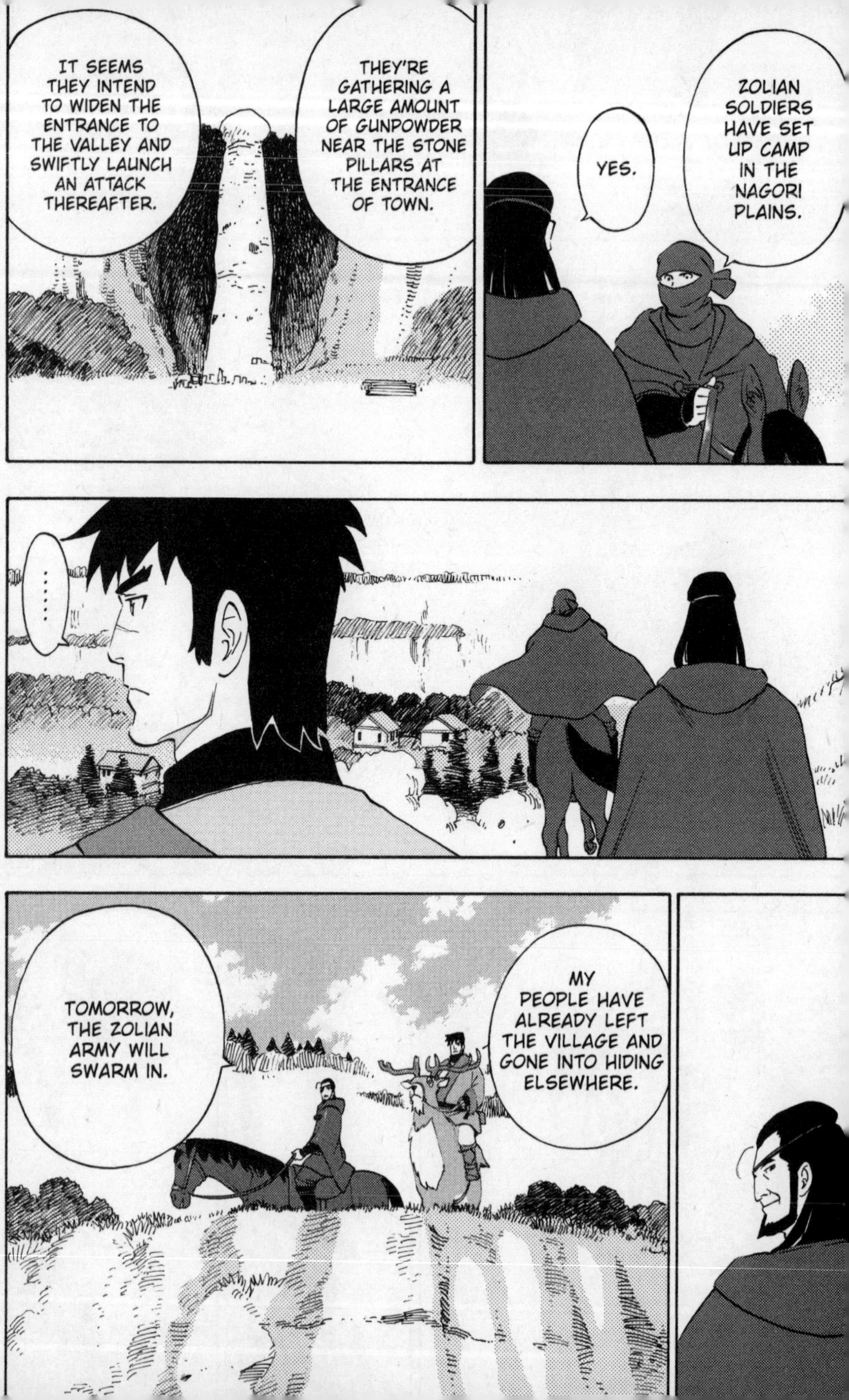
ZOLIAN SOLDIERS HAVE SET UP CAMP IN THE NAGORI PLAINS.
YES.
THEY'RE GATHERING A LARGE AMOUNT OF GUNPOWDER NEAR THE STONE PILLARS AT THE ENTRANCE OF TOWN.
IT SEEMS THEY INTEND TO WIDEN THE ENTRANCE TO THE VALLEY AND SWIFTLY LAUNCH AN ATTACK THEREAFTER.
......
MY PEOPLE HAVE ALREADY LEFT THE VILLAGE AND GONE INTO HIDING ELSEWHERE.
TOMORROW, THE ZOLIAN ARMY WILL SWARM IN.

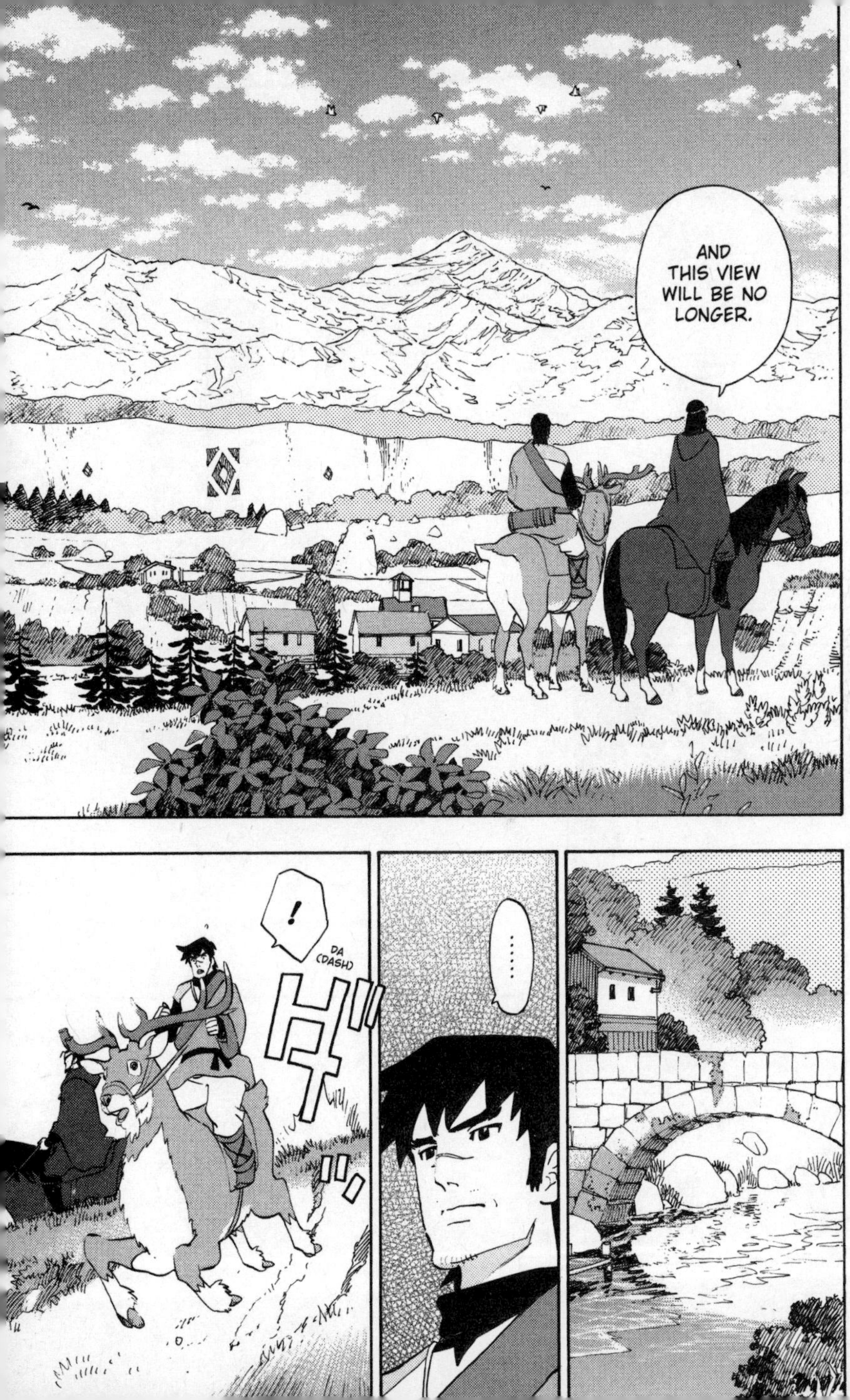
AND THIS VIEW WILL BE NO LONGER.
......
!
DA (DASH)

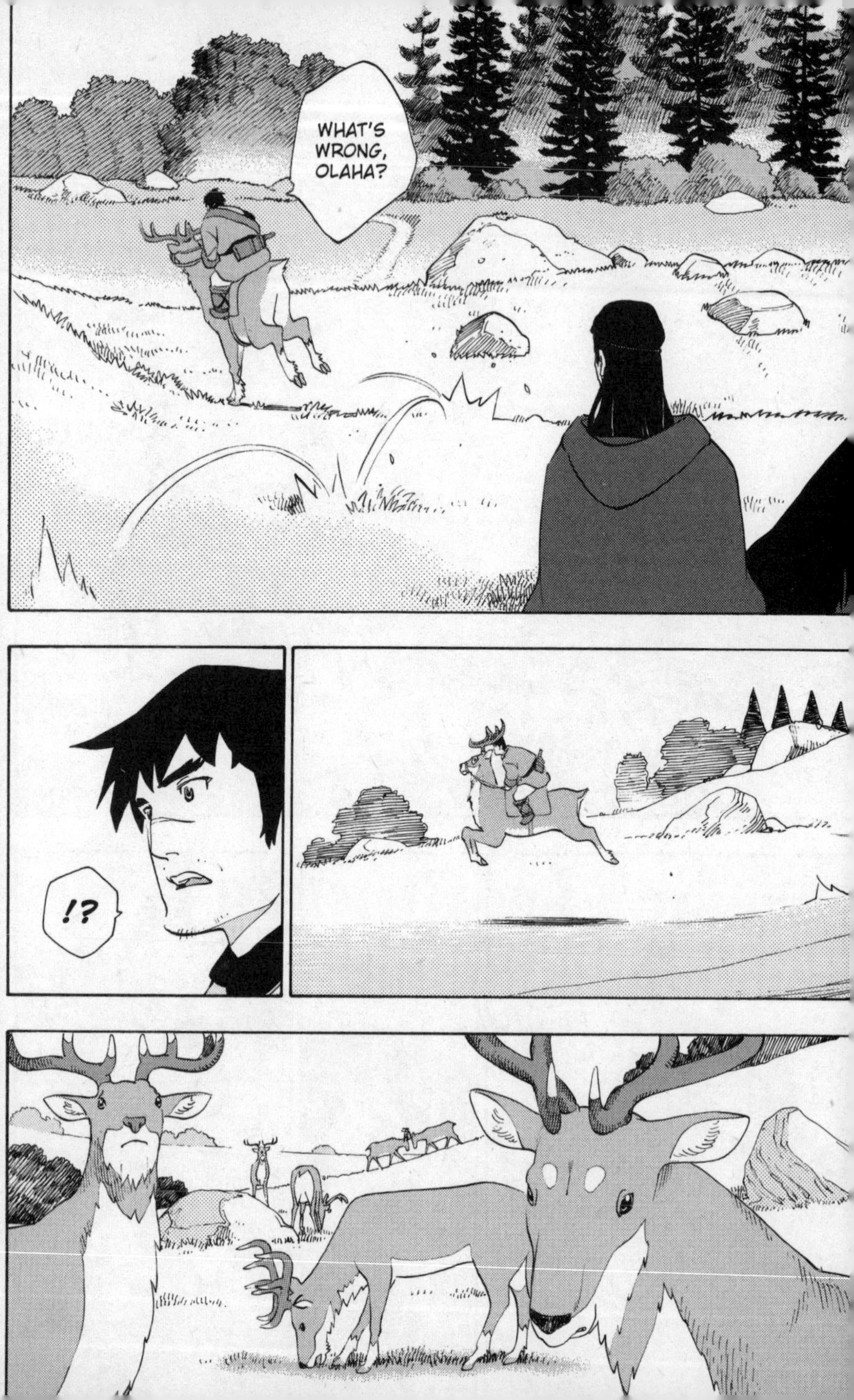
WHAT'S WRONG, OLAHA?
!?

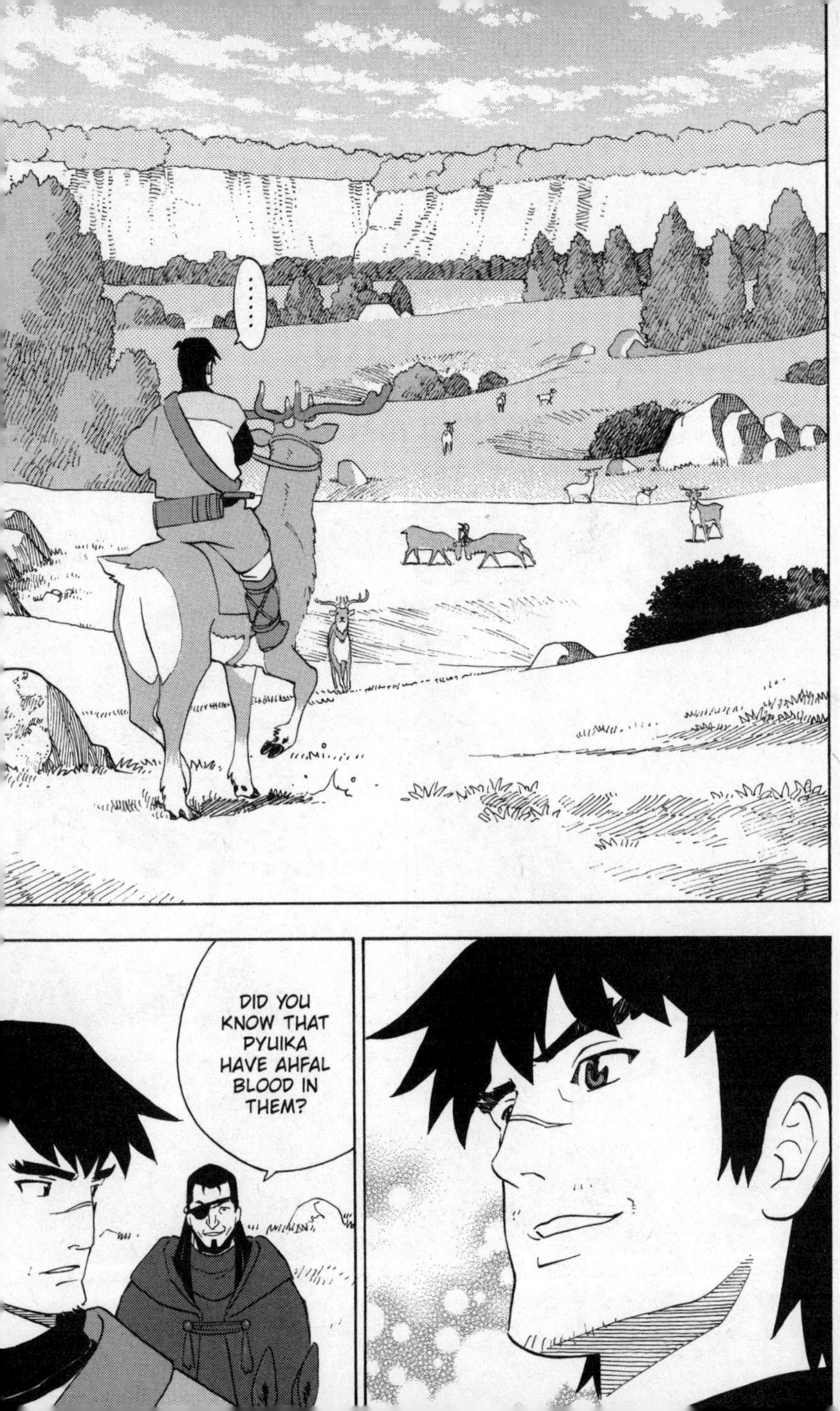
.....
DID YOU KNOW THAT PYUIKA HAVE AHFAL BLOOD IN THEM?

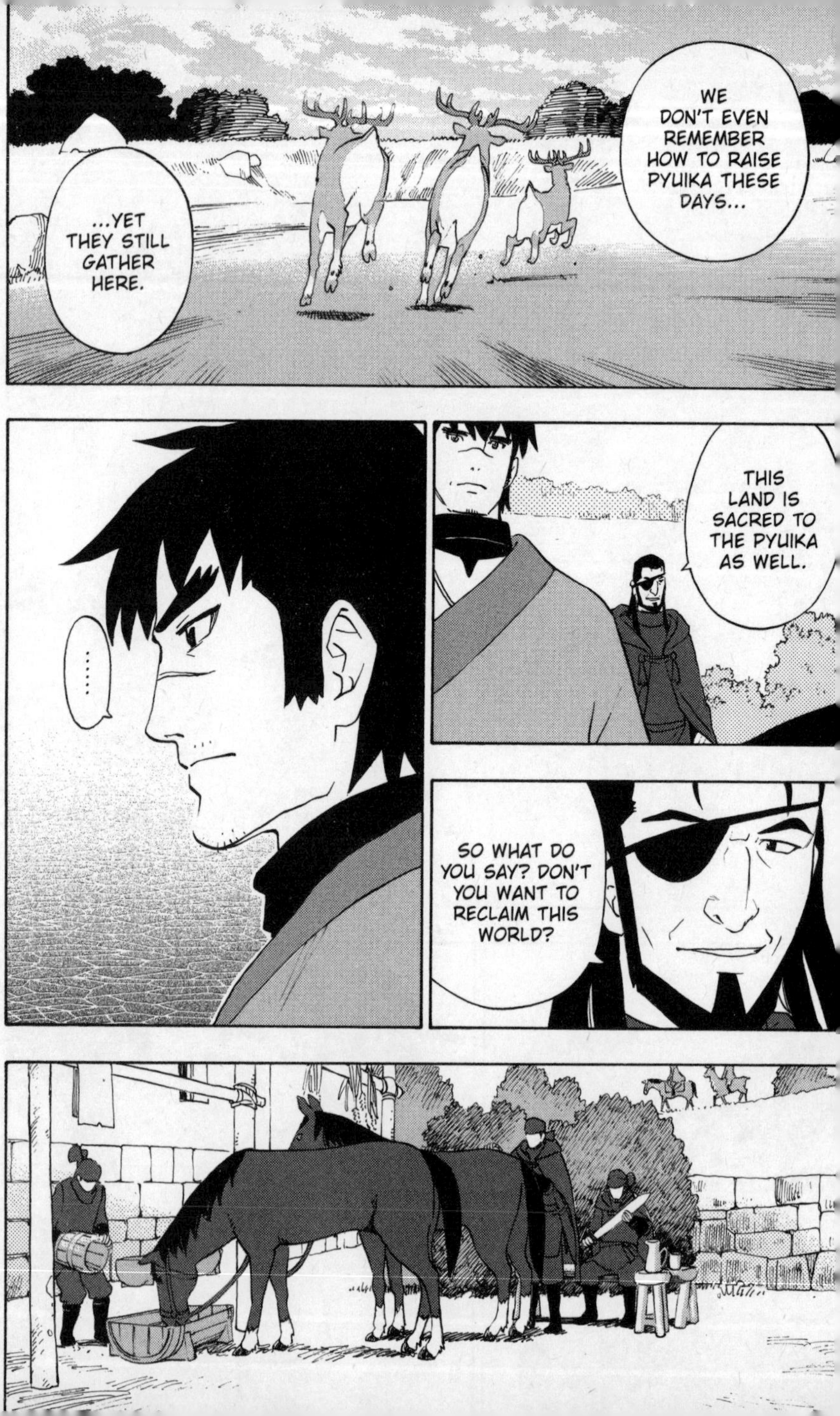
WE DON'T EVEN REMEMBER HOW TO RAISE PYUIKA THESE DAYS...
...YET THEY STILL GATHER HERE.
THIS LAND IS SACRED TO THE PYUIKA AS WELL.
SO WHAT DO YOU SAY? DON'T YOU WANT TO RECLAIM THIS WORLD?
......

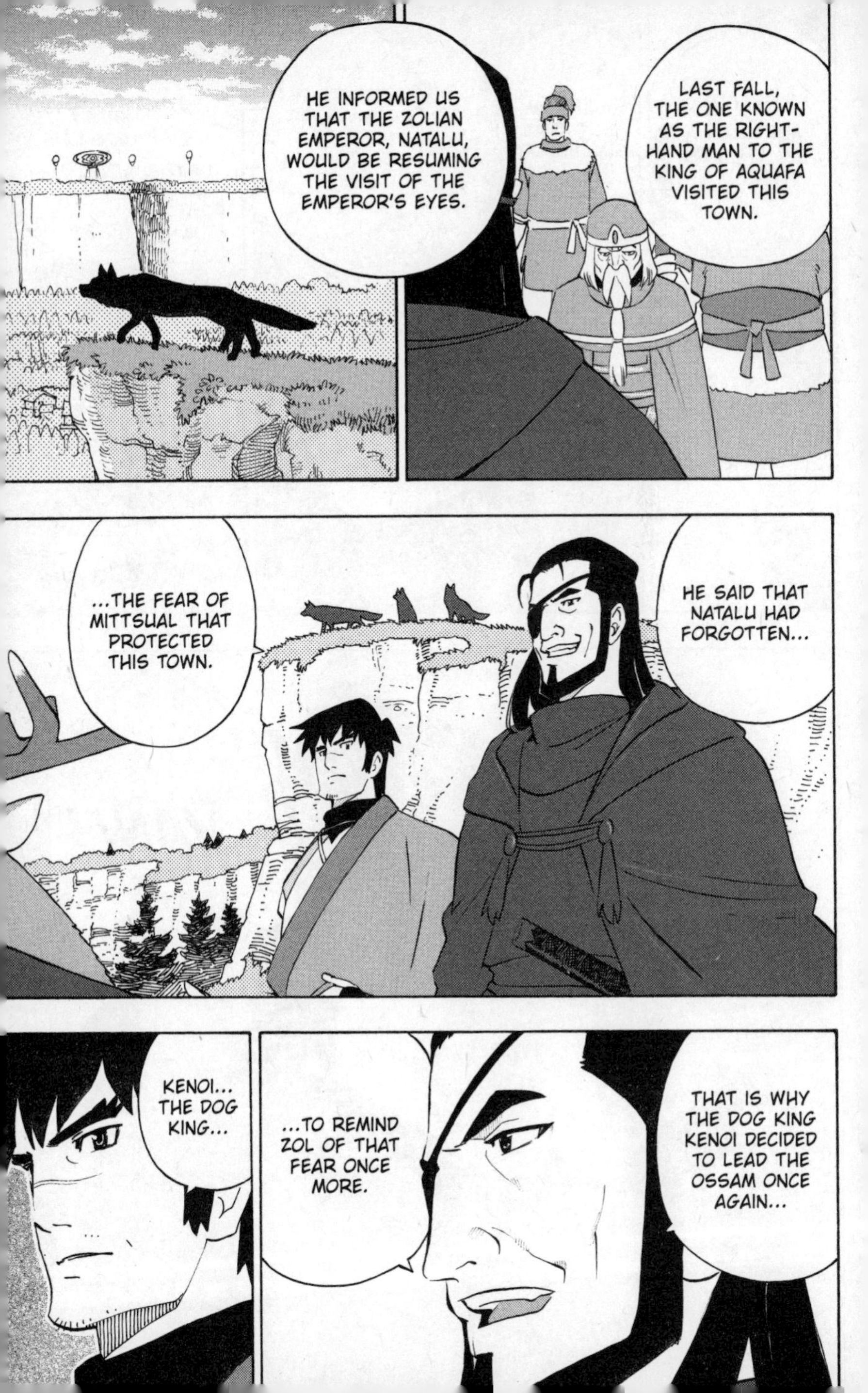
LAST FALL, THE ONE KNOWN AS THE RIGHT-HAND MAN TO THE KING OF AQUAFA VISITED THIS TOWN.
HE INFORMED US THAT THE ZOLIAN EMPEROR, NATALU, WOULD BE RESUMING THE VISIT OF THE EMPEROR'S EYES.
HE SAID THAT NATALU HAD FORGOTTEN...
...THE FEAR OF MITTSUAL THAT PROTECTED THIS TOWN.
THAT IS WHY THE DOG KING KENOI DECIDED TO LEAD THE OSSAM ONCE AGAIN...
...TO REMIND ZOL OF THAT FEAR ONCE MORE.
KENOI... THE DOG KING...
...

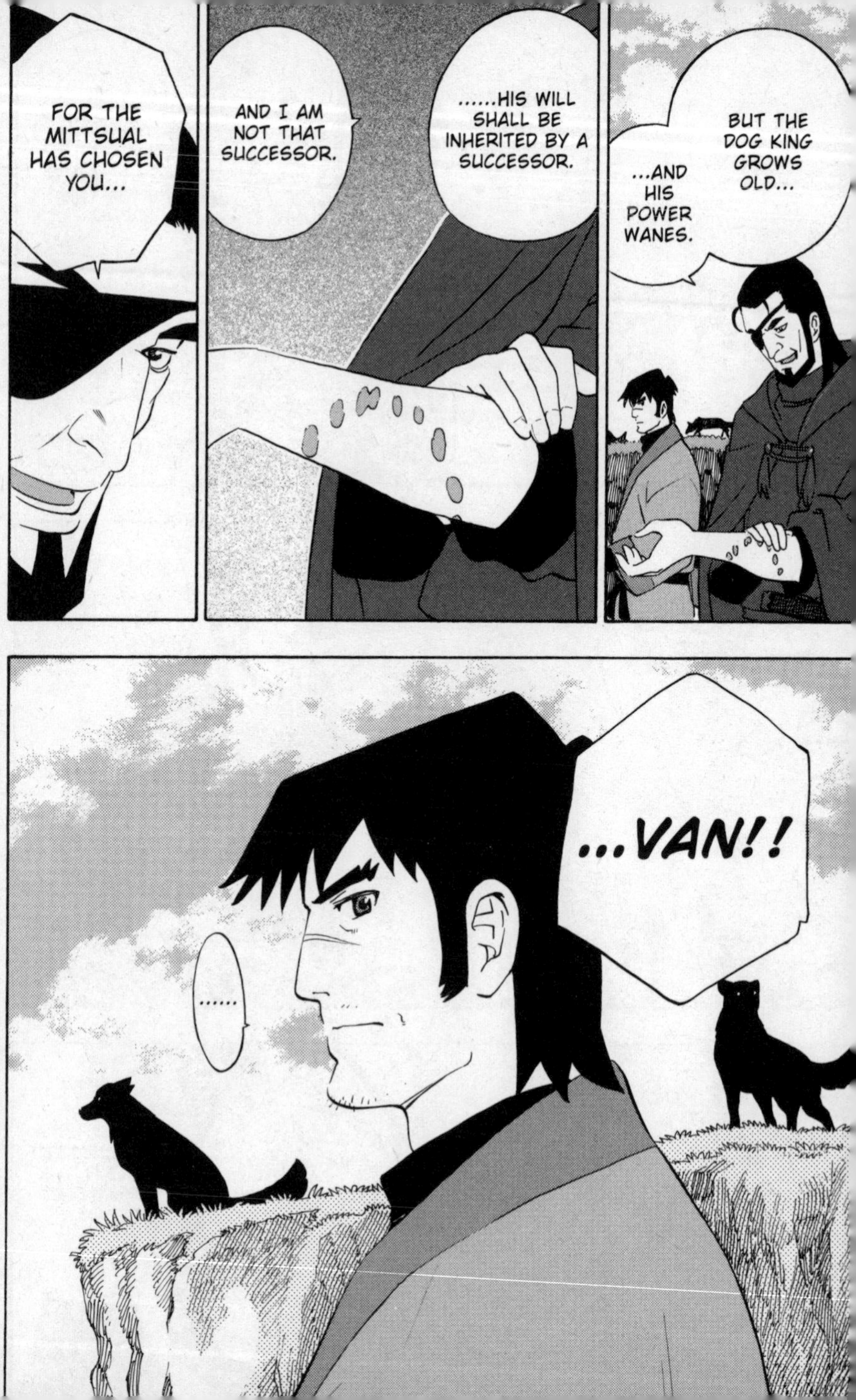
BUT THE DOG KING GROWS OLD...
...AND HIS POWER WANES.
......HIS WILL SHALL BE INHERITED BY A SUCCESSOR.
AND I AM NOT THAT SUCCESSOR.
FOR THE MITTSUAL HAS CHOSEN YOU...
...VAN!!
......

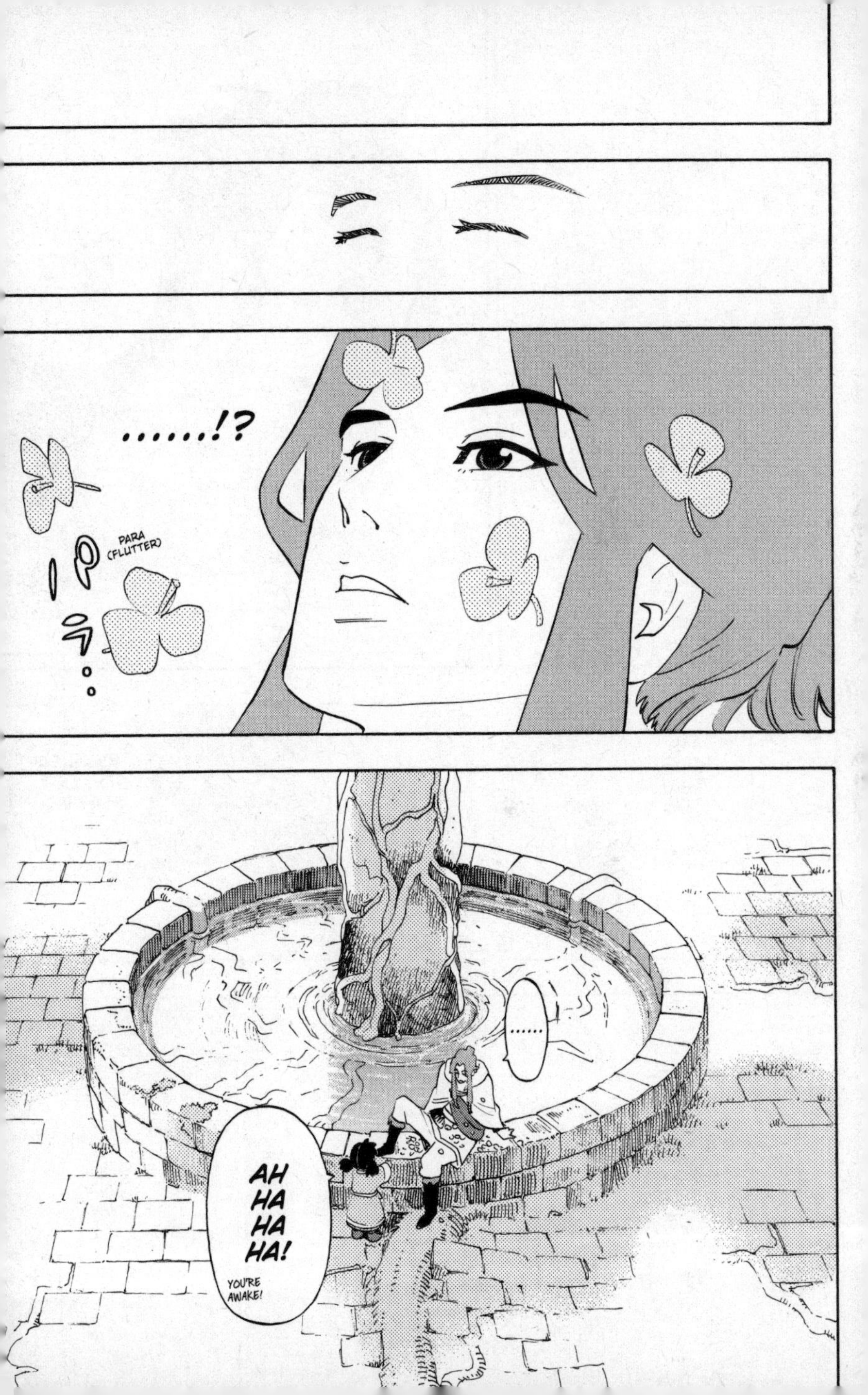
......!?
PARA (FLUTTER)
......
AH HA HA HA HA!
YOU'RE AWAKE!

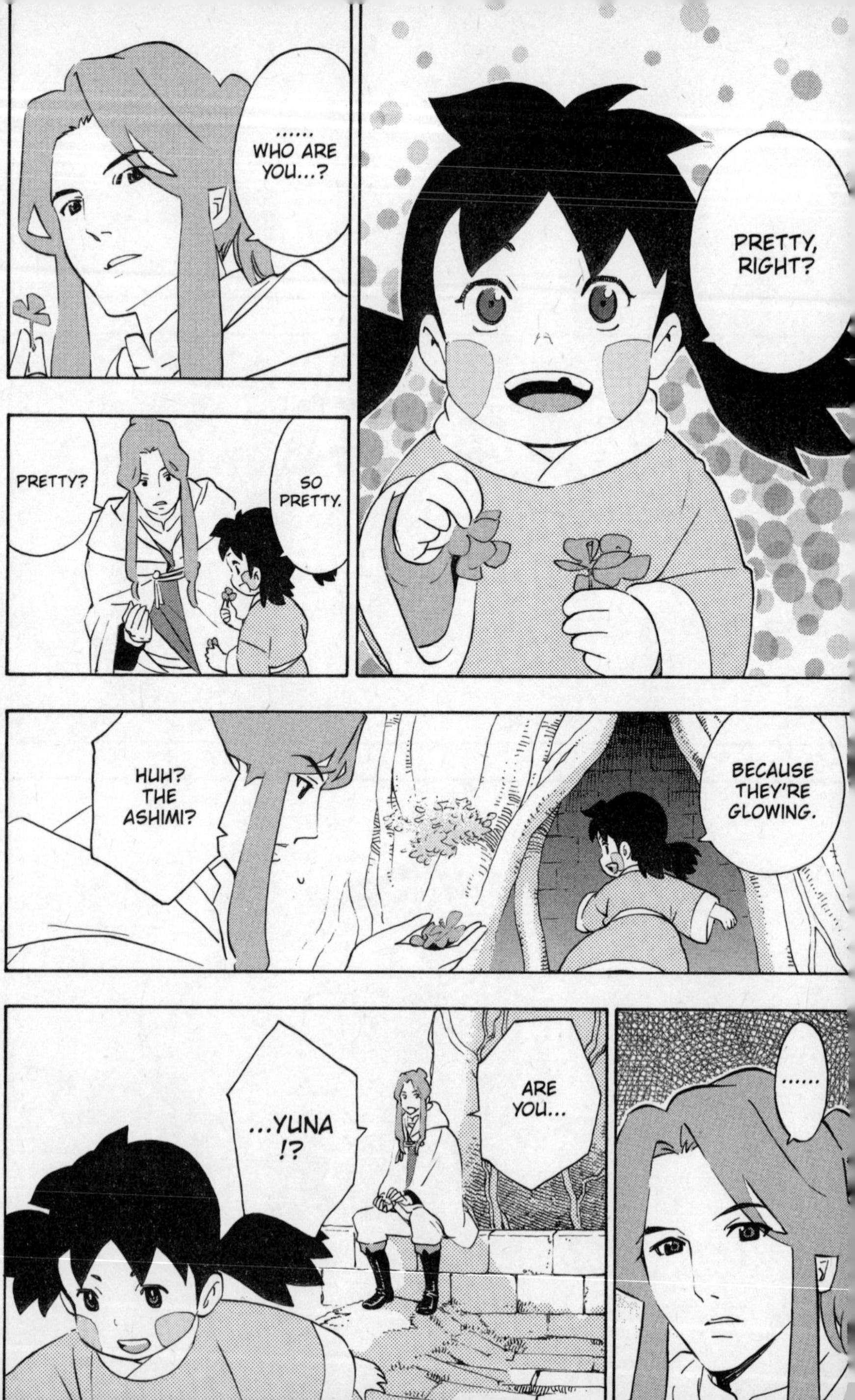
PRETTY, RIGHT?
...... WHO ARE YOU...?
SO PRETTY.
PRETTY?
BECAUSE THEY'RE GLOWING.
HUH? THE ASHIMI?
......
ARE YOU...
...YUNA !?

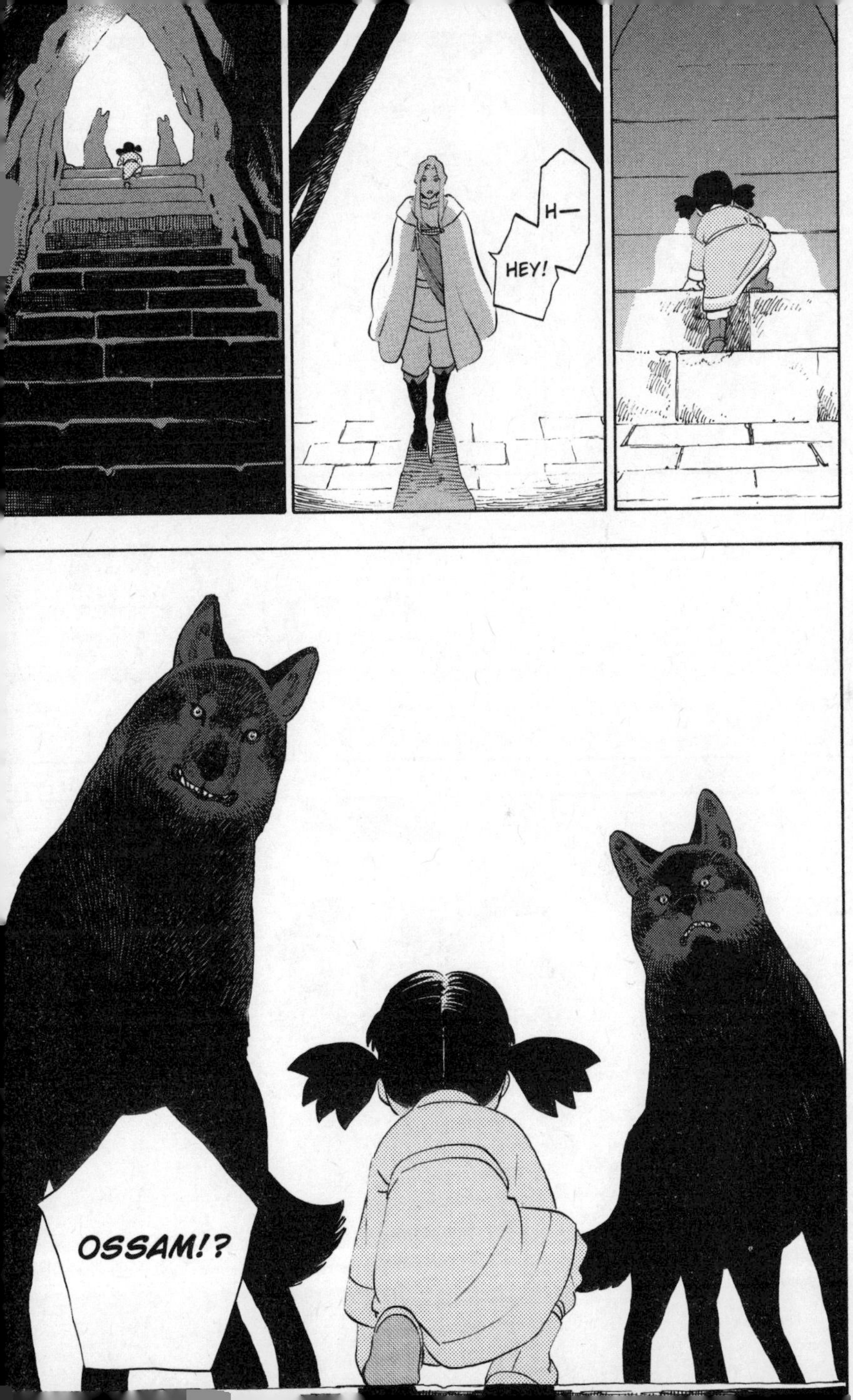
H—
HEY!
OSSAM!?

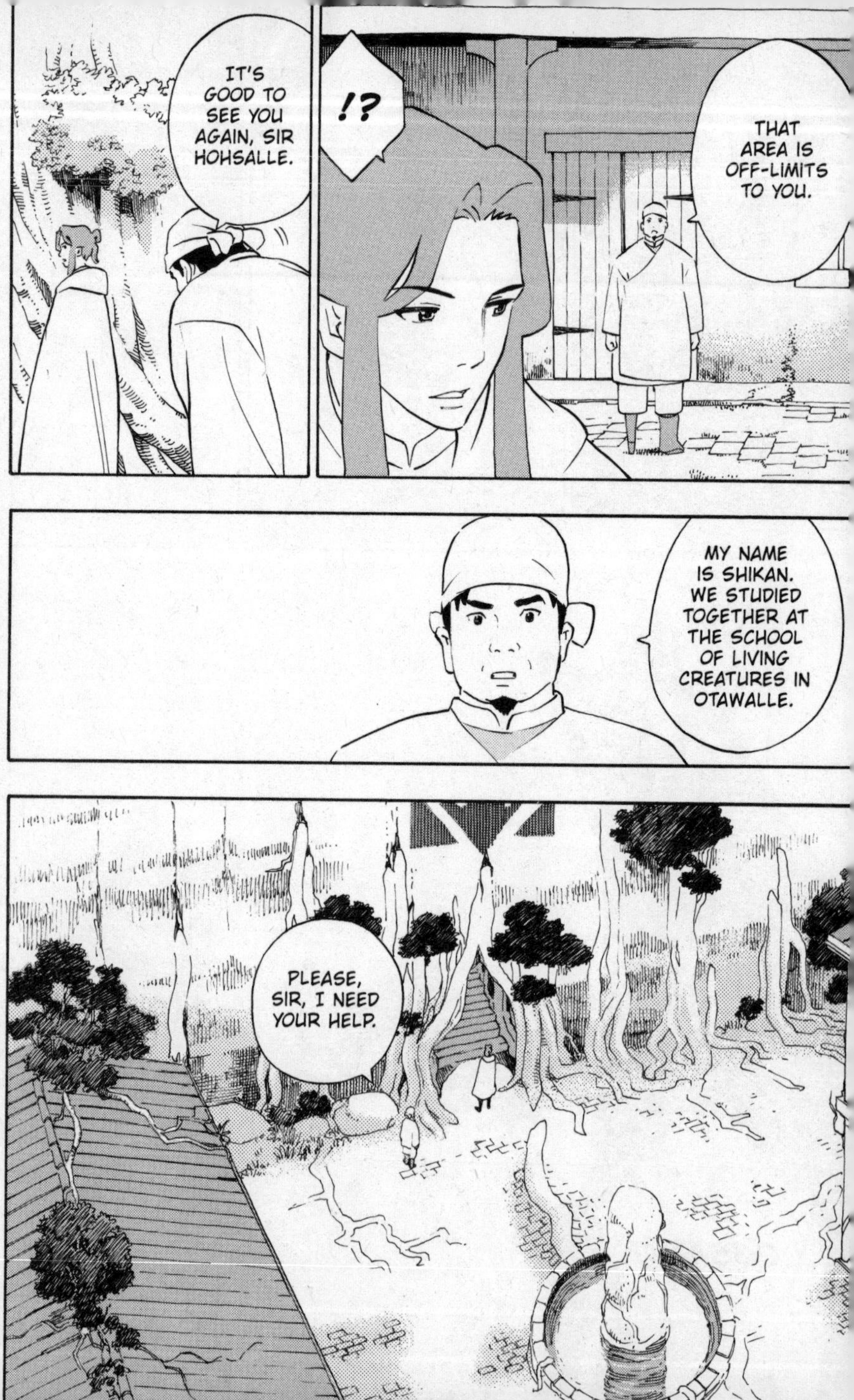
THAT AREA IS OFF-LIMITS TO YOU.
!?
IT'S GOOD TO SEE YOU AGAIN, SIR HOHSALLE.
MY NAME IS SHIKAN. WE STUDIED TOGETHER AT THE SCHOOL OF LIVING CREATURES IN OTAWALLE.
PLEASE, SIR, I NEED YOUR HELP.

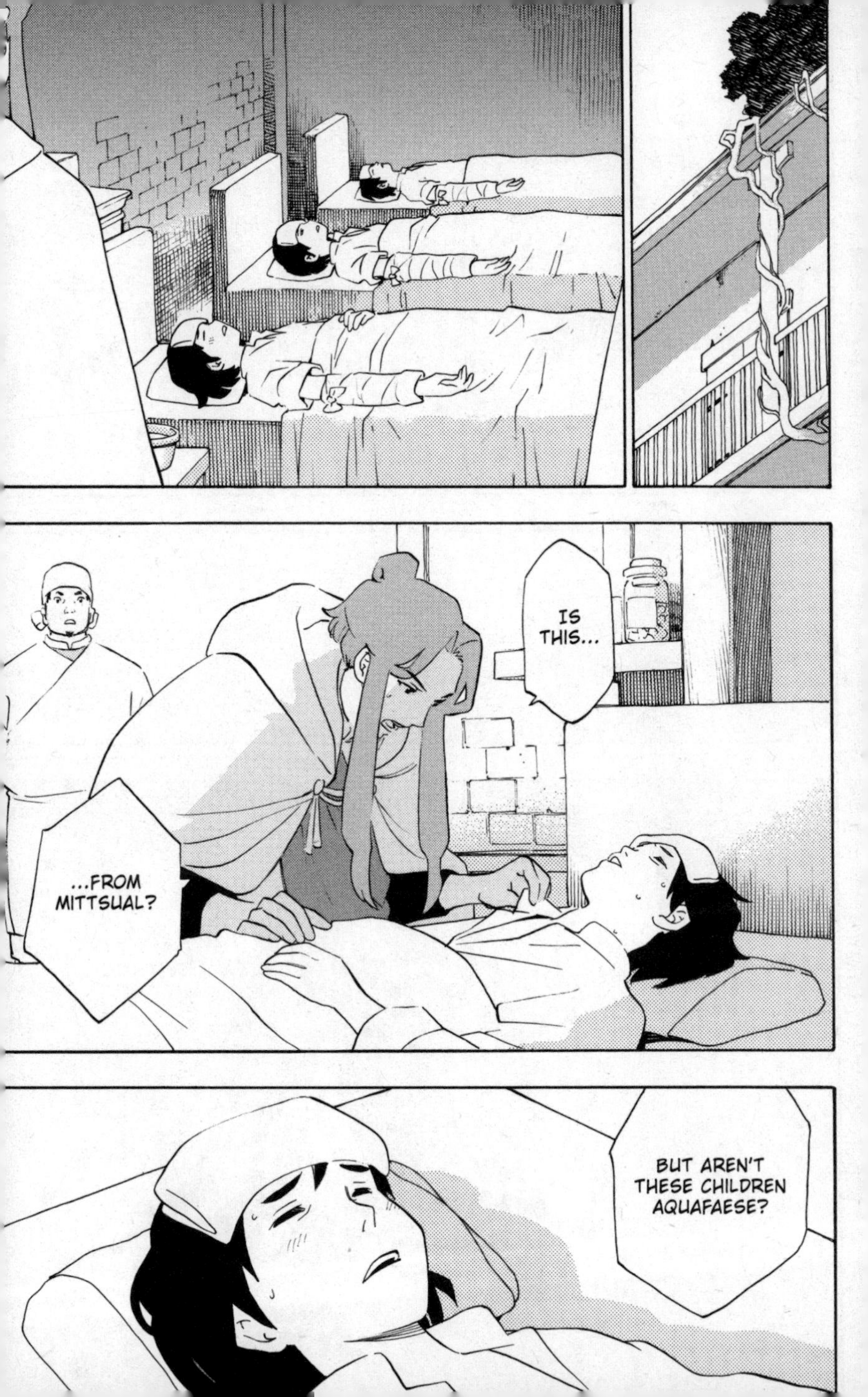
IS THIS...
...FROM MITTSUAL?
BUT AREN'T THESE CHILDREN AQUAFAESE?

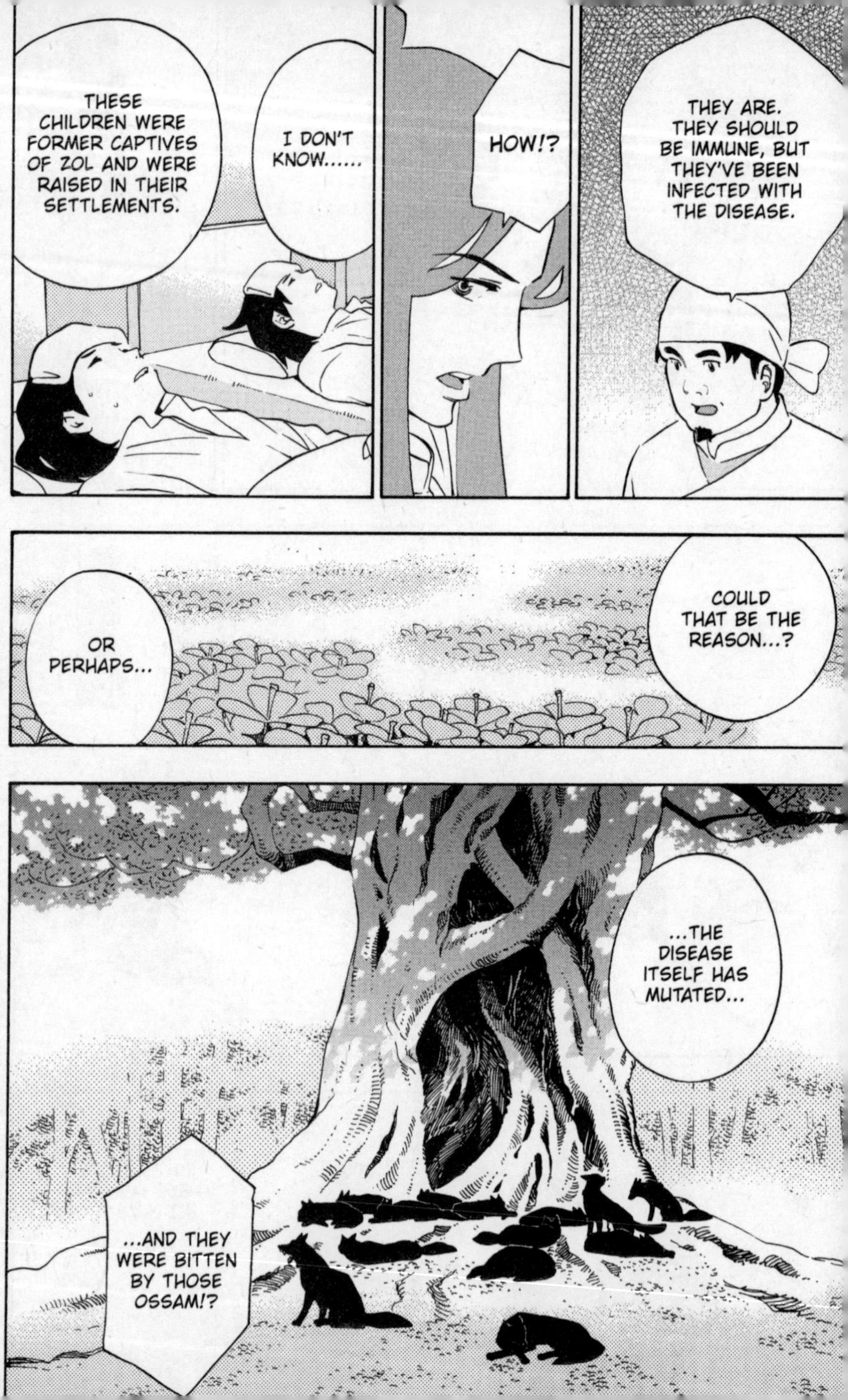
THEY ARE. THEY SHOULD BE IMMUNE, BUT THEY'VE BEEN INFECTED WITH THE DISEASE.
HOW!?
I DON'T KNOW......
THESE CHILDREN WERE FORMER CAPTIVES OF ZOL AND WERE RAISED IN THEIR SETTLEMENTS.
COULD THAT BE THE REASON...?
OR PERHAPS...
...THE DISEASE ITSELF HAS MUTATED...
...AND THEY WERE BITTEN BY THOSE OSSAM!?

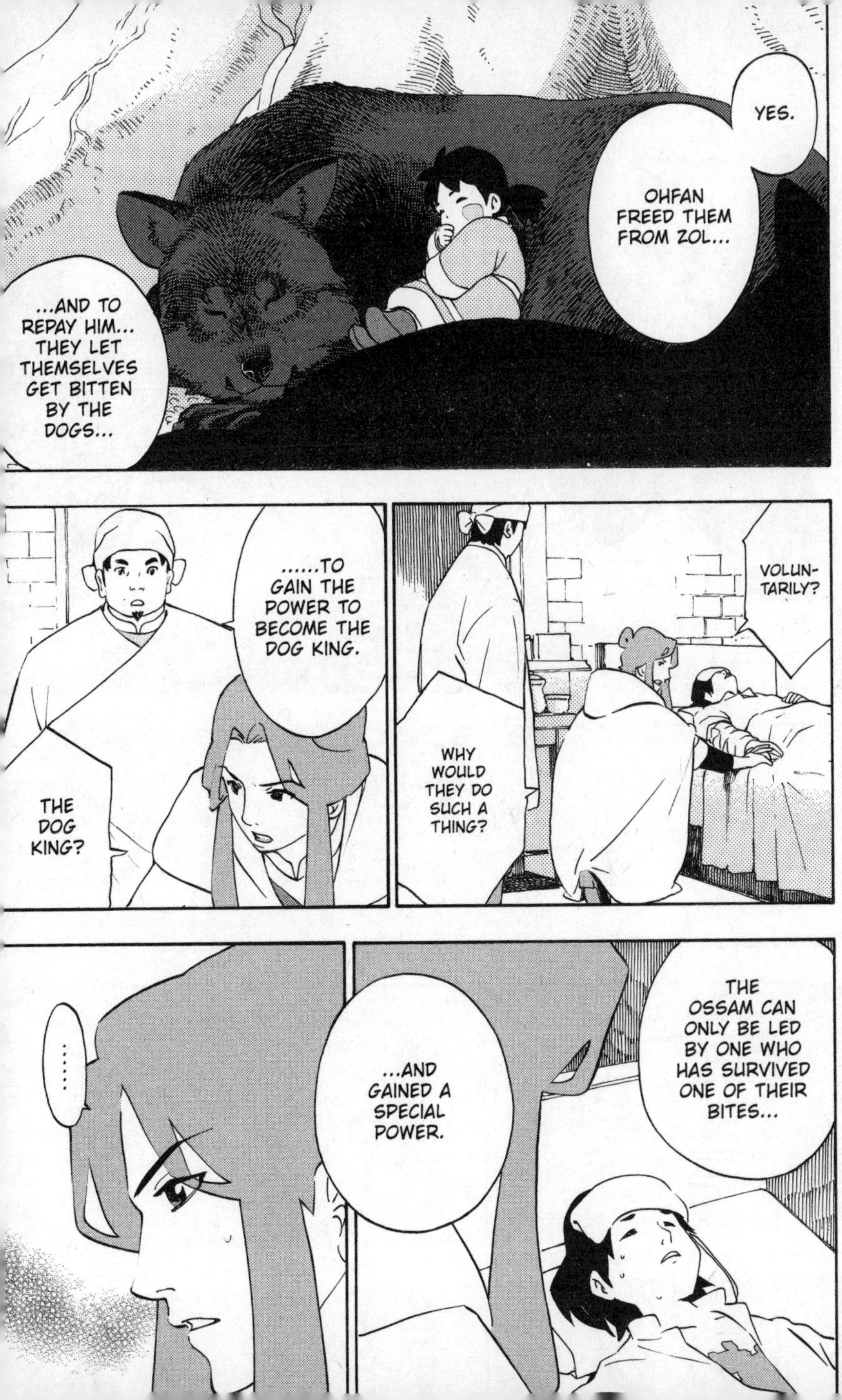
YES.
OHFAN FREED THEM FROM ZOL...
...AND TO REPAY HIM... THEY LET THEMSELVES GET BITTEN BY THE DOGS...
VOLUN-TARILY?
WHY WOULD THEY DO SUCH A THING?
......TO GAIN THE POWER TO BECOME THE DOG KING.
THE DOG KING?
THE OSSAM CAN ONLY BE LED BY ONE WHO HAS SURVIVED ONE OF THEIR BITES...
...AND GAINED A SPECIAL POWER.
......

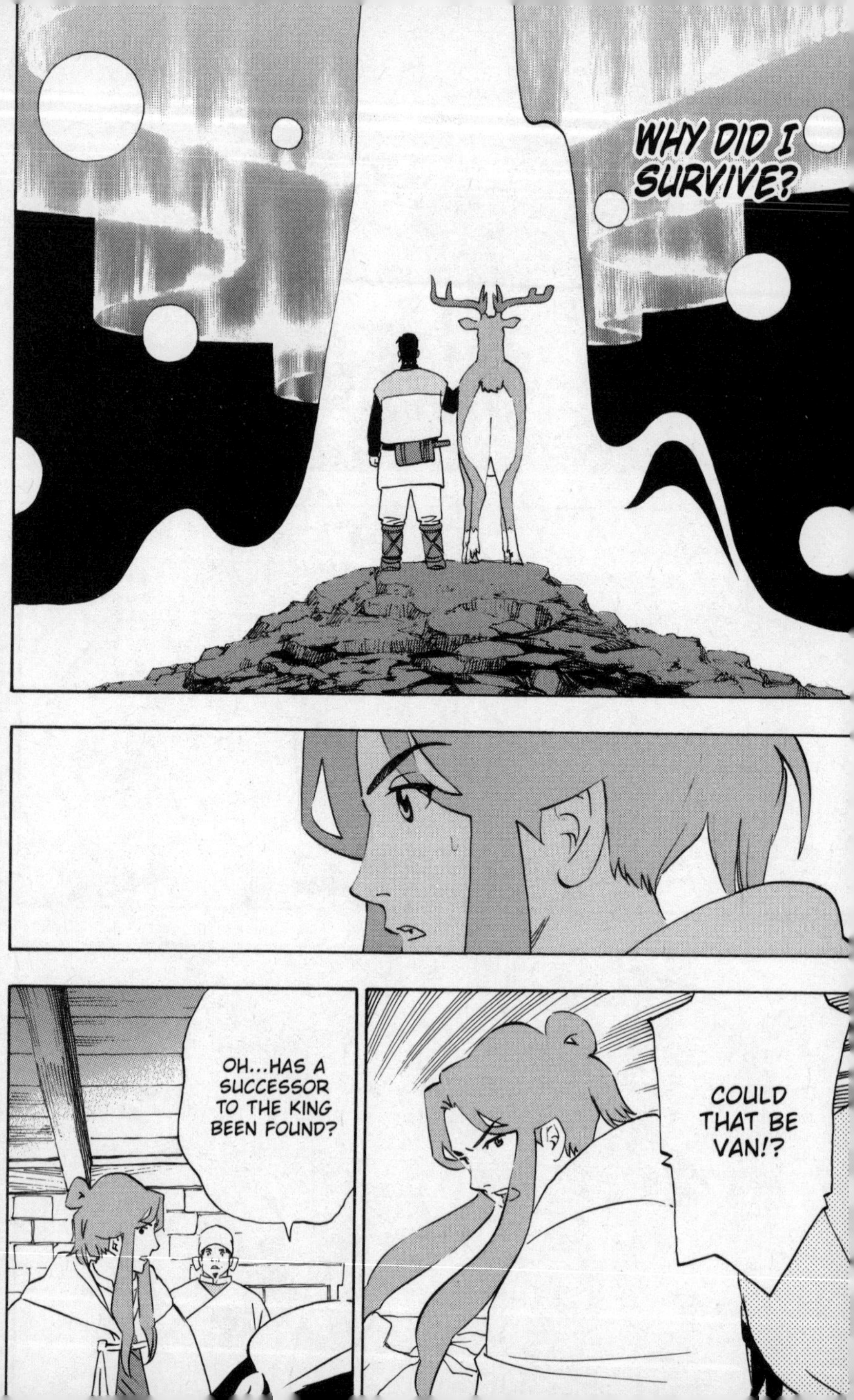
WHY DID I SURVIVE?
COULD THAT BE VAN!?
OH...HAS A SUCCESSOR TO THE KING BEEN FOUND?

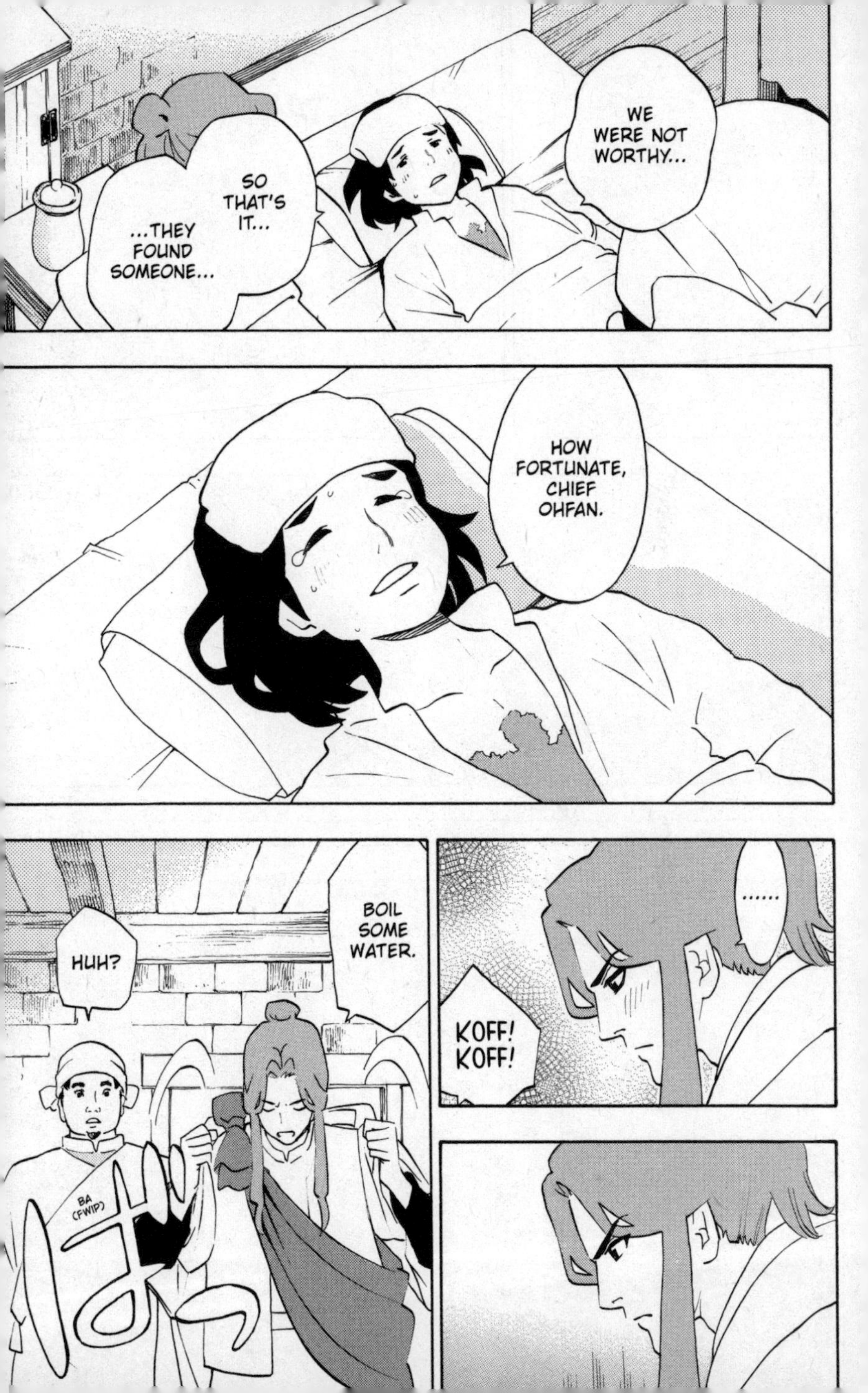
WE WERE NOT WORTHY...
SO THAT'S IT... ...THEY FOUND SOMEONE...
HOW FORTUNATE, CHIEF OHFAN.
......
KOFF! KOFF!
BOIL SOME WATER.
HUH?
BA (FWIP)

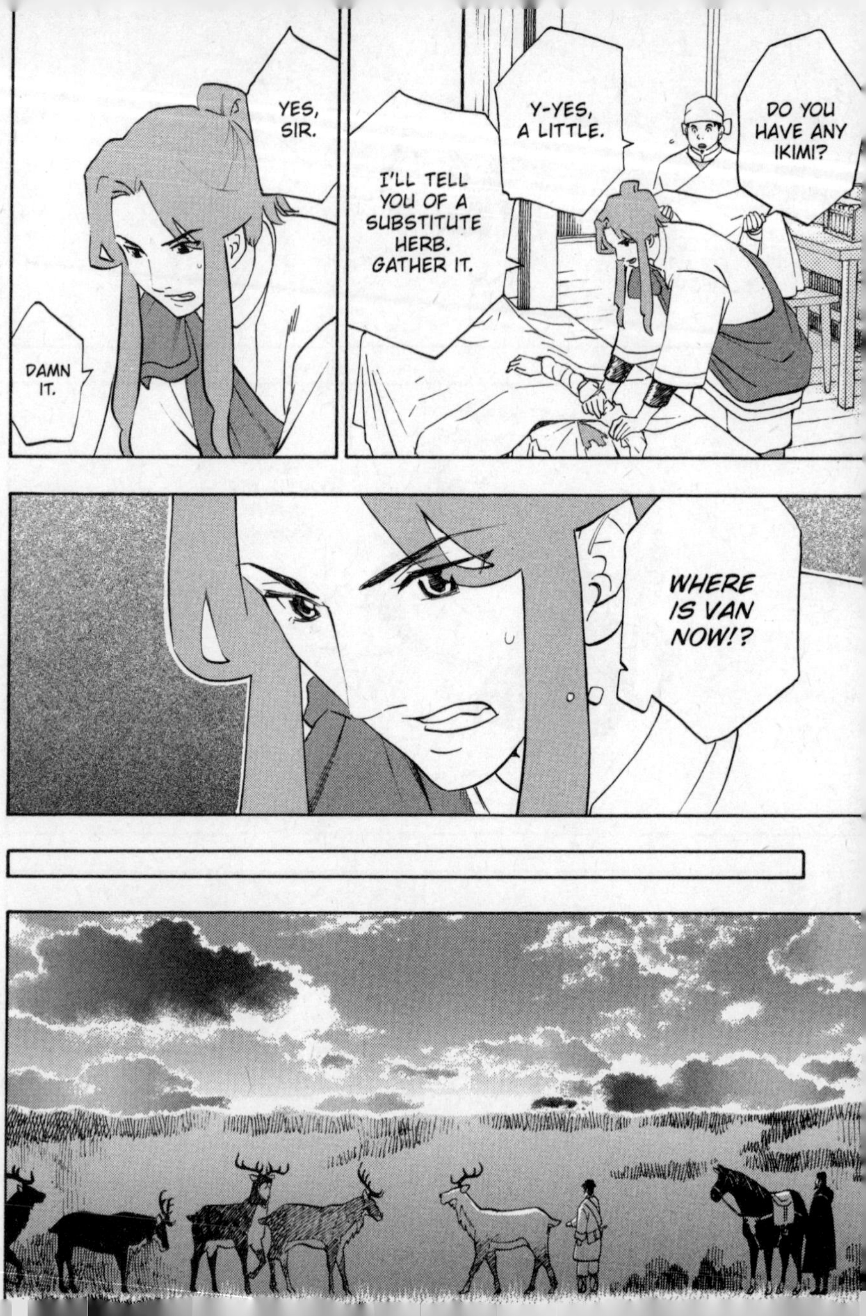
DO YOU HAVE ANY IKIMI?
Y-YES, A LITTLE.
I'LL TELL YOU OF A SUBSTITUTE HERB. GATHER IT.
YES, SIR.
DAMN IT.
WHERE IS VAN NOW!?

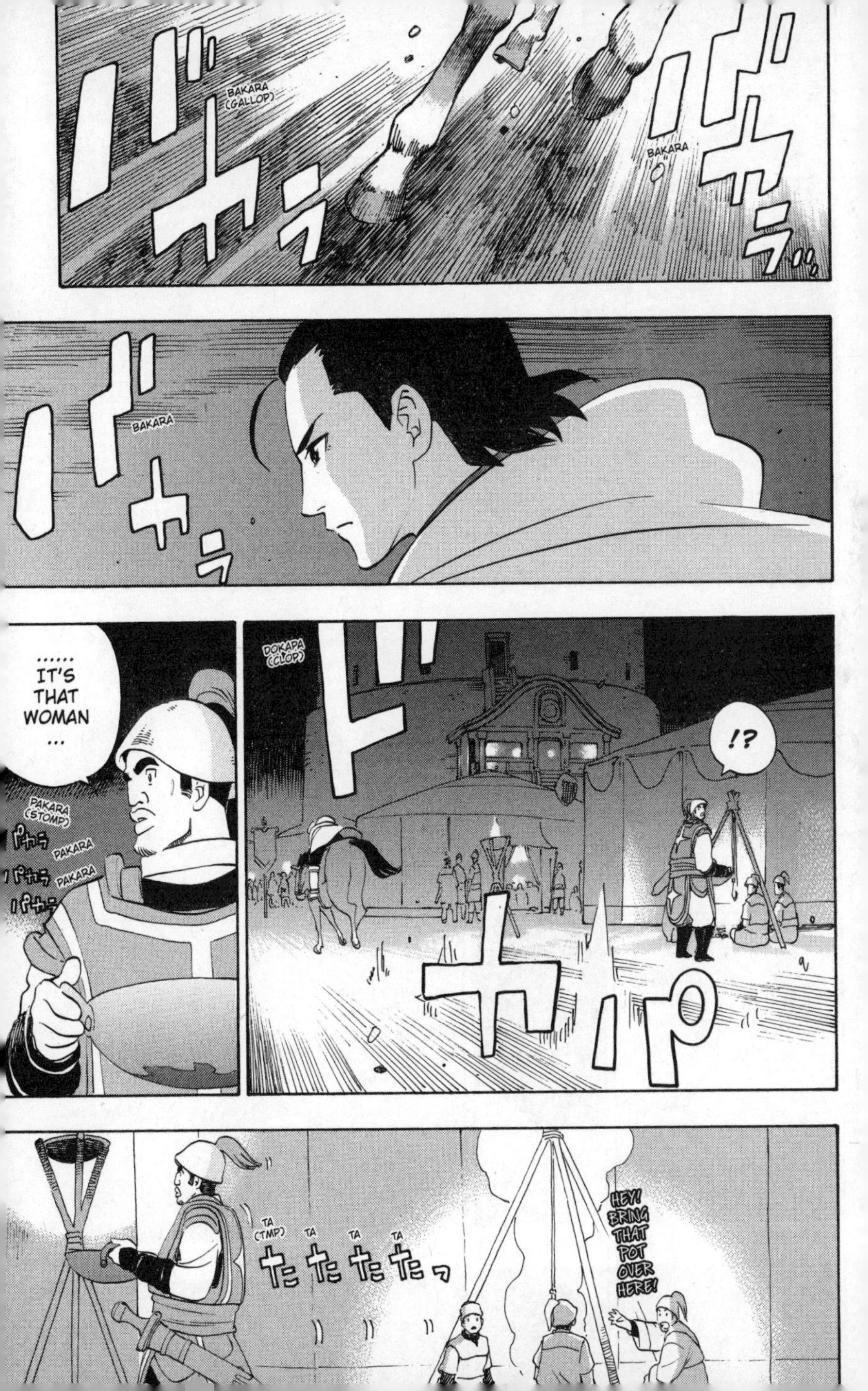
BAKARA (GALLOP)
BAKARA
BAKARA
DOKAPA (CLOP)
!?
...... IT'S THAT WOMAN ...
PAKARA (STOMP)
PAKARA
PAKARA
HEY! BRING THAT POT OVER HERE!
TA (TMP) TA TA TA

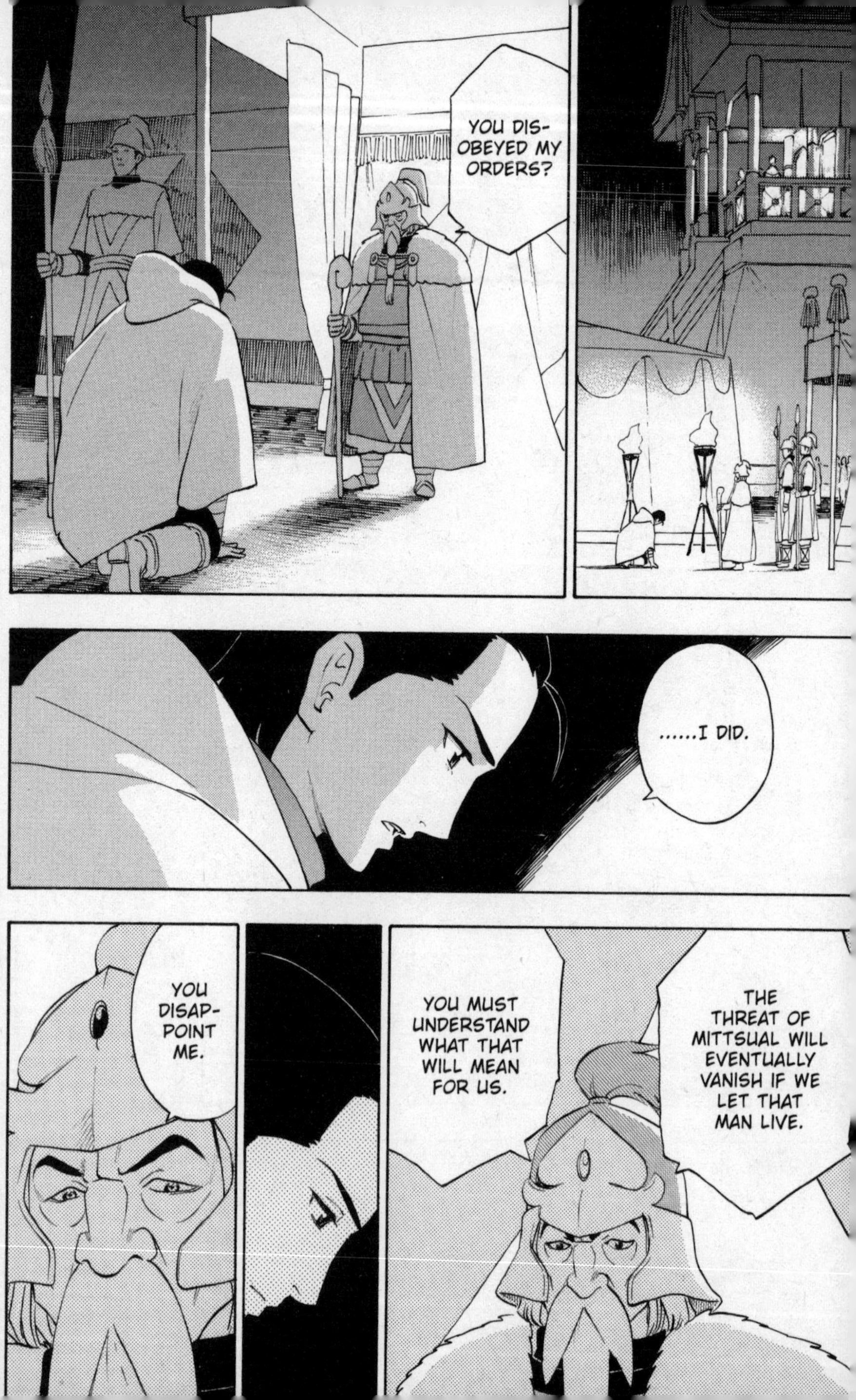

YOU DIS-OBEYED MY ORDERS?
......I DID.
THE THREAT OF MITTSUAL WILL EVENTUALLY VANISH IF WE LET THAT MAN LIVE.
YOU MUST UNDERSTAND WHAT THAT WILL MEAN FOR US.
YOU DISAP-POINT ME.

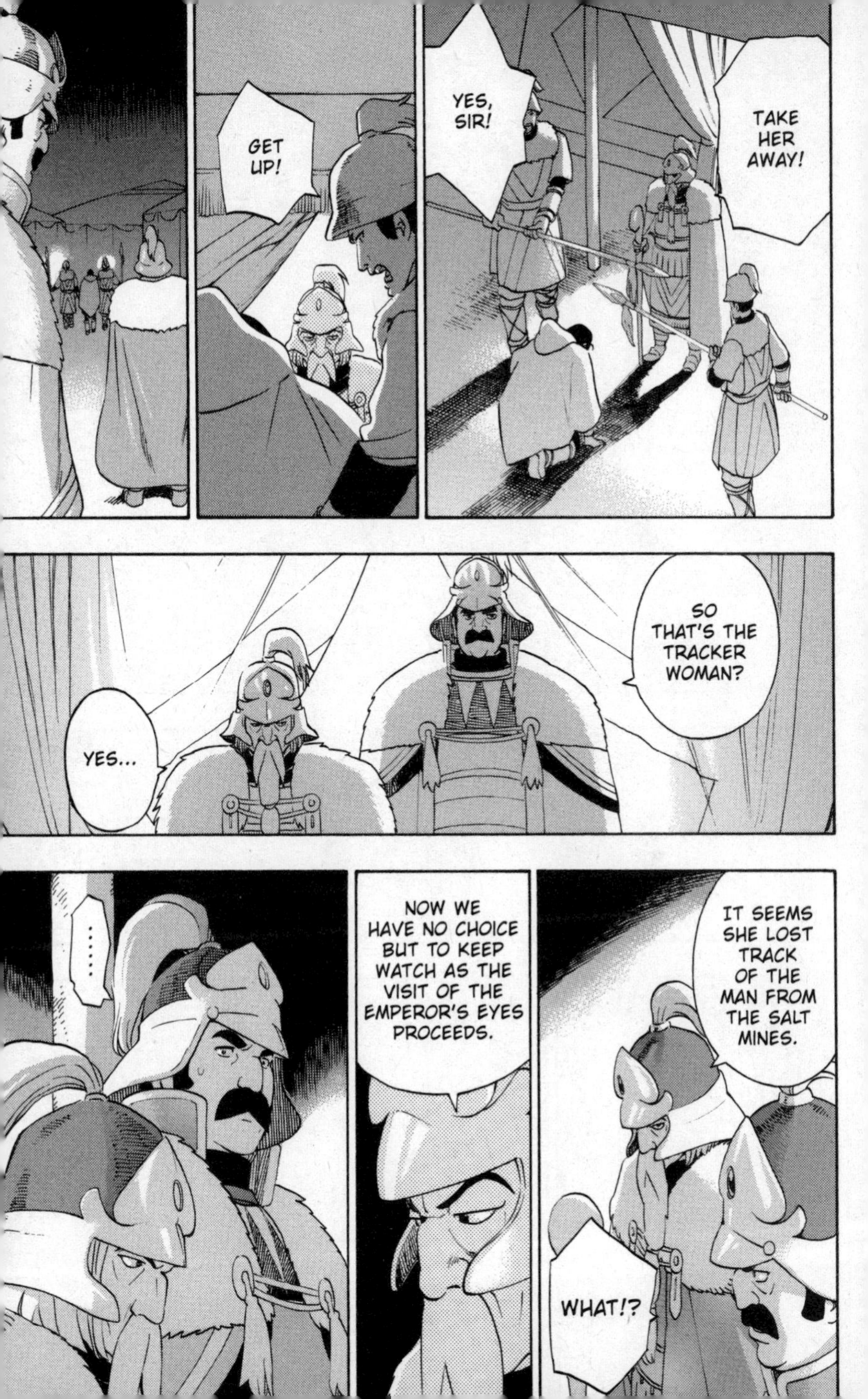
TAKE HER AWAY!
YES, SIR!
GET UP!
SO THAT'S THE TRACKER WOMAN?
YES...
IT SEEMS SHE LOST TRACK OF THE MAN FROM THE SALT MINES.
WHAT!?
NOW WE HAVE NO CHOICE BUT TO KEEP WATCH AS THE VISIT OF THE EMPEROR'S EYES PROCEEDS.
......

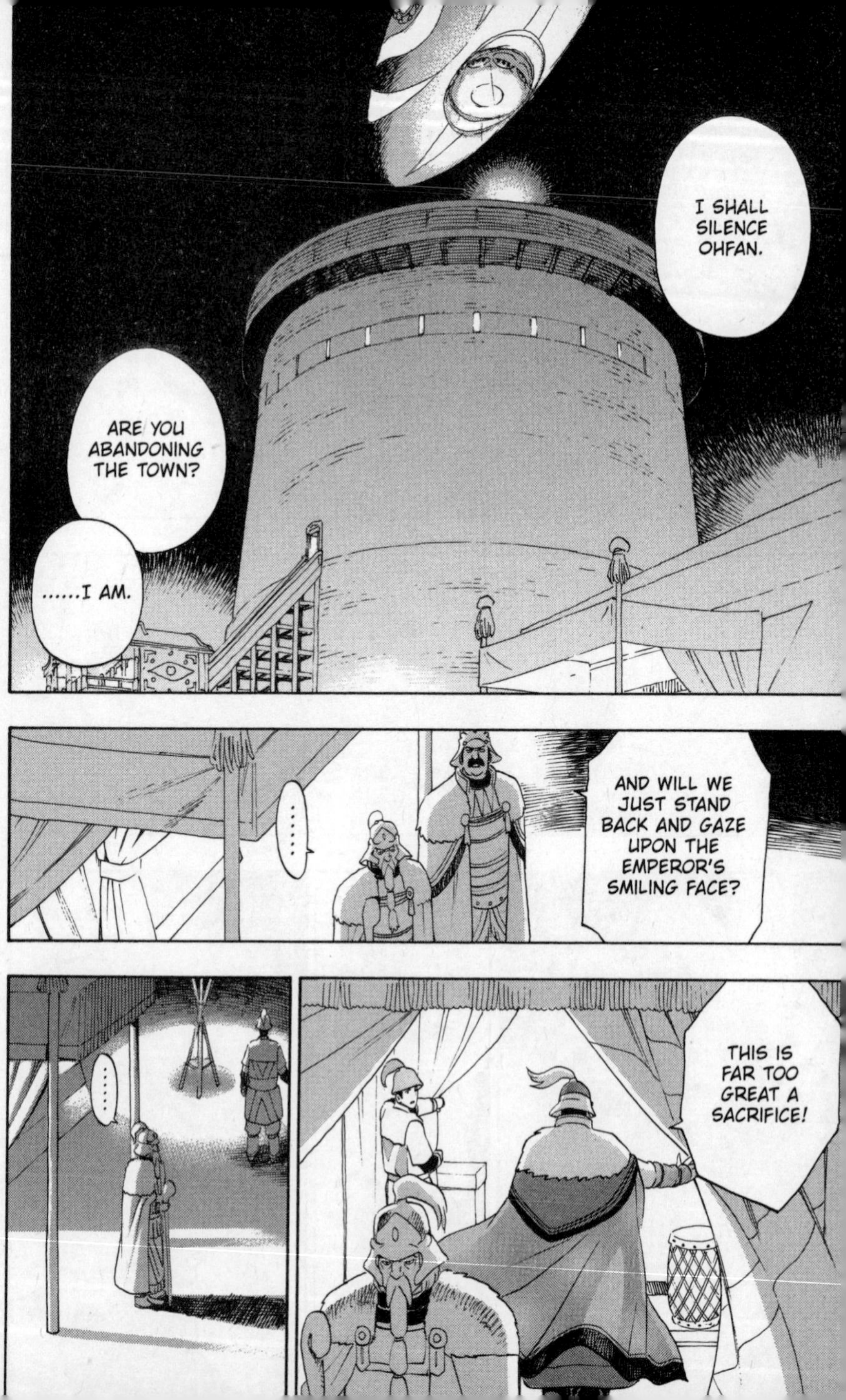
I SHALL SILENCE OHFAN.
ARE YOU ABANDONING THE TOWN?
......I AM.
AND WILL WE JUST STAND BACK AND GAZE UPON THE EMPEROR'S SMILING FACE?
......
THIS IS FAR TOO GREAT A SACRIFICE!
......

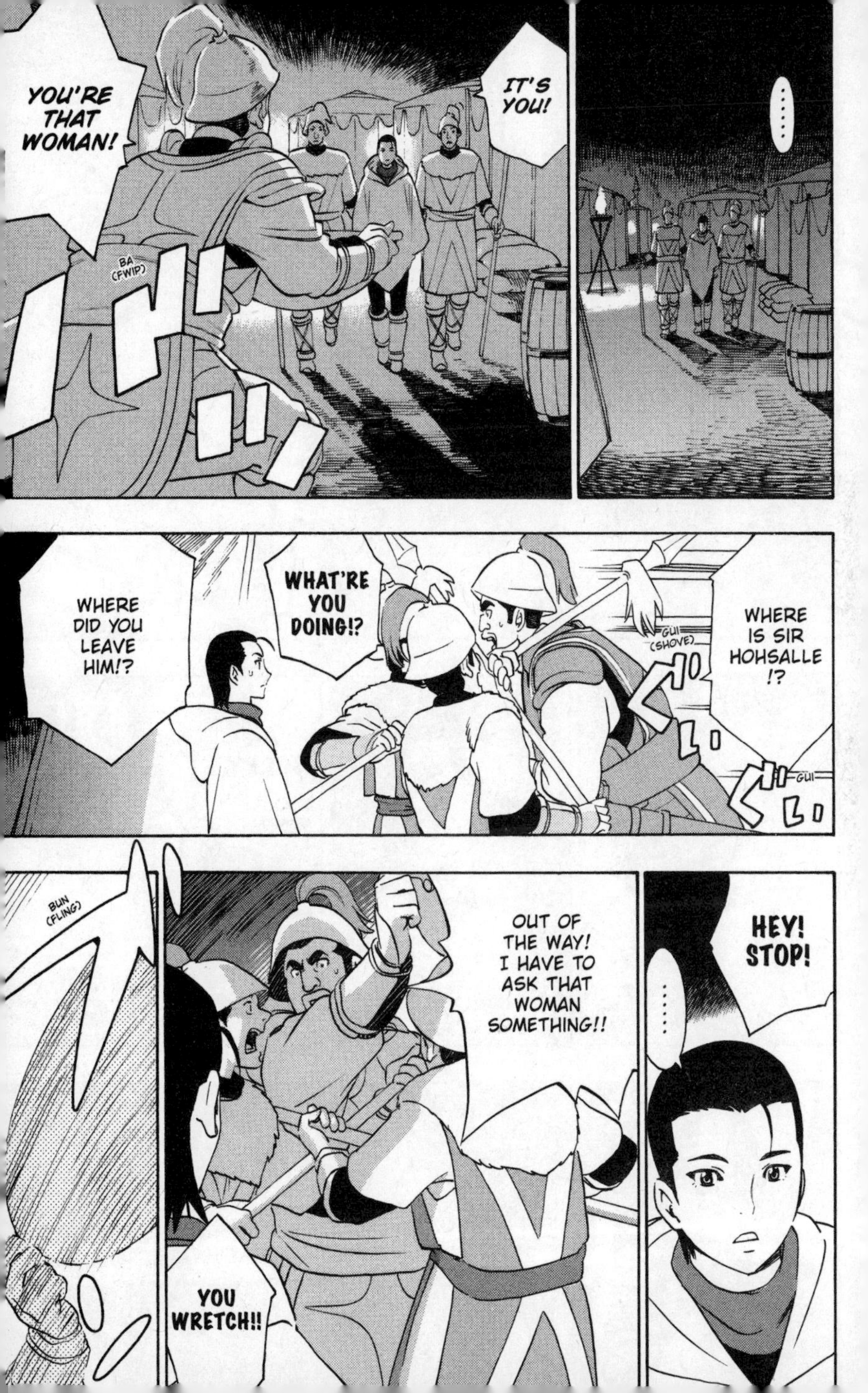
......
IT'S YOU!
YOU'RE THAT WOMAN!
BA (FWIP)
WHERE IS SIR HOHSALLE!?
GUI (SHOVE)
GUI
WHAT'RE YOU DOING!?
WHERE DID YOU LEAVE HIM!?
HEY! STOP!
......
OUT OF THE WAY! I HAVE TO ASK THAT WOMAN SOMETHING!!
YOU WRETCH!!
BUN (FLING)

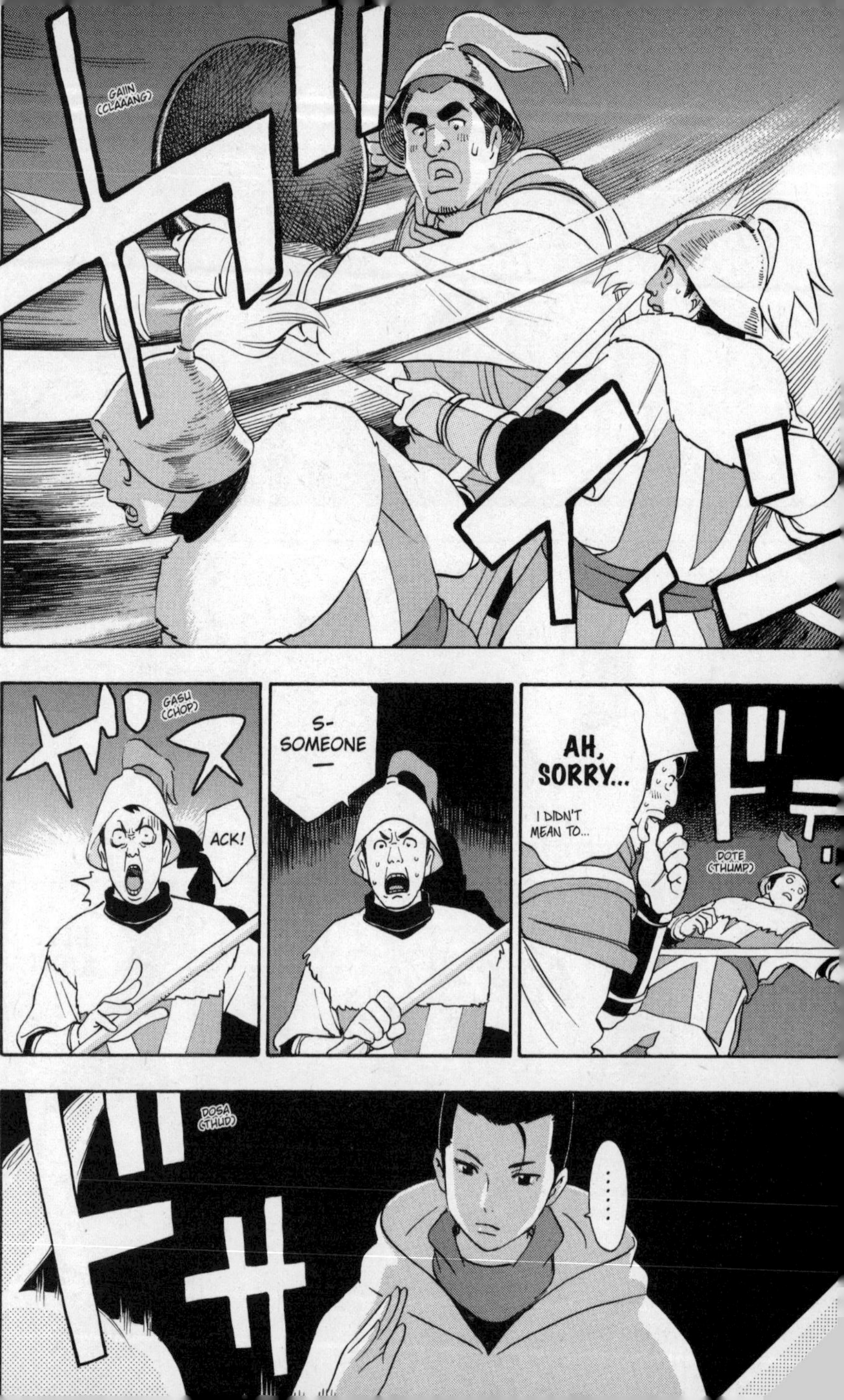
GAIIN (CLAAANG)
AH, SORRY...
I DIDN'T MEAN TO...
DOTE (THUMP)
S-SOMEONE—
GASU (CHOP)
ACK!
DOSA (THUD)
......

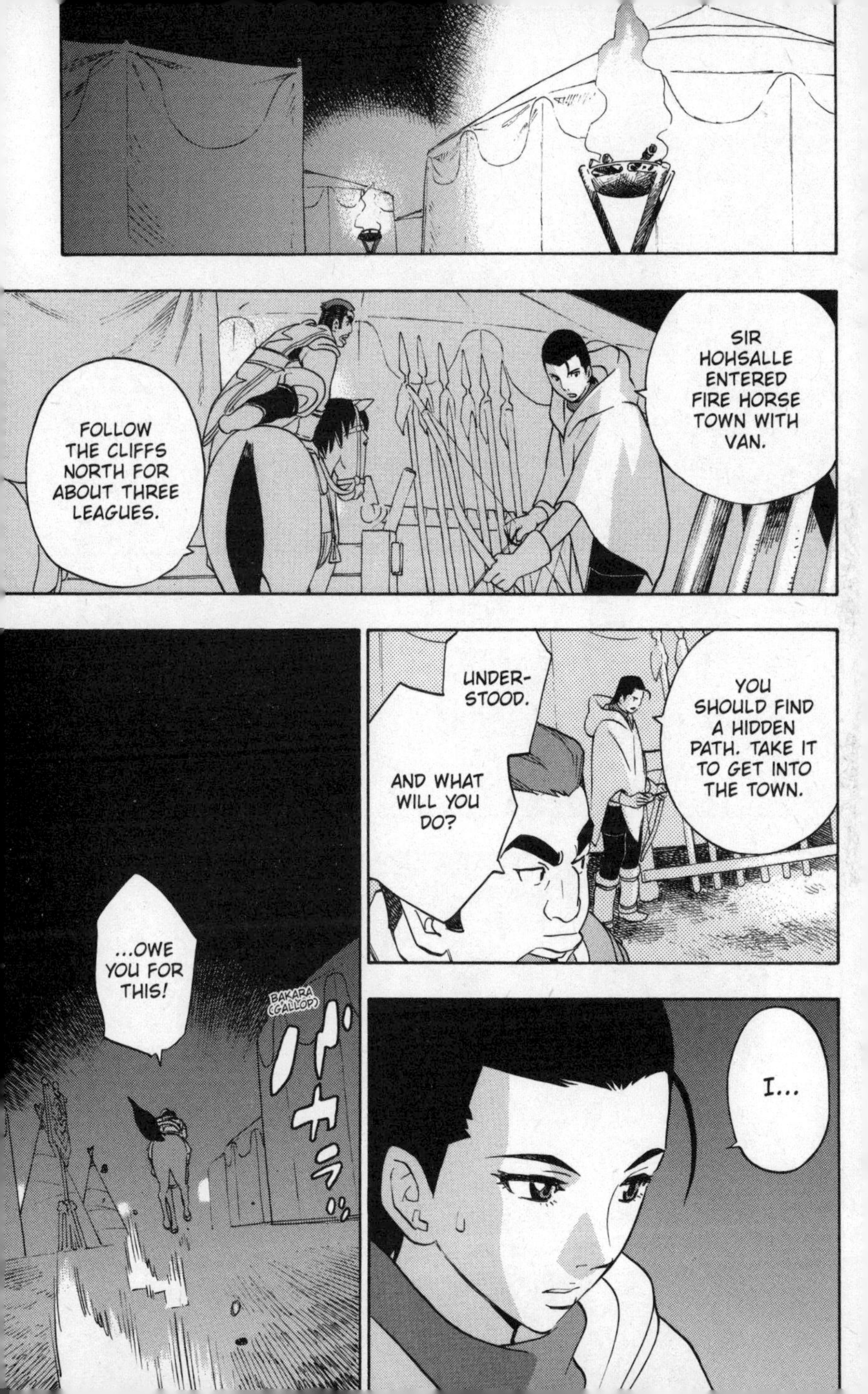
SIR HOHSALLE ENTERED FIRE HORSE TOWN WITH VAN.
FOLLOW THE CLIFFS NORTH FOR ABOUT THREE LEAGUES.
YOU SHOULD FIND A HIDDEN PATH. TAKE IT TO GET INTO THE TOWN.
UNDER-STOOD.
AND WHAT WILL YOU DO?
I...
...OWE YOU FOR THIS!
BAKARA (GALLOP)

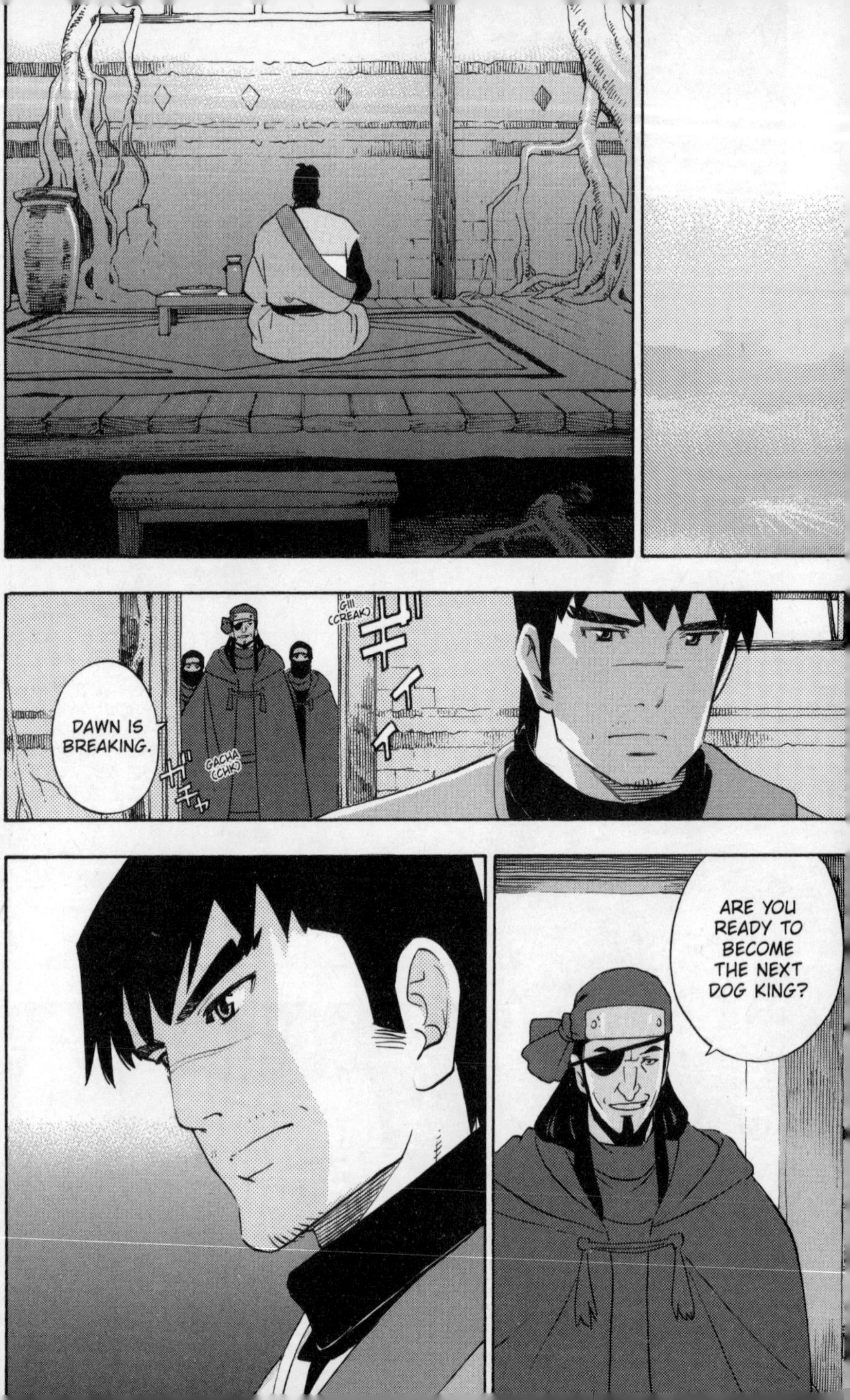
GIII (CREAK)
GACHA (CHK)
DAWN IS BREAKING.
ARE YOU READY TO BECOME THE NEXT DOG KING?

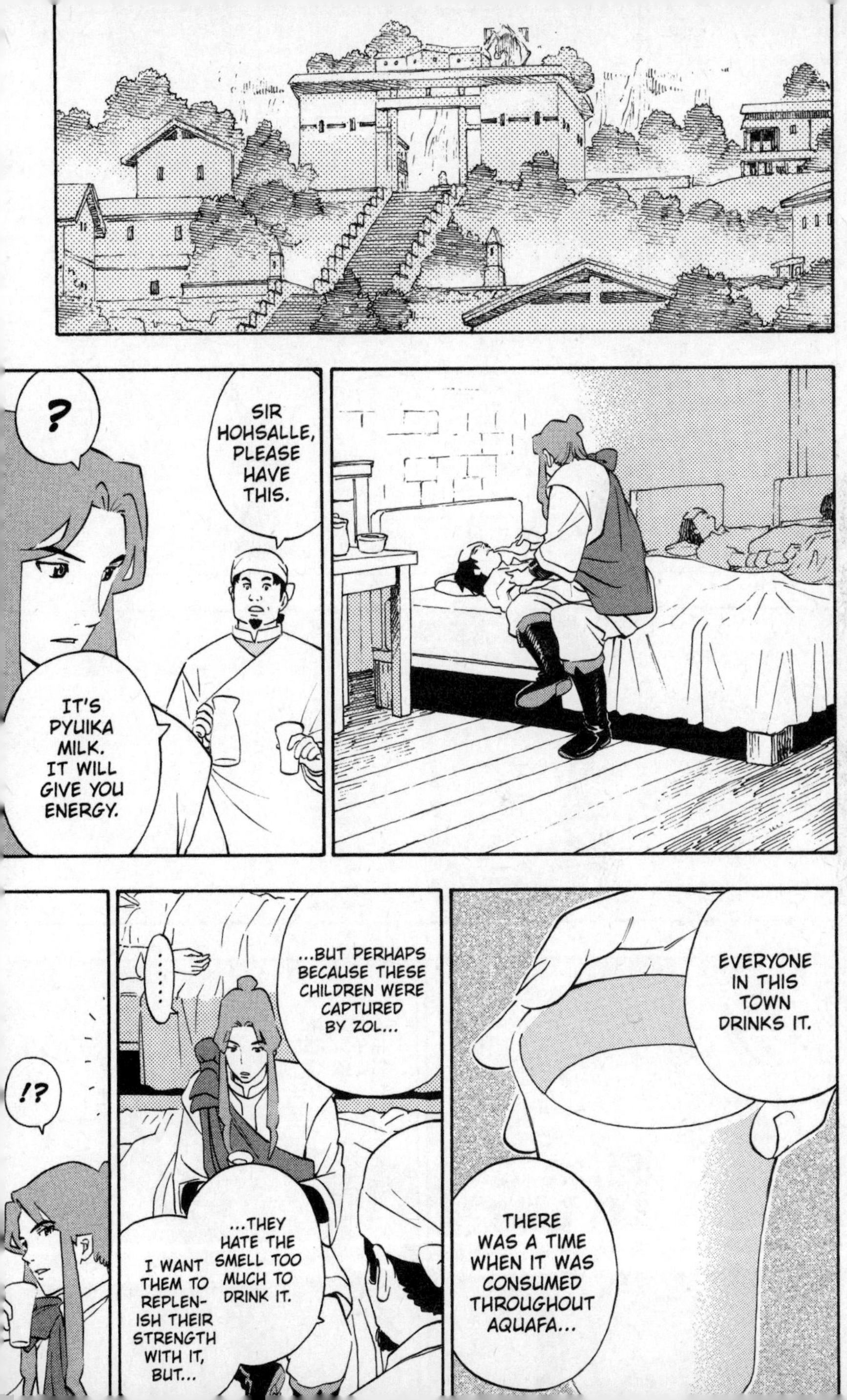
SIR HOHSALLE, PLEASE HAVE THIS.
?
IT'S PYUIKA MILK. IT WILL GIVE YOU ENERGY.
EVERYONE IN THIS TOWN DRINKS IT.
THERE WAS A TIME WHEN IT WAS CONSUMED THROUGHOUT AQUAFA...
I WANT THEM TO REPLEN-ISH THEIR STRENGTH WITH IT, BUT...
...BUT PERHAPS BECAUSE THESE CHILDREN WERE CAPTURED BY ZOL...
......
...THEY HATE THE SMELL TOO MUCH TO DRINK IT.
!?

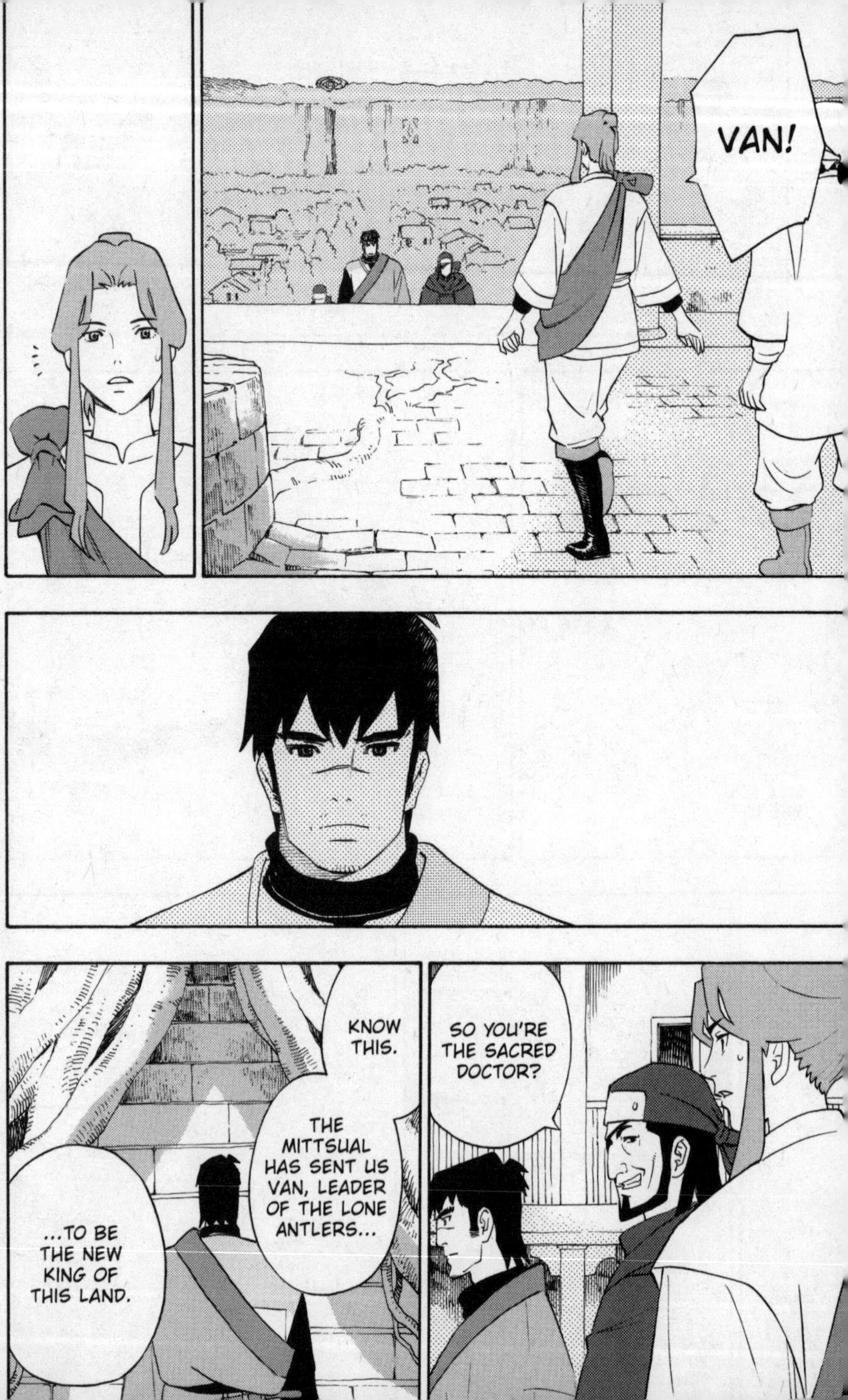
VAN!
SO YOU'RE THE SACRED DOCTOR?
KNOW THIS.
THE MITTSUAL HAS SENT US VAN, LEADER OF THE LONE ANTLERS...
...TO BE THE NEW KING OF THIS LAND.

THIS IS AN ORDER FROM GOD.

THIS DISEASE ONLY SPARES THE CHOSEN.

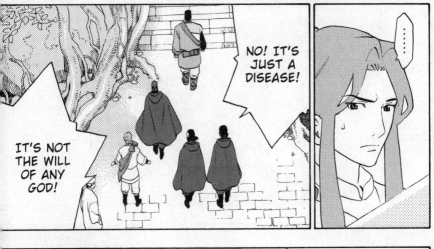

NO! IT'S JUST A DISEASE!

IT'S NOT THE WILL OF ANY GOD!

I SHOULD BE ABLE TO SAVE THOSE CHILDREN WITH VAN'S BLOOD!

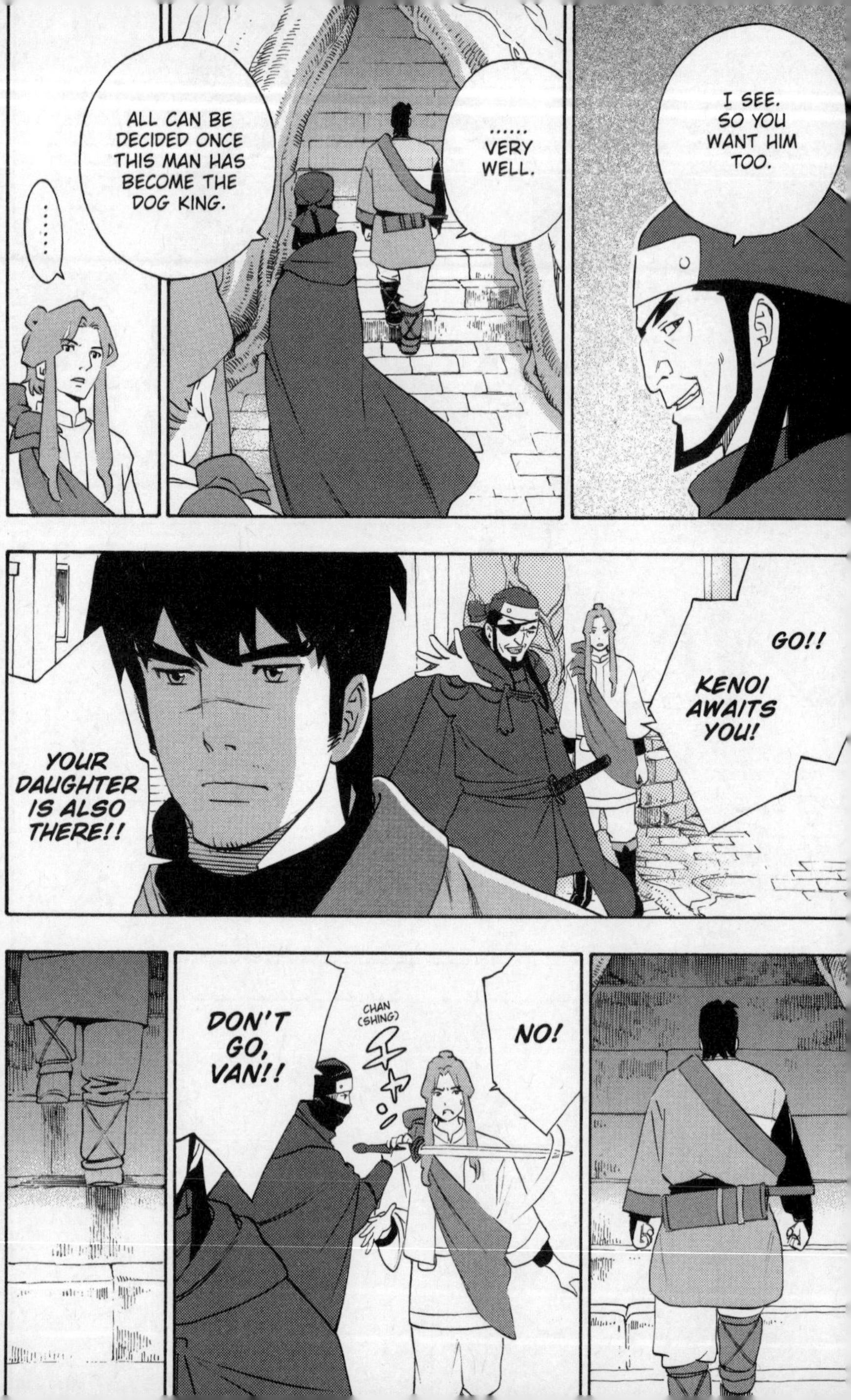
I SEE. SO YOU WANT HIM TOO.
...... VERY WELL.
ALL CAN BE DECIDED ONCE THIS MAN HAS BECOME THE DOG KING.
......
GO!!
KENOI AWAITS YOU!
YOUR DAUGHTER IS ALSO THERE!!
NO!
CHAN (SHING)
DON'T GO, VAN!!

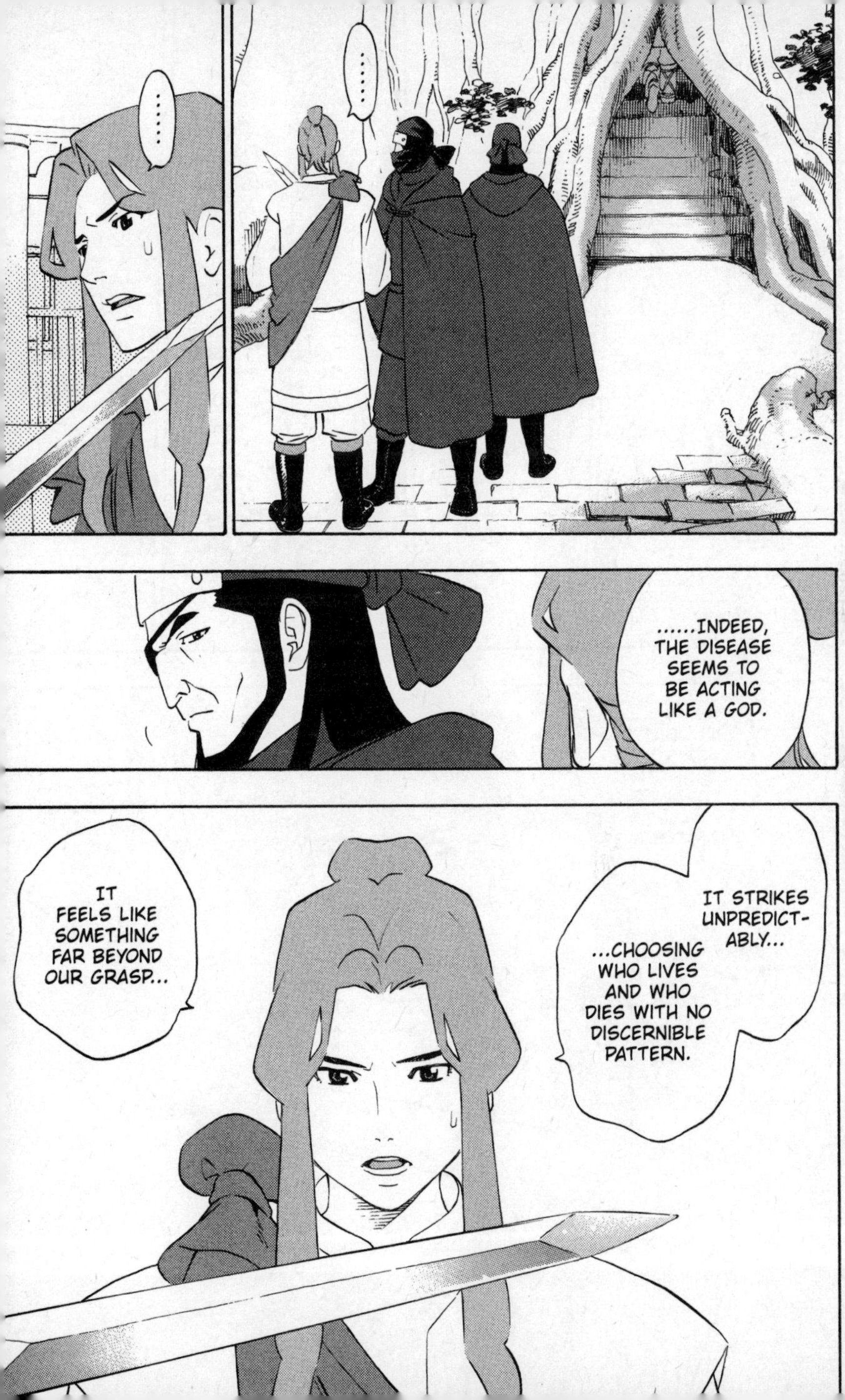
......
......
......INDEED, THE DISEASE SEEMS TO BE ACTING LIKE A GOD.
IT STRIKES UNPREDICT-ABLY...
...CHOOSING WHO LIVES AND WHO DIES WITH NO DISCERNIBLE PATTERN.
IT FEELS LIKE SOMETHING FAR BEYOND OUR GRASP...

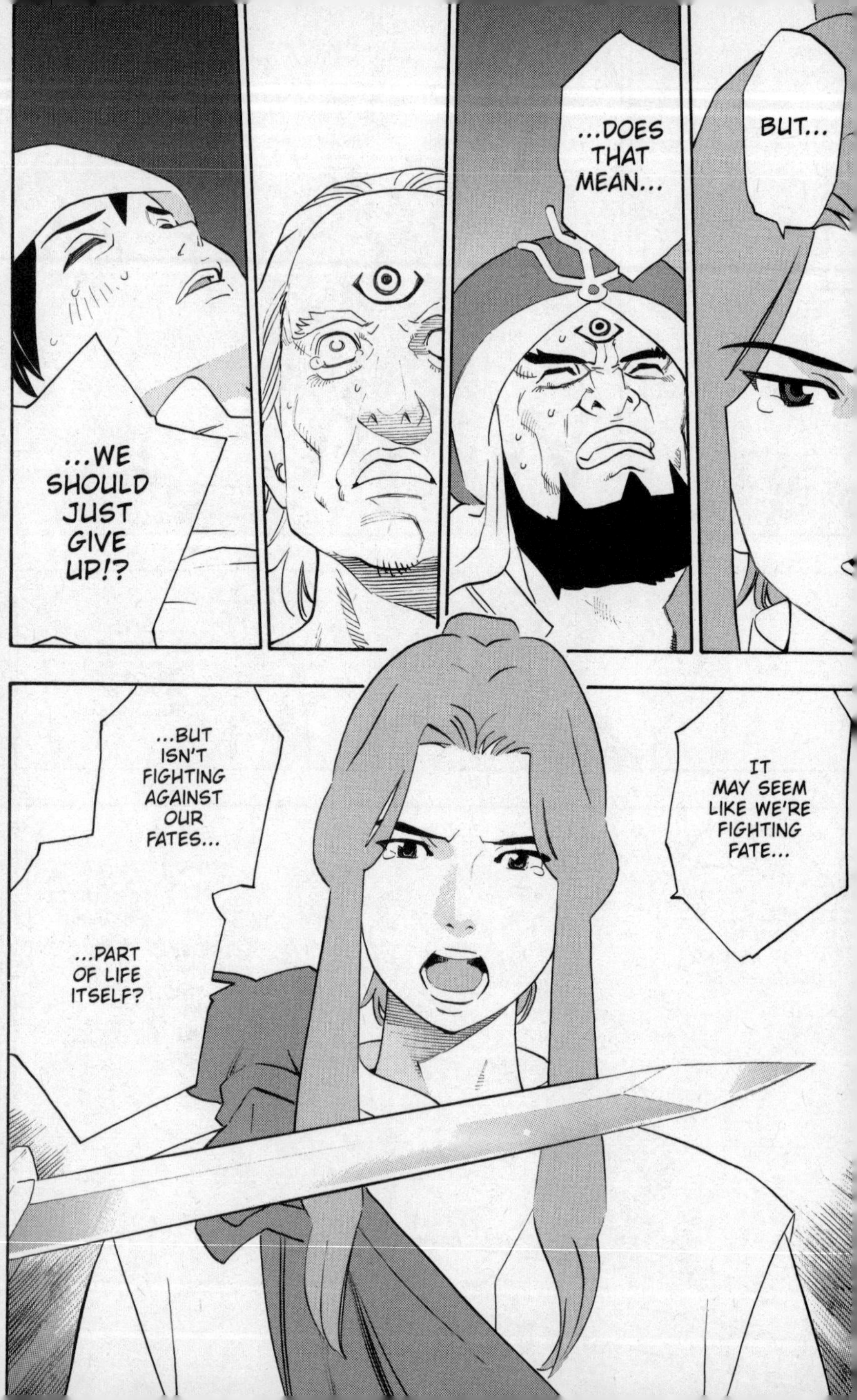
BUT...
...DOES THAT MEAN...
...WE SHOULD JUST GIVE UP!?
IT MAY SEEM LIKE WE'RE FIGHTING FATE...
...BUT ISN'T FIGHTING AGAINST OUR FATES...
...PART OF LIFE ITSELF?

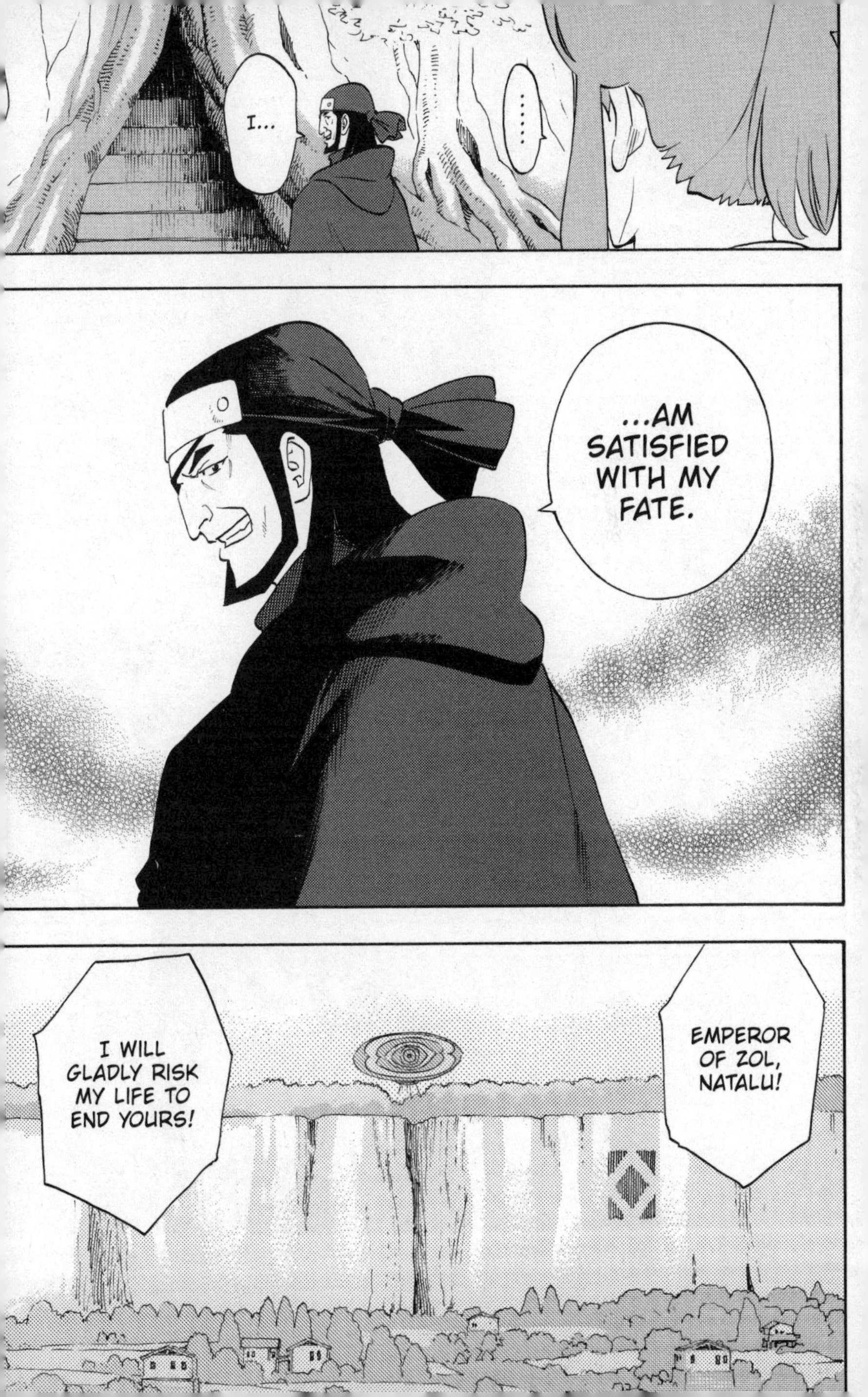
......
I...
...AM SATISFIED WITH MY FATE.
EMPEROR OF ZOL, NATALU!
I WILL GLADLY RISK MY LIFE TO END YOURS!

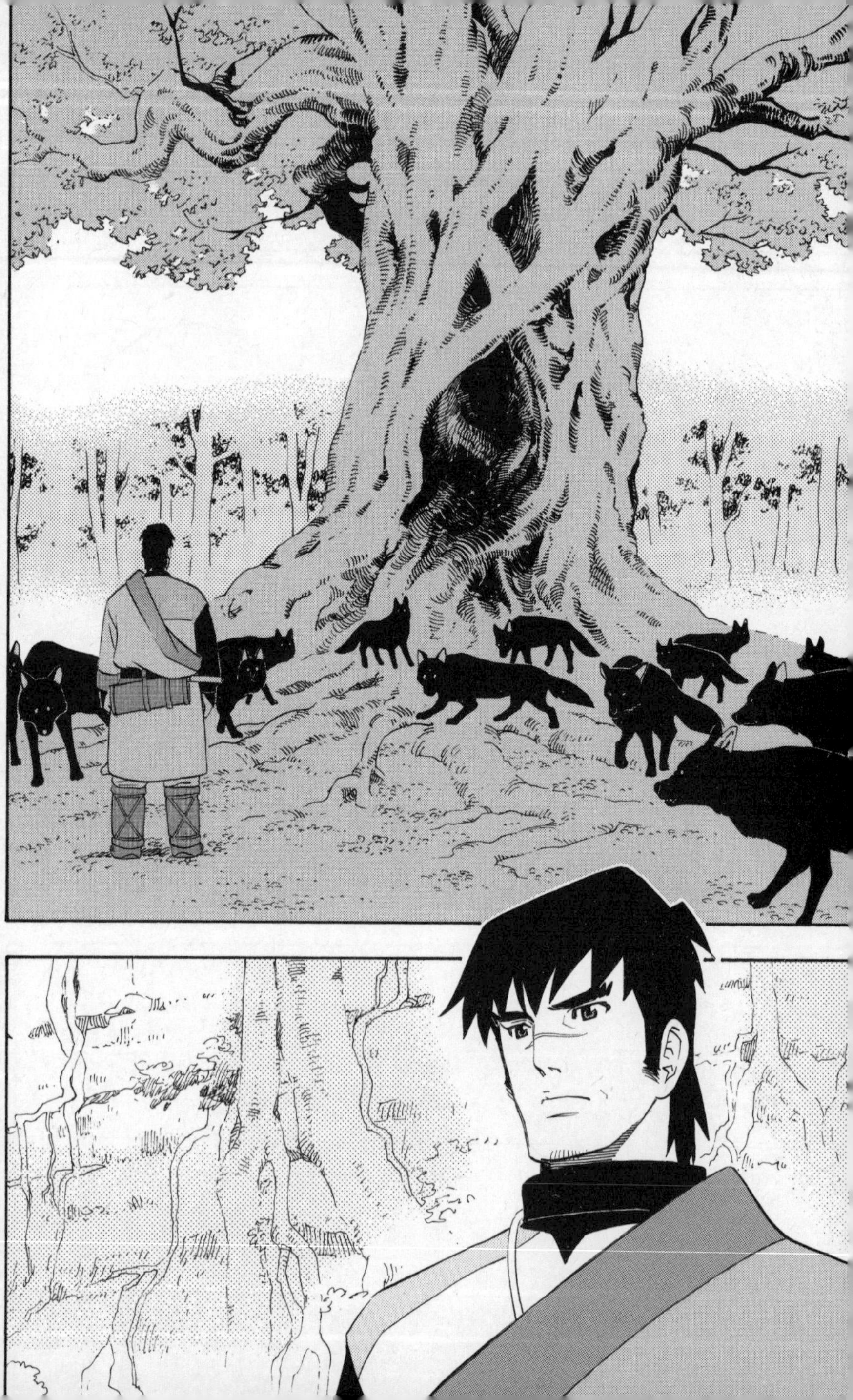

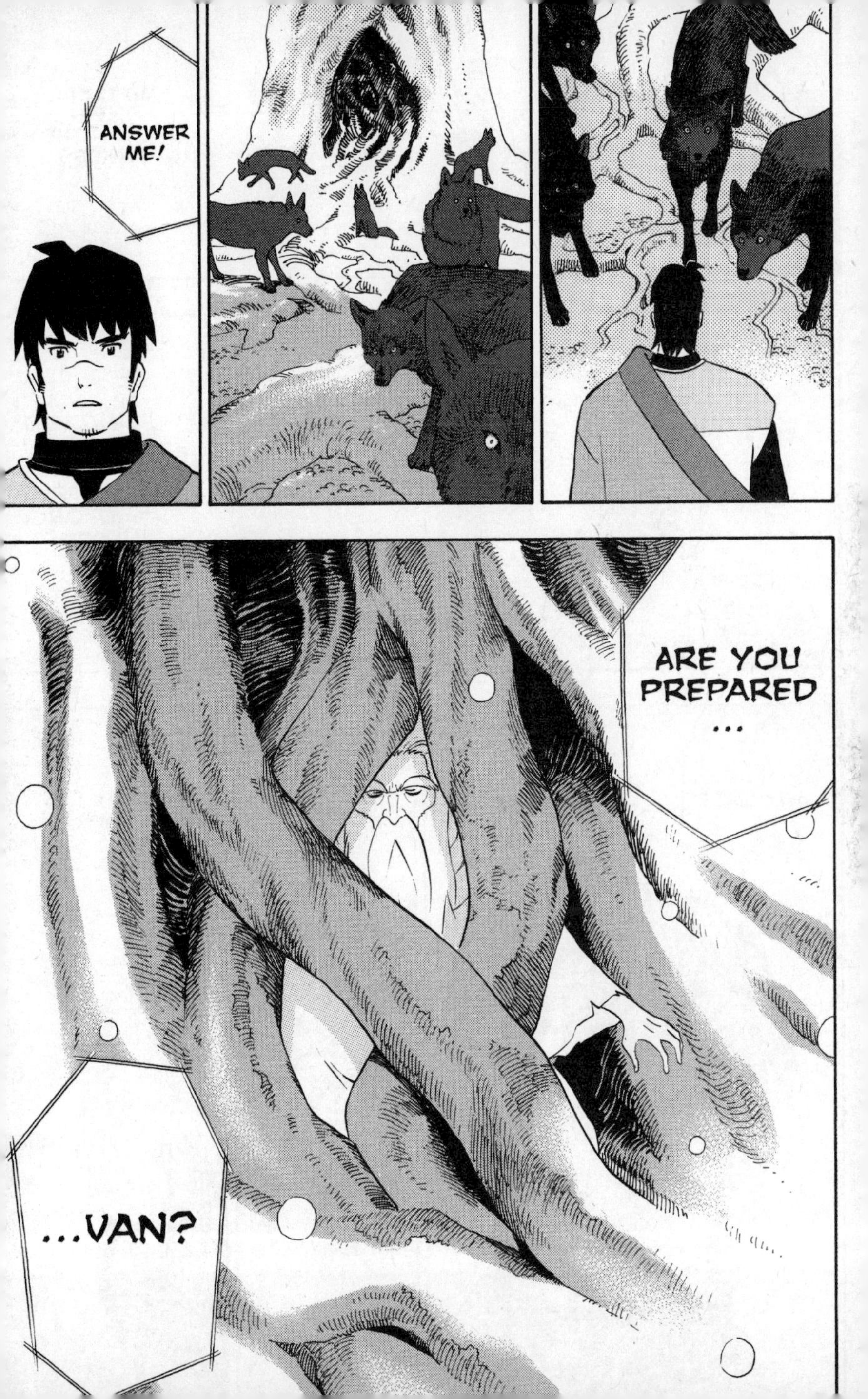
ANSWER ME!
ARE YOU PREPARED ...
...VAN?

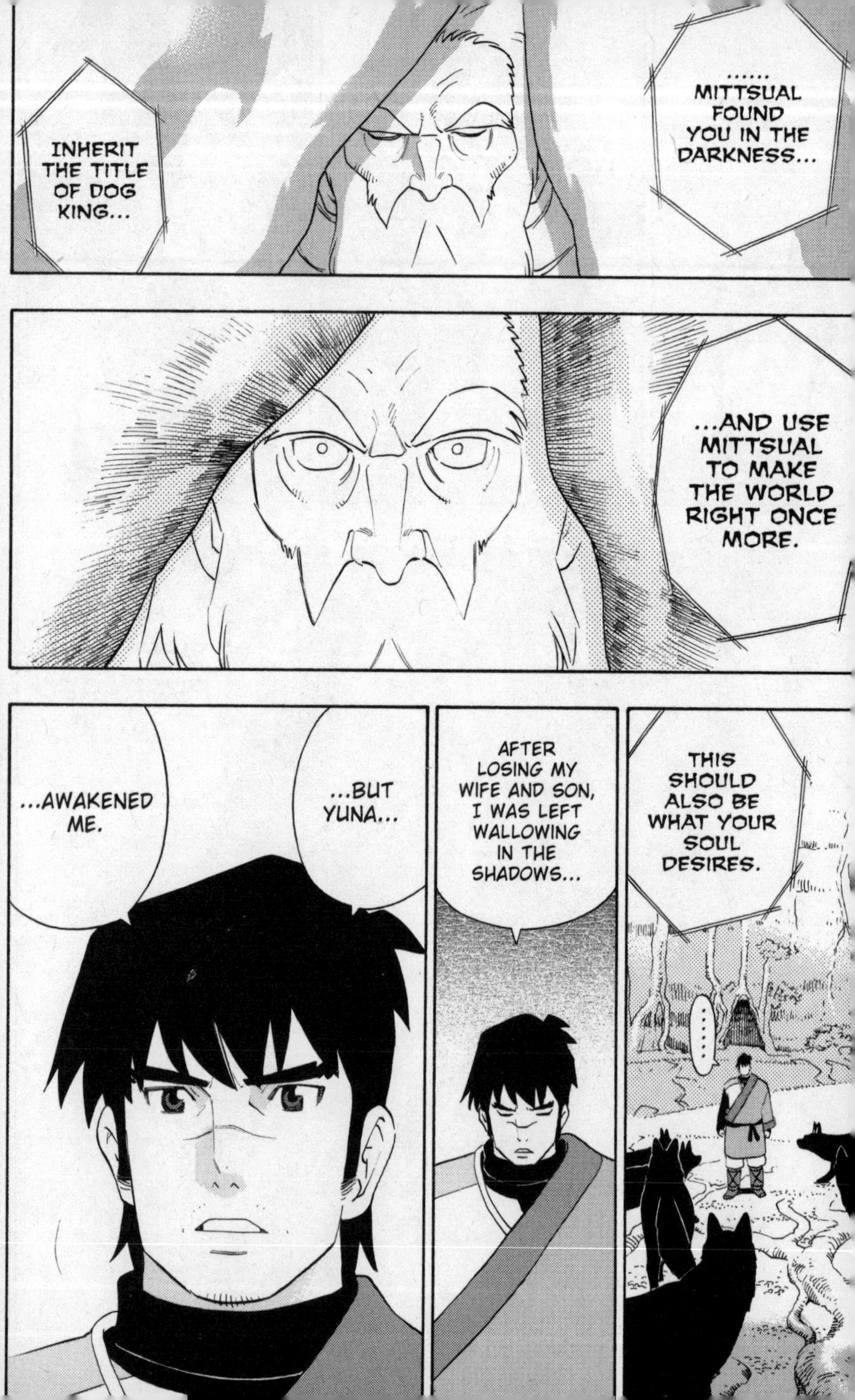
......
MITTSUAL FOUND YOU IN THE DARKNESS...
INHERIT THE TITLE OF DOG KING...
...AND USE MITTSUAL TO MAKE THE WORLD RIGHT ONCE MORE.
THIS SHOULD ALSO BE WHAT YOUR SOUL DESIRES.
......
AFTER LOSING MY WIFE AND SON, I WAS LEFT WALLOWING IN THE SHADOWS...
...BUT YUNA...
...AWAKENED ME.

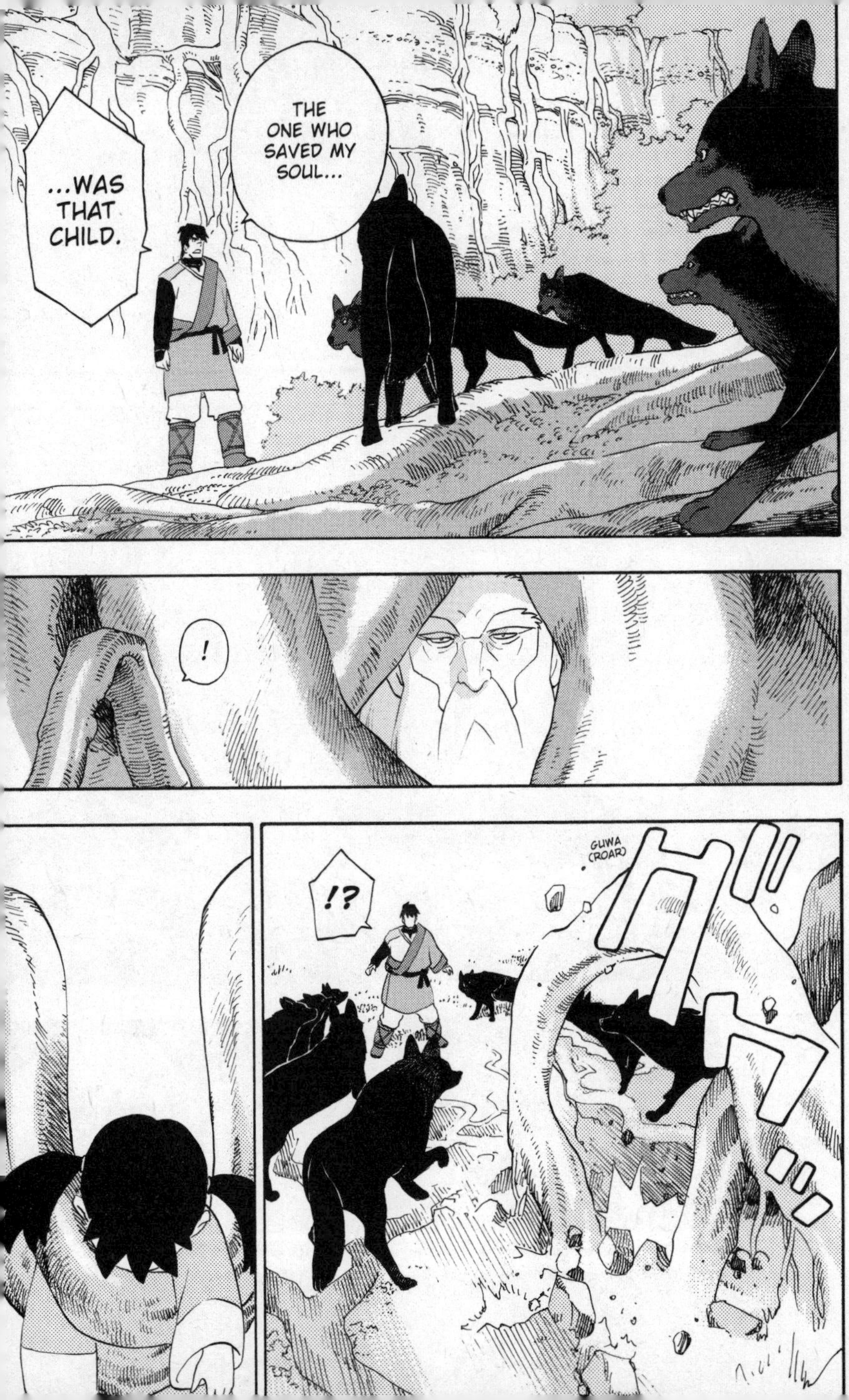
THE ONE WHO SAVED MY SOUL...
...WAS THAT CHILD.
!
GUWA (ROAR)
!?

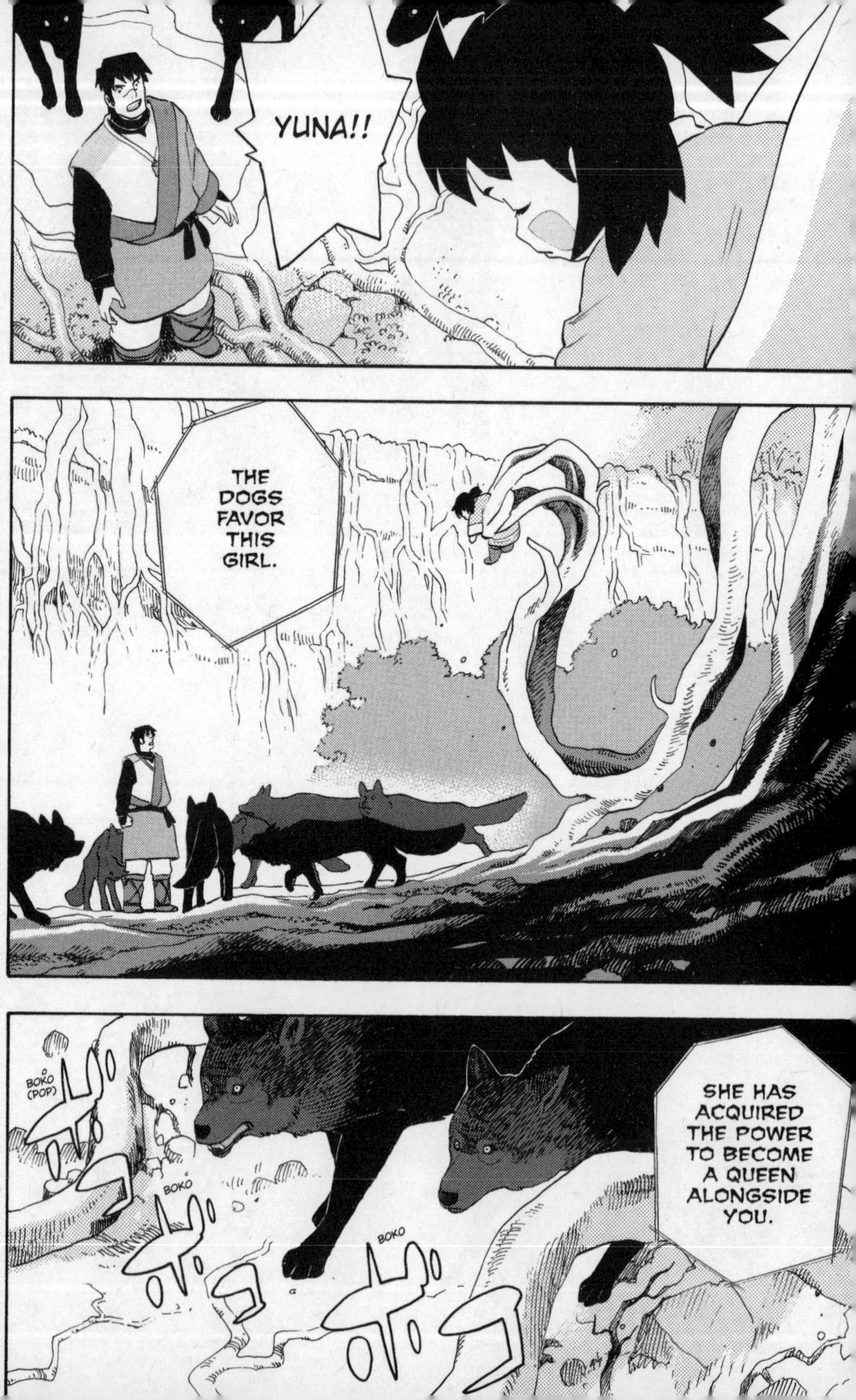
YUNA!!
THE DOGS FAVOR THIS GIRL.
SHE HAS ACQUIRED THE POWER TO BECOME A QUEEN ALONGSIDE YOU.
BOKO (POP)
BOKO
BOKO

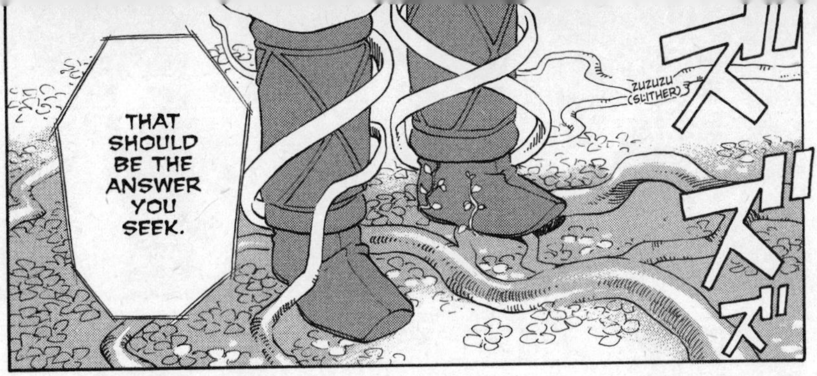
ZUZUZU (SLITHER)
THAT SHOULD BE THE ANSWER YOU SEEK.
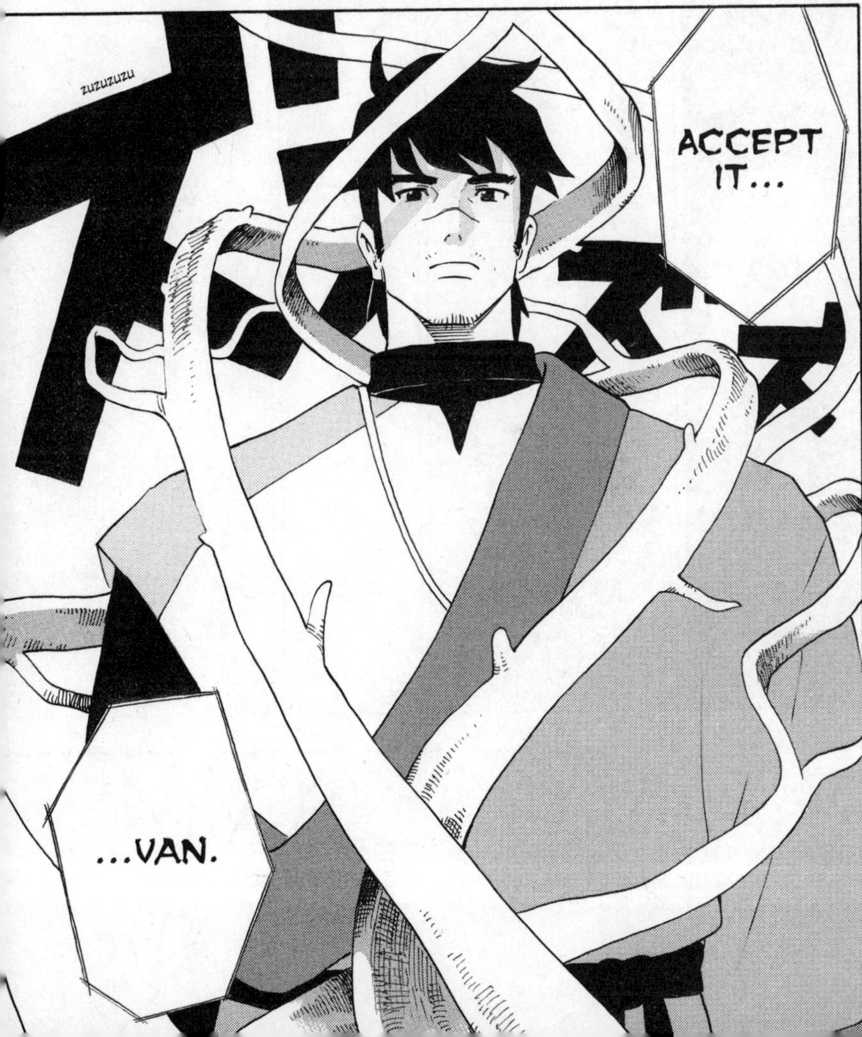
ACCEPT IT...
ZUZUZUZU
...VAN.

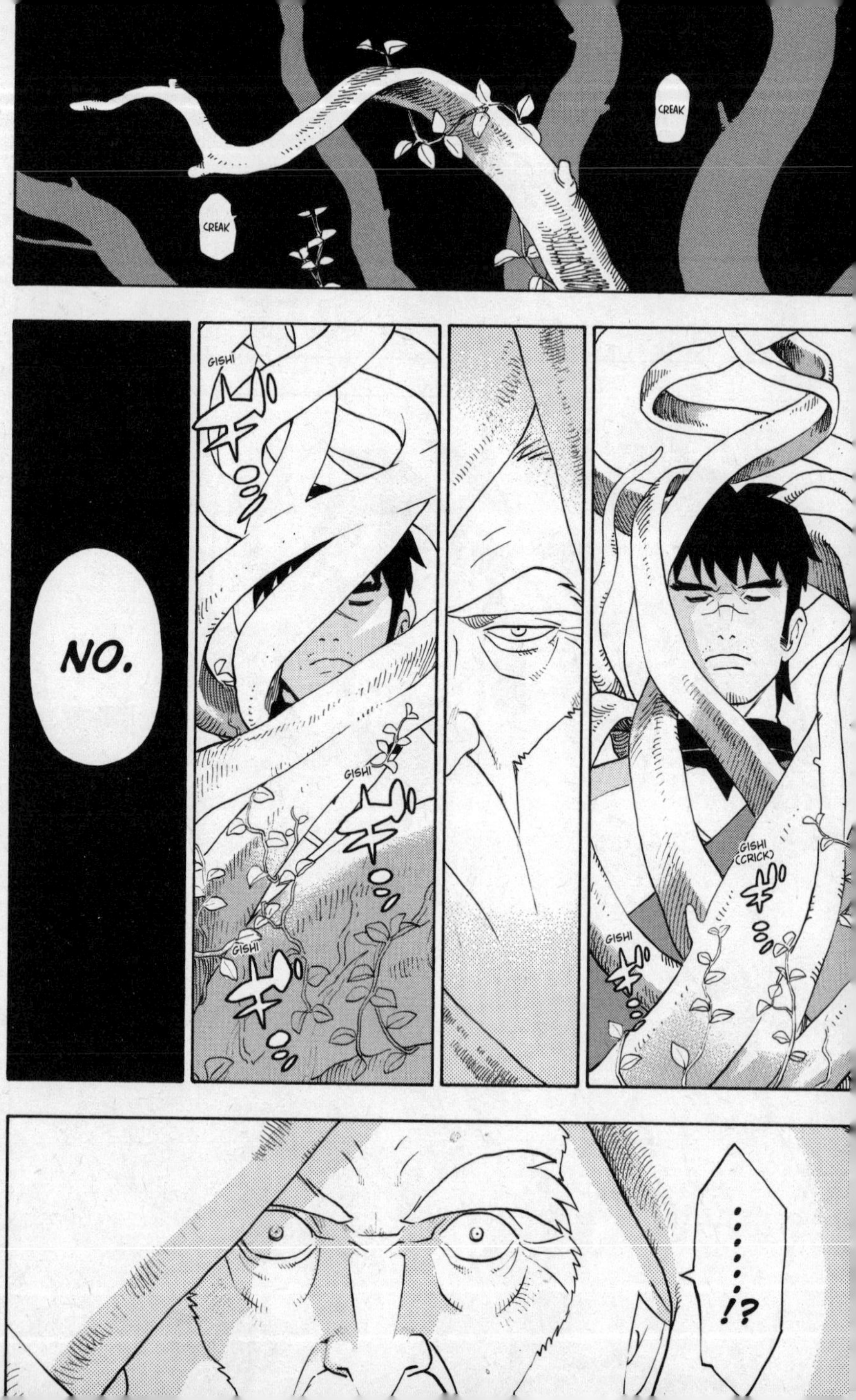

CREAK
CREAK
GISHI (CRICK)
GISHI
GISHI
GISHI
GISHI
NO.
......!?

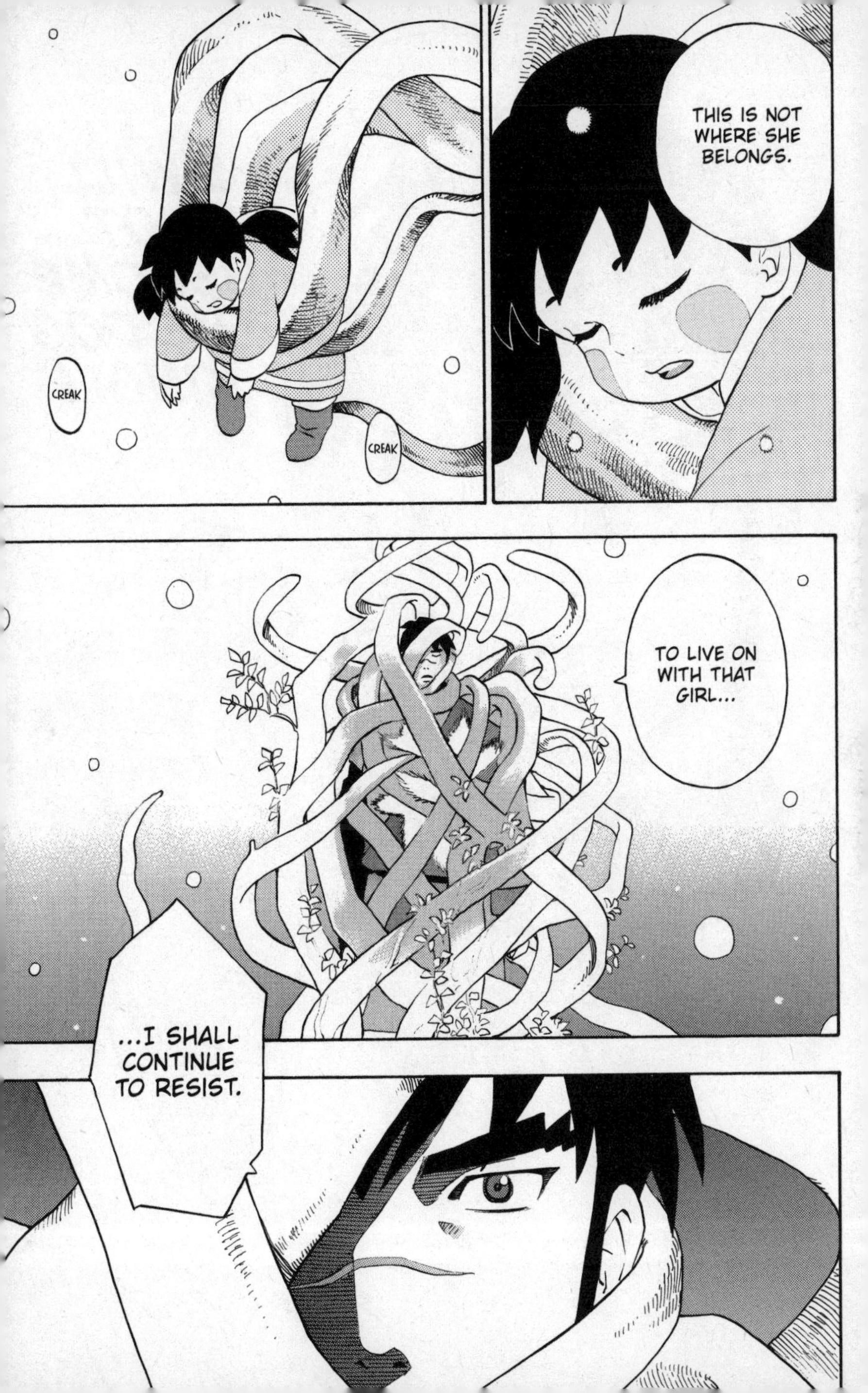
THIS IS NOT WHERE SHE BELONGS.
CREAK
CREAK
TO LIVE ON WITH THAT GIRL...
...I SHALL CONTINUE TO RESIST.

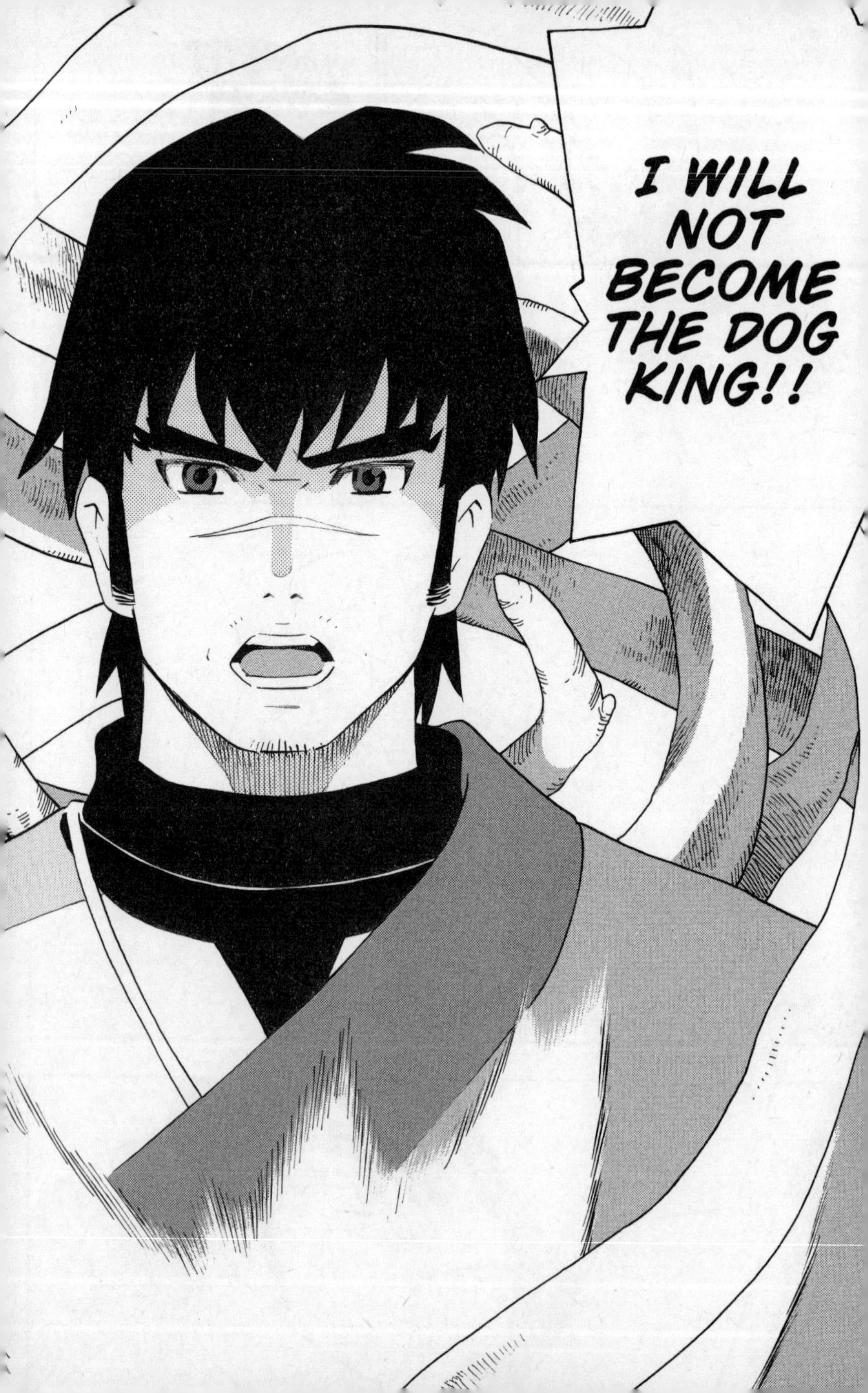
I WILL NOT BECOME THE DOG KING!!

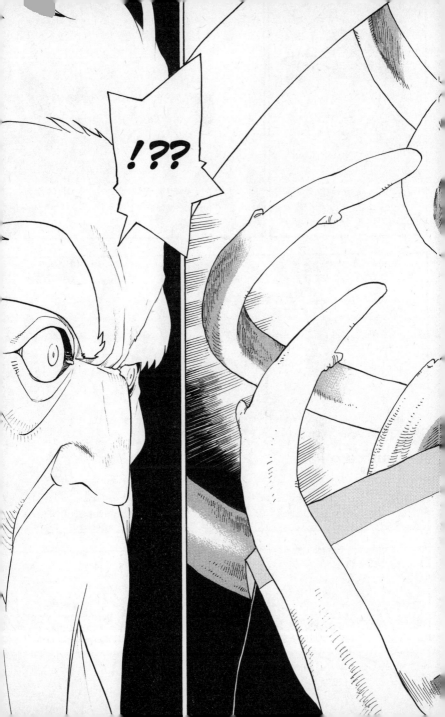

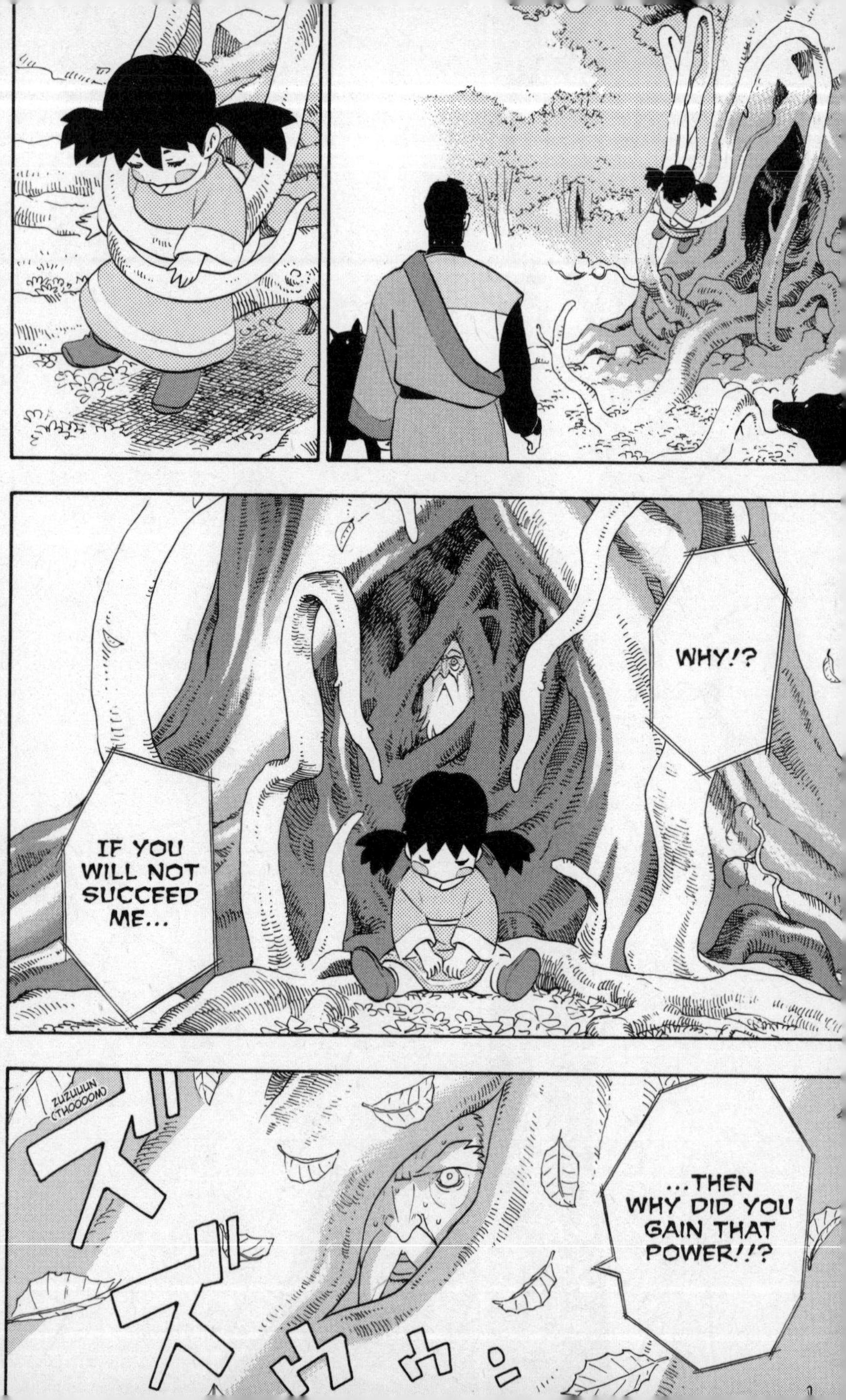
WHY!?
IF YOU WILL NOT SUCCEED ME...
...THEN WHY DID YOU GAIN THAT POWER!!?
ZUZUUUN (THOOOOM)

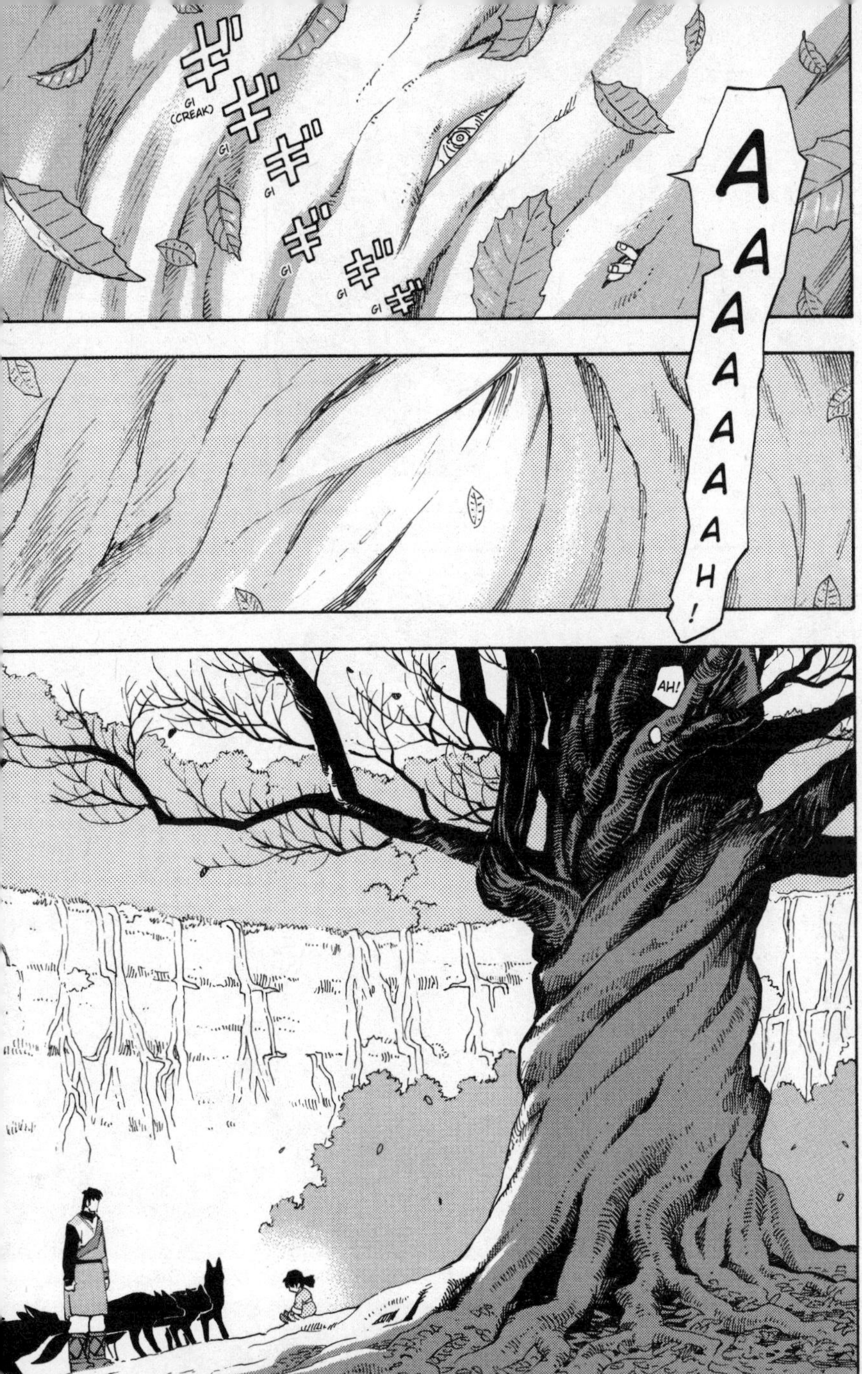

AAAAAAAAH!
ギ
GI (CREAK)
ギ
GI
ギ
GI
ギ
GI
ギ
GI
ギ
GI
AH!

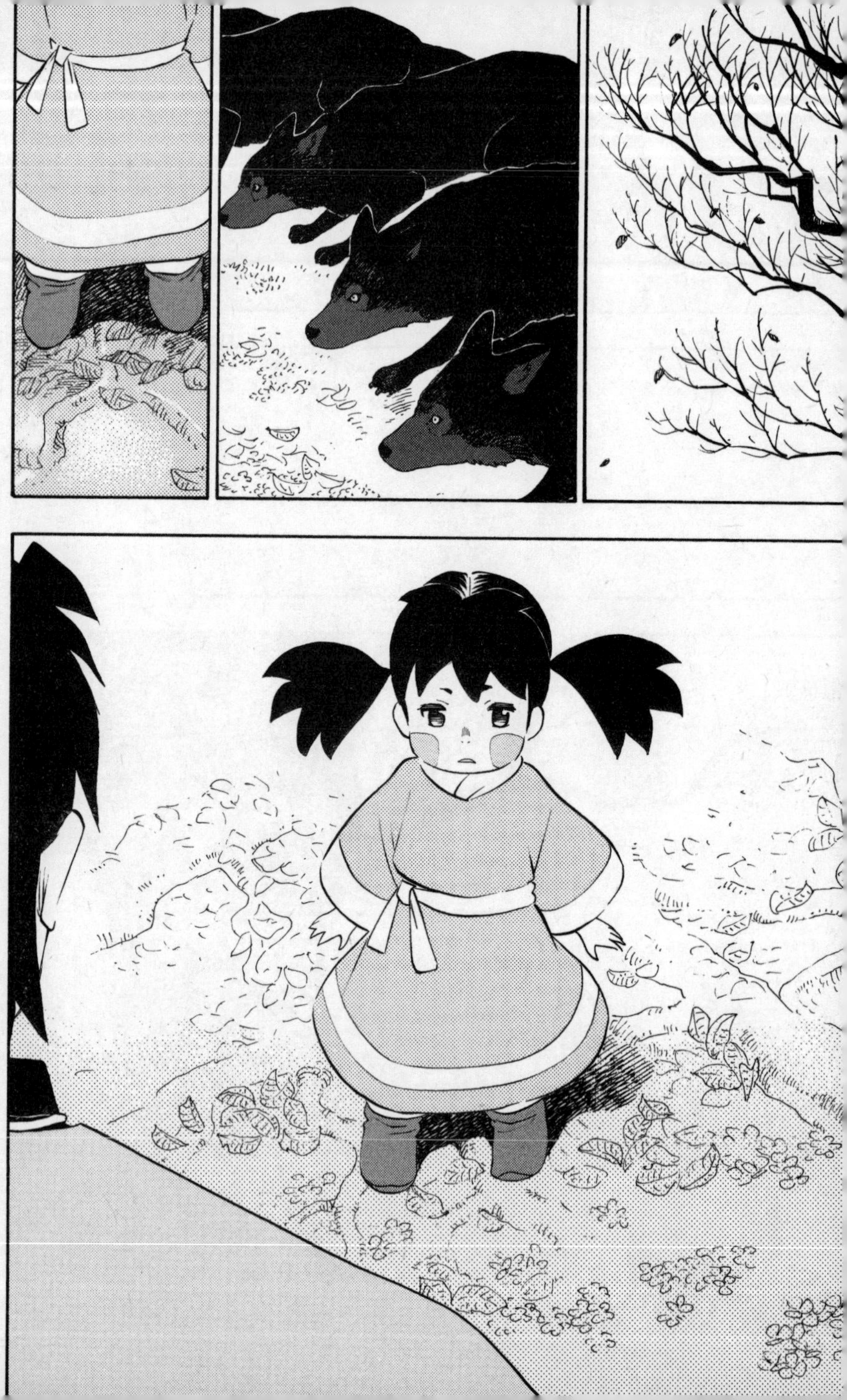

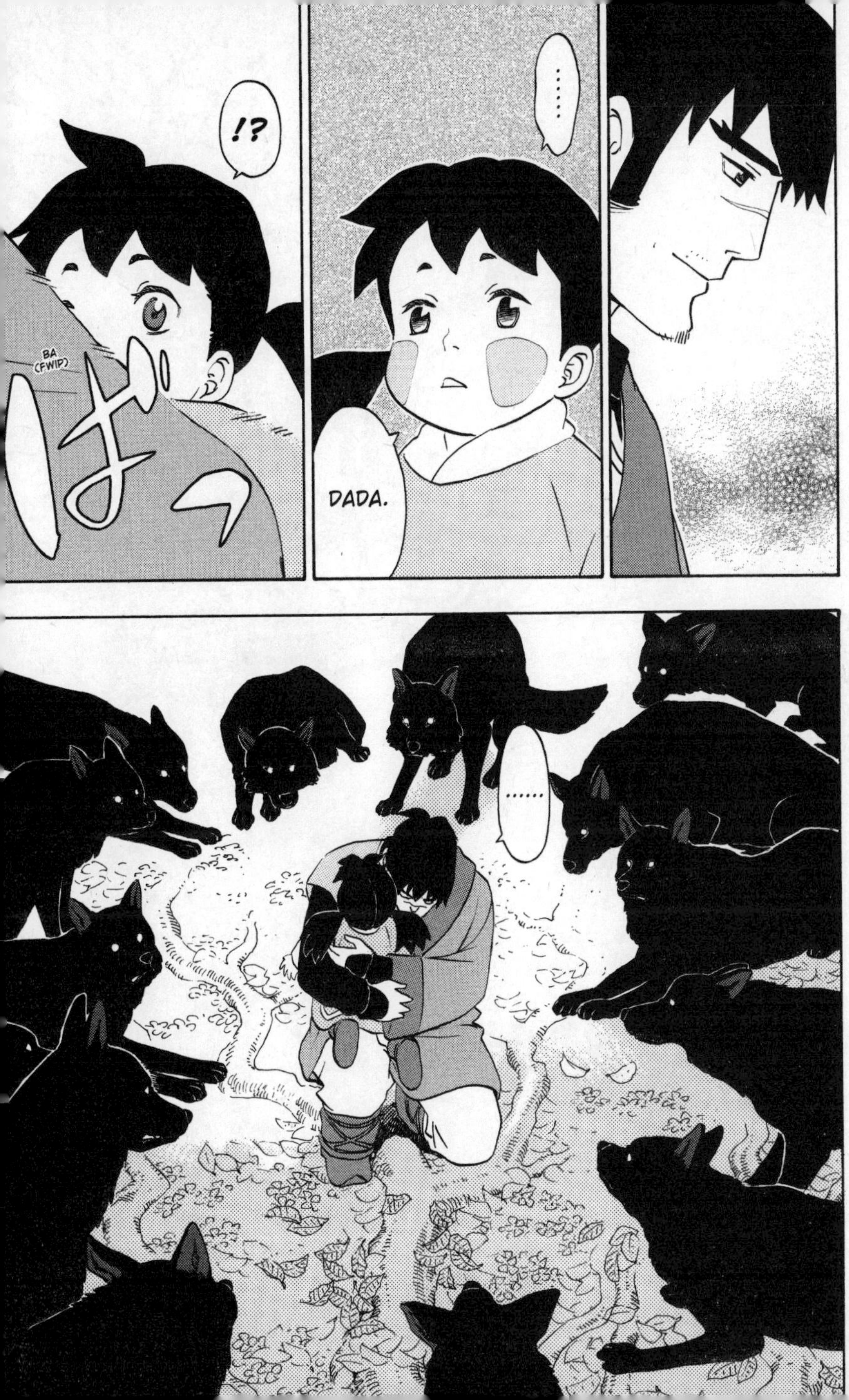
......
DADA.
!?
BA (FWIP)
......

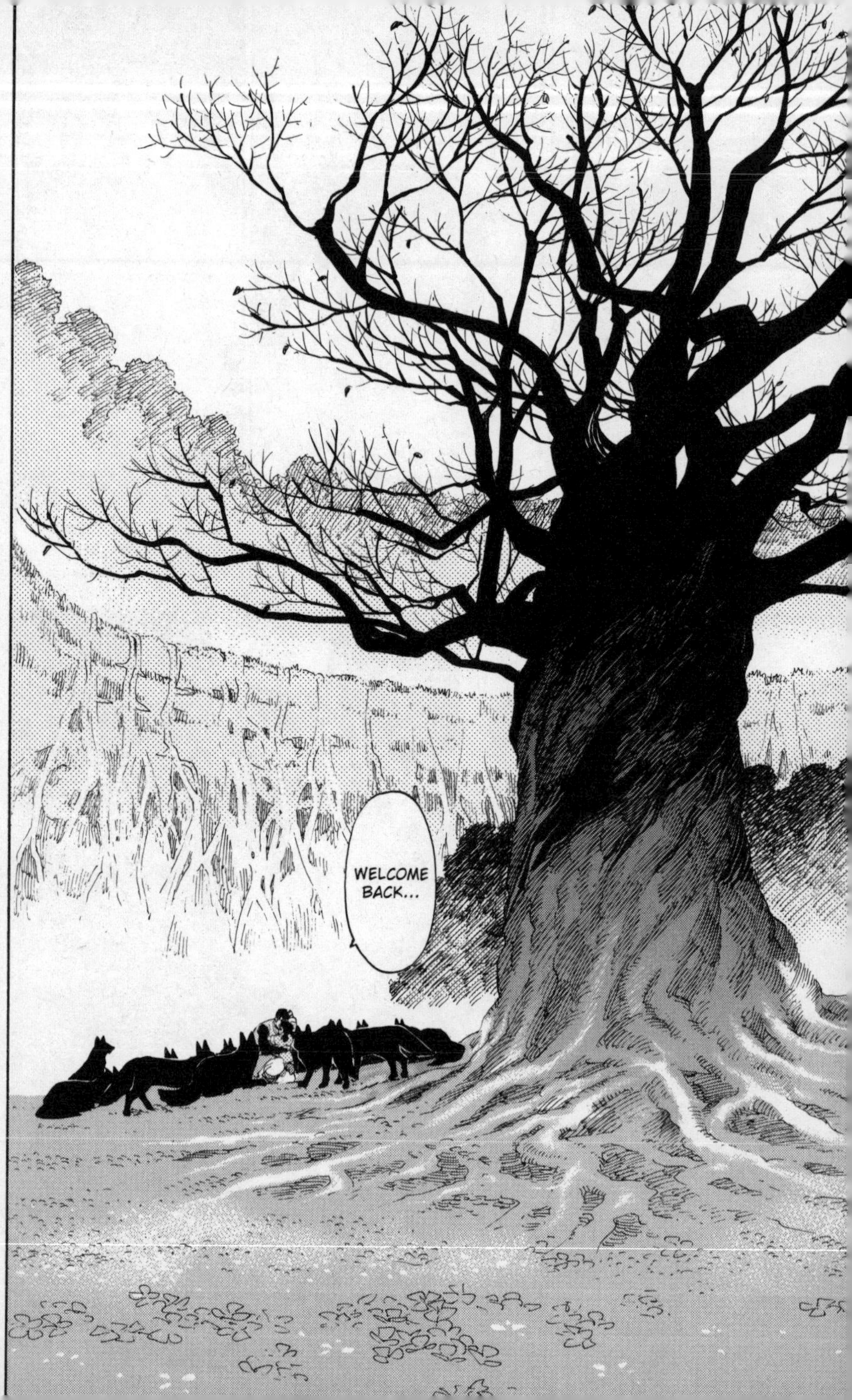
WELCOME BACK...

# Chapter 10: Antibody

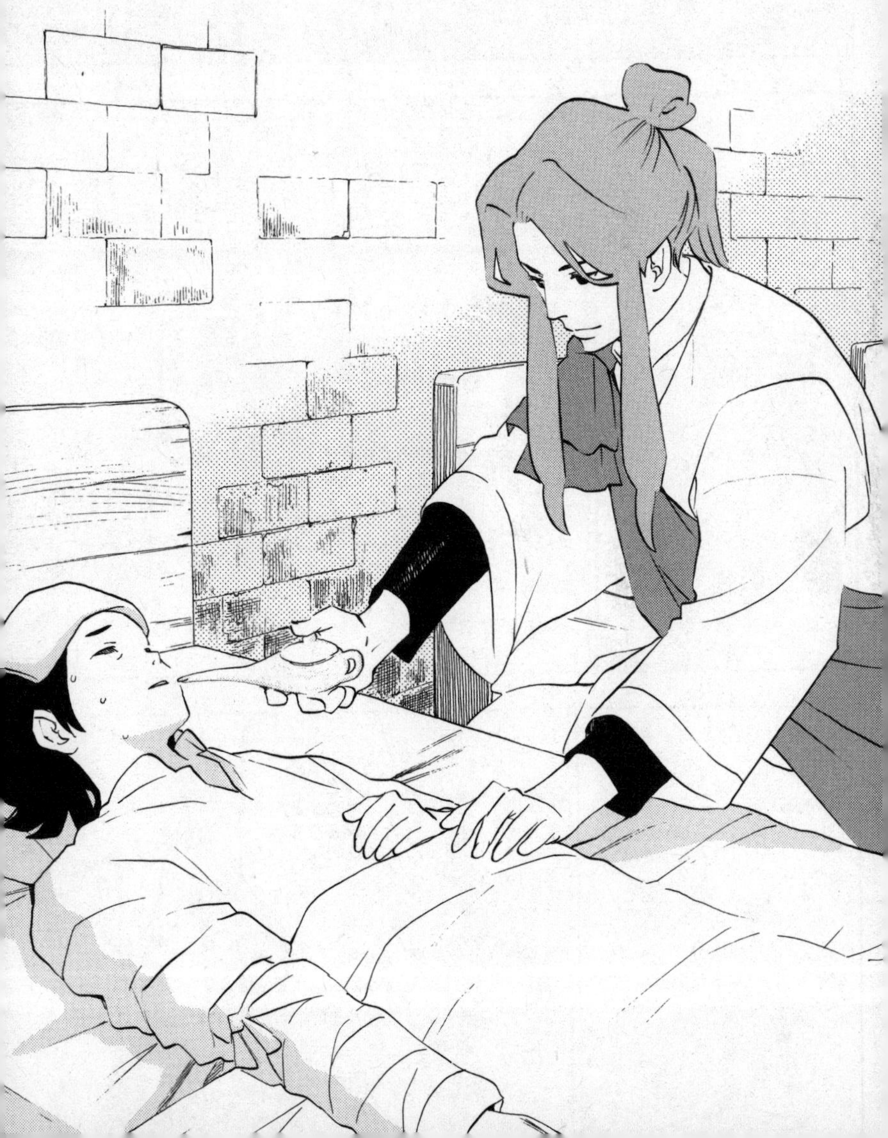

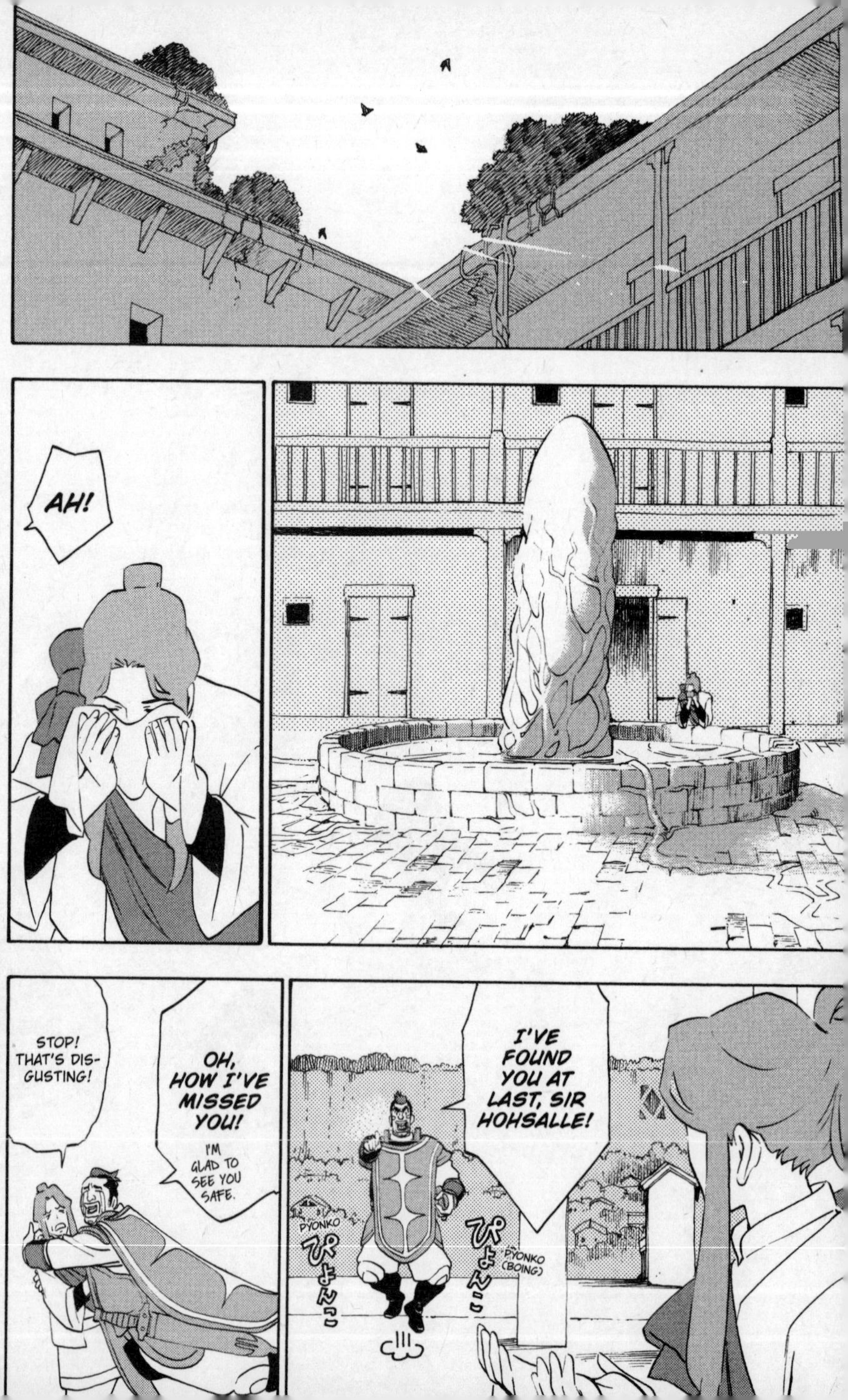
AH!
I'VE FOUND YOU AT LAST, SIR HOHSALLE!
ぴょんっ
PYONKO (BOING)
ぴょんっ
PYONKO
OH, HOW I'VE MISSED YOU!
I'M GLAD TO SEE YOU SAFE.
STOP! THAT'S DISGUSTING!

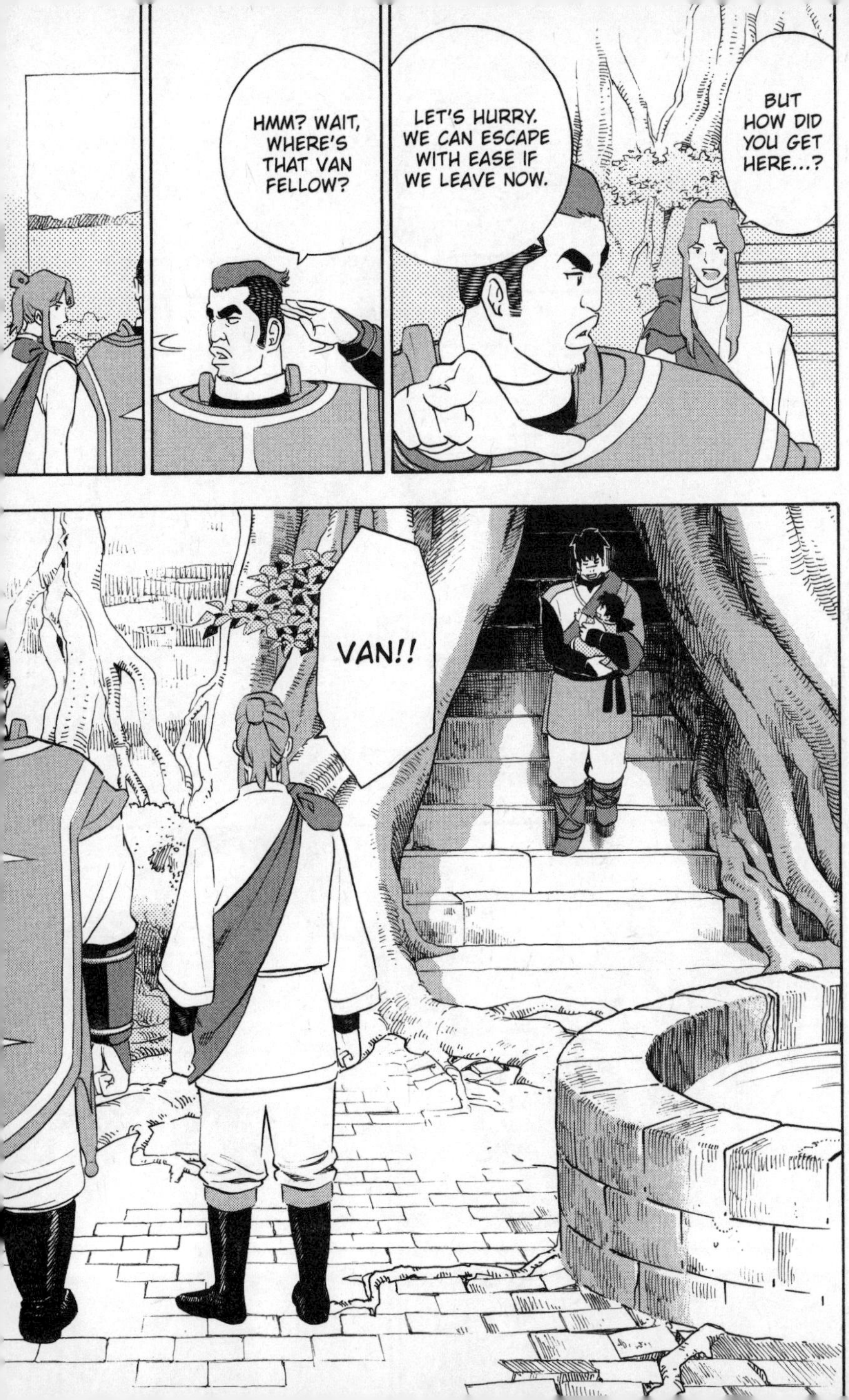
BUT HOW DID YOU GET HERE...?
LET'S HURRY. WE CAN ESCAPE WITH EASE IF WE LEAVE NOW.
HMM? WAIT, WHERE'S THAT VAN FELLOW?
VAN!!

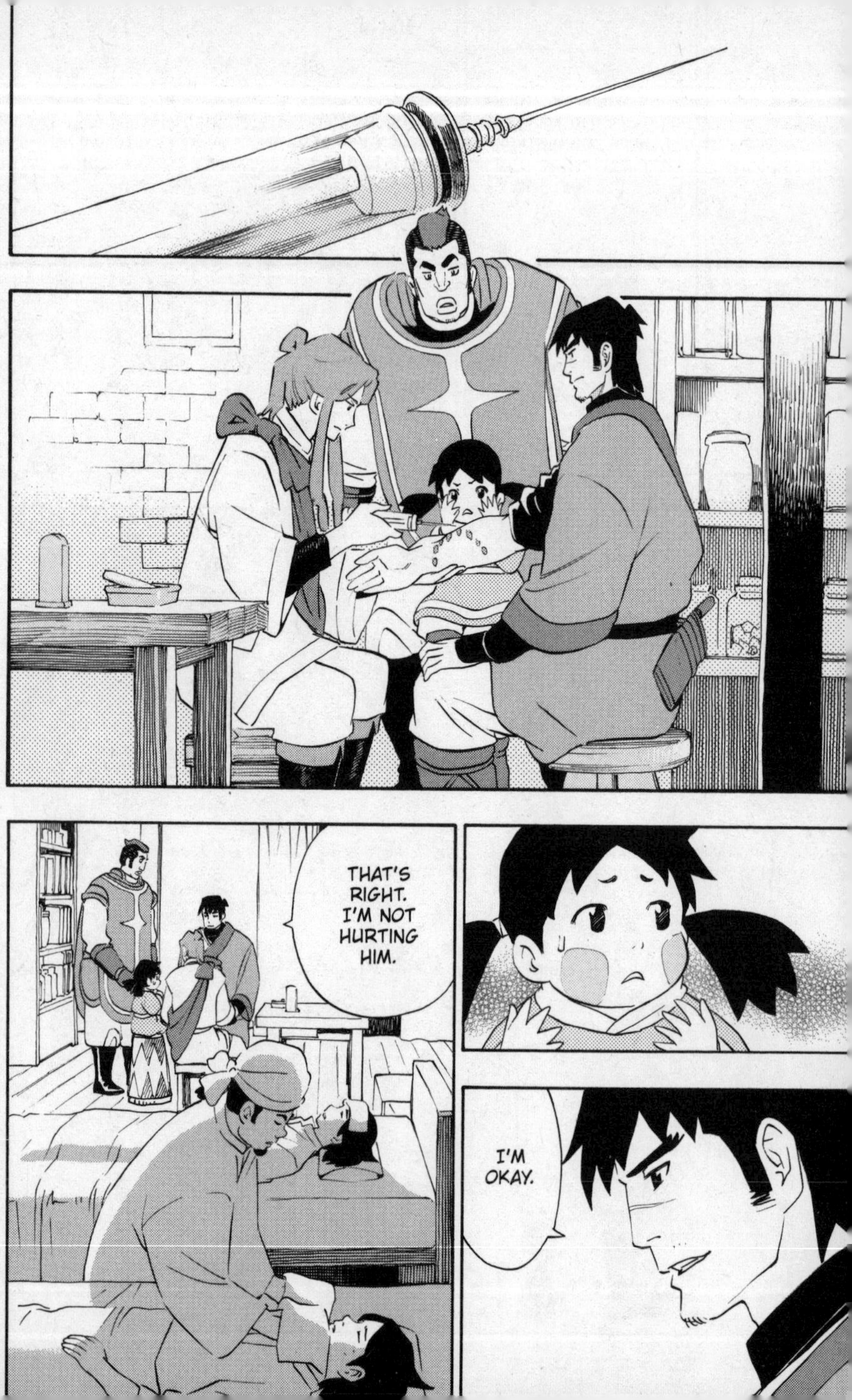
THAT'S RIGHT. I'M NOT HURTING HIM.
I'M OKAY.

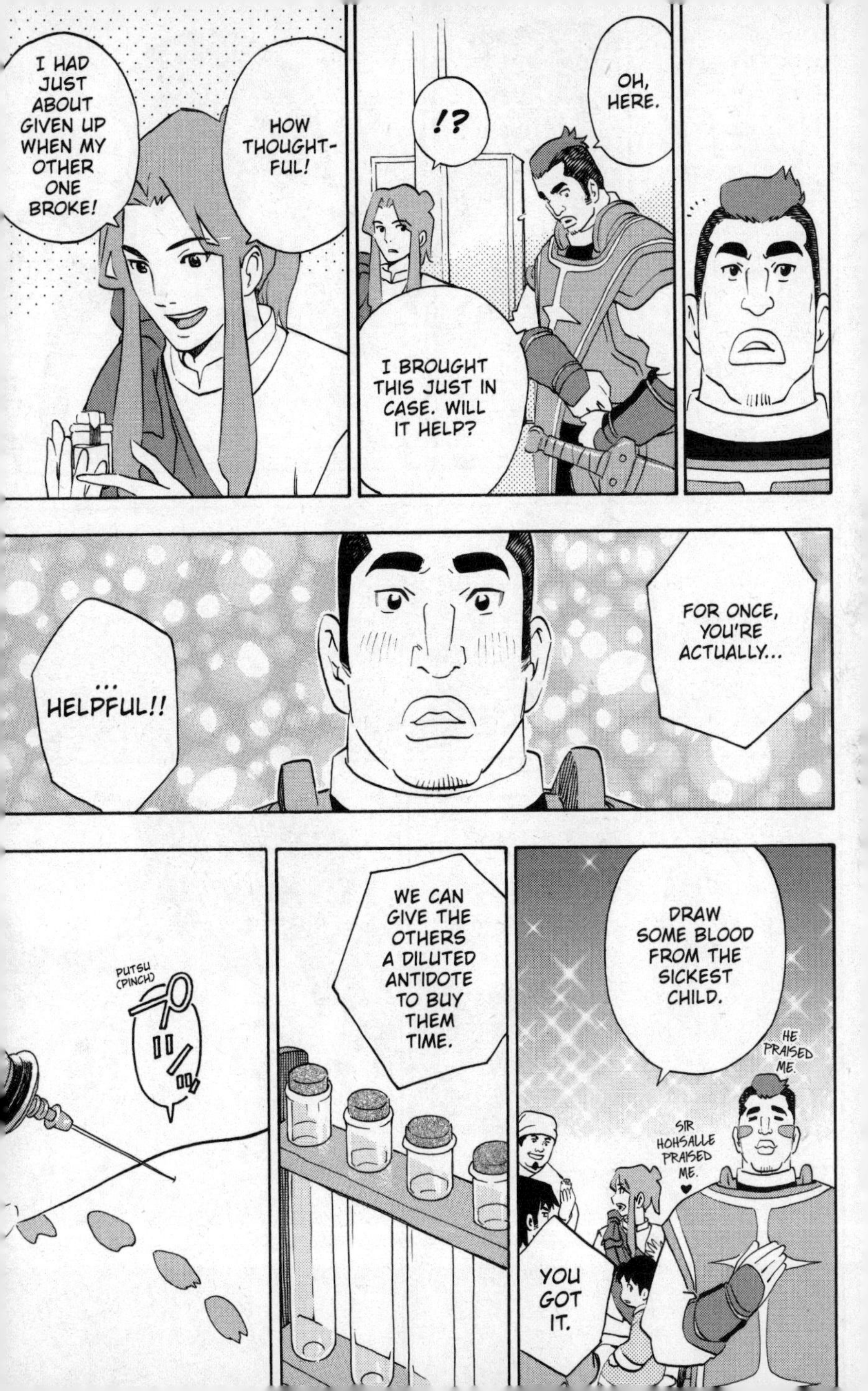
OH, HERE.
!?
I BROUGHT THIS JUST IN CASE. WILL IT HELP?
HOW THOUGHT-FUL!
I HAD JUST ABOUT GIVEN UP WHEN MY OTHER ONE BROKE!
FOR ONCE, YOU'RE ACTUALLY...
... HELPFUL!!
DRAW SOME BLOOD FROM THE SICKEST CHILD.
HE PRAISED ME.
SIR HOHSALLE PRAISED ME. ♥
YOU GOT IT.
WE CAN GIVE THE OTHERS A DILUTED ANTIDOTE TO BUY THEM TIME.
PUTSU (PINCH)

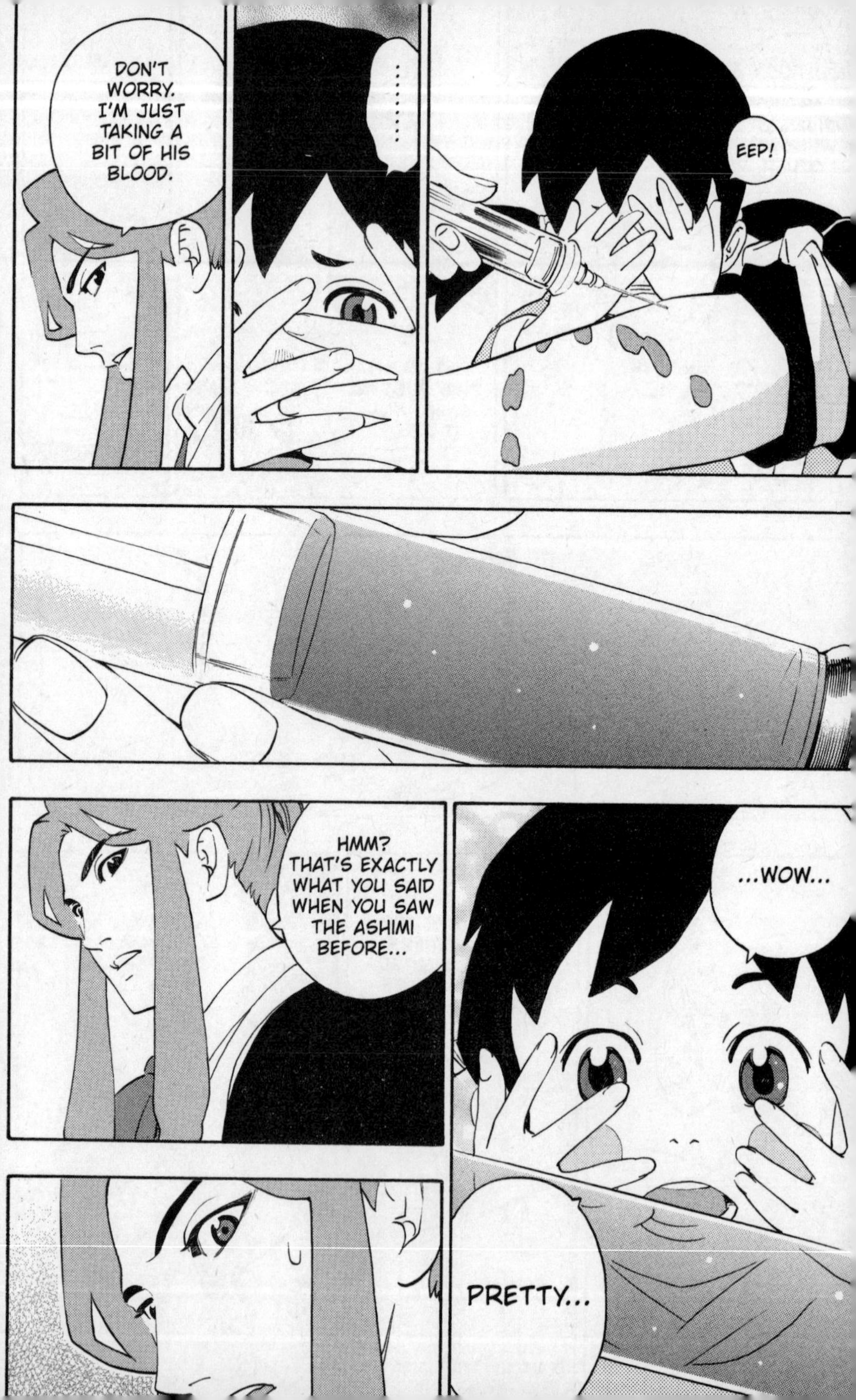

EEP!
......
DON'T WORRY. I'M JUST TAKING A BIT OF HIS BLOOD.
...WOW...
PRETTY...
HMM? THAT'S EXACTLY WHAT YOU SAID WHEN YOU SAW THE ASHIMI BEFORE...

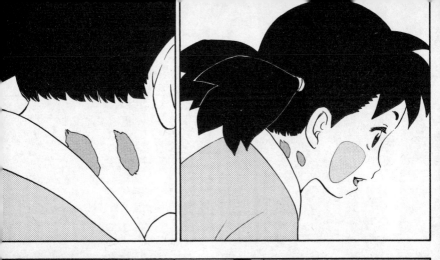

......

KA
(FLASH)

...ALSO
BITTEN
BY A
DOG!?

WAS
SHE...

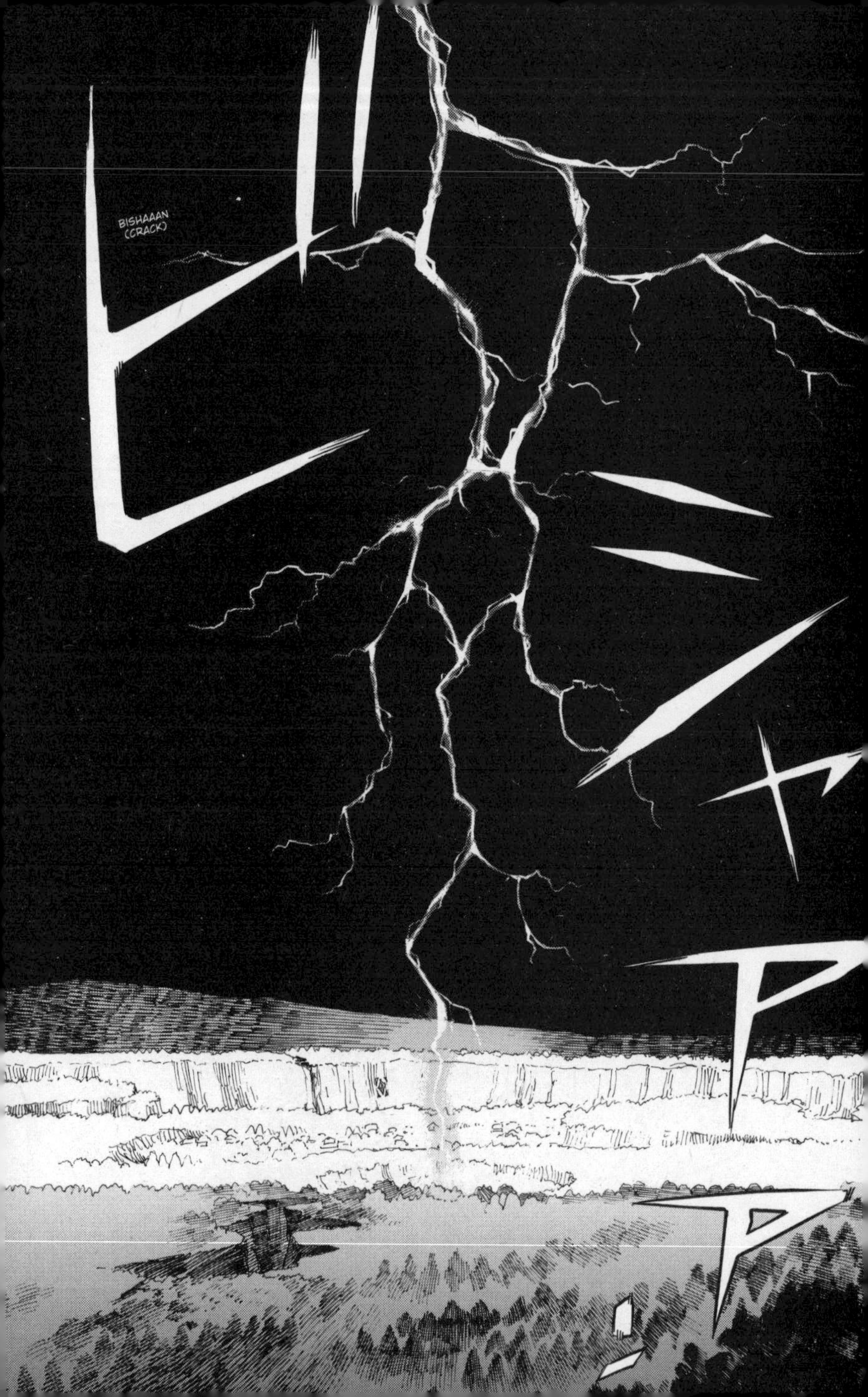
BISHAAAN
(CRACK)

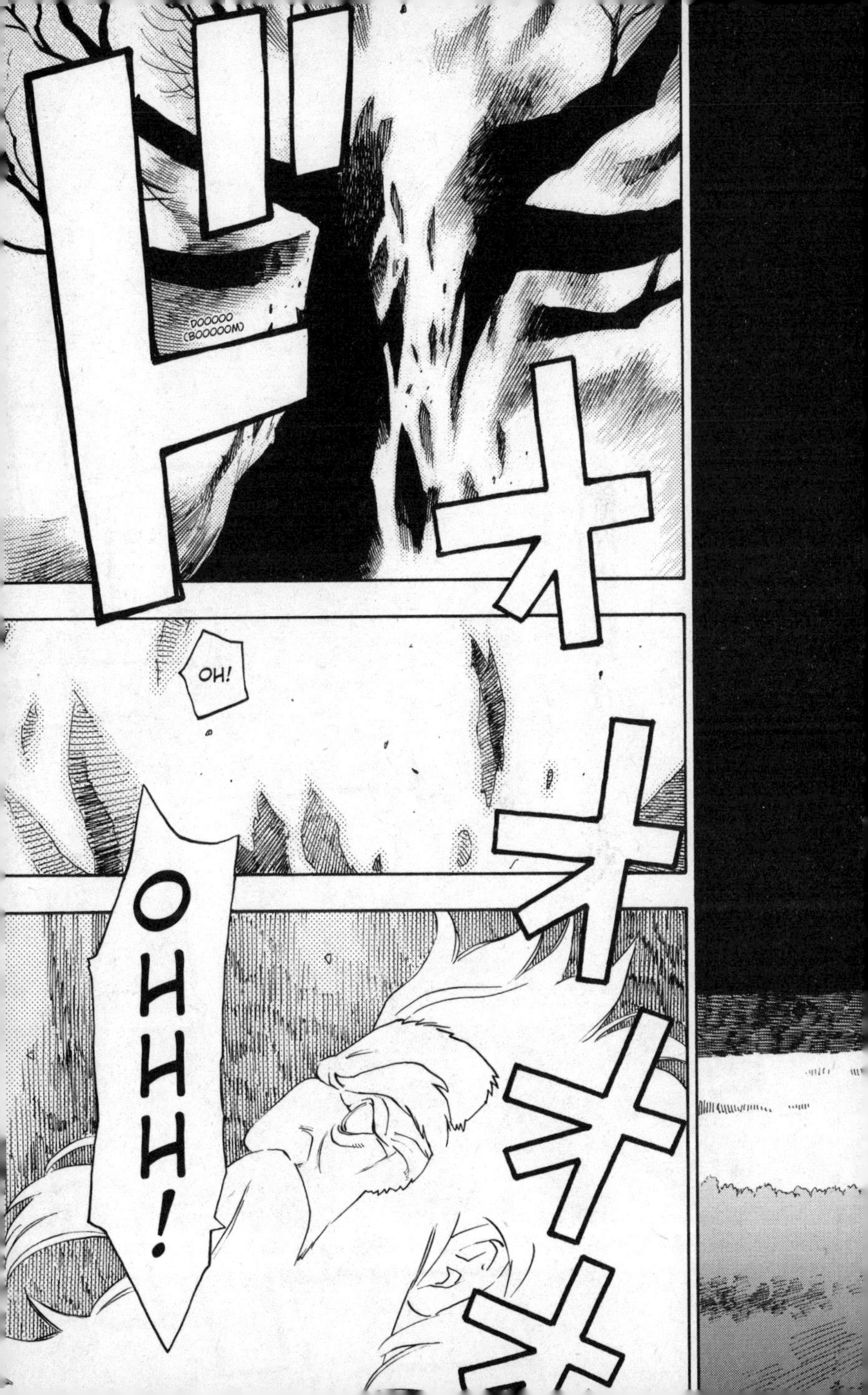
DOOOOO (BOOOOOM)
OH!
OHHH!

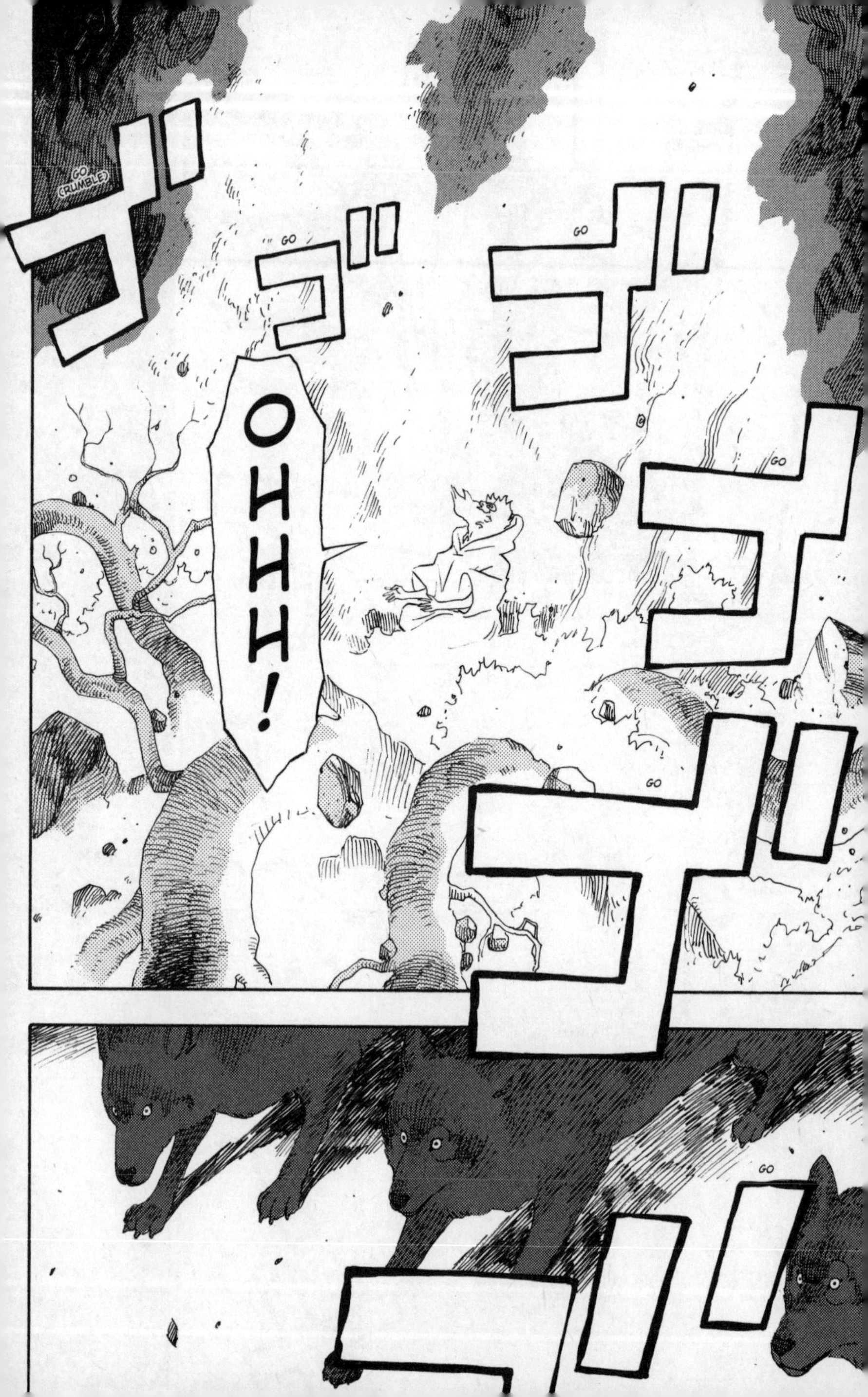
GO (RUMBLE)
ゴ
GO
ゴ
GO
ゴ
OHHH!
GO
ゴ
GO
ゴ
GO
ゴ

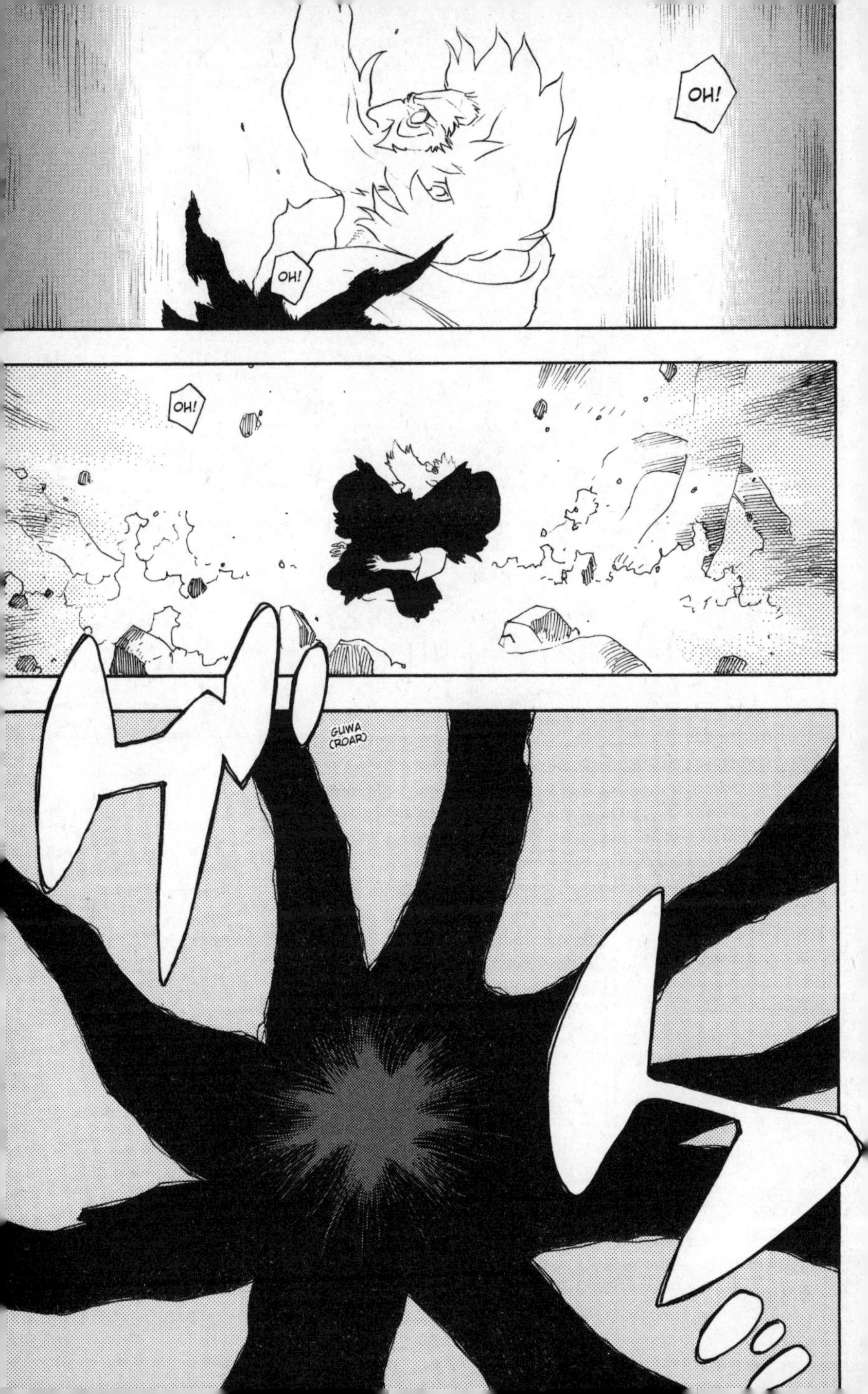
OH!
OH!
OH!
GUWA (ROAR)

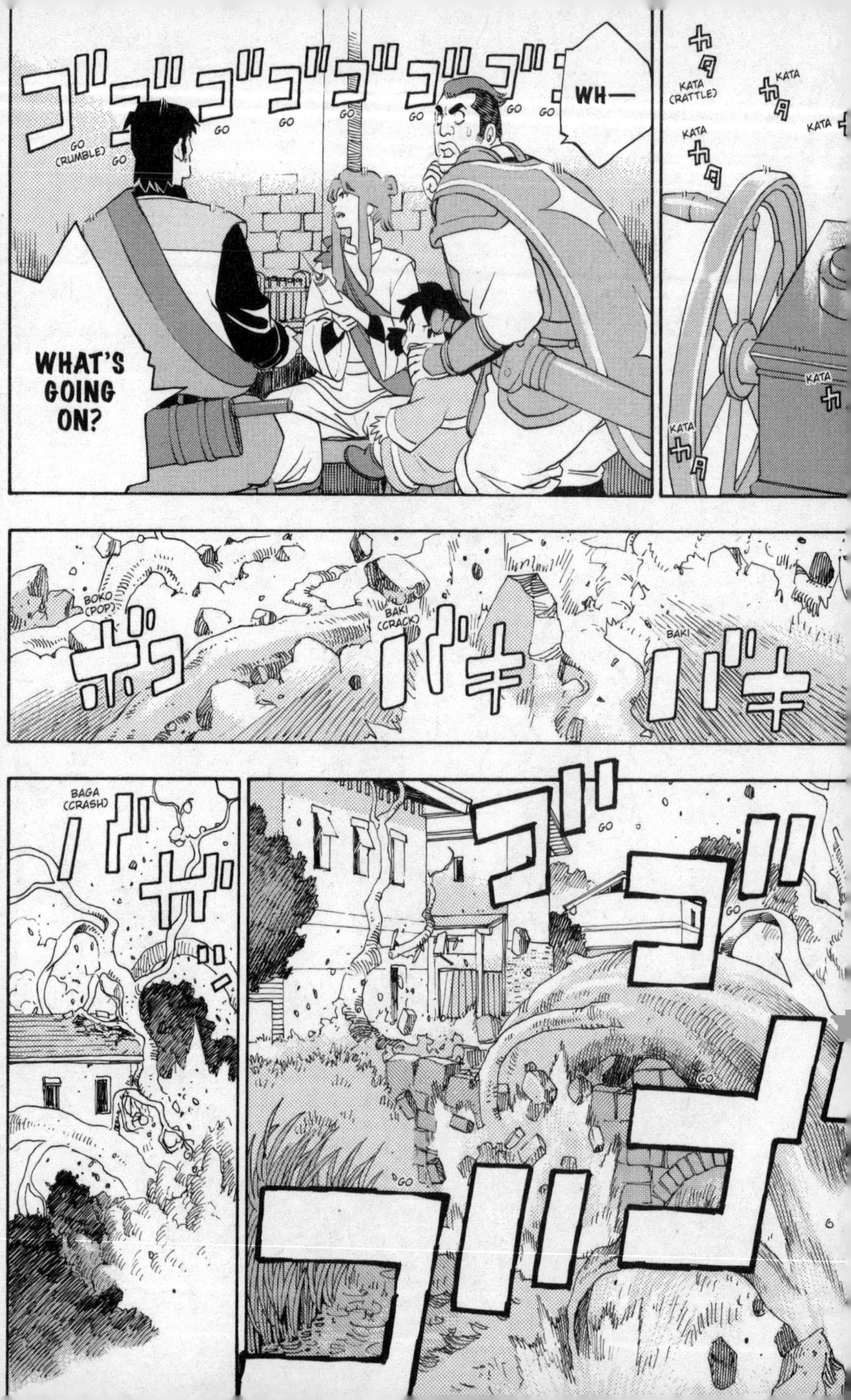
KATA (RATTLE)
KATA
KATA
KATA
KATA
KATA
WH—
GO GO
GO
GO
GO
GO
GO (RUMBLE) GO
WHAT'S GOING ON?
BAKI
BAKI (CRACK)
BOKO (POP)
GO
GO
GO
GO
BAGA (CRASH)

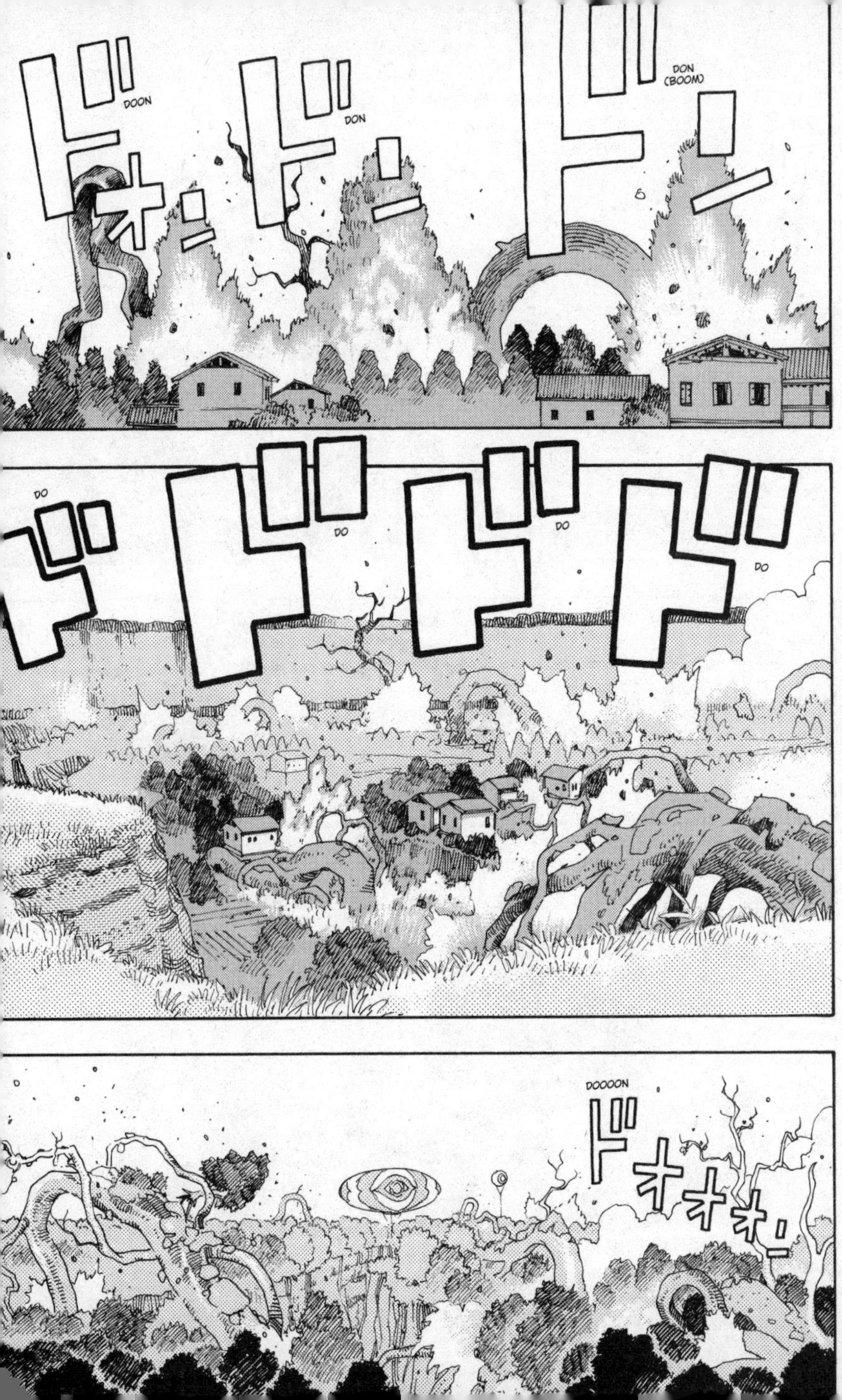
DON (BOOM)
DON
DOON
DO
DO
DO
DO
DOOOON

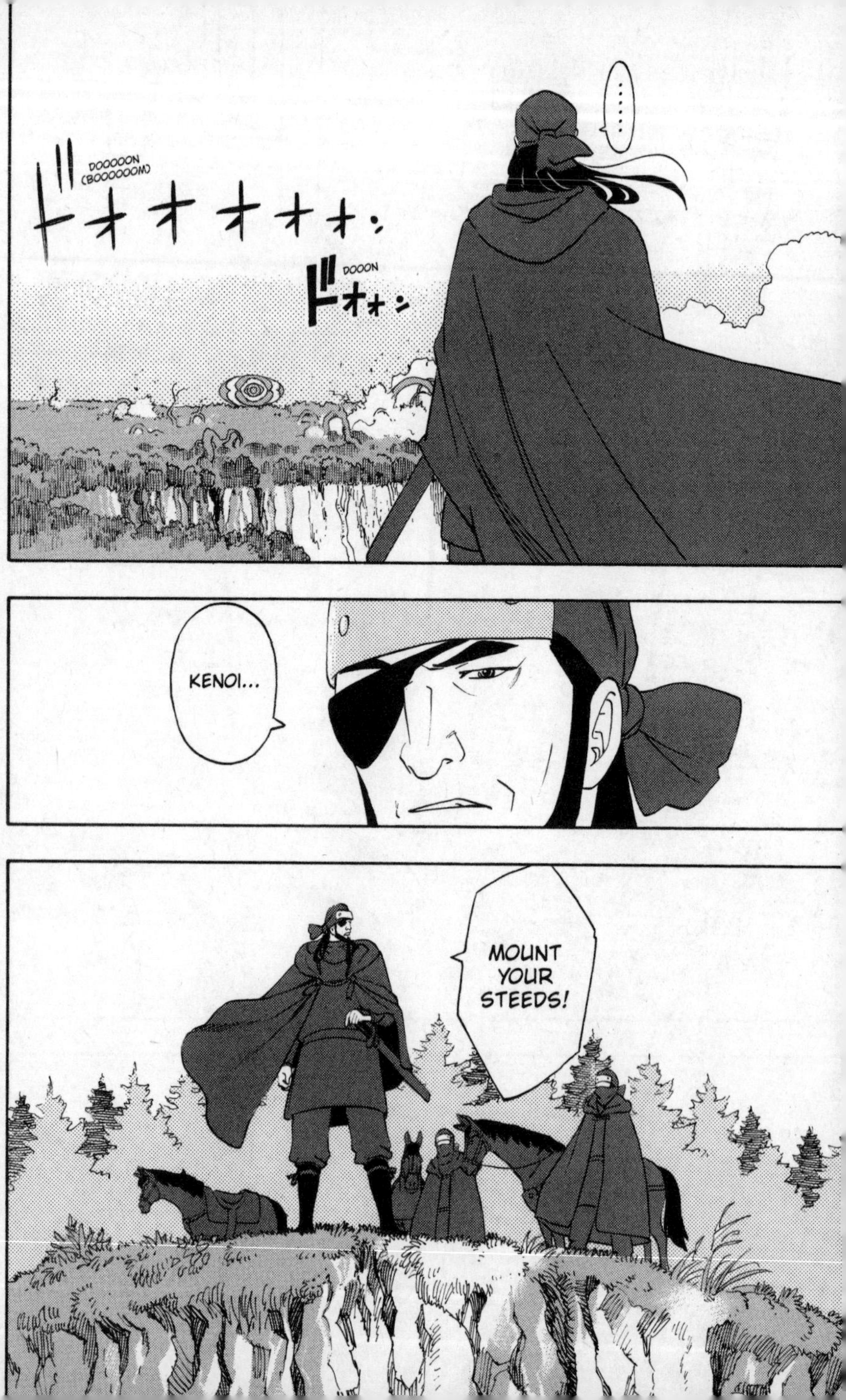
……
ドオオオオオン DOOOOON (BOOOOOOM)
ドオオン DOOON
KENOI...
MOUNT YOUR STEEDS!

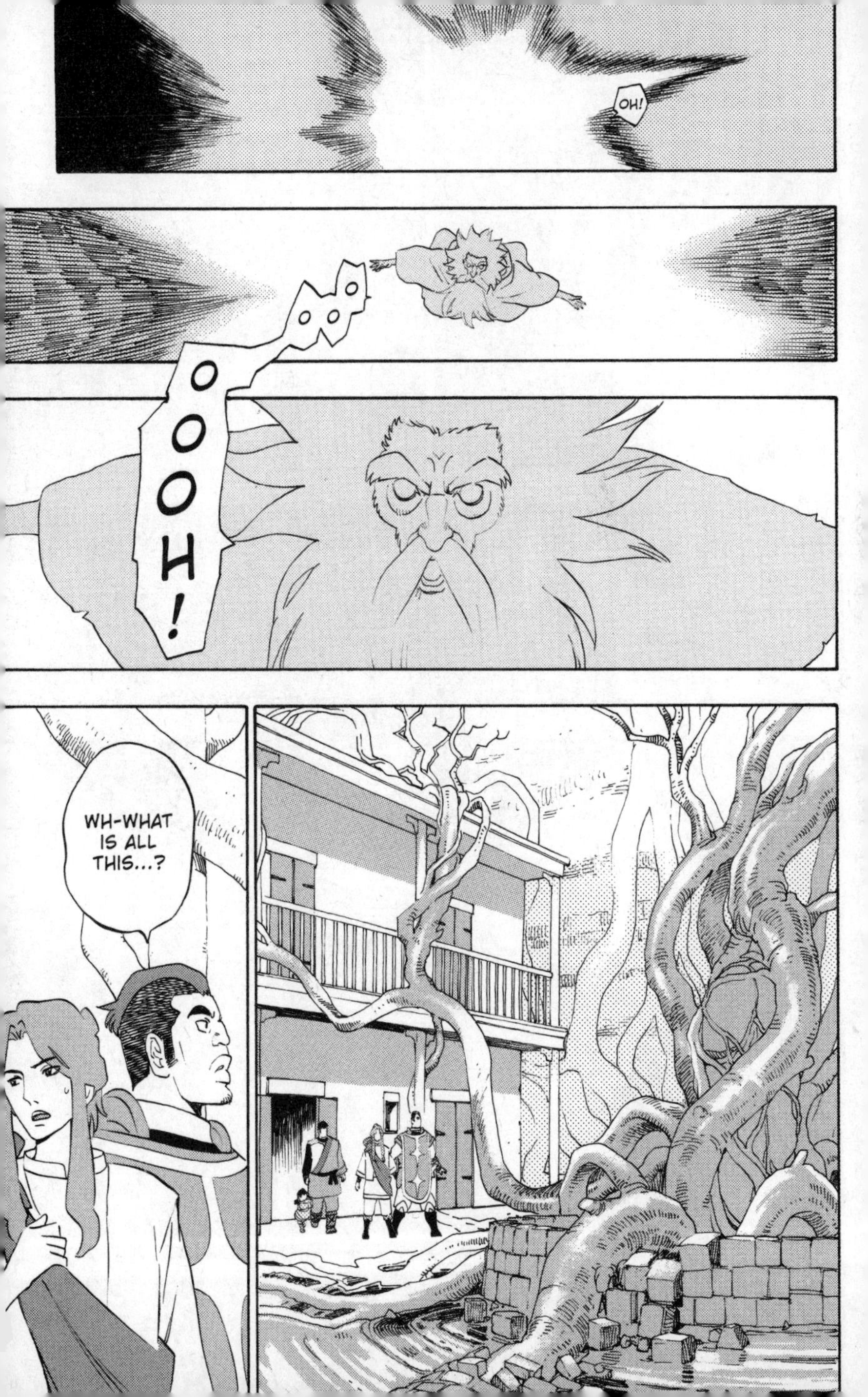
OH!
OOOOOOH!
WH-WHAT IS ALL THIS...?

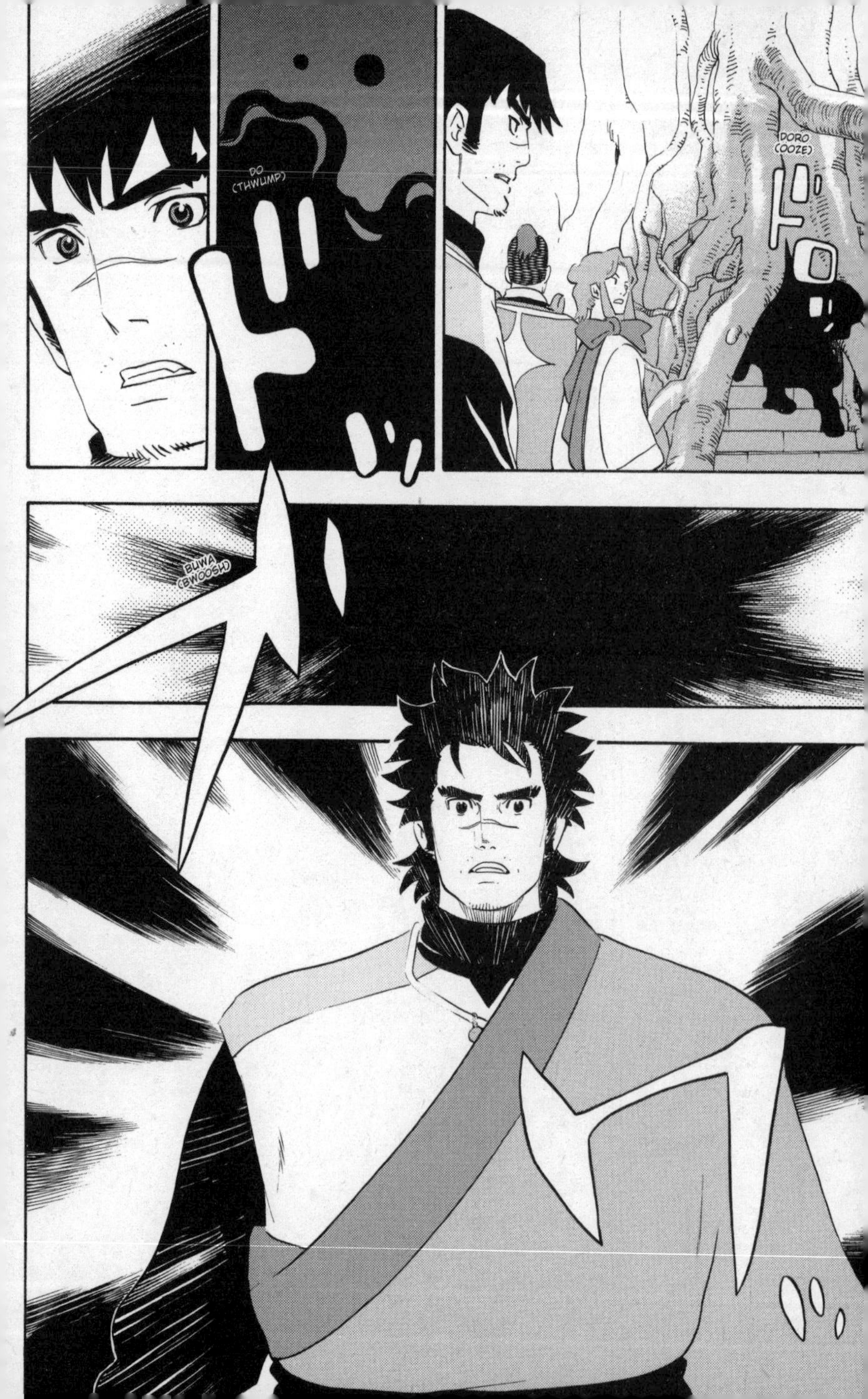
DORO (OOZE)
DO (THWUMP)
BUWA (BWOOSH)

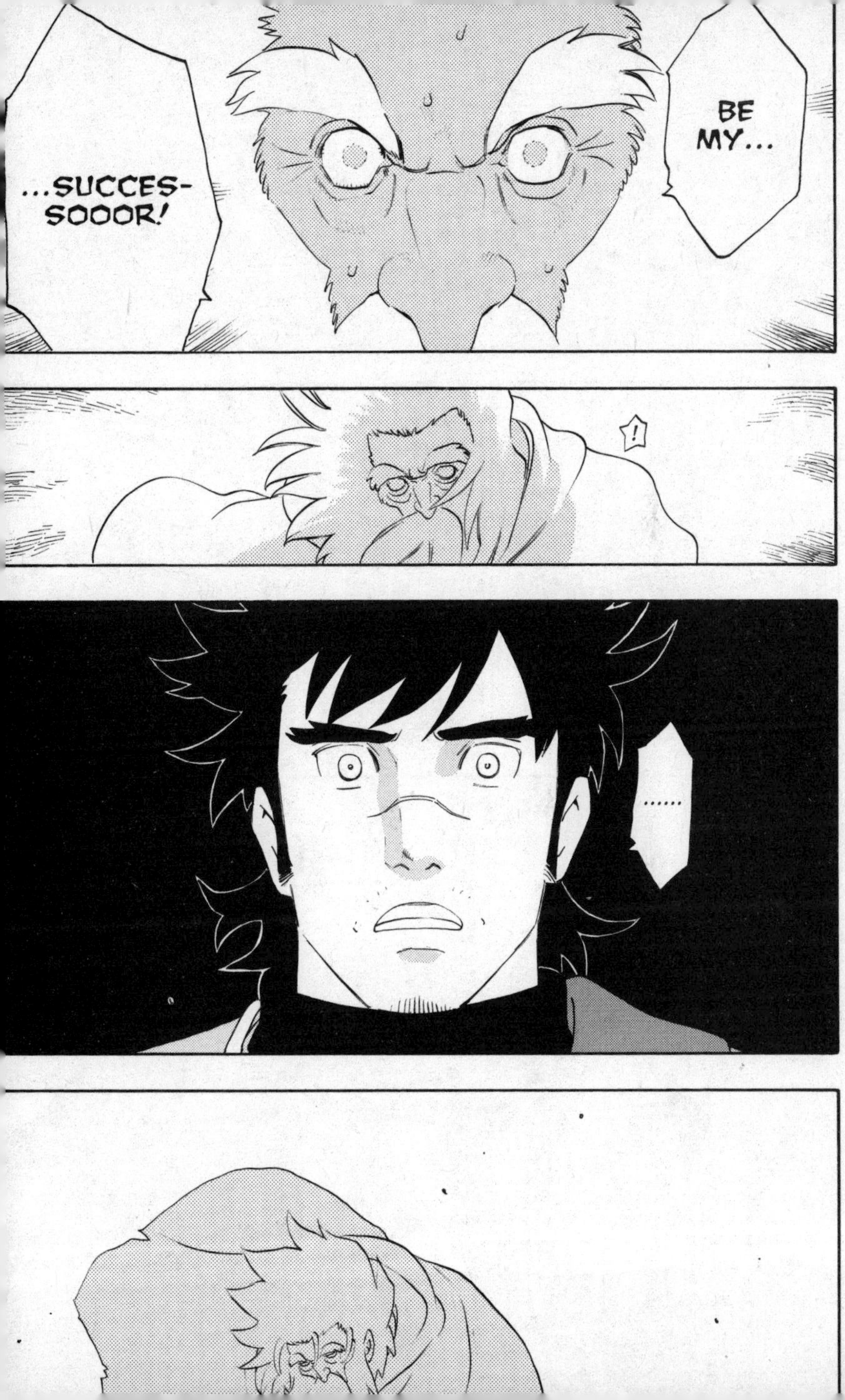
BE MY...
...SUCCES-SOOOR!
!
......

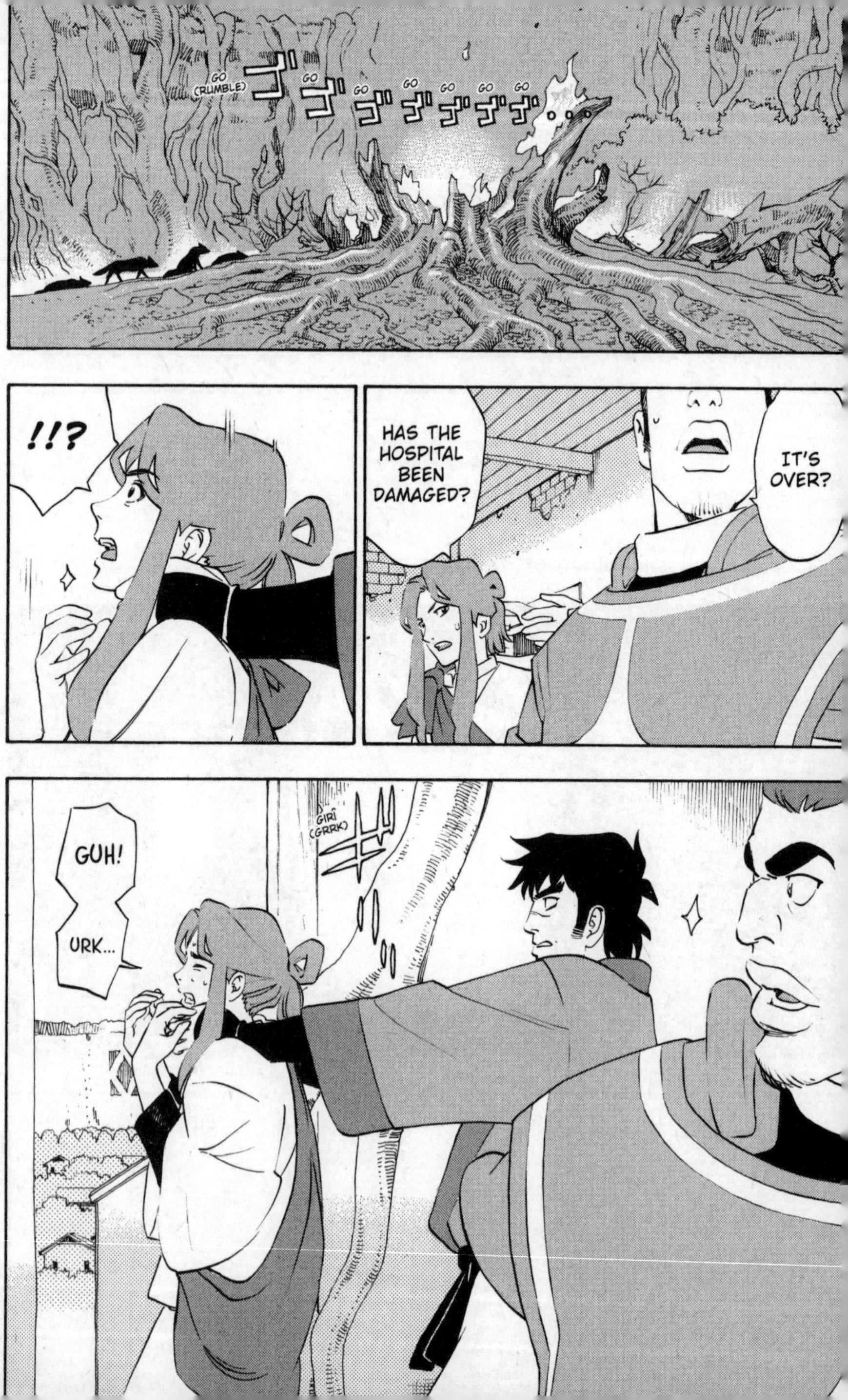
GO (RUMBLE)
GO GO GO GO GO GO
IT'S OVER?
HAS THE HOSPITAL BEEN DAMAGED?
!!?
GIRI (GRRK)
GUH!
URK...

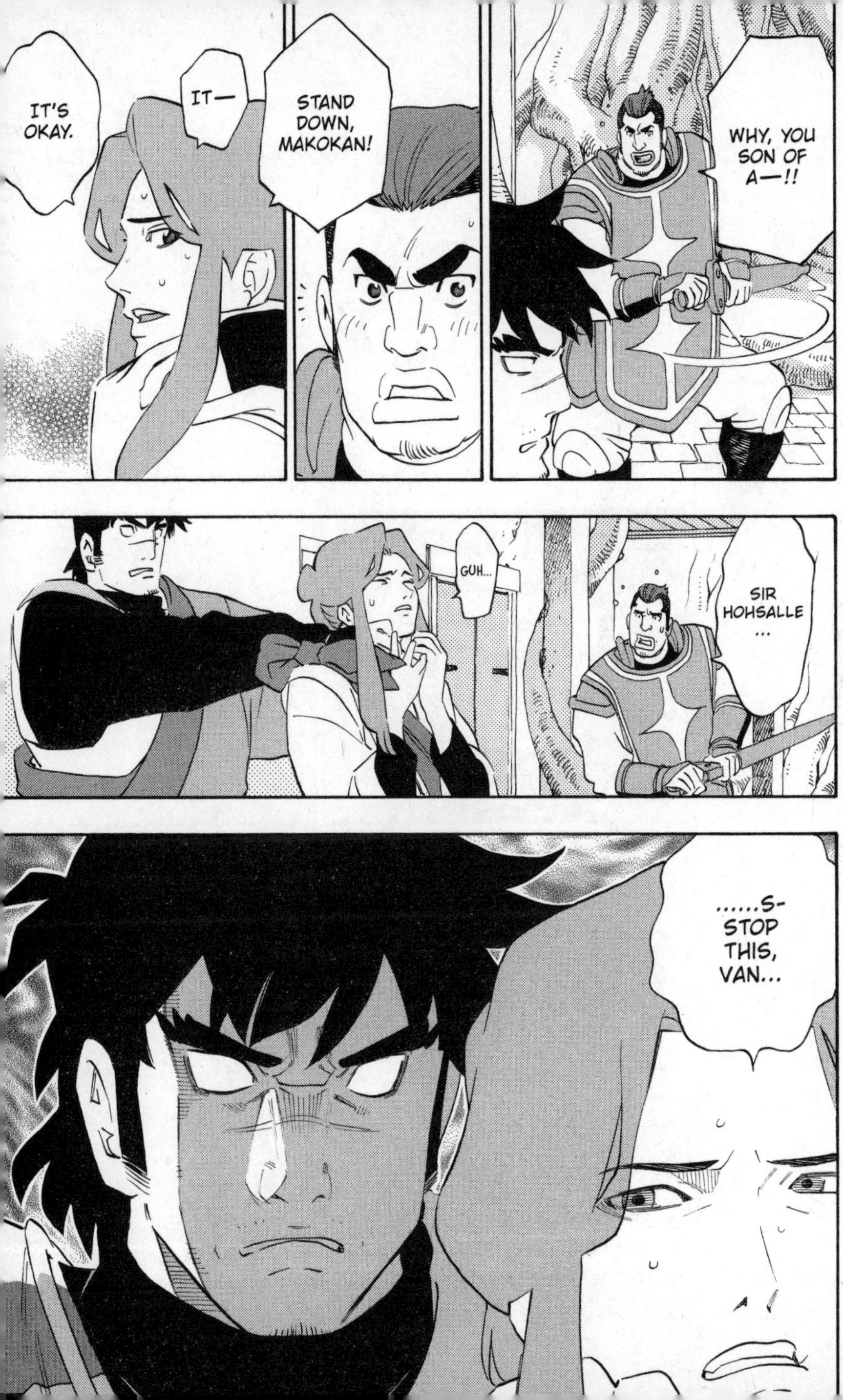
WHY, YOU SON OF A—!!
STAND DOWN, MAKOKAN!
IT—
IT'S OKAY.
SIR HOHSALLE ...
GUH...
......S-STOP THIS, VAN...

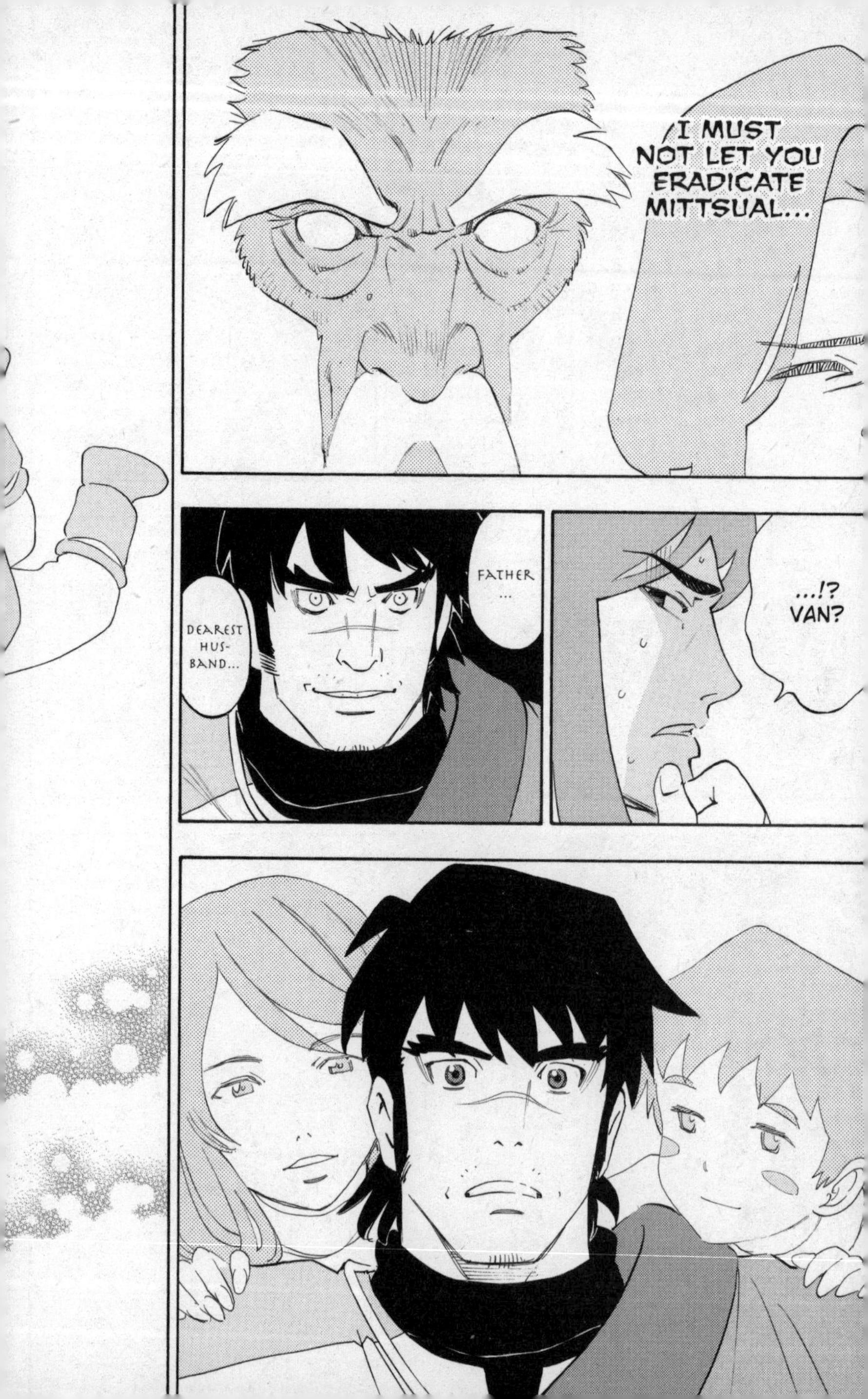
I MUST NOT LET YOU ERADICATE MITTSUAL...
...!? VAN?
FATHER ...
DEAREST HUS-BAND...

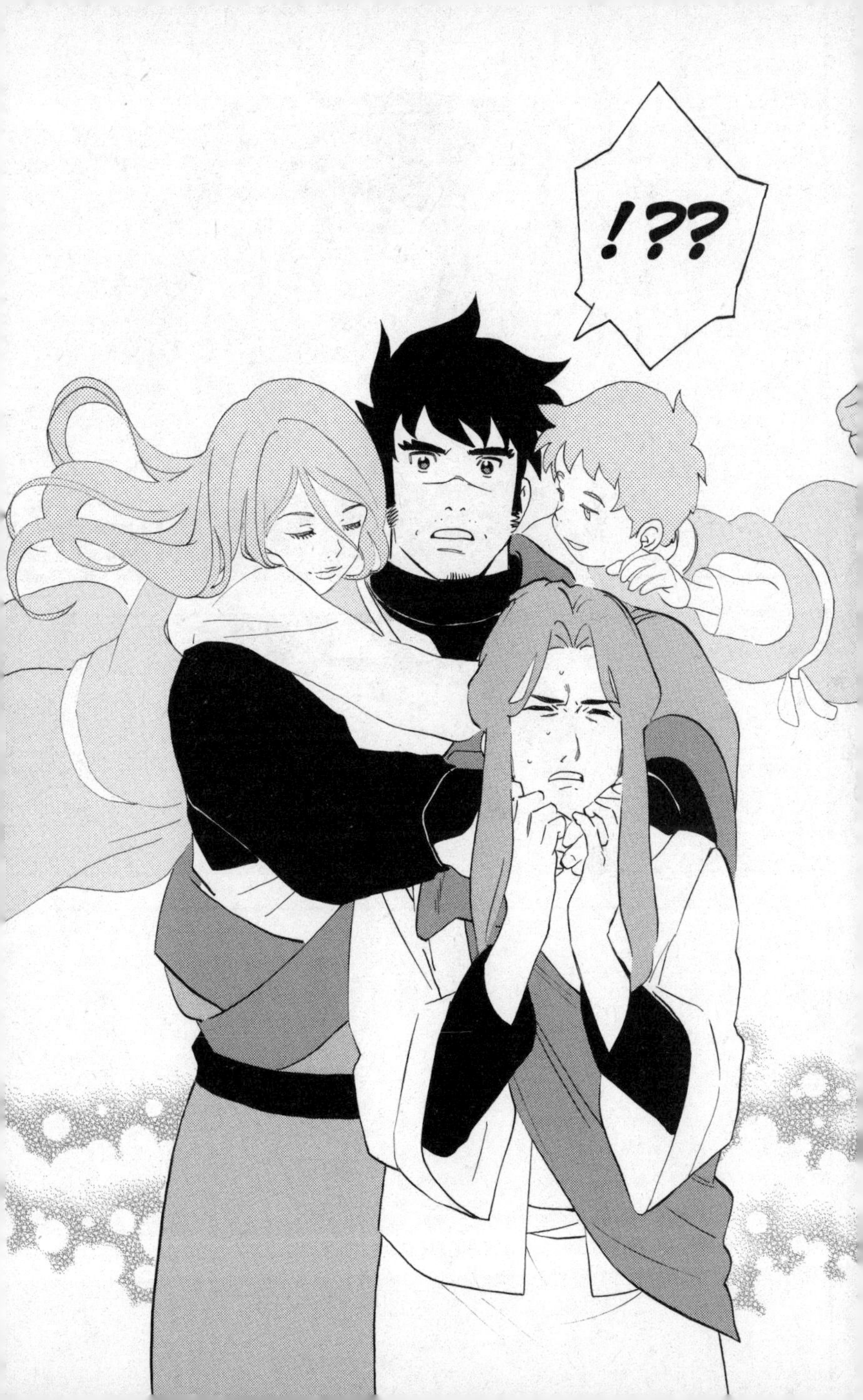
!??

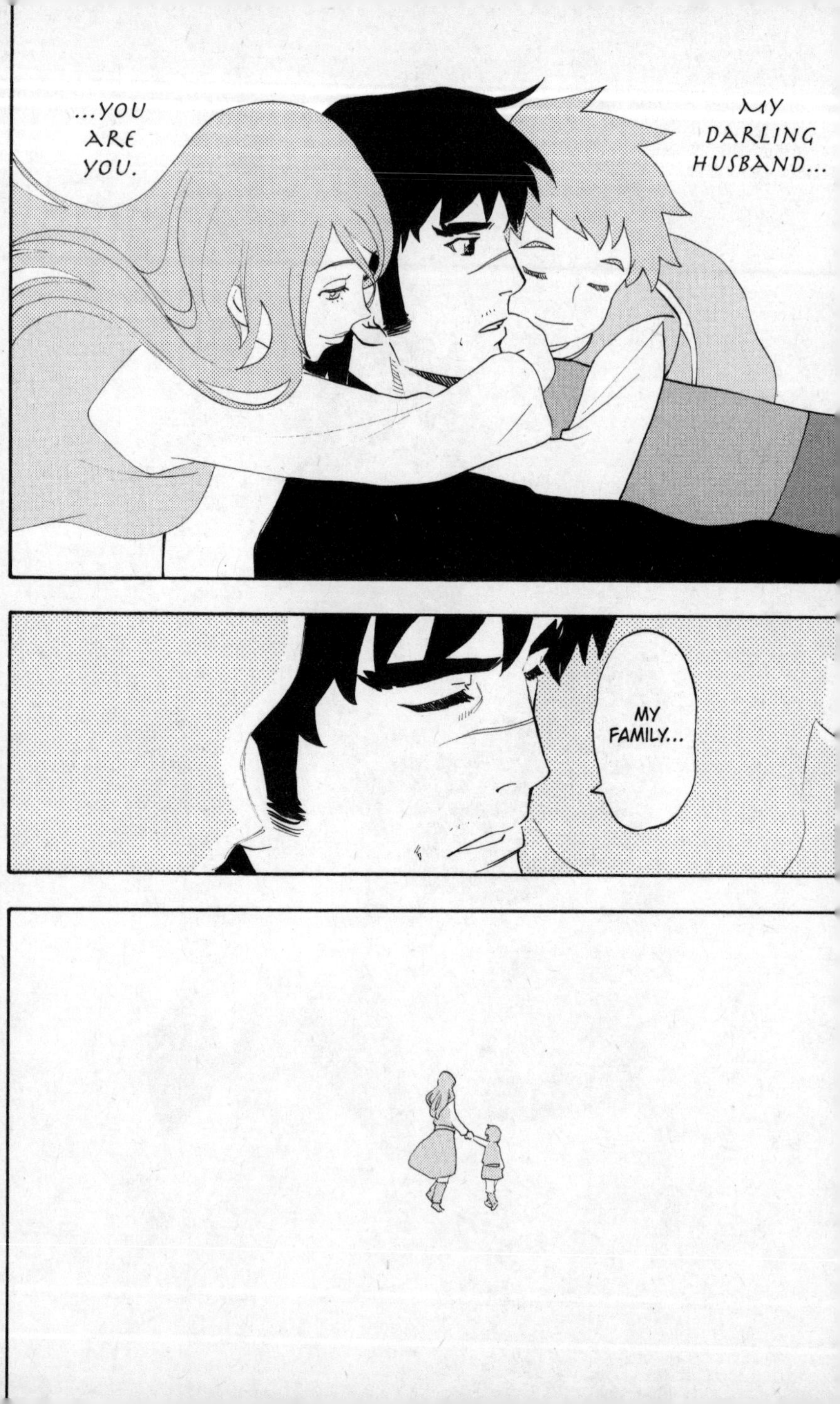
MY DARLING HUSBAND...
...YOU ARE YOU.
MY FAMILY...

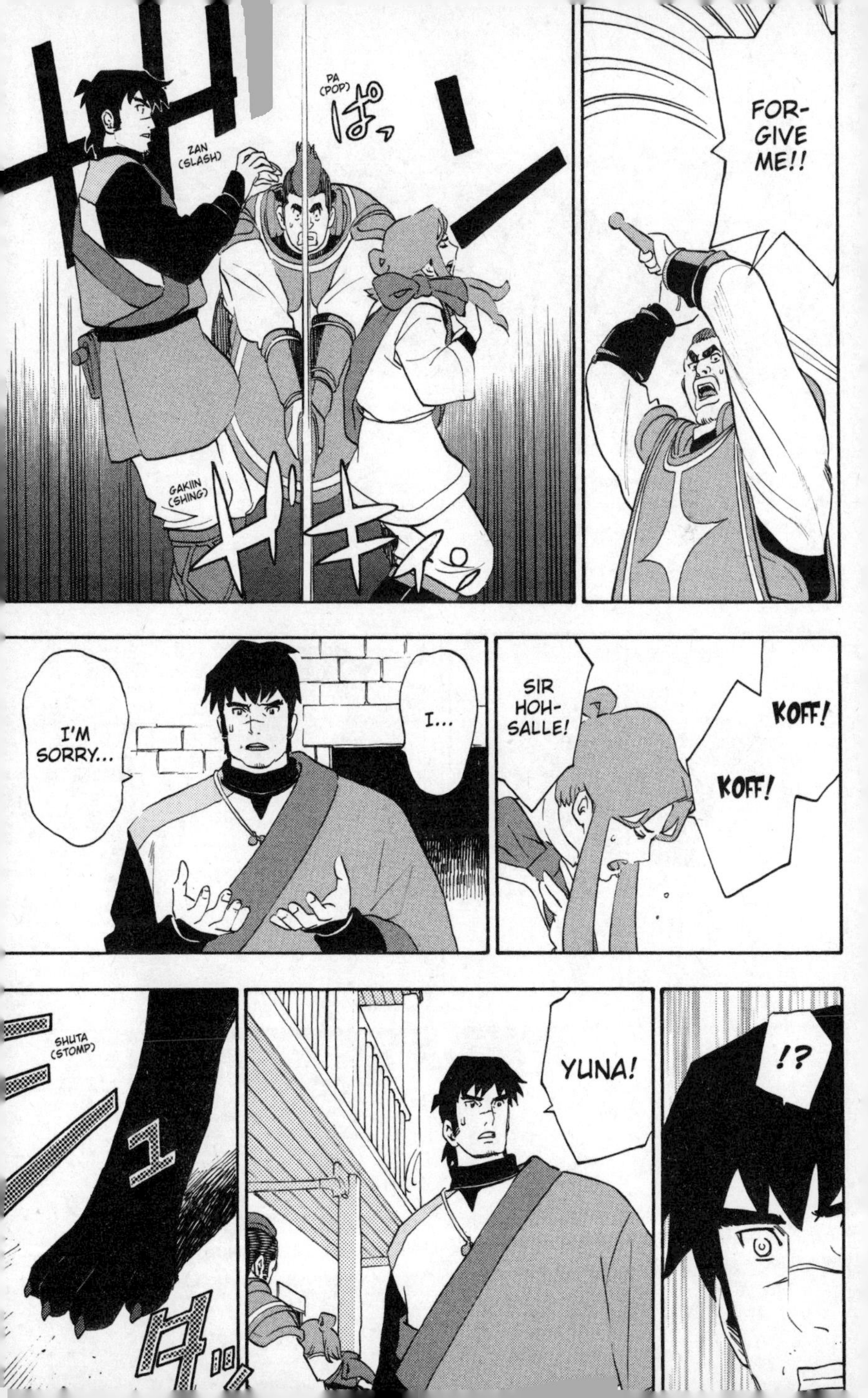
FOR-
GIVE
ME!!
PA
(POP)
ZAN
(SLASH)
GAKIIN
(SHING)
KOFF!
SIR
HOH-
SALLE!
KOFF!
I...
I'M
SORRY...
!?
YUNA!
SHUTA
(STOMP)

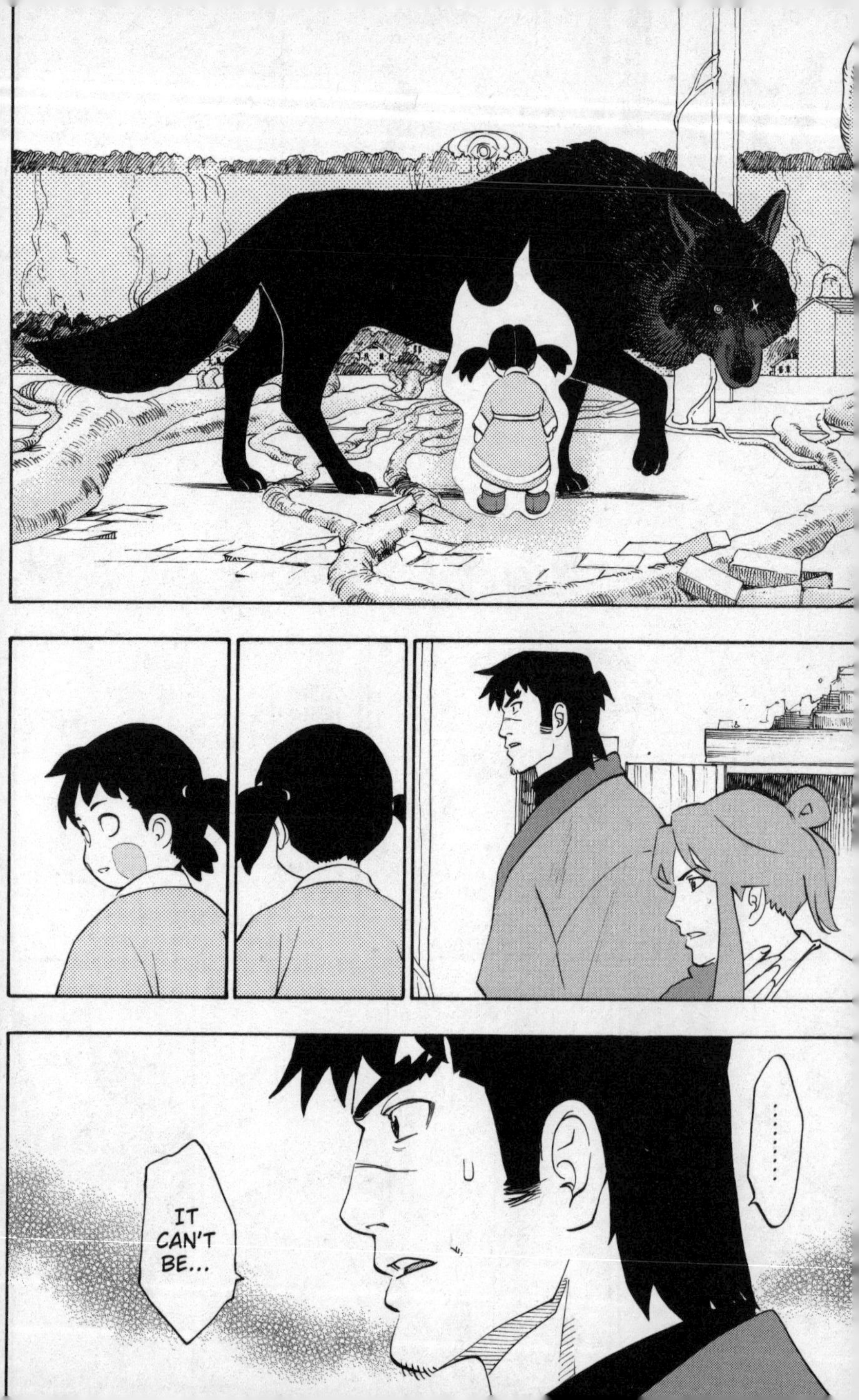
......
IT CAN'T BE...

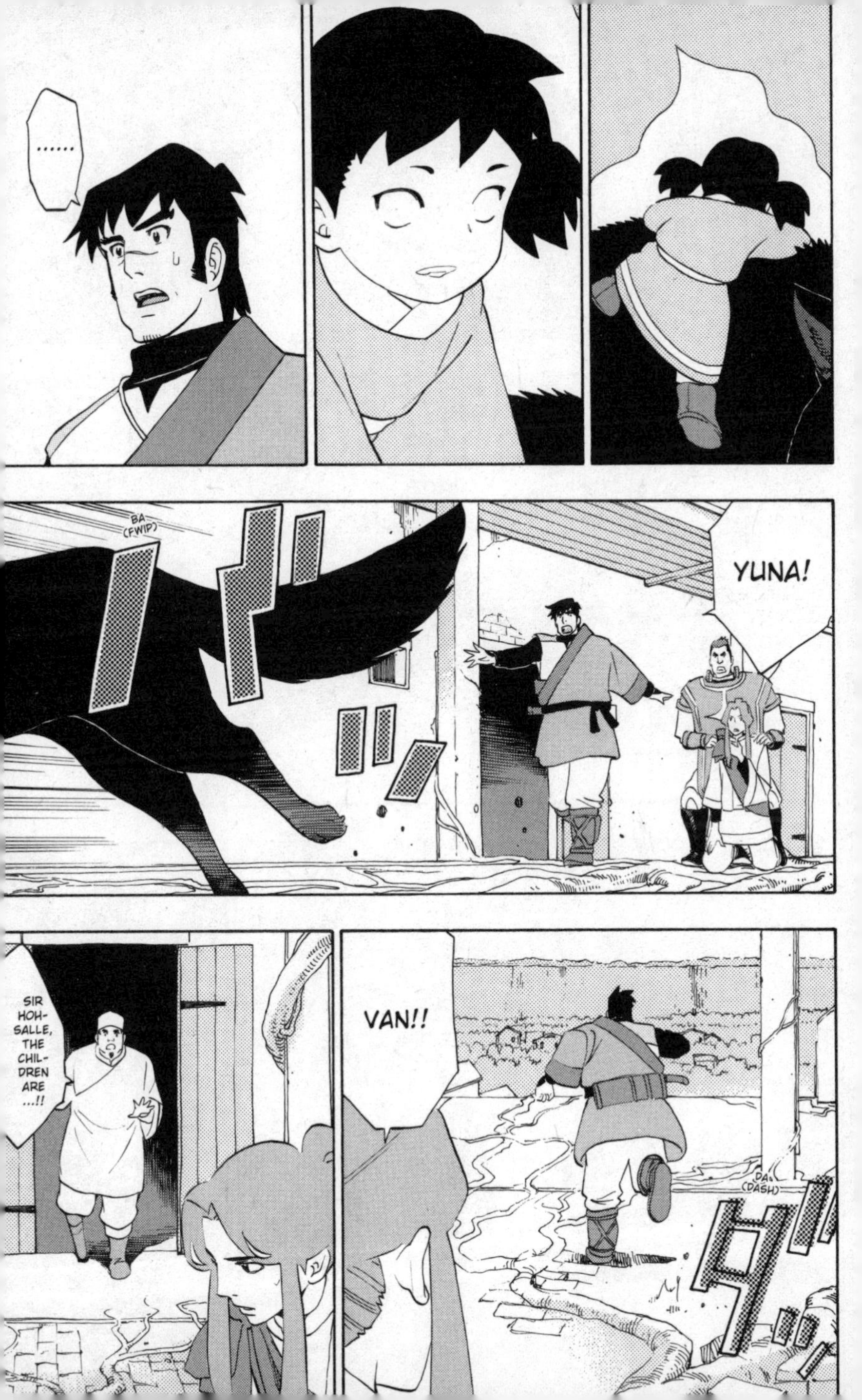
......
YUNA!
BA
(FWIP)
VAN!!
DA
(DASH)
SIR HOH-SALLE, THE CHILDREN ARE ...!!

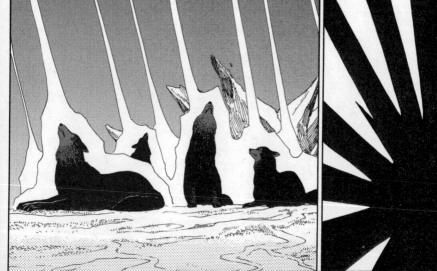

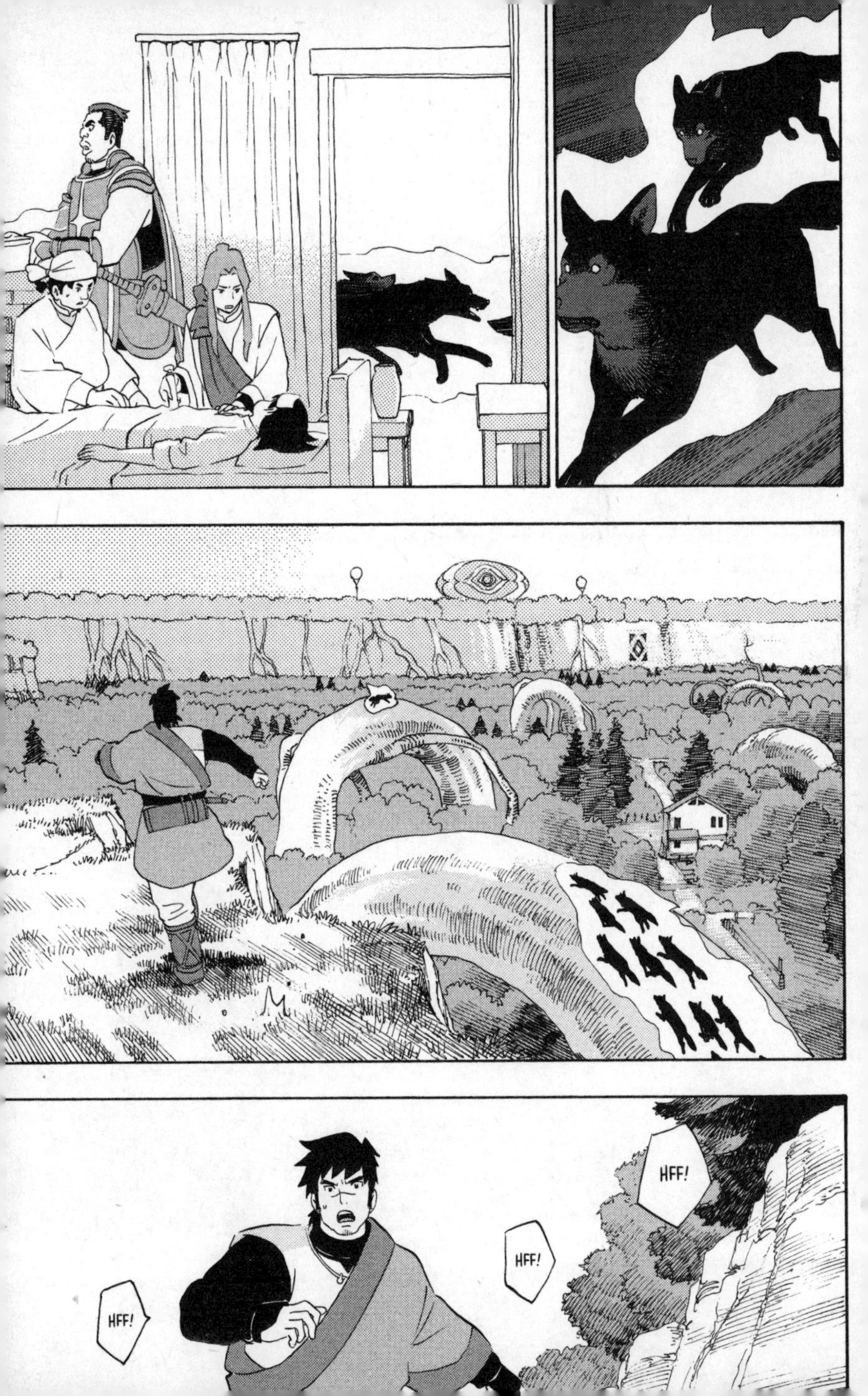
HFF!
HFF!
HFF!

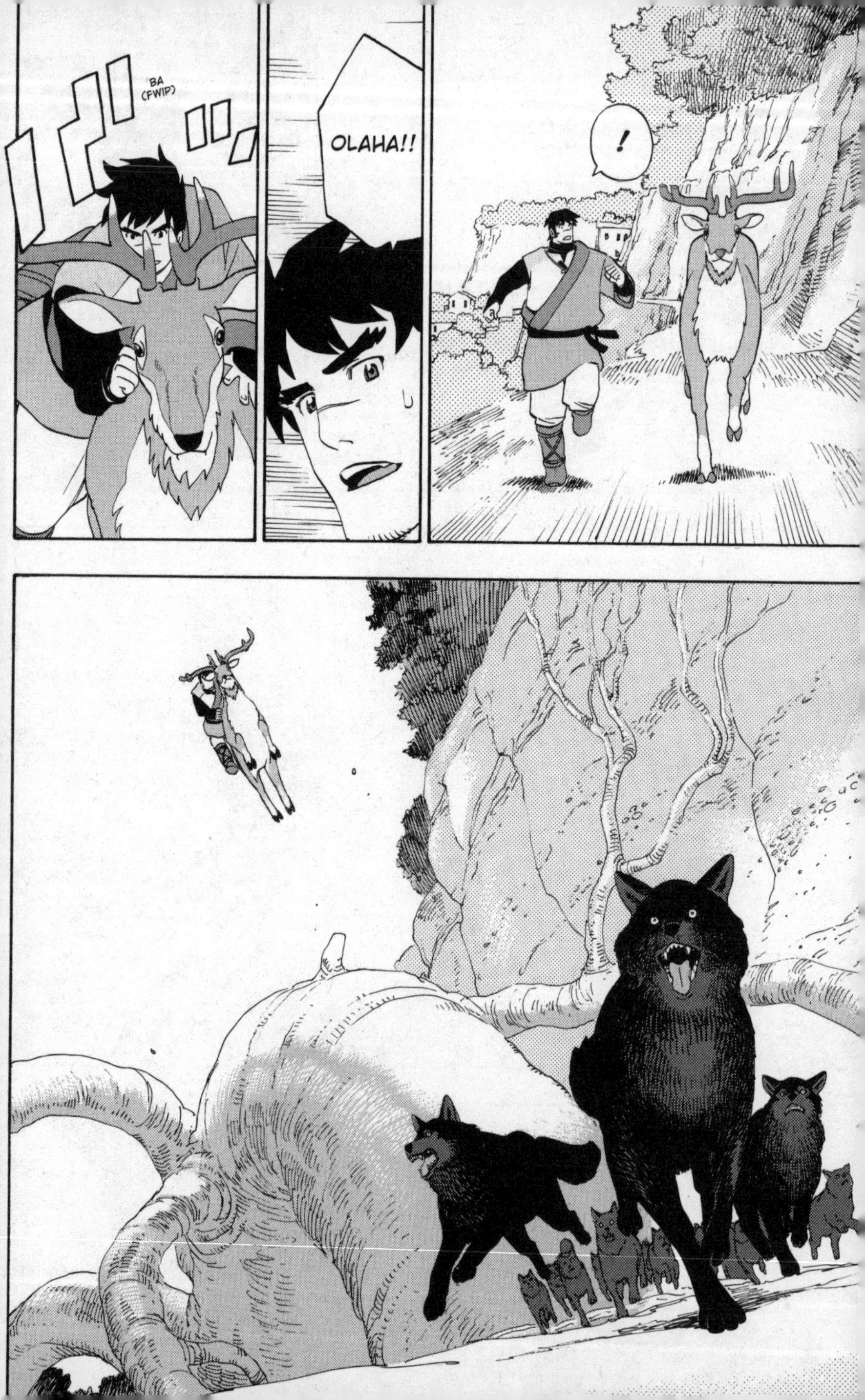
!
OLAHA!!
BA
(FWIP)

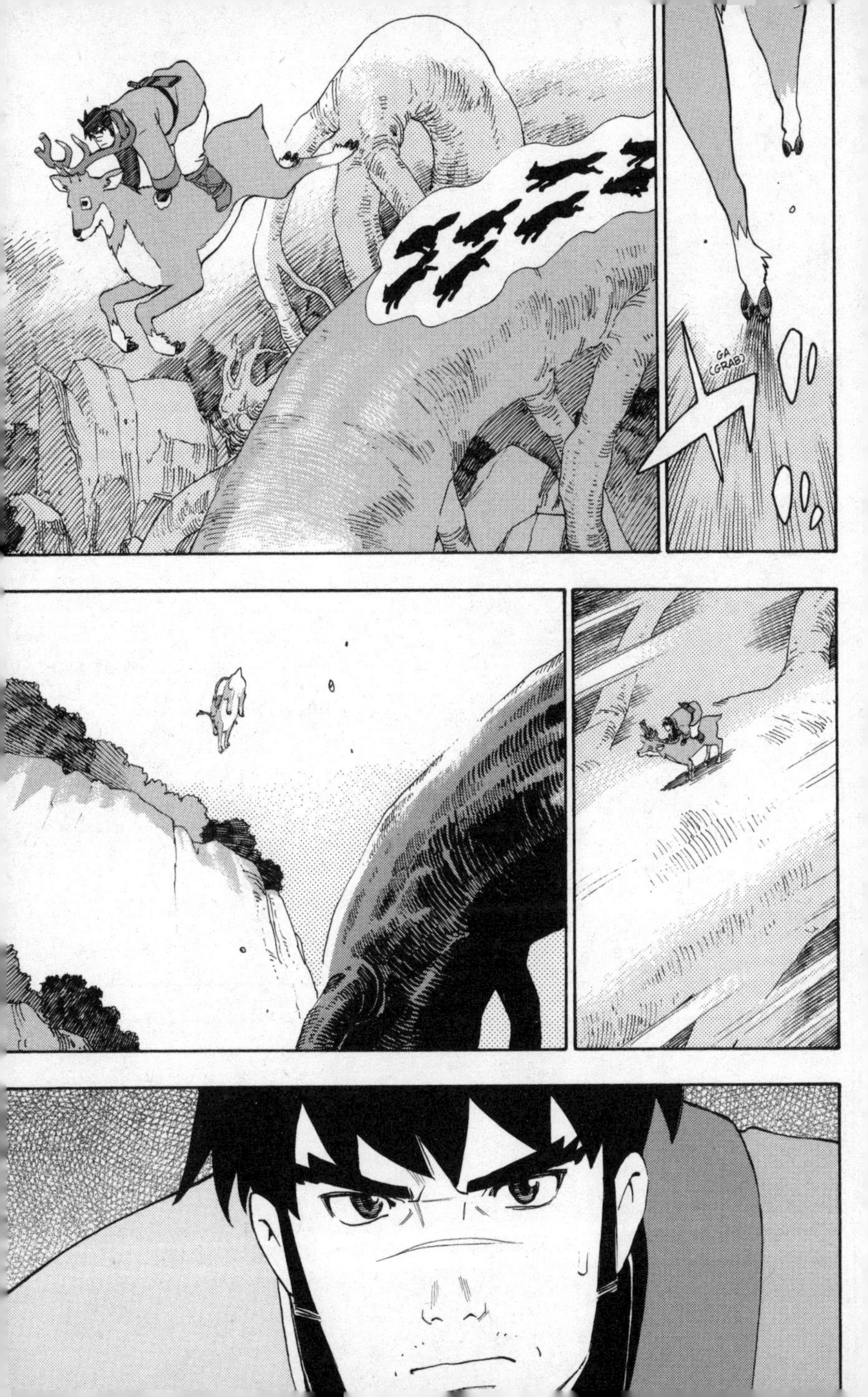
GA
(GRAB)

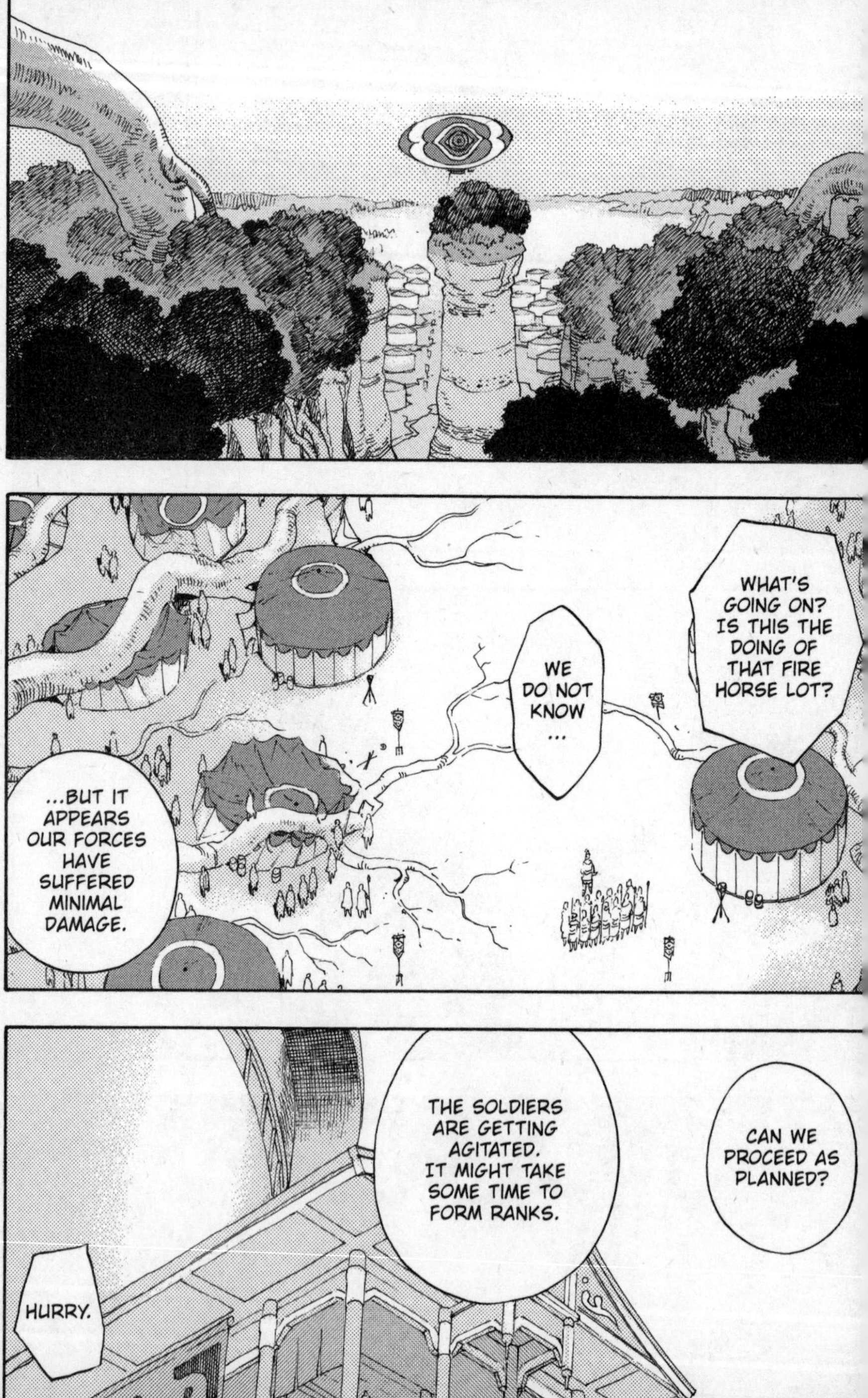
WHAT'S GOING ON? IS THIS THE DOING OF THAT FIRE HORSE LOT?
WE DO NOT KNOW ...
...BUT IT APPEARS OUR FORCES HAVE SUFFERED MINIMAL DAMAGE.
CAN WE PROCEED AS PLANNED?
THE SOLDIERS ARE GETTING AGITATED. IT MIGHT TAKE SOME TIME TO FORM RANKS.
HURRY.

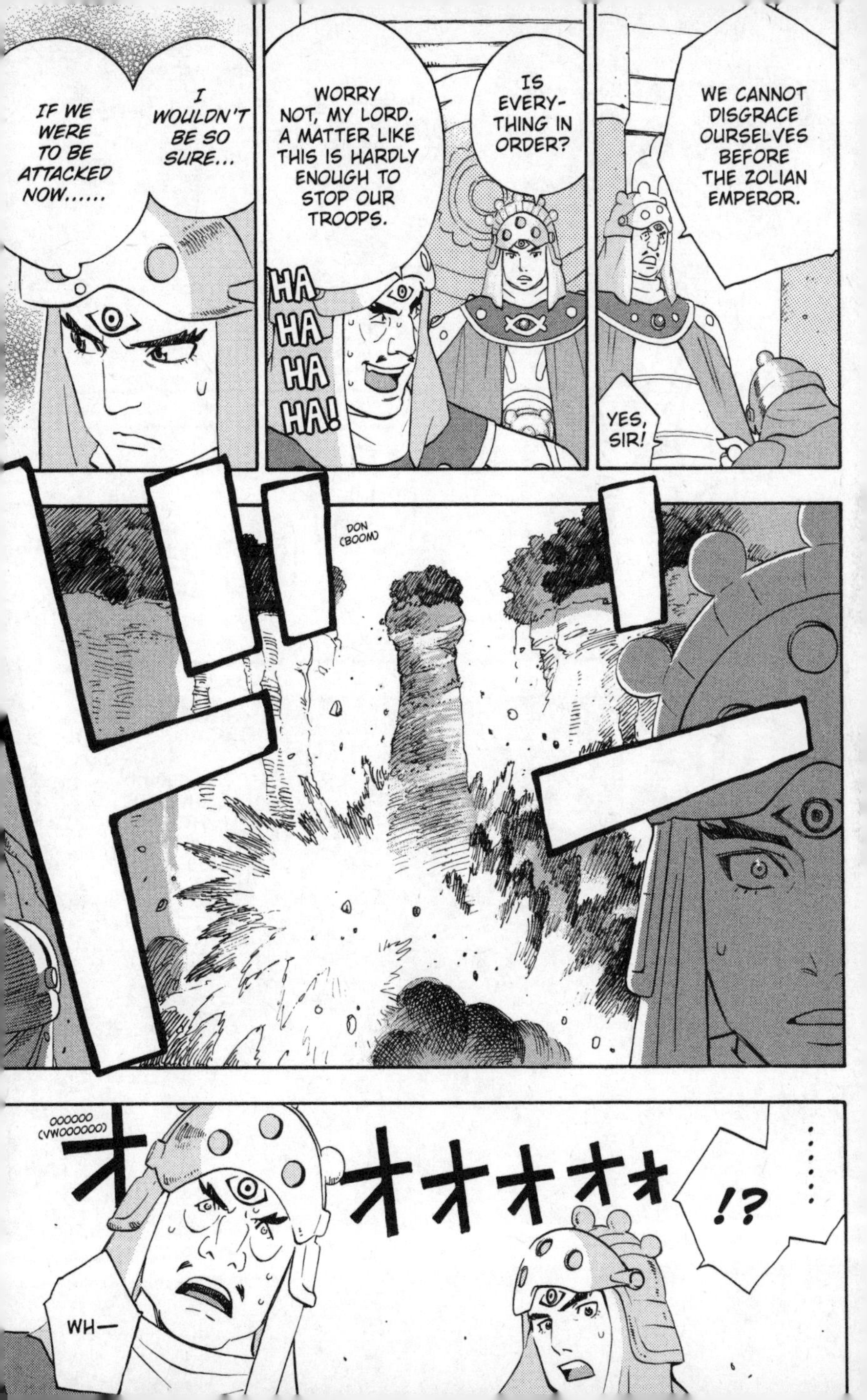
WE CANNOT DISGRACE OURSELVES BEFORE THE ZOLIAN EMPEROR.
YES, SIR!
IS EVERY-THING IN ORDER?
WORRY NOT, MY LORD. A MATTER LIKE THIS IS HARDLY ENOUGH TO STOP OUR TROOPS.
HA HA HA HA HA!
I WOULDN'T BE SO SURE...
IF WE WERE TO BE ATTACKED NOW......
DON (BOOM)
......
!?
オオオオオオ
OOOOOO (VWOOOOOO)
WH—

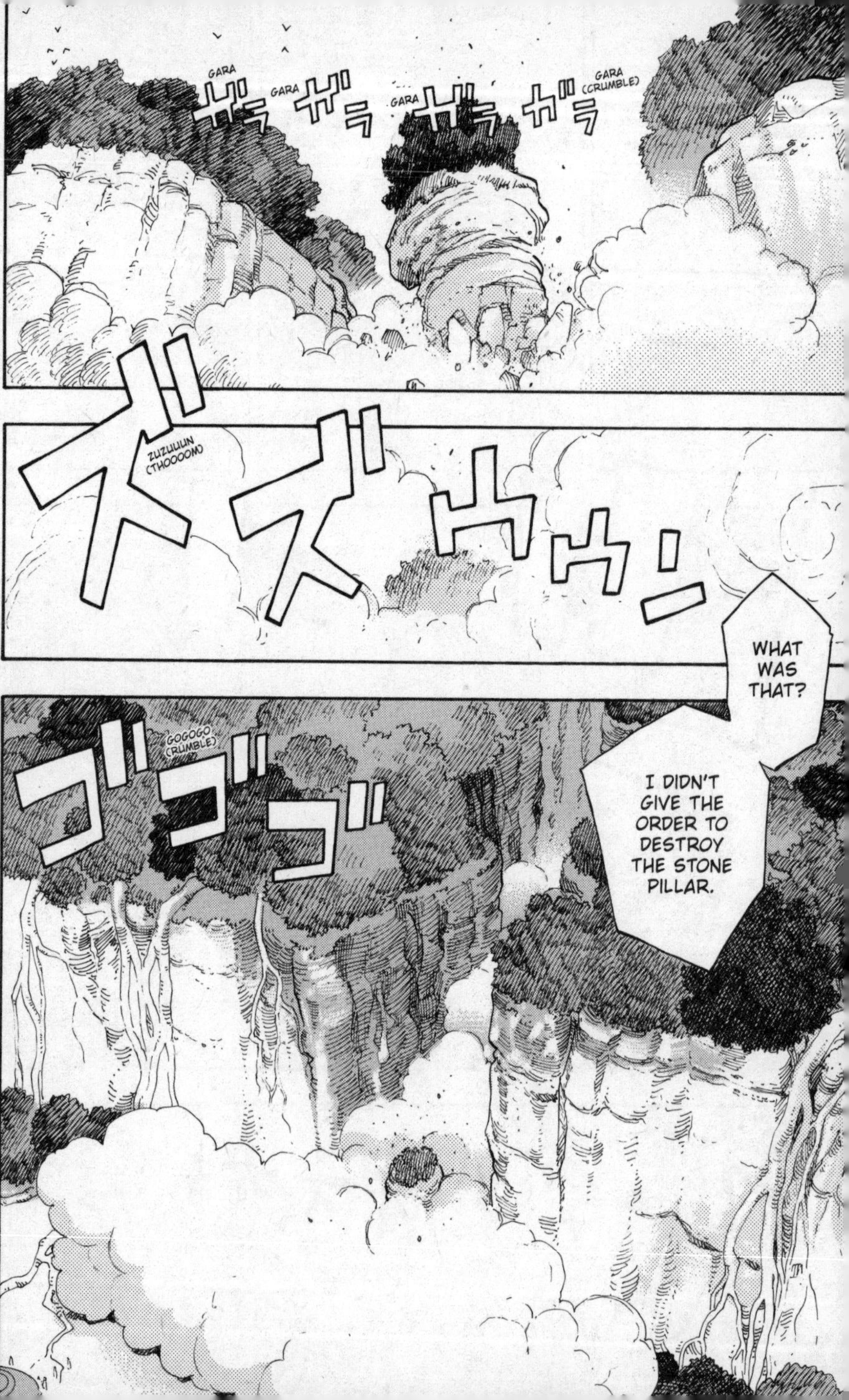
GARA (CRUMBLE)
GARA
GARA
GARA
ZUZUUUN (THOOOOM)
WHAT WAS THAT?
I DIDN'T GIVE THE ORDER TO DESTROY THE STONE PILLAR.
GOGOGO (RUMBLE)

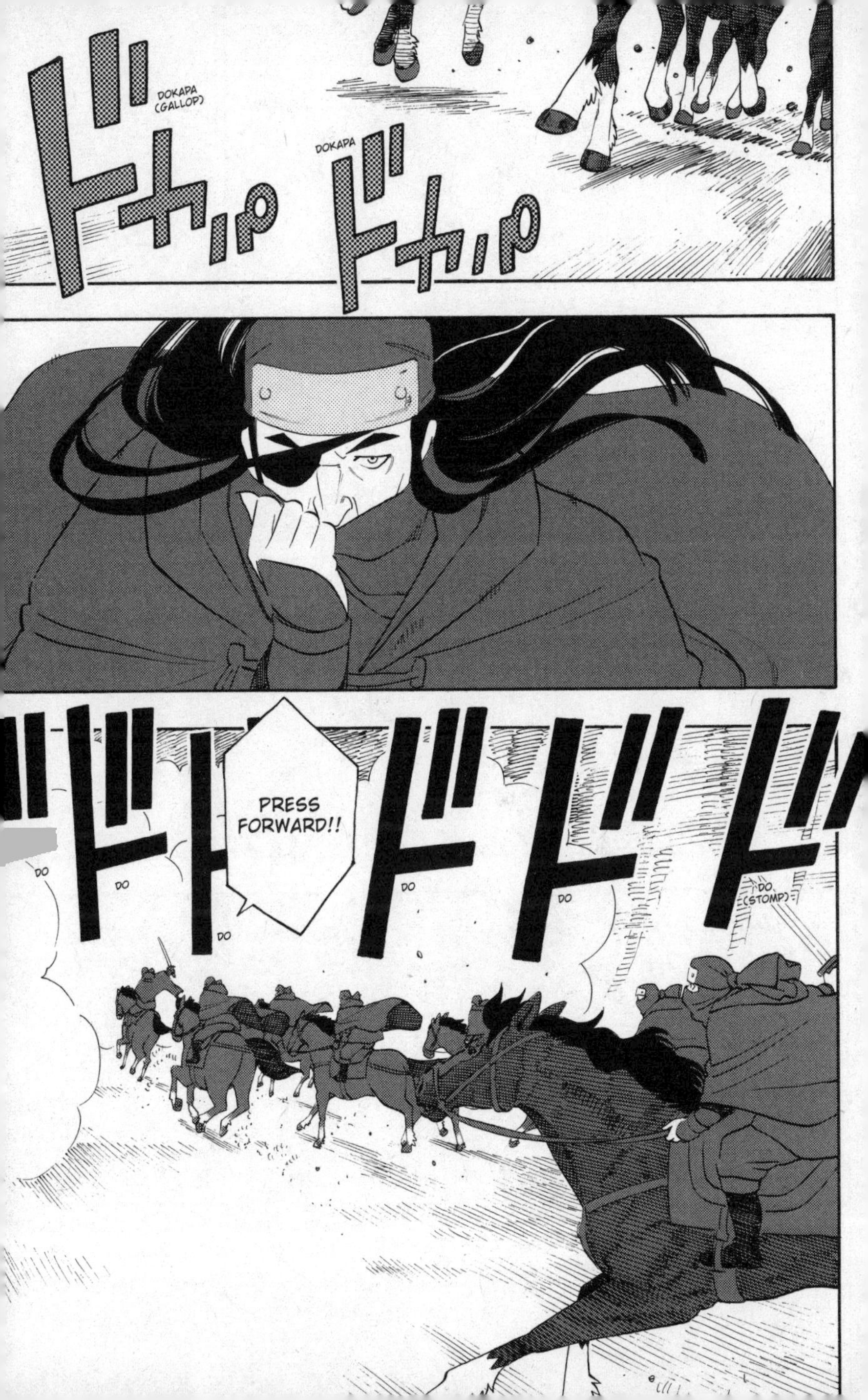
DOKAPA
DOKAPA (GALLOP)
DO (STOMP)
DO
DO
PRESS FORWARD!!
DO
DO
DO

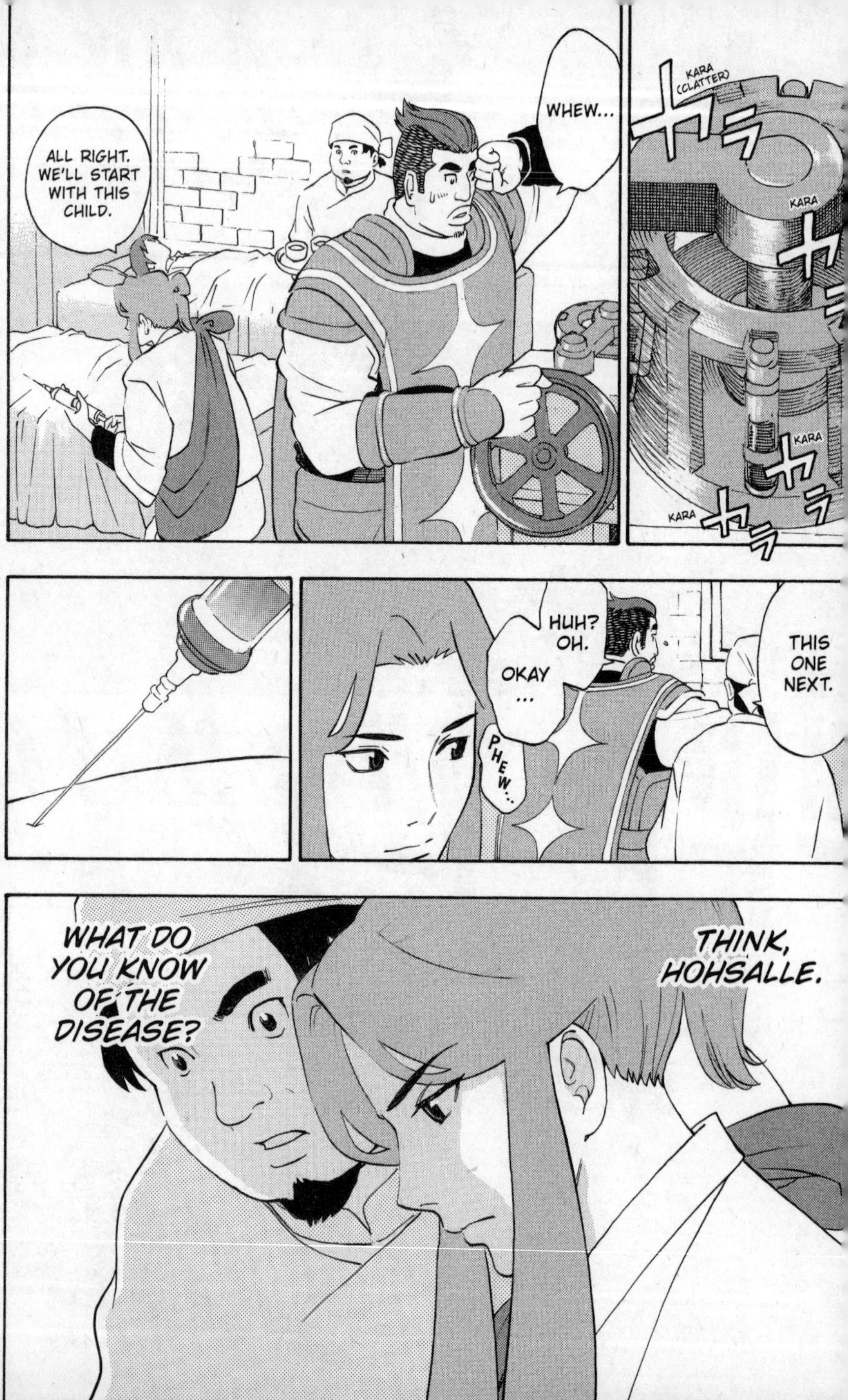
KARA (CLATTER)
KARA
KARA
KARA
WHEW...
ALL RIGHT. WE'LL START WITH THIS CHILD.
THIS ONE NEXT.
HUH? OH.
OKAY ...
PHEW...
THINK, HOHSALLE.
WHAT DO YOU KNOW OF THE DISEASE?

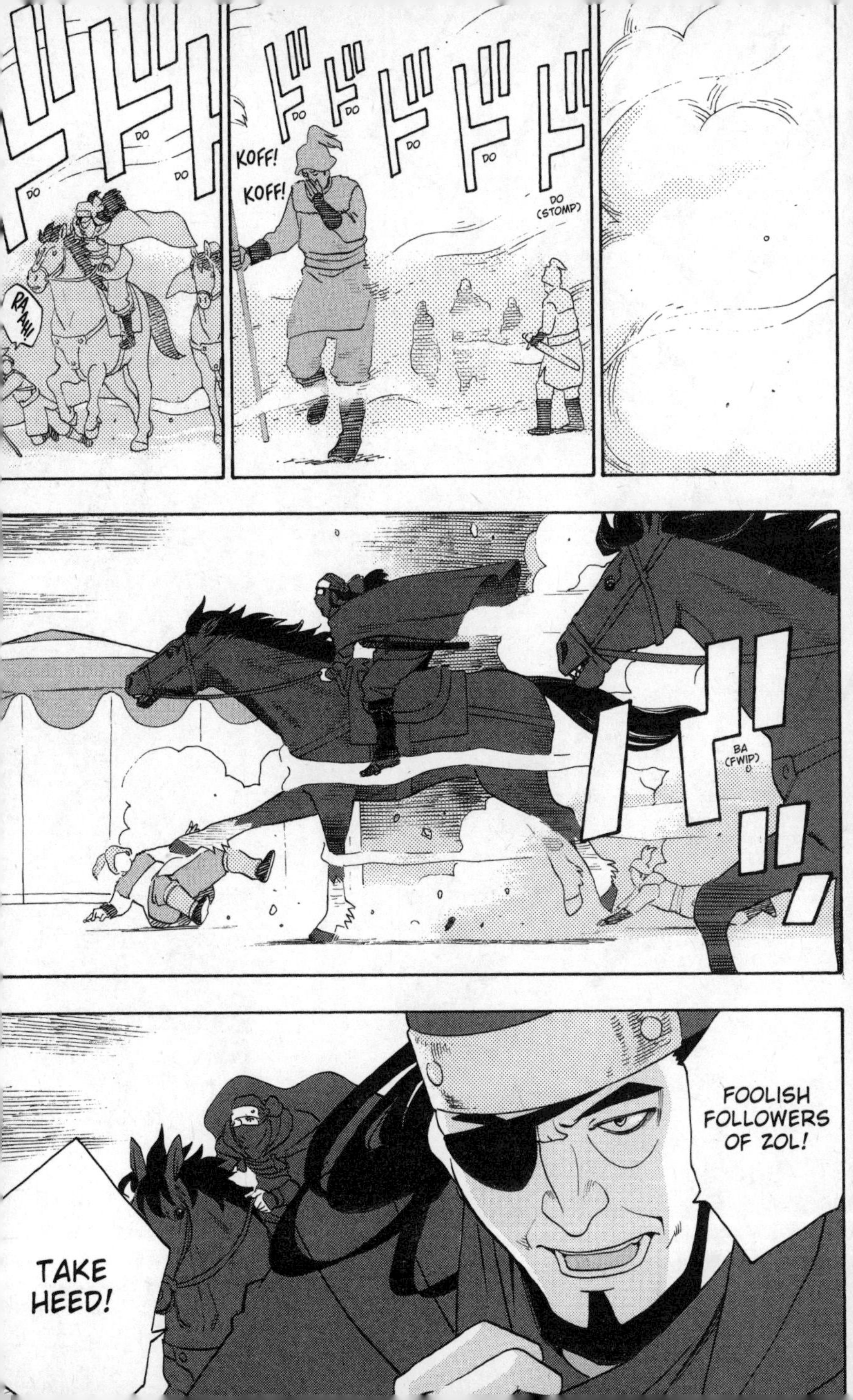
DO
(STOMP)
DO
DO
DO
DO
KOFF!
KOFF!
DO
DO
DO
RAAAH!
BA
(FWIP)
FOOLISH
FOLLOWERS
OF ZOL!
TAKE
HEED!

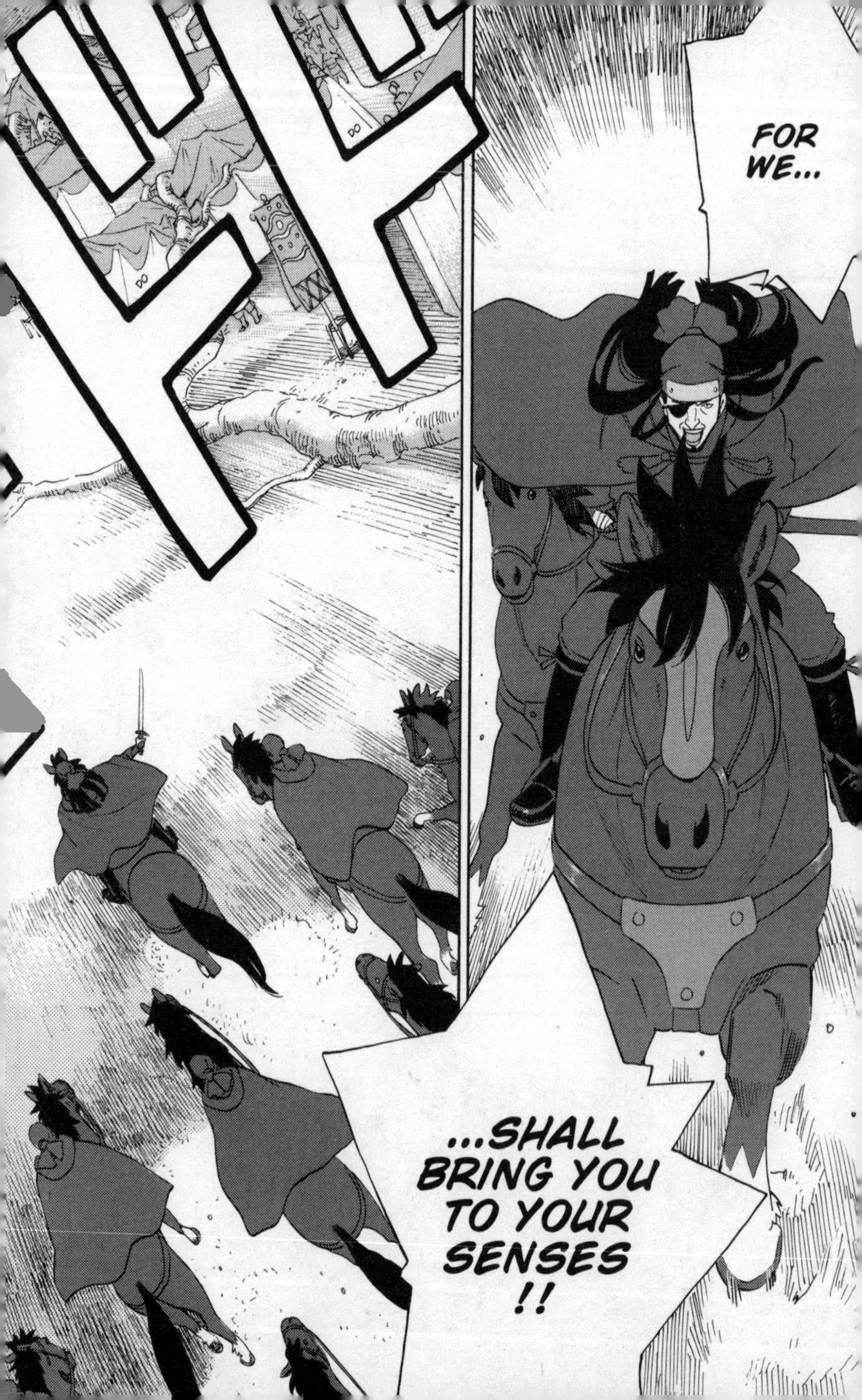
FOR WE...
...SHALL BRING YOU TO YOUR SENSES !!
DO
DO

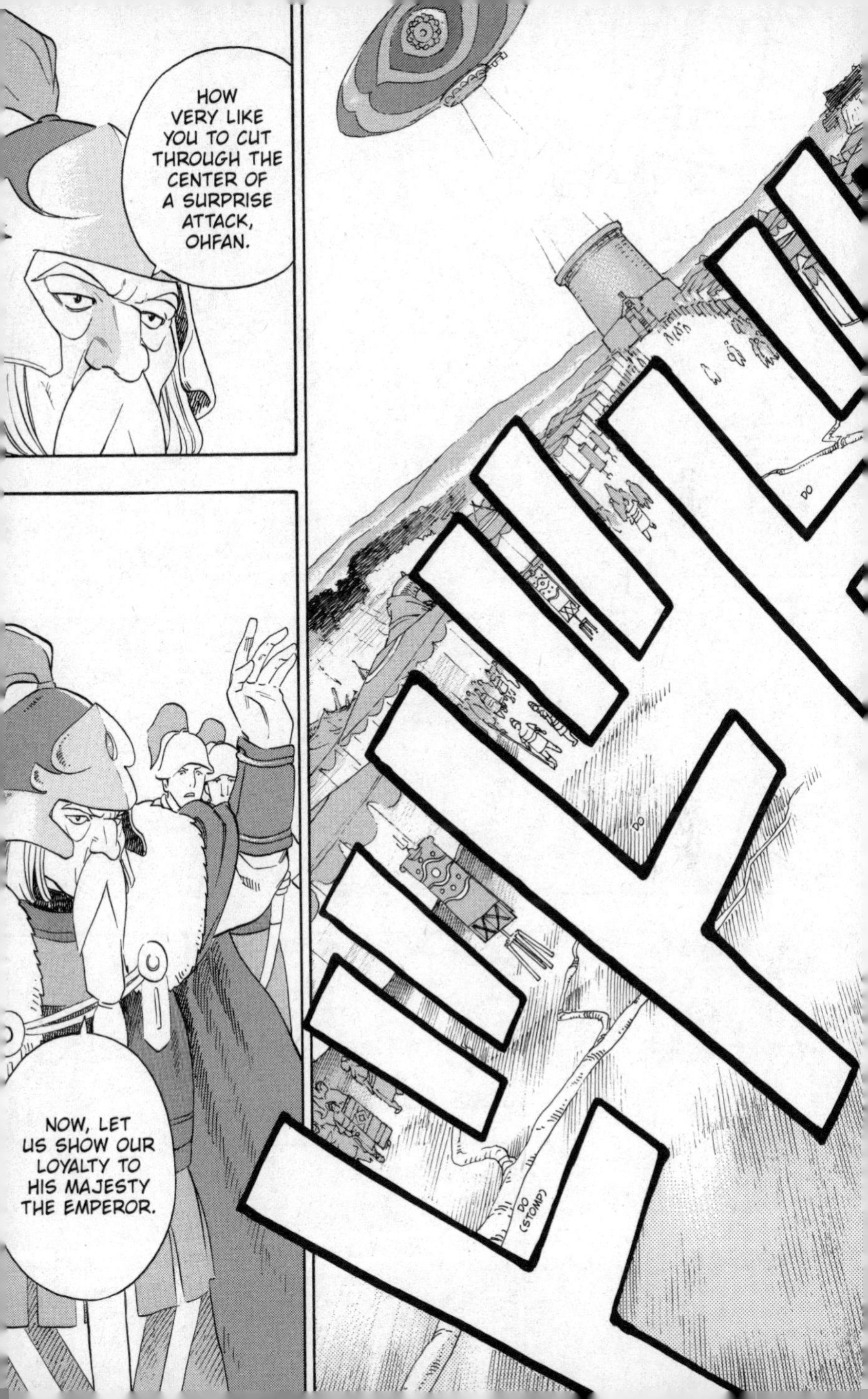
DO
DO
DO (STOMP)
HOW VERY LIKE YOU TO CUT THROUGH THE CENTER OF A SURPRISE ATTACK, OHFAN.
NOW, LET US SHOW OUR LOYALTY TO HIS MAJESTY THE EMPEROR.

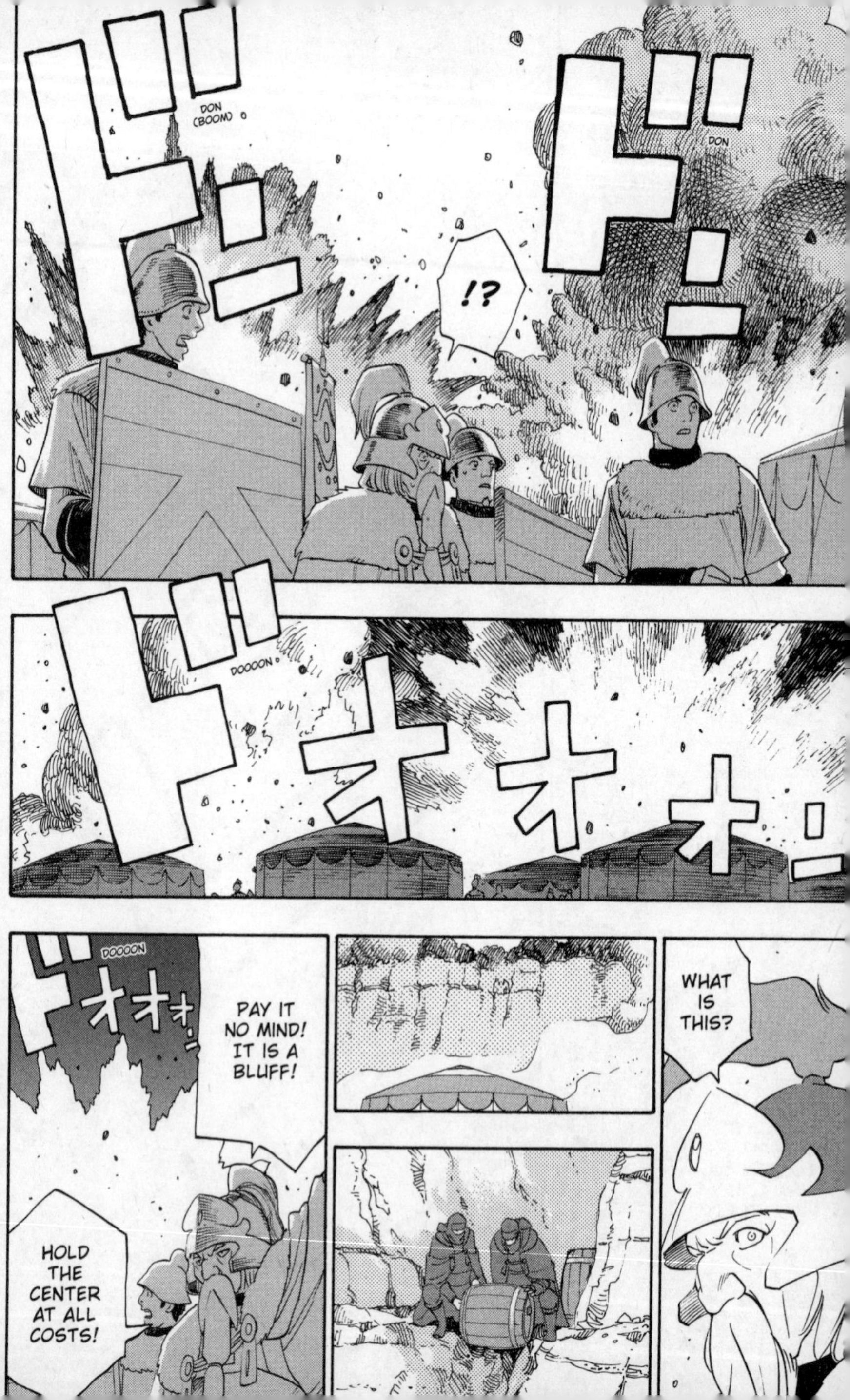
DON
DON (BOOM)
!?
DOOOON
WHAT IS THIS?
DOOOON
PAY IT NO MIND! IT IS A BLUFF!
HOLD THE CENTER AT ALL COSTS!

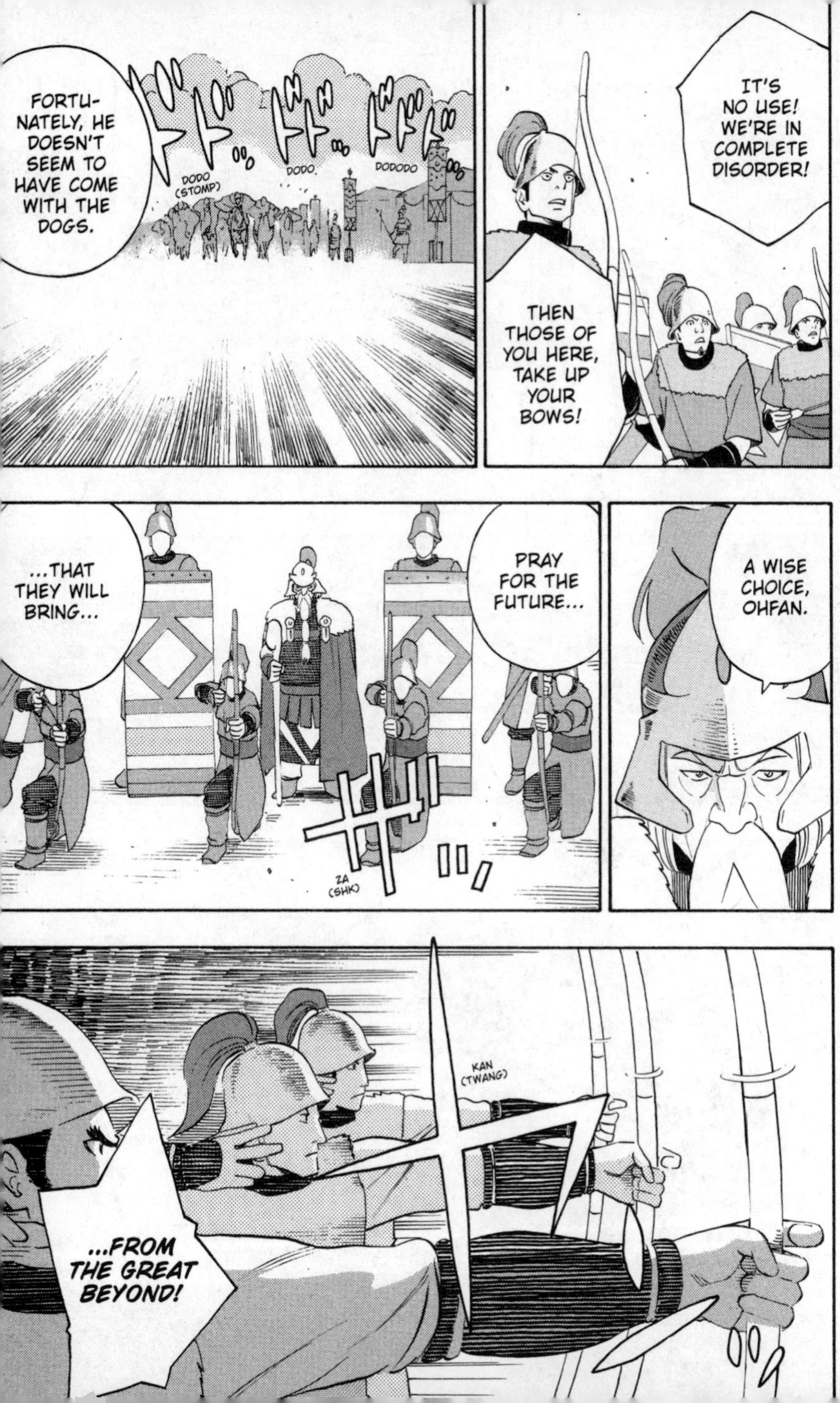
IT'S NO USE! WE'RE IN COMPLETE DISORDER!
THEN THOSE OF YOU HERE, TAKE UP YOUR BOWS!
FORTU-NATELY, HE DOESN'T SEEM TO HAVE COME WITH THE DOGS.
DODO (STOMP)
DODO
DODODO
A WISE CHOICE, OHFAN.
PRAY FOR THE FUTURE...
...THAT THEY WILL BRING...
ZA (SHK)
KAN (TWANG)
...FROM THE GREAT BEYOND!

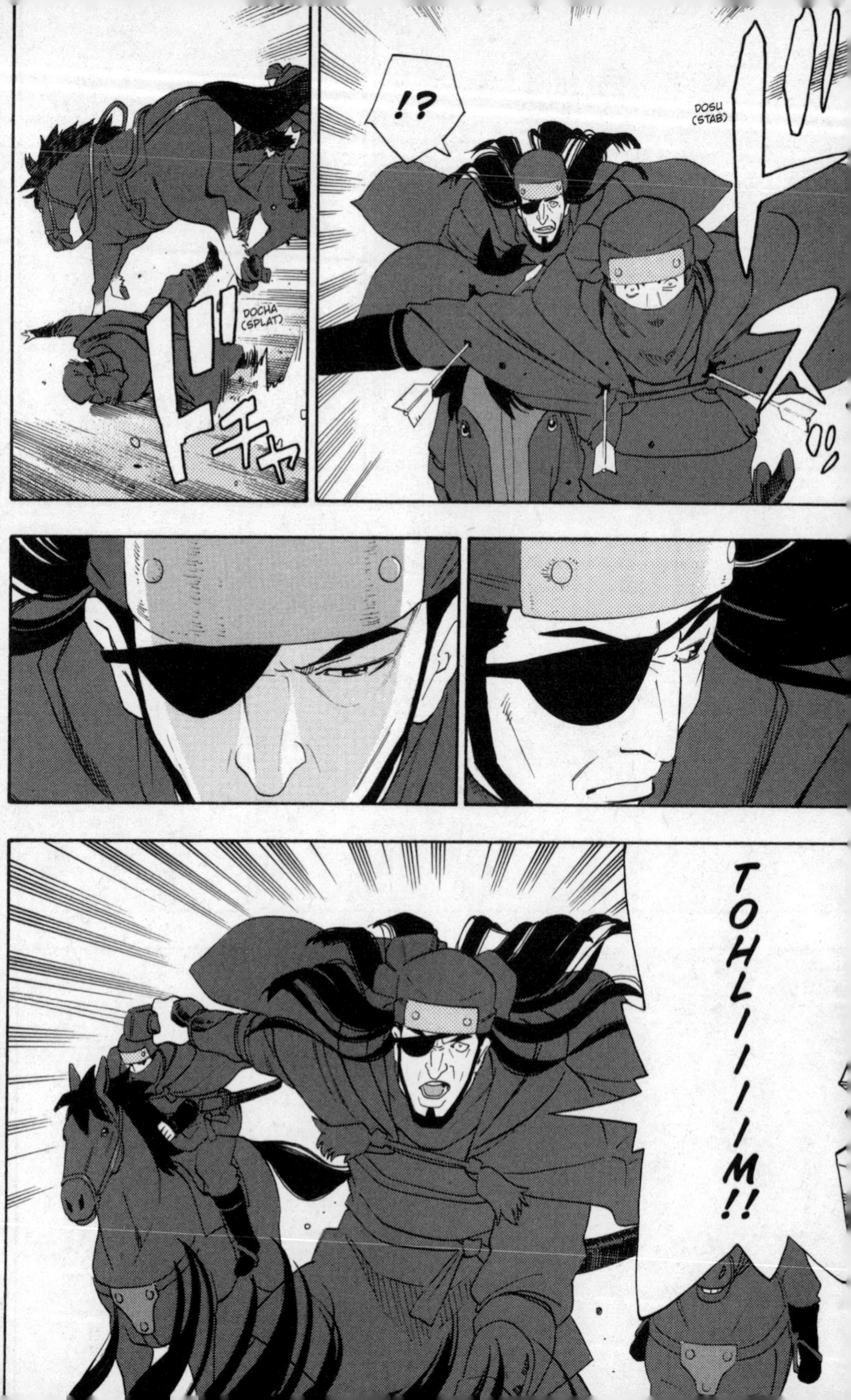
DOSU (STAB)
!?
DOCHA (SPLAT)
TOHLIIIIM!!

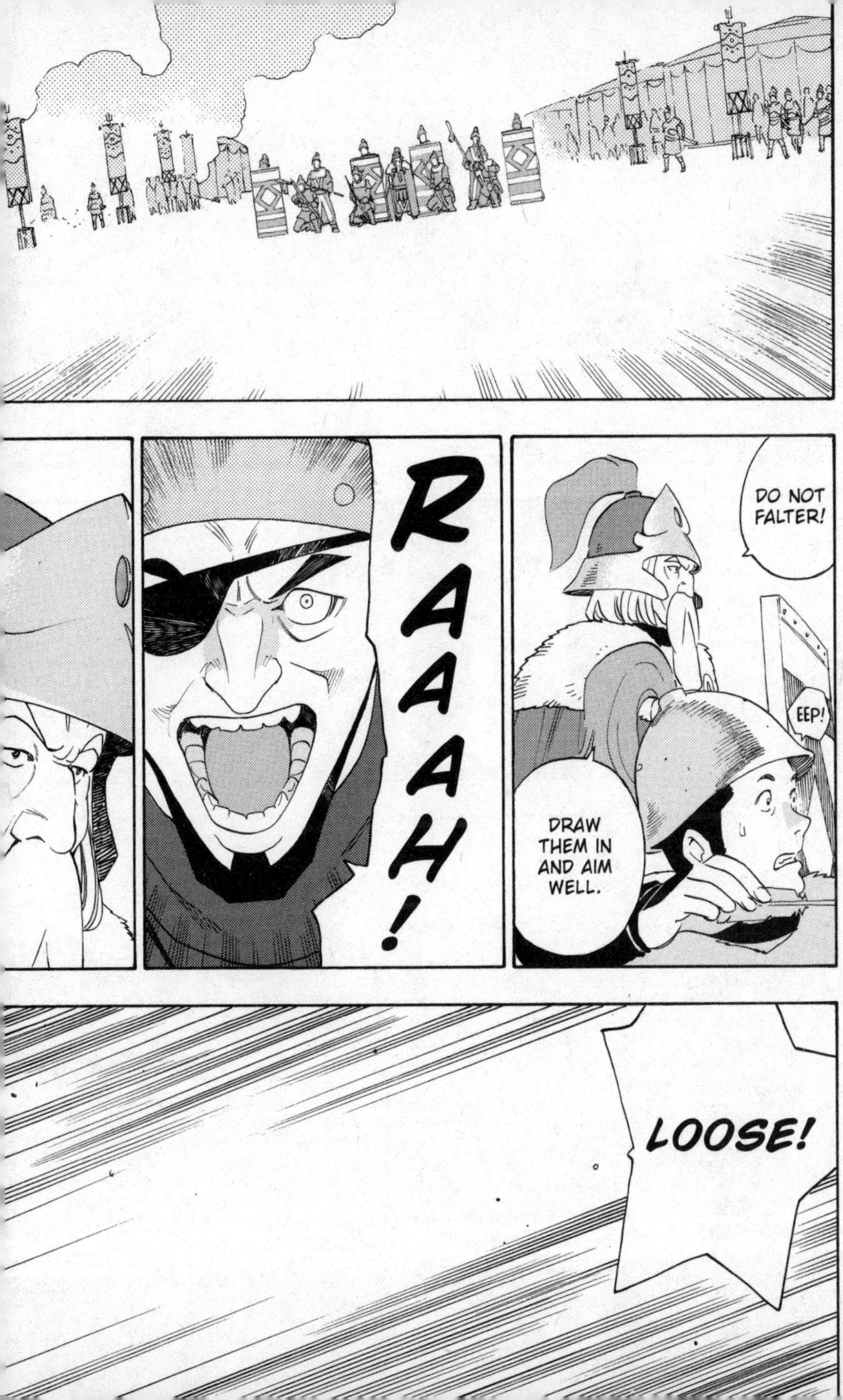
DO NOT FALTER!
EEP!
DRAW THEM IN AND AIM WELL.
RAAAAH!
LOOSE!

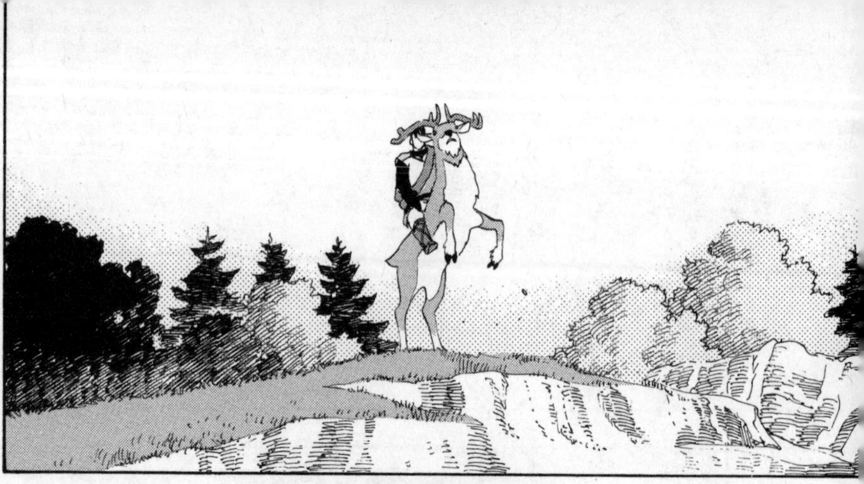

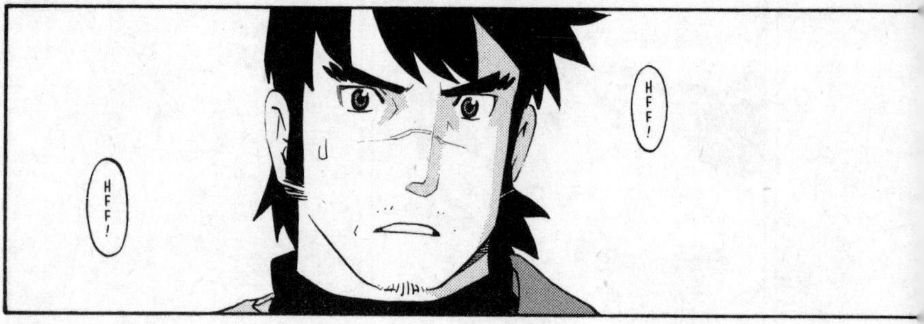
HFF!
HFF!

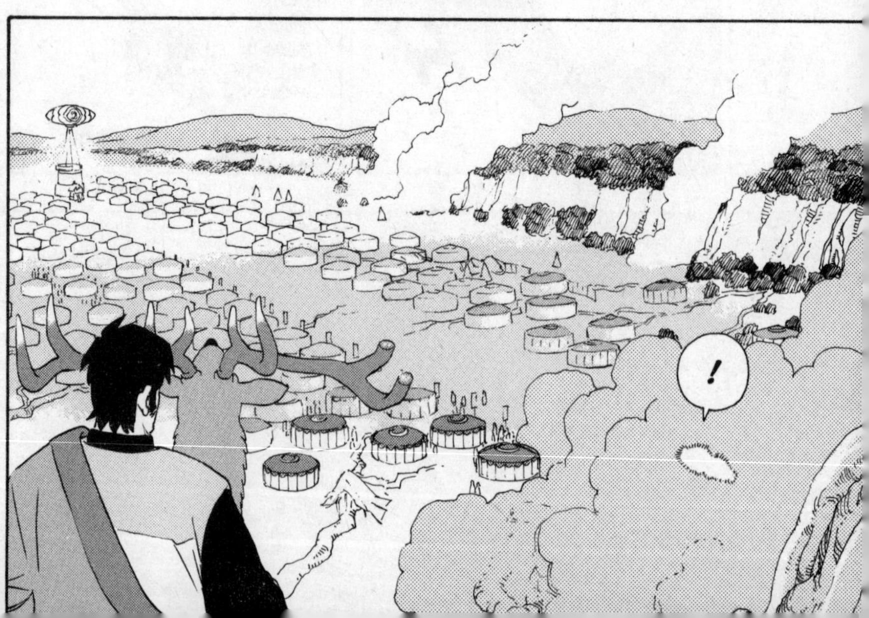
!

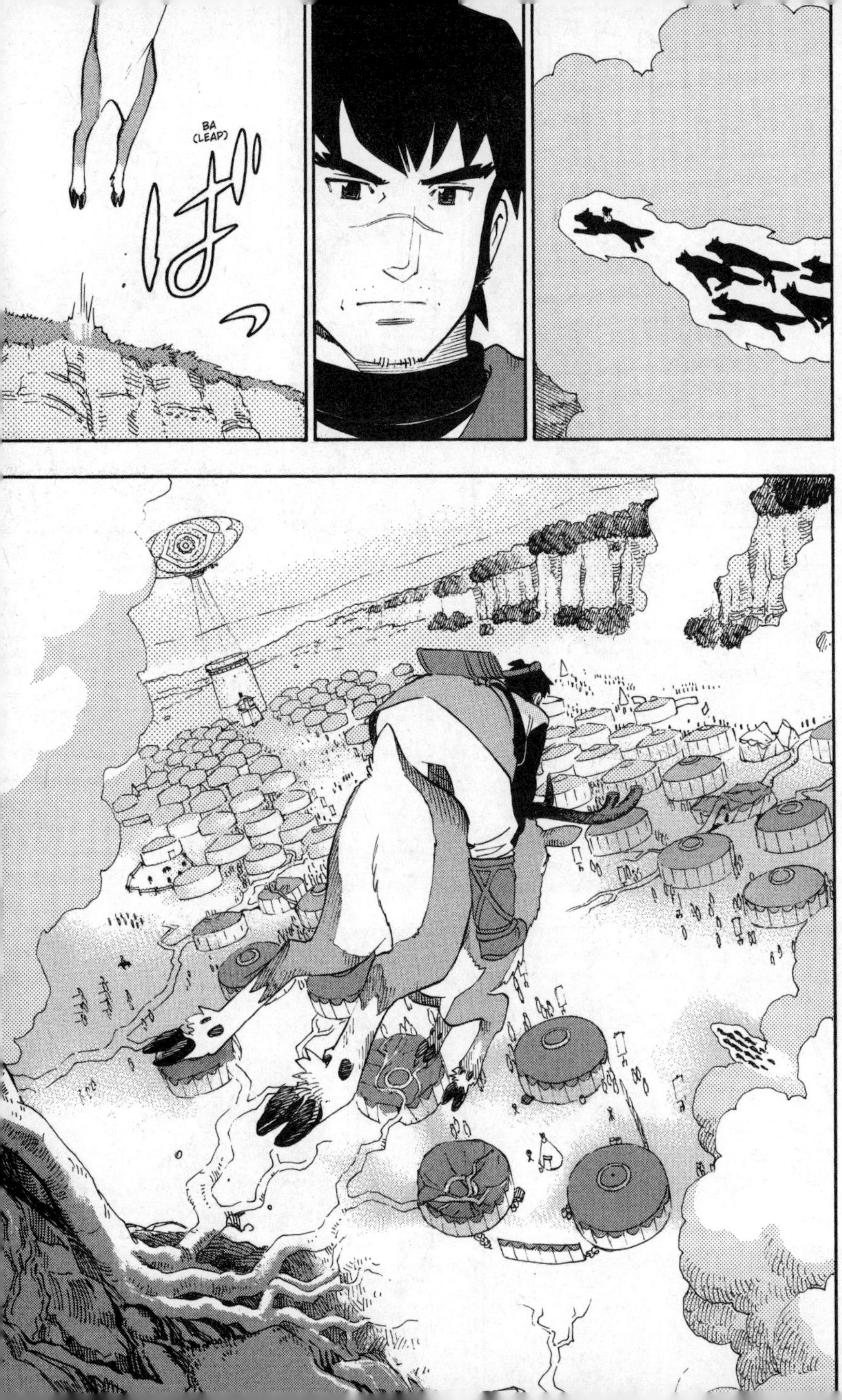
BA
(LEAP)

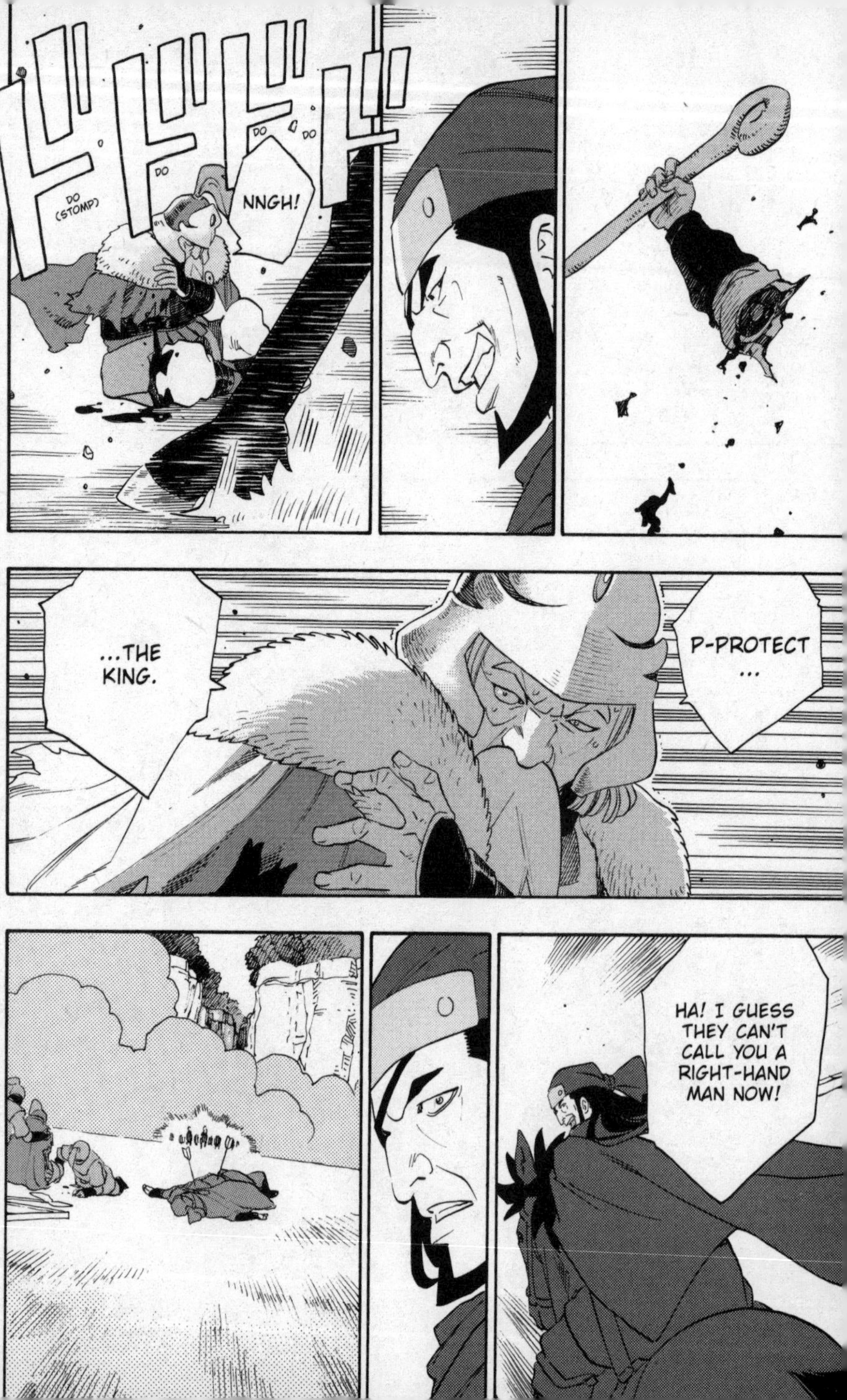
DO
DO
DO
DO (STOMP)
NNGH!
P-PROTECT...
...THE KING.
HA! I GUESS THEY CAN'T CALL YOU A RIGHT-HAND MAN NOW!

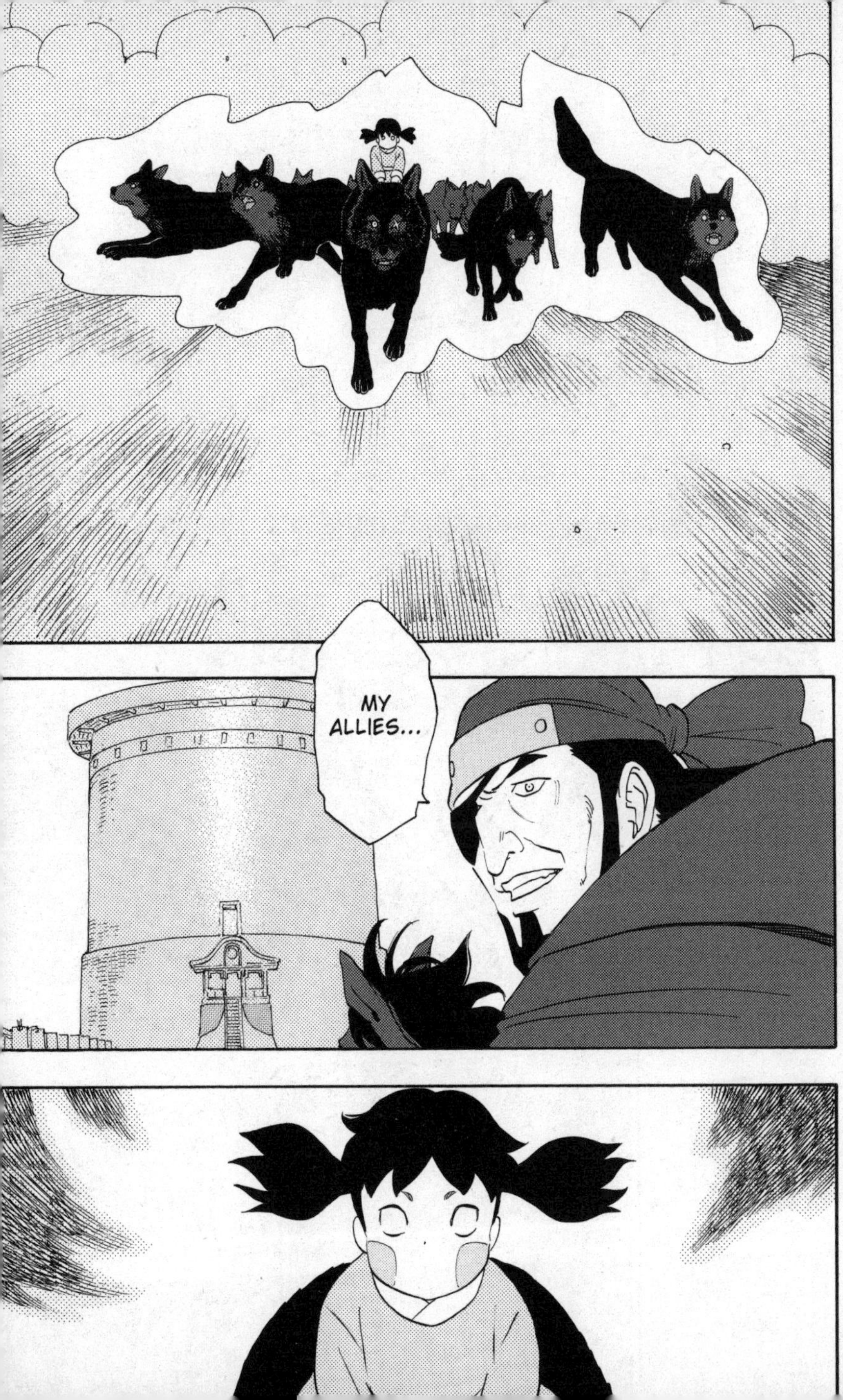
MY ALLIES...

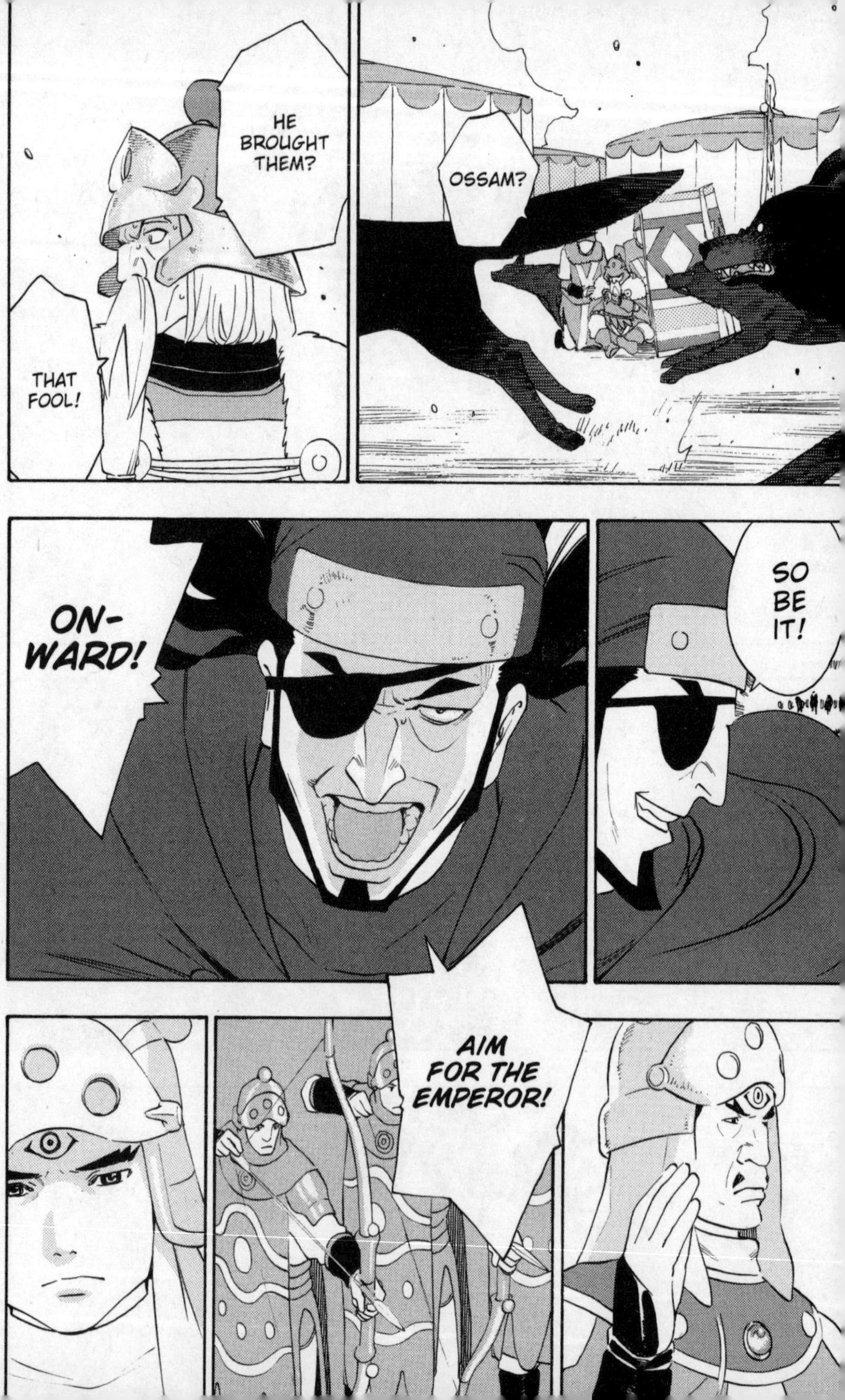
OSSAM?
HE BROUGHT THEM?
THAT FOOL!
SO BE IT!
ON-WARD!
AIM FOR THE EMPEROR!

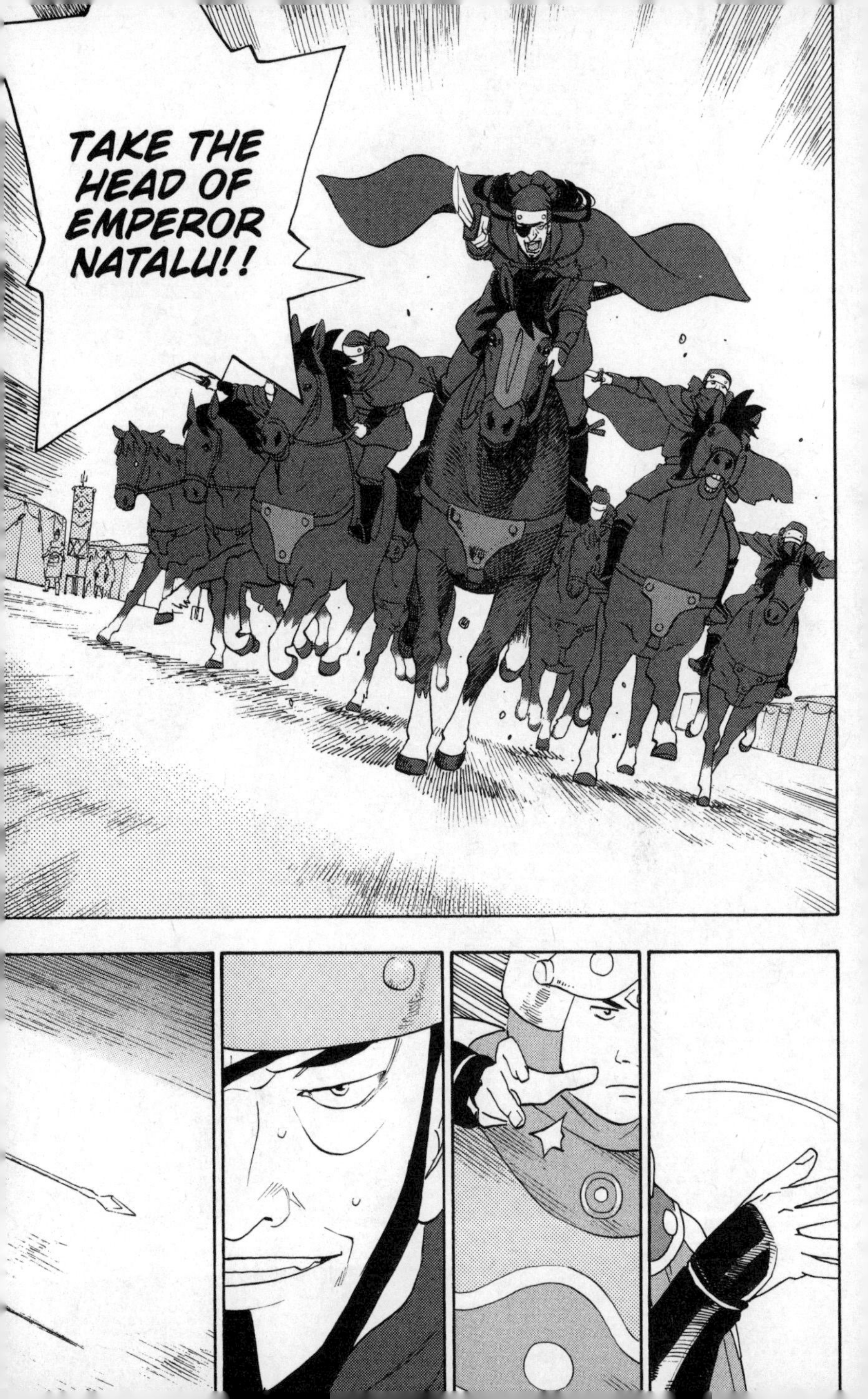
TAKE THE HEAD OF EMPEROR NATALU!!

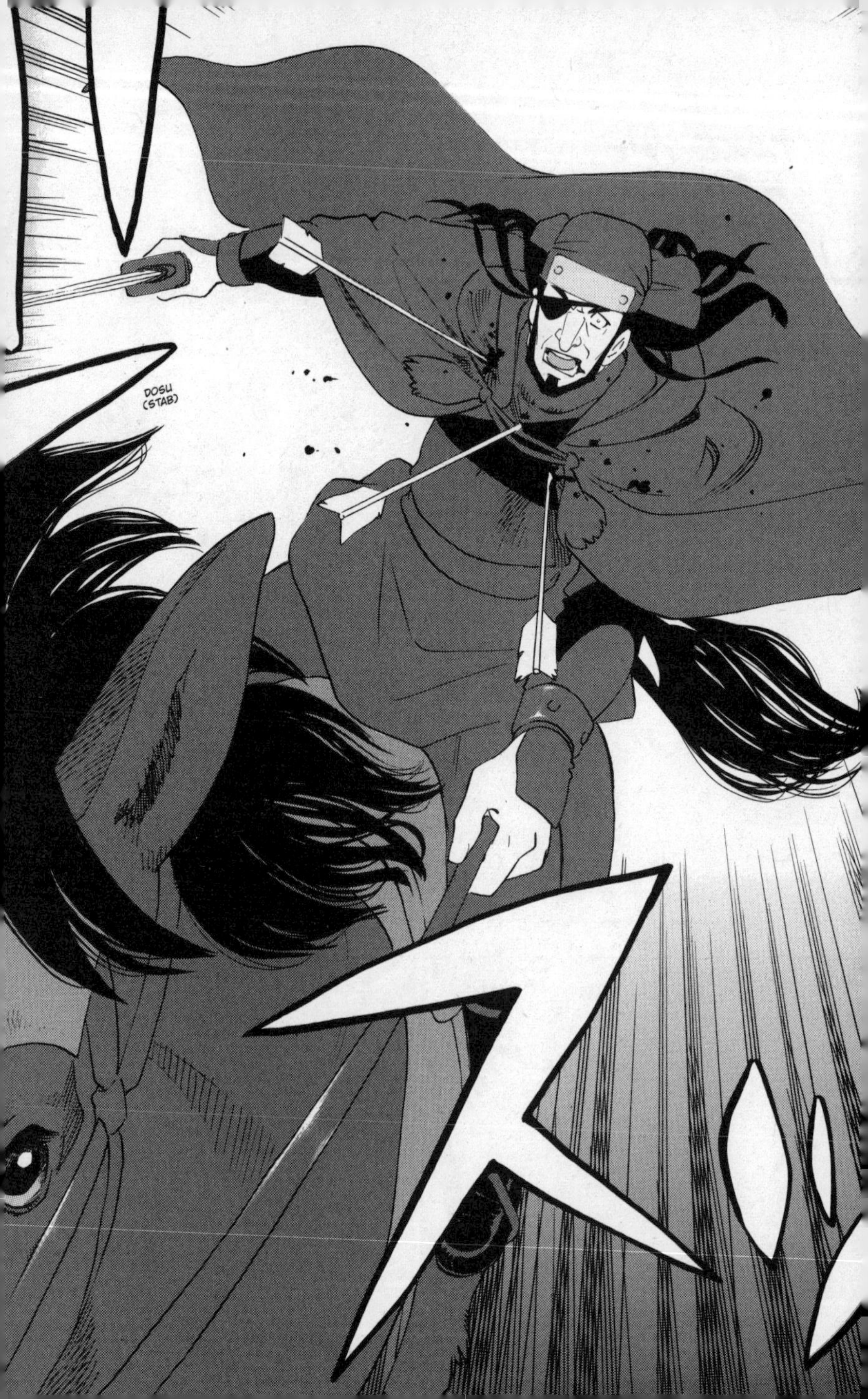
DOSU
(STAB)

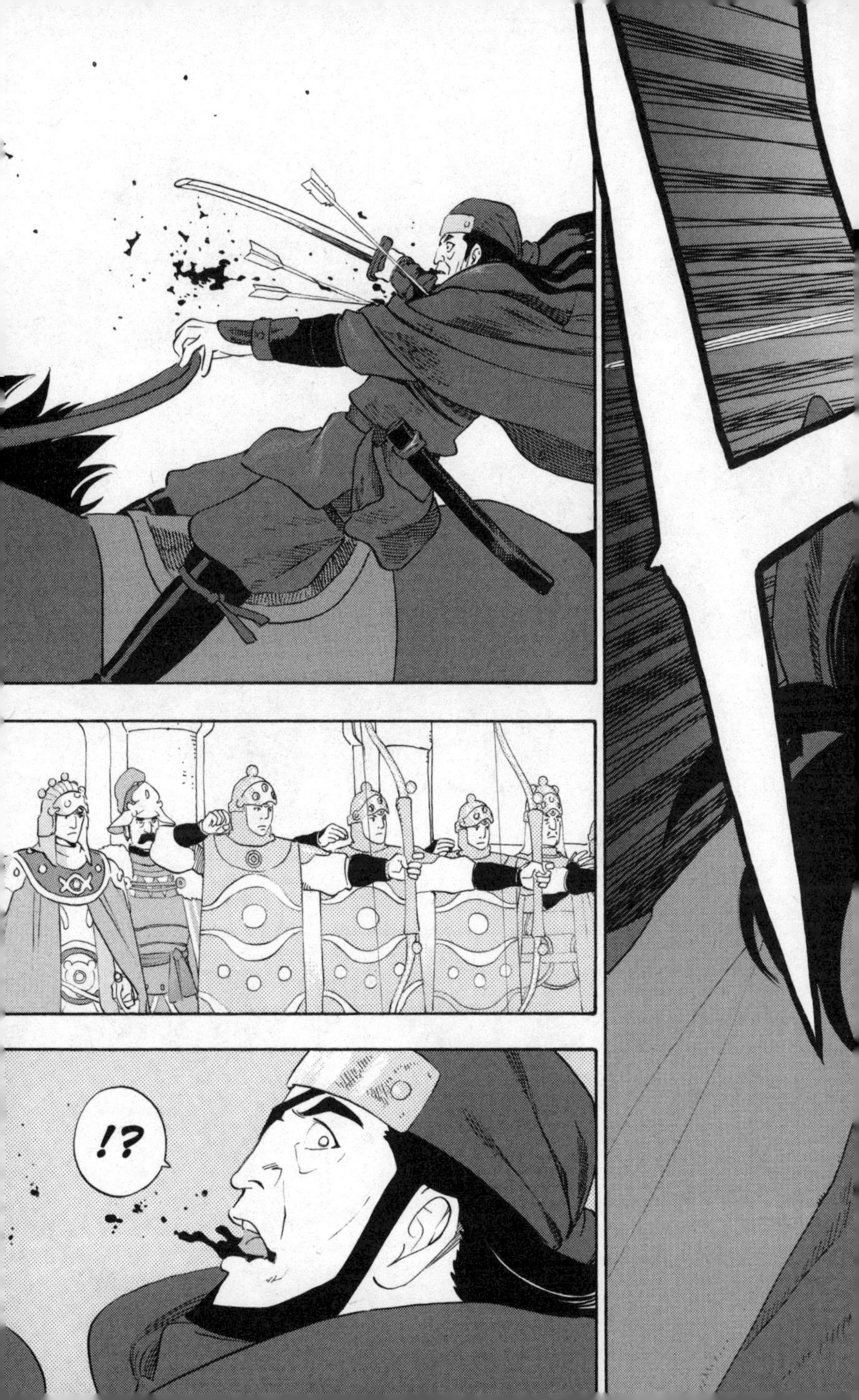
!?

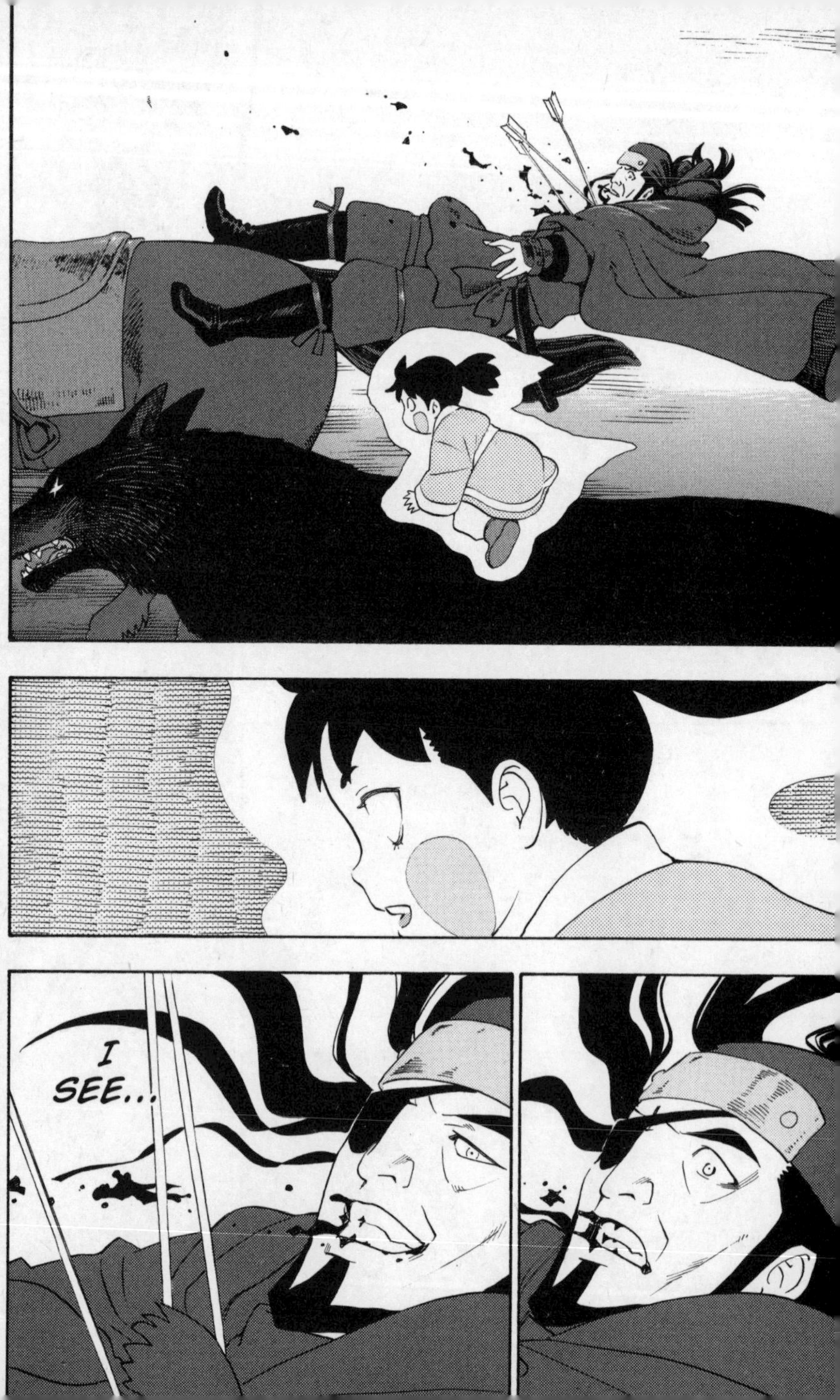
I SEE...

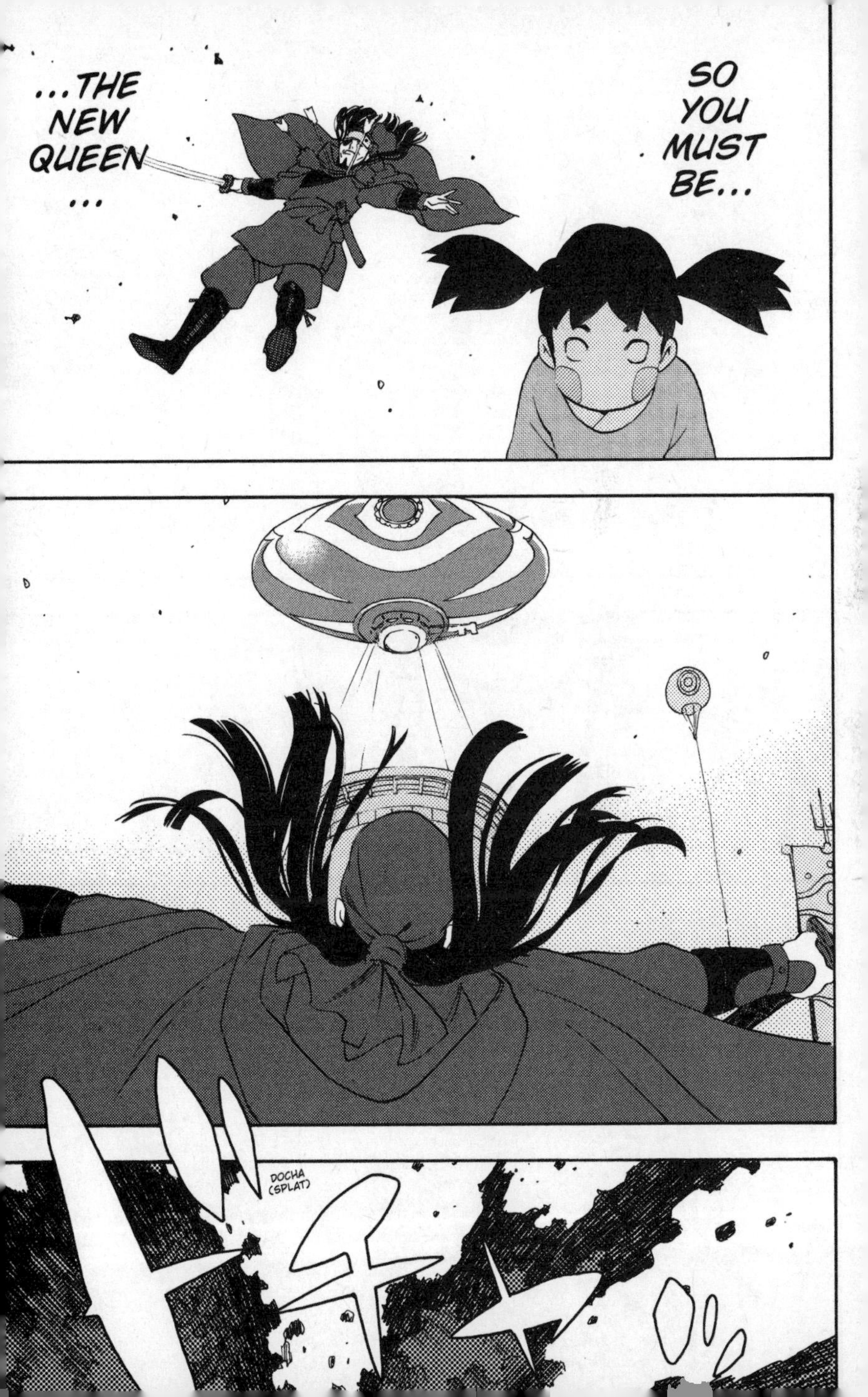
SO YOU MUST BE...
...THE NEW QUEEN...
DOCHA (SPLAT)

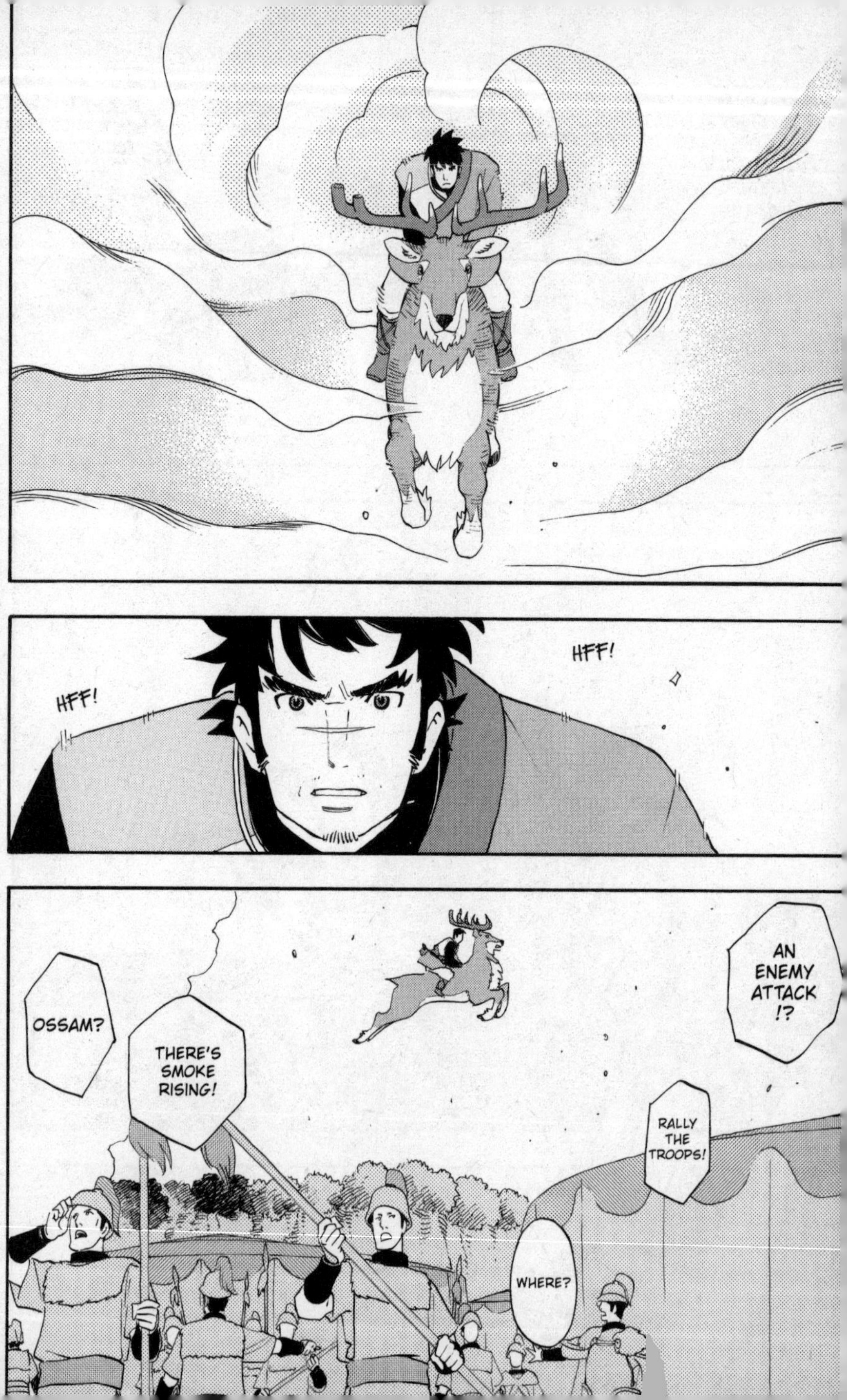
HFF!
HFF!
AN ENEMY ATTACK!?
RALLY THE TROOPS!
WHERE?
THERE'S SMOKE RISING!
OSSAM?

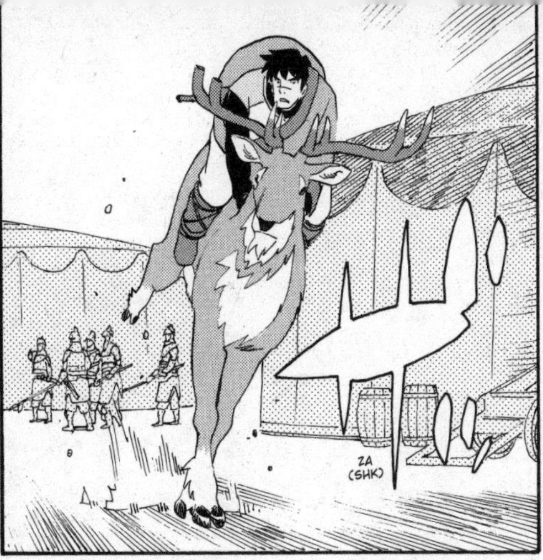
ZA
(SHK)
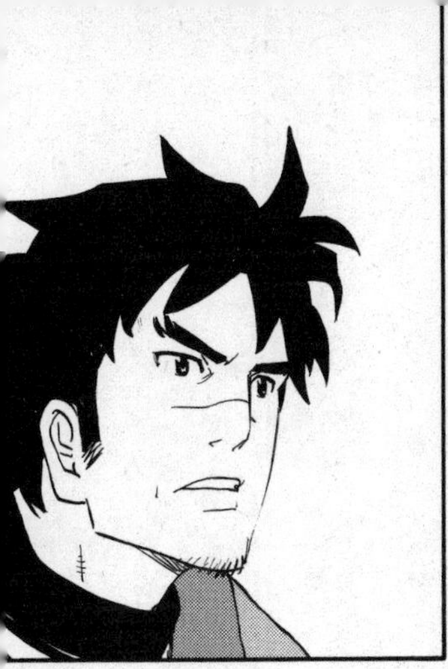
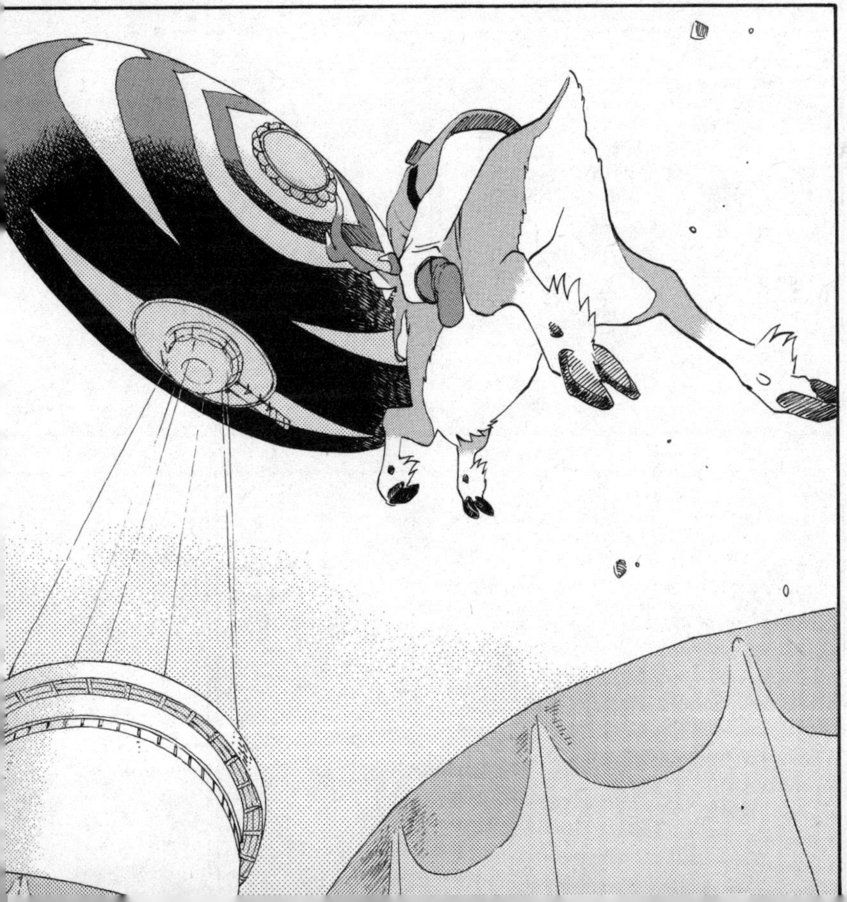

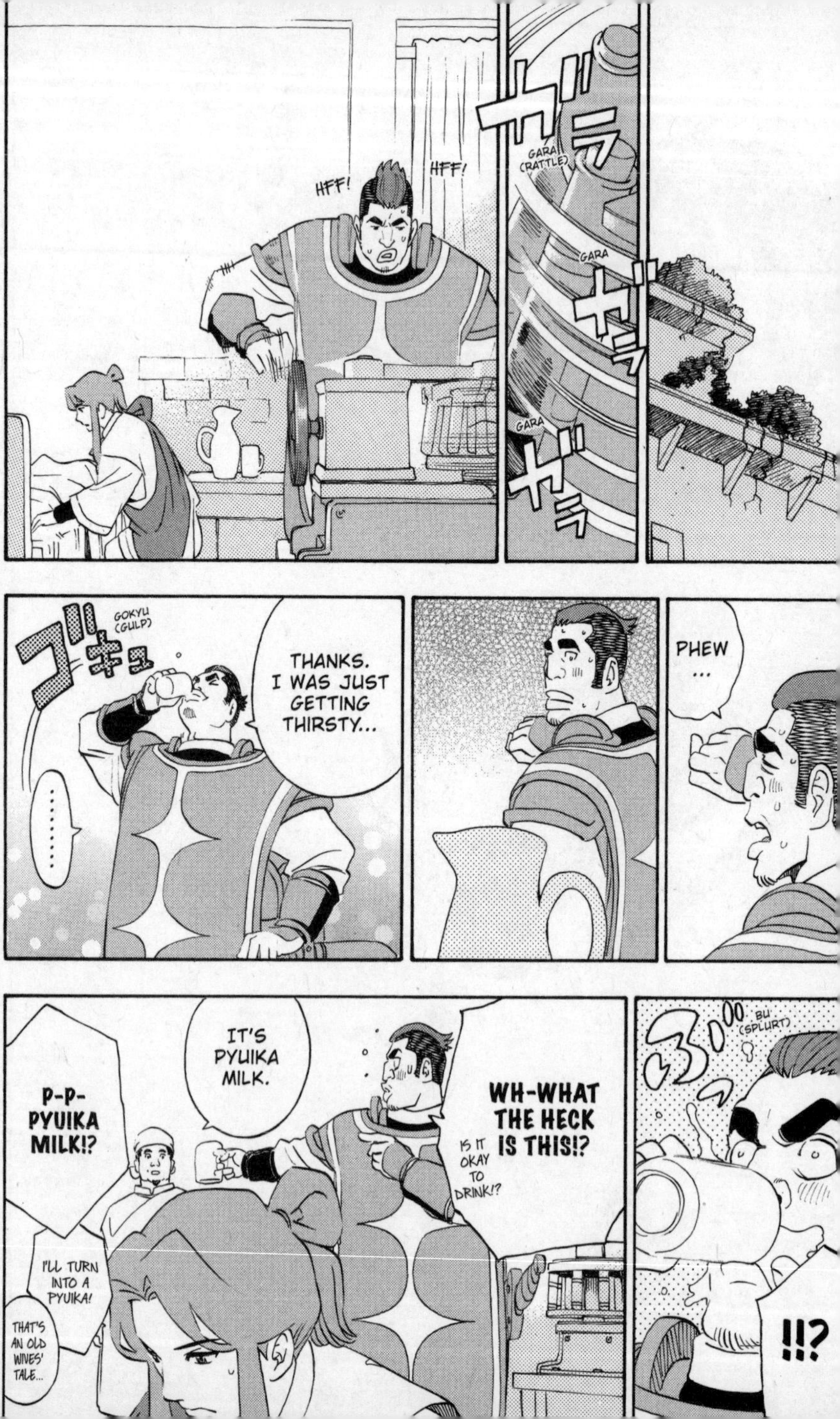
GARA (RATTLE)
GARA
GARA
HFF!
HFF!
PHEW...
GOKYU (GULP)
THANKS. I WAS JUST GETTING THIRSTY...
......
BU (SPLURT)
!!?
WH-WHAT THE HECK IS THIS!?
IS IT OKAY TO DRINK!?
IT'S PYUIKA MILK.
P-P-PYUIKA MILK!?
I'LL TURN INTO A PYUIKA!
THAT'S AN OLD WIVES' TALE...

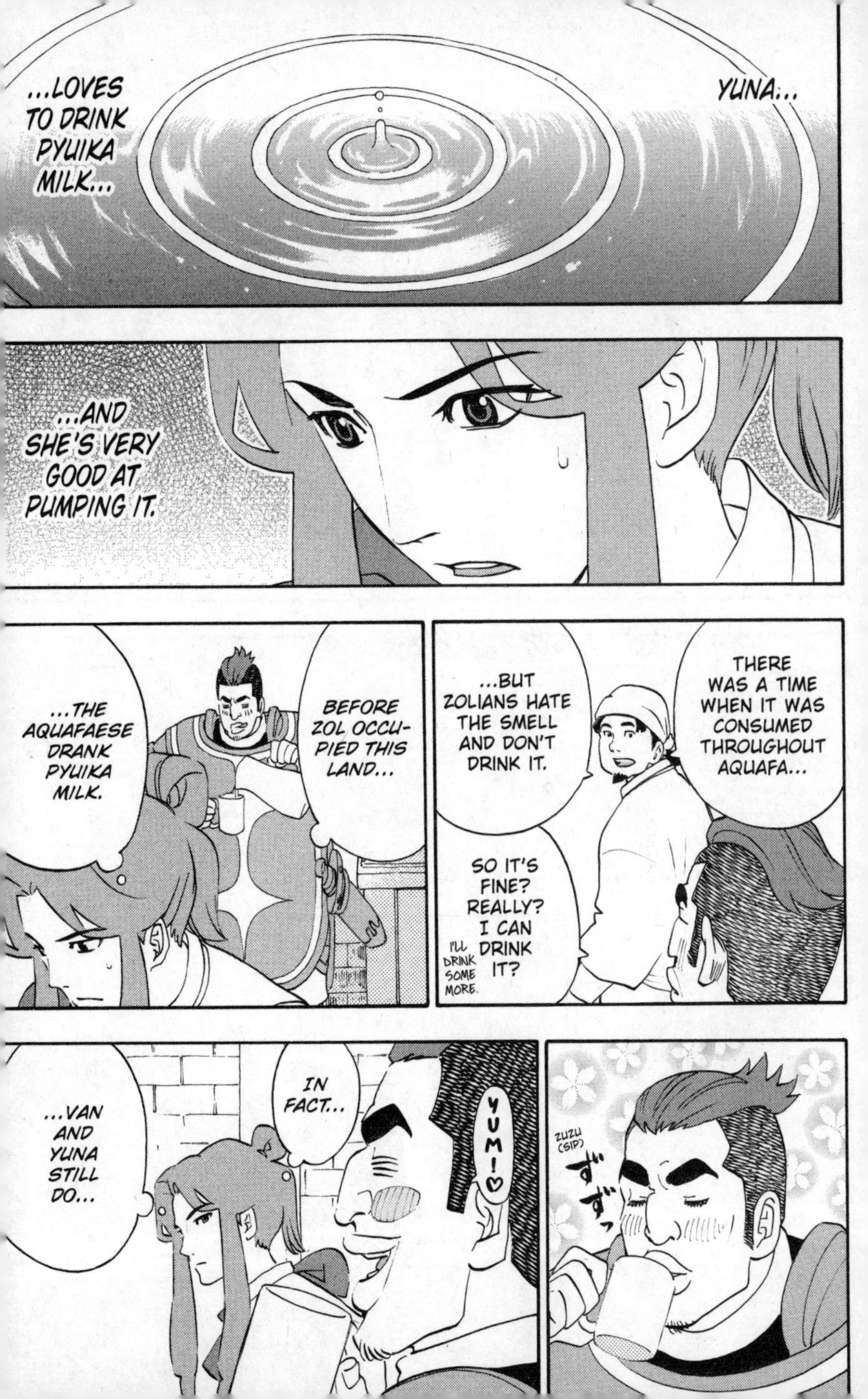
YUNA...
...LOVES TO DRINK PYUIKA MILK...
...AND SHE'S VERY GOOD AT PUMPING IT.
THERE WAS A TIME WHEN IT WAS CONSUMED THROUGHOUT AQUAFA...
...BUT ZOLIANS HATE THE SMELL AND DON'T DRINK IT.
SO IT'S FINE? REALLY? I CAN DRINK IT?
I'LL DRINK SOME MORE.
BEFORE ZOL OCCUPIED THIS LAND...
...THE AQUAFAESE DRANK PYUIKA MILK.
ZUZU (SIP)
YUM!♥
IN FACT...
...VAN AND YUNA STILL DO...

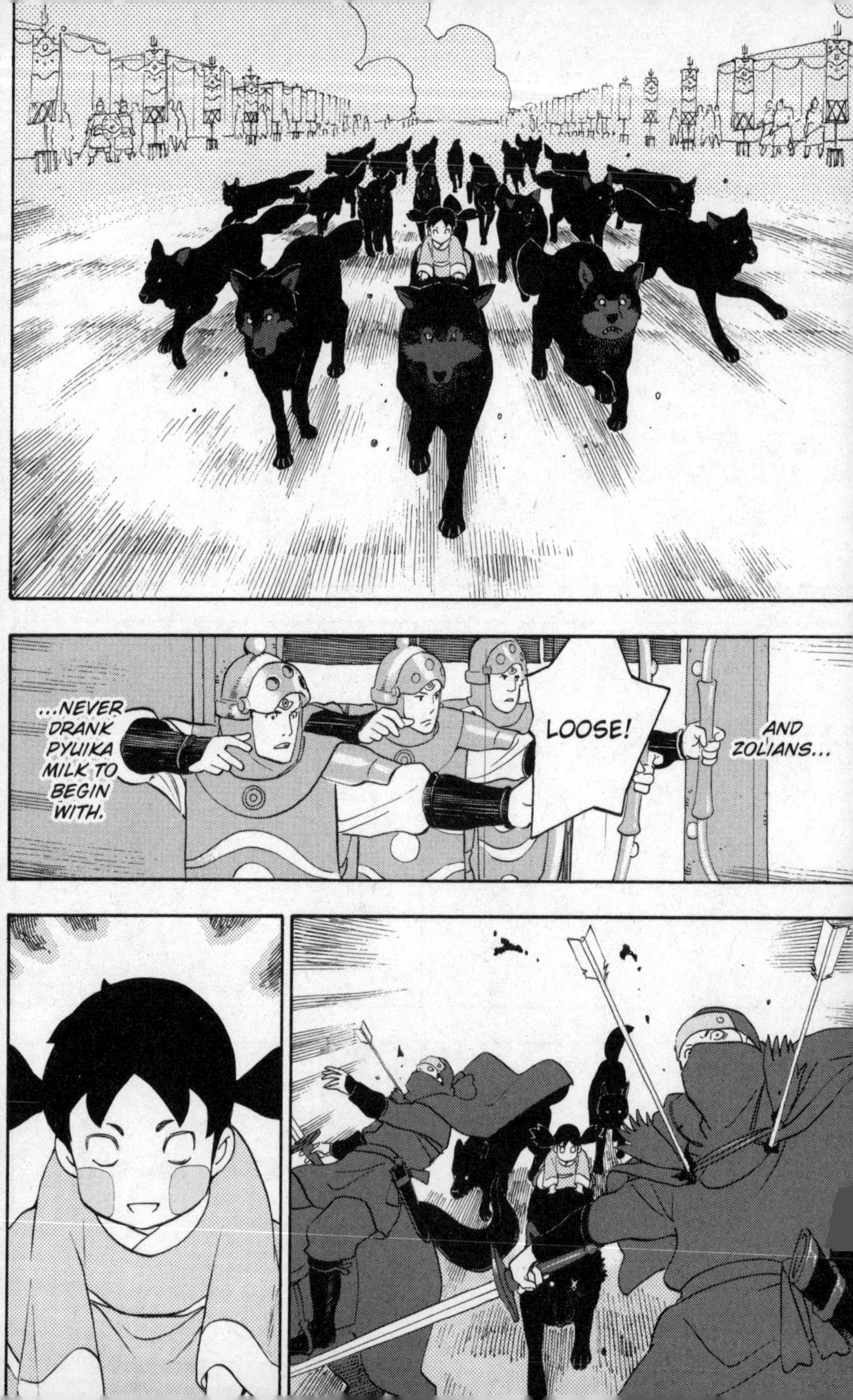
AND ZOLIANS...
LOOSE!
...NEVER DRANK PYUIKA MILK TO BEGIN WITH.

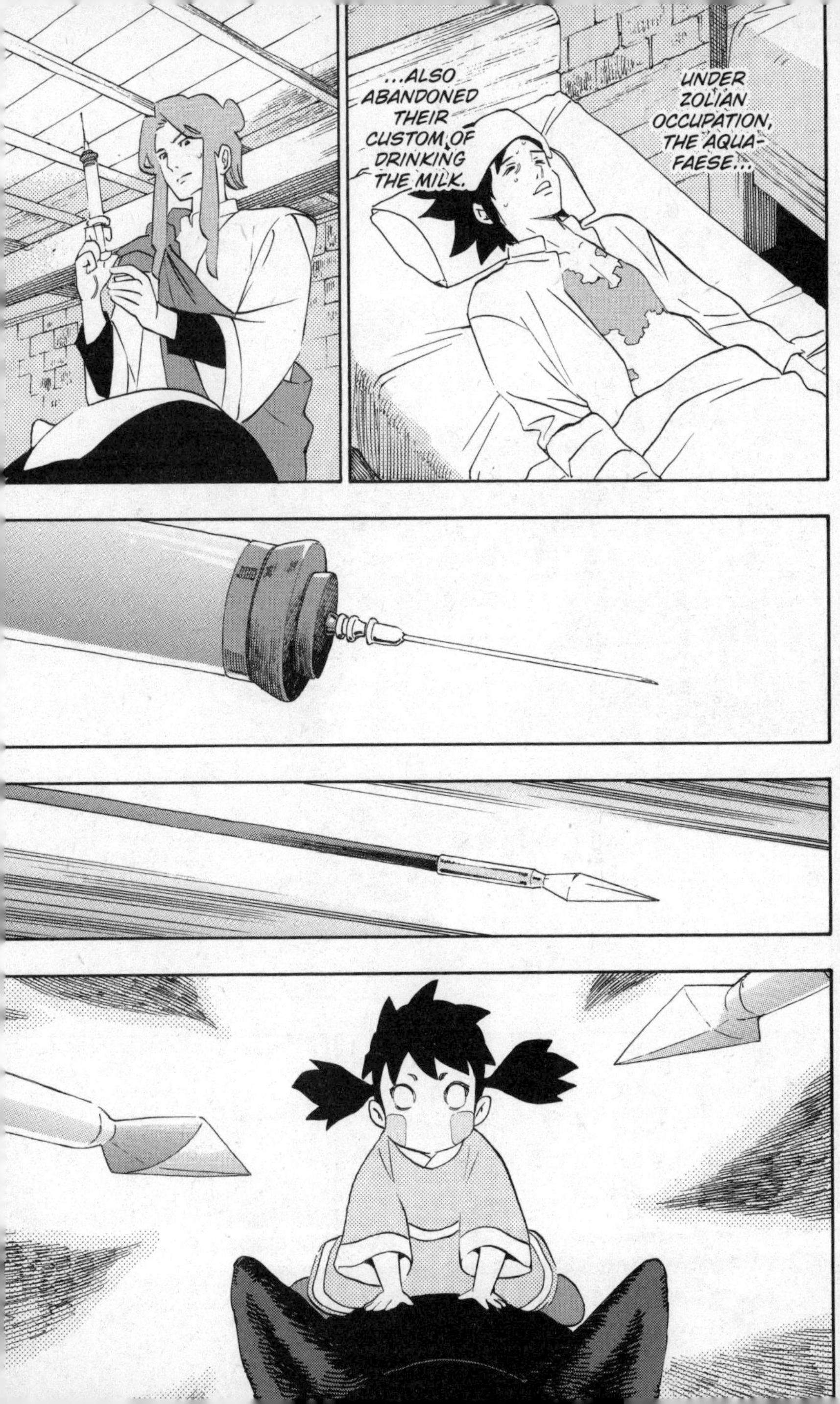
UNDER ZOLIAN OCCUPATION, THE AQUA-FAESE...
...ALSO ABANDONED THEIR CUSTOM OF DRINKING THE MILK.

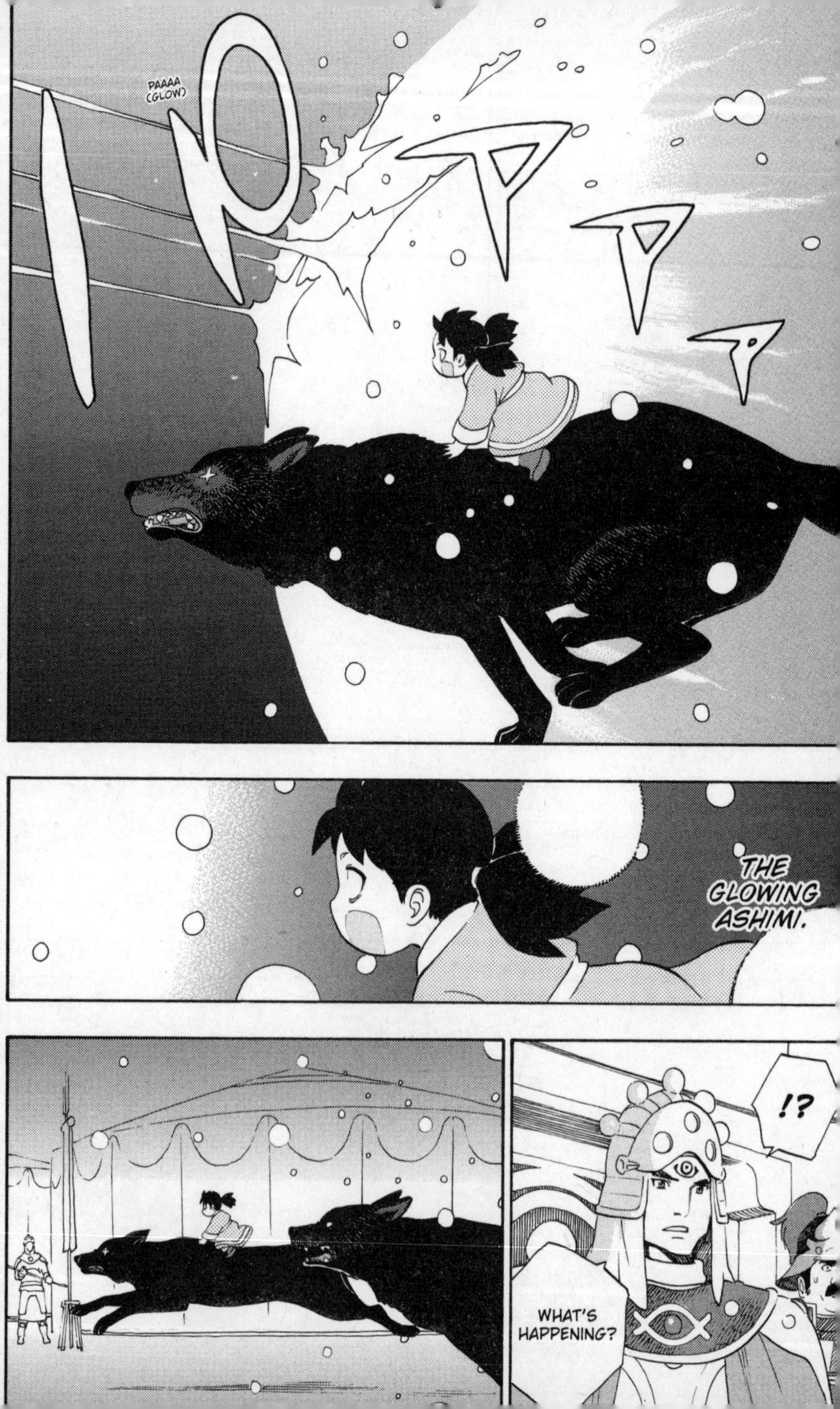
PAAAA (GLOW)
THE GLOWING ASHIMI.
!?
WHAT'S HAPPENING?

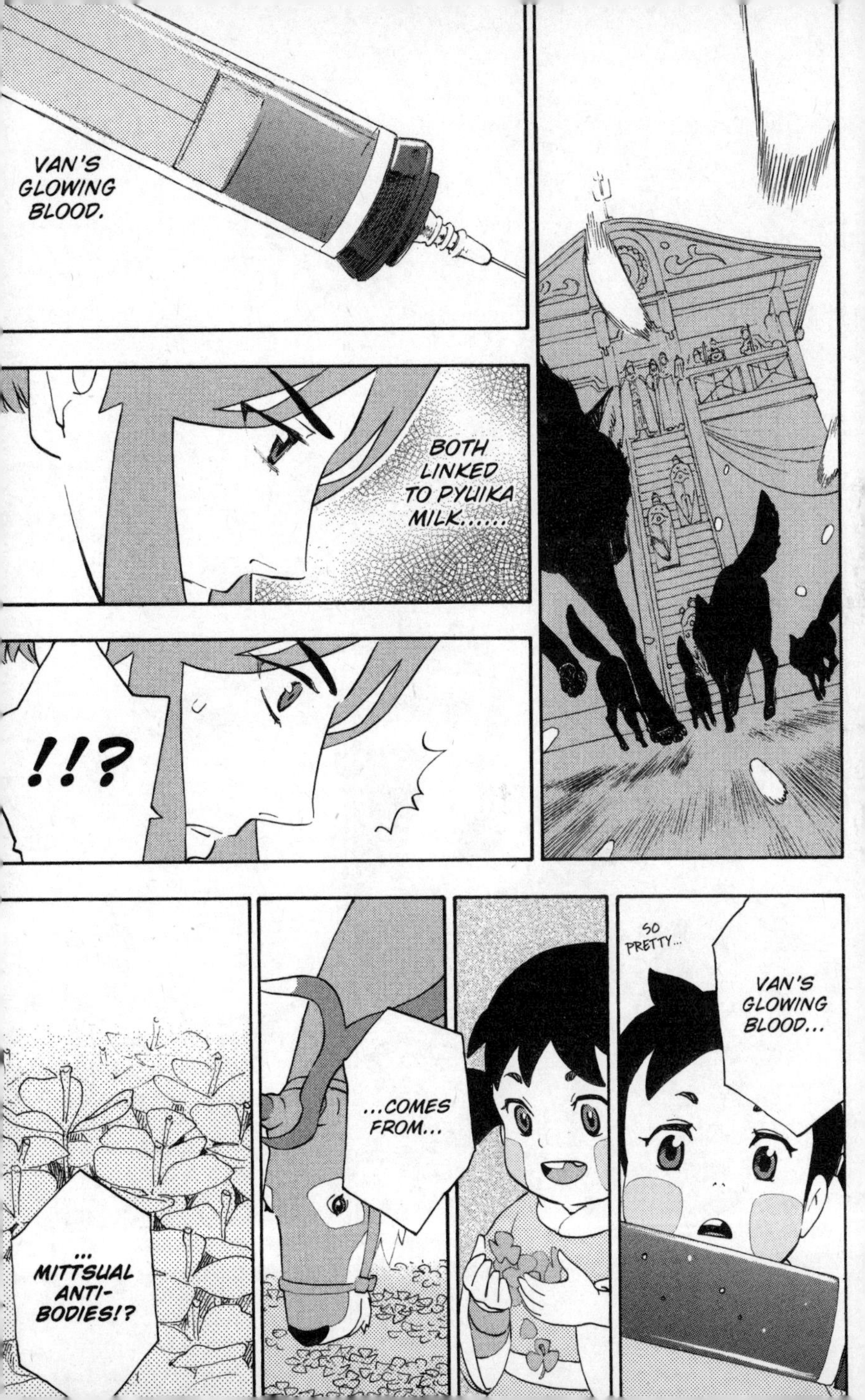
VAN'S GLOWING BLOOD.
BOTH LINKED TO PYUIKA MILK......
!!?
SO PRETTY...
VAN'S GLOWING BLOOD...
...COMES FROM...
... MITTSUAL ANTI-BODIES!?

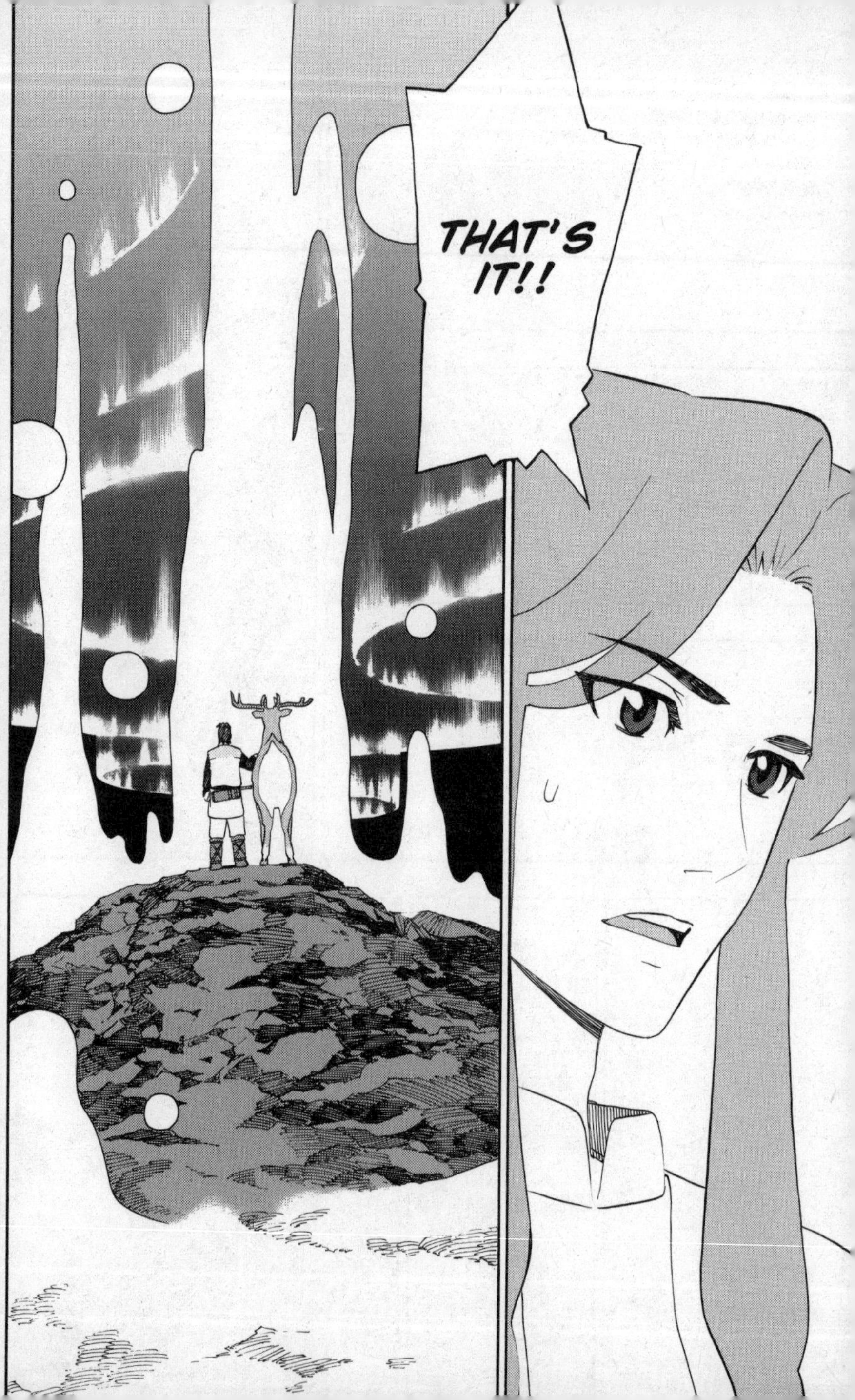
THAT'S IT!!

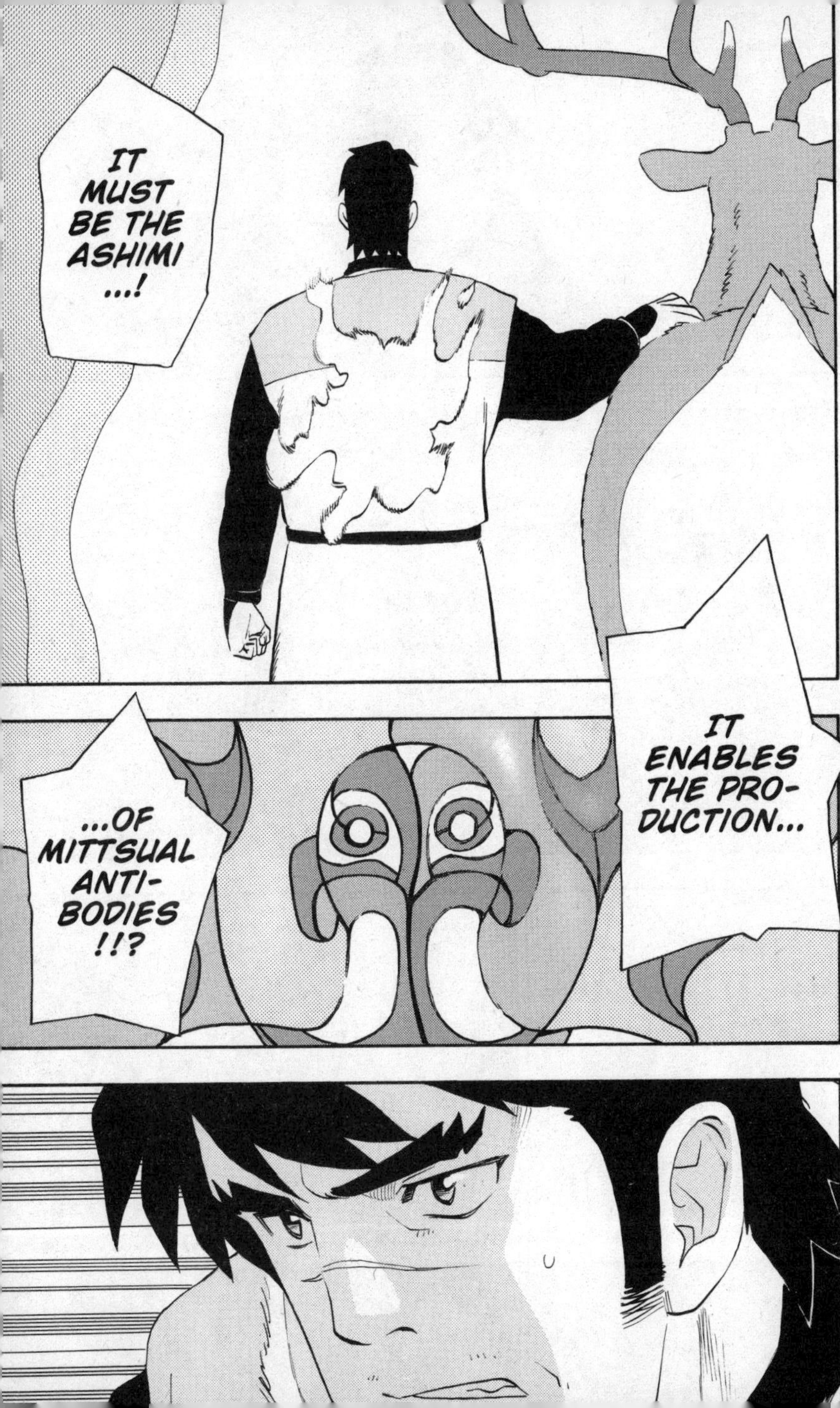
IT MUST BE THE ASHIMI ...!
IT ENABLES THE PRO-DUCTION...
...OF MITTSUAL ANTI-BODIES !!?

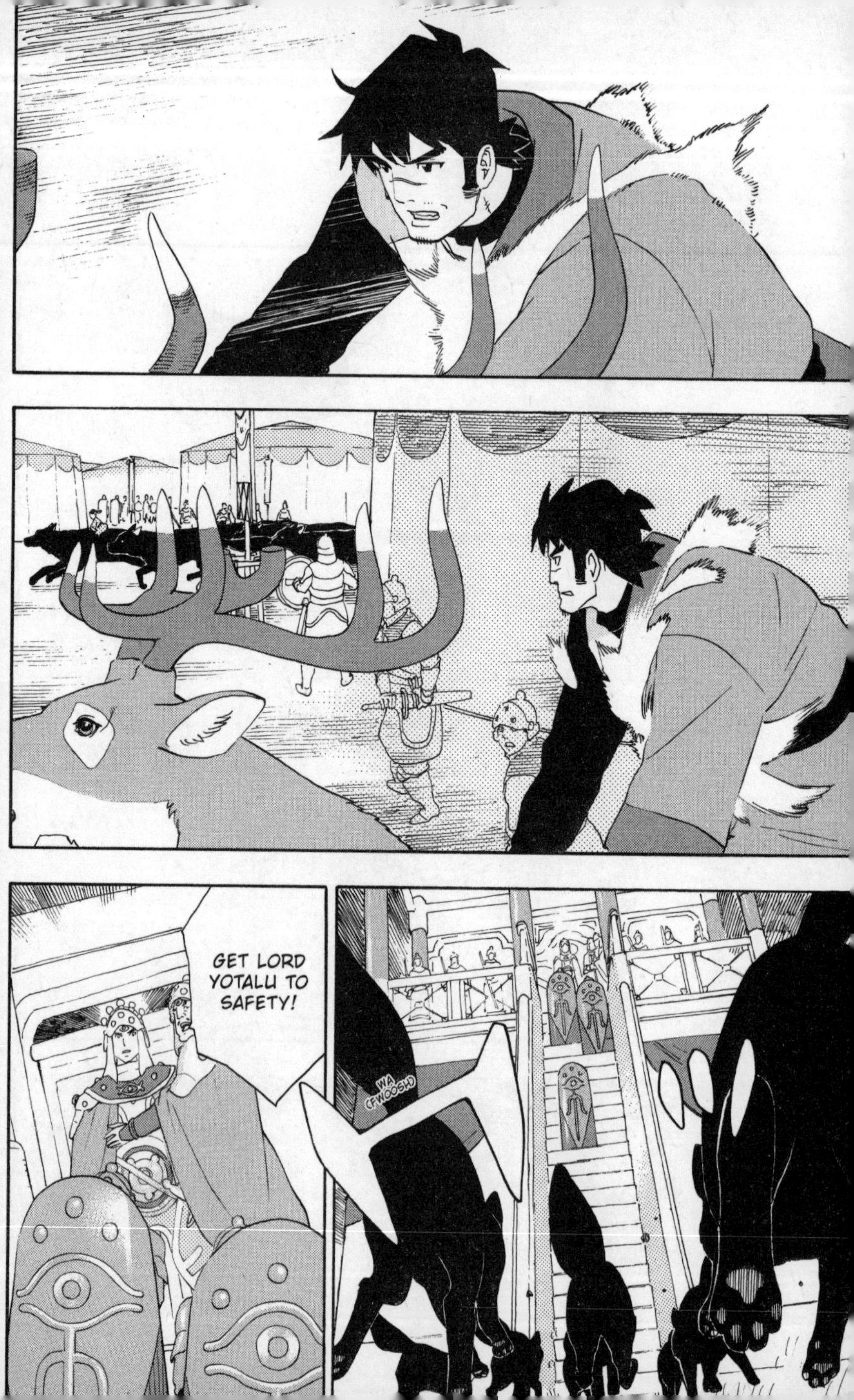
WA (FWOOSH)
GET LORD YOTALU TO SAFETY!

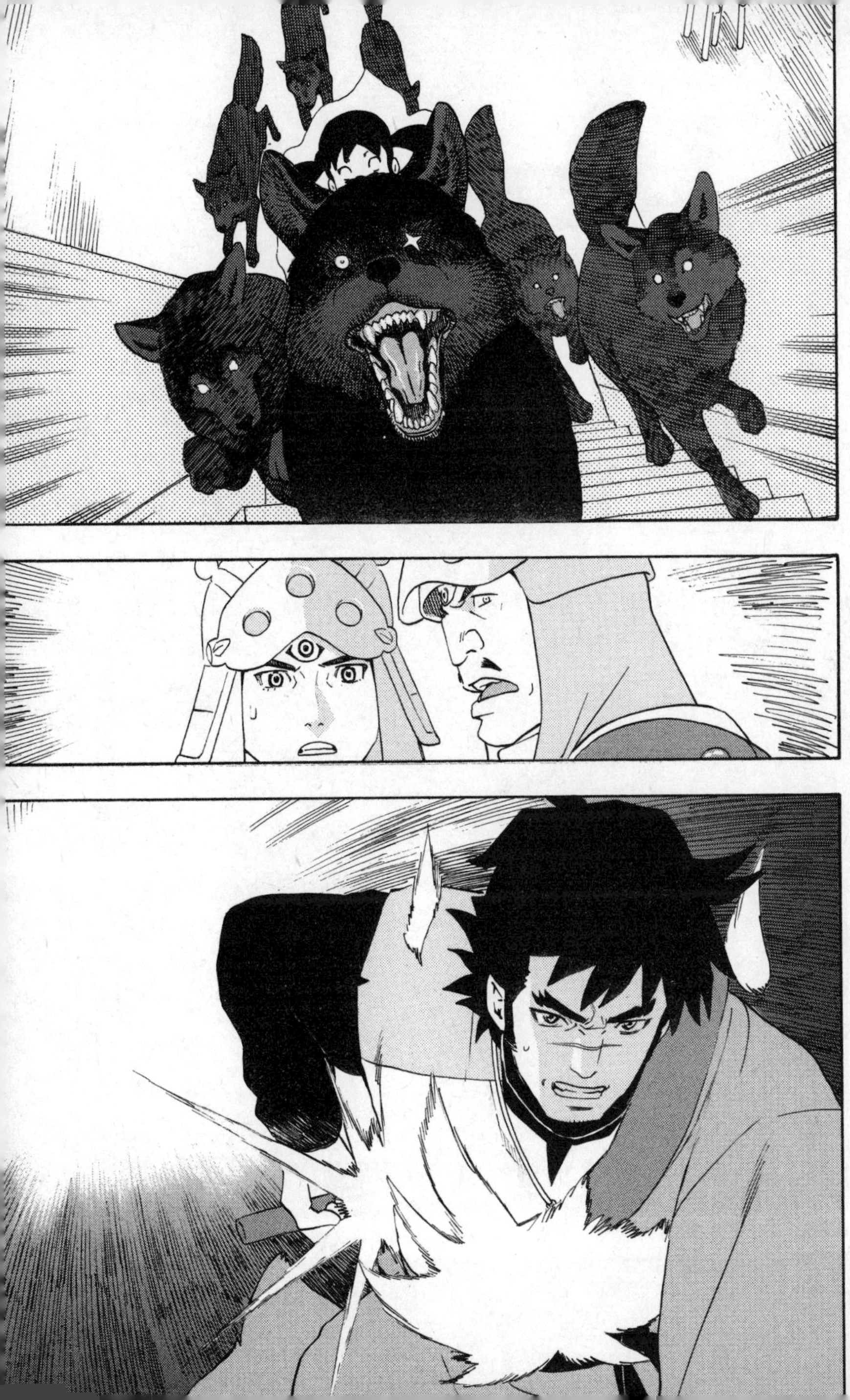

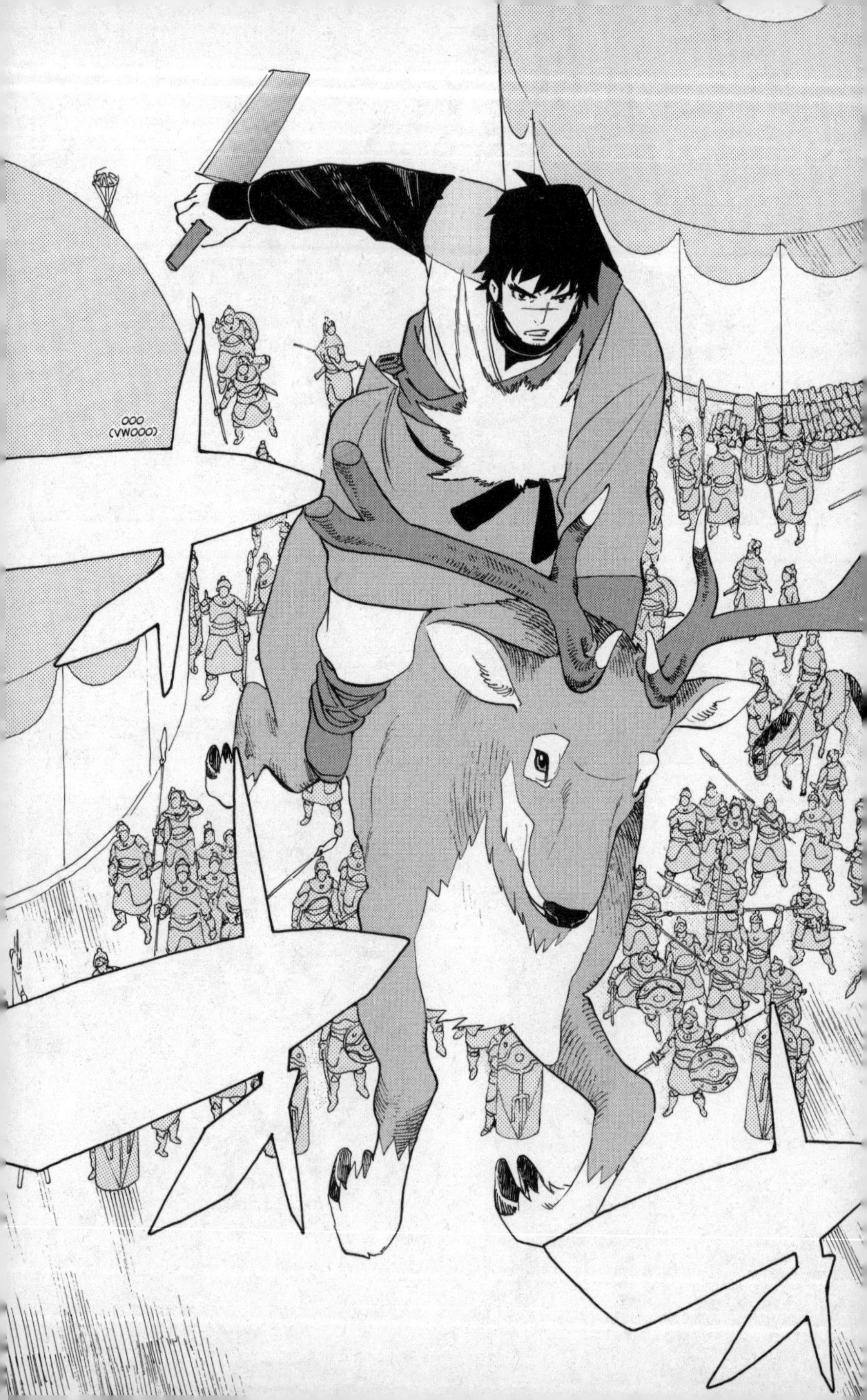
OOO
(VWOOO)

THE
DEER
KING

YUNA AND THE
PROMISED JOURNEY

# Final Chapter:
# Reunion

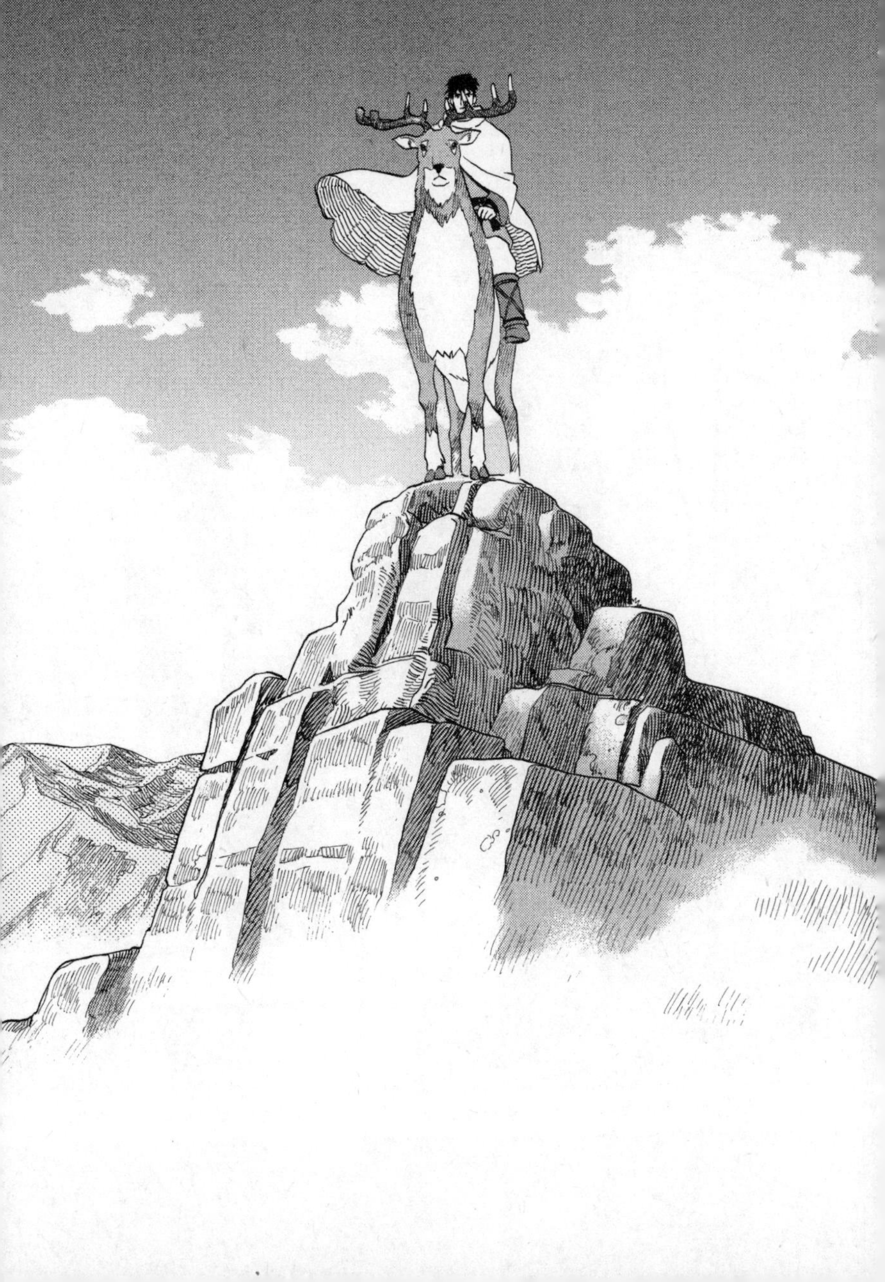

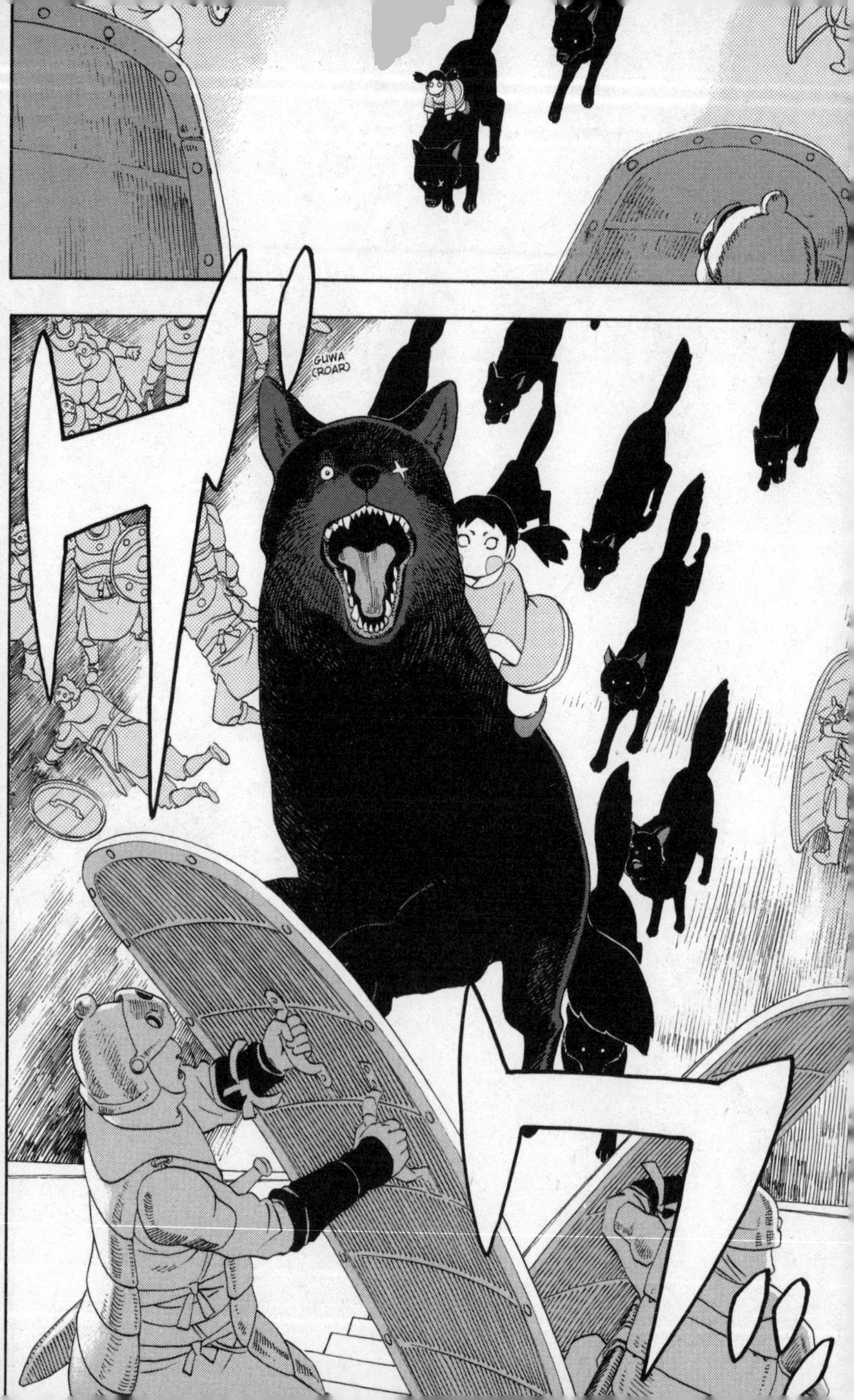
GUWA
(ROAR)

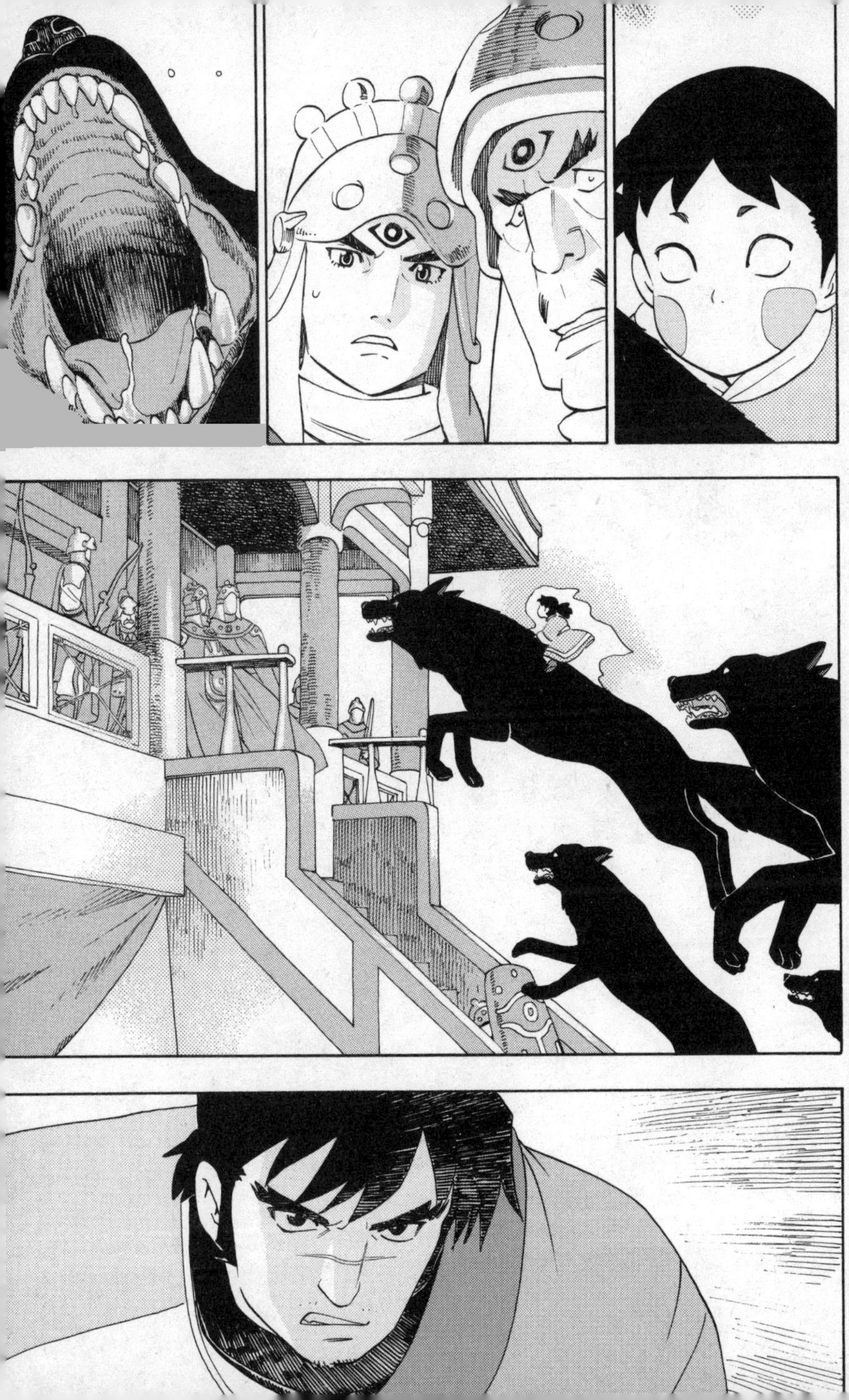

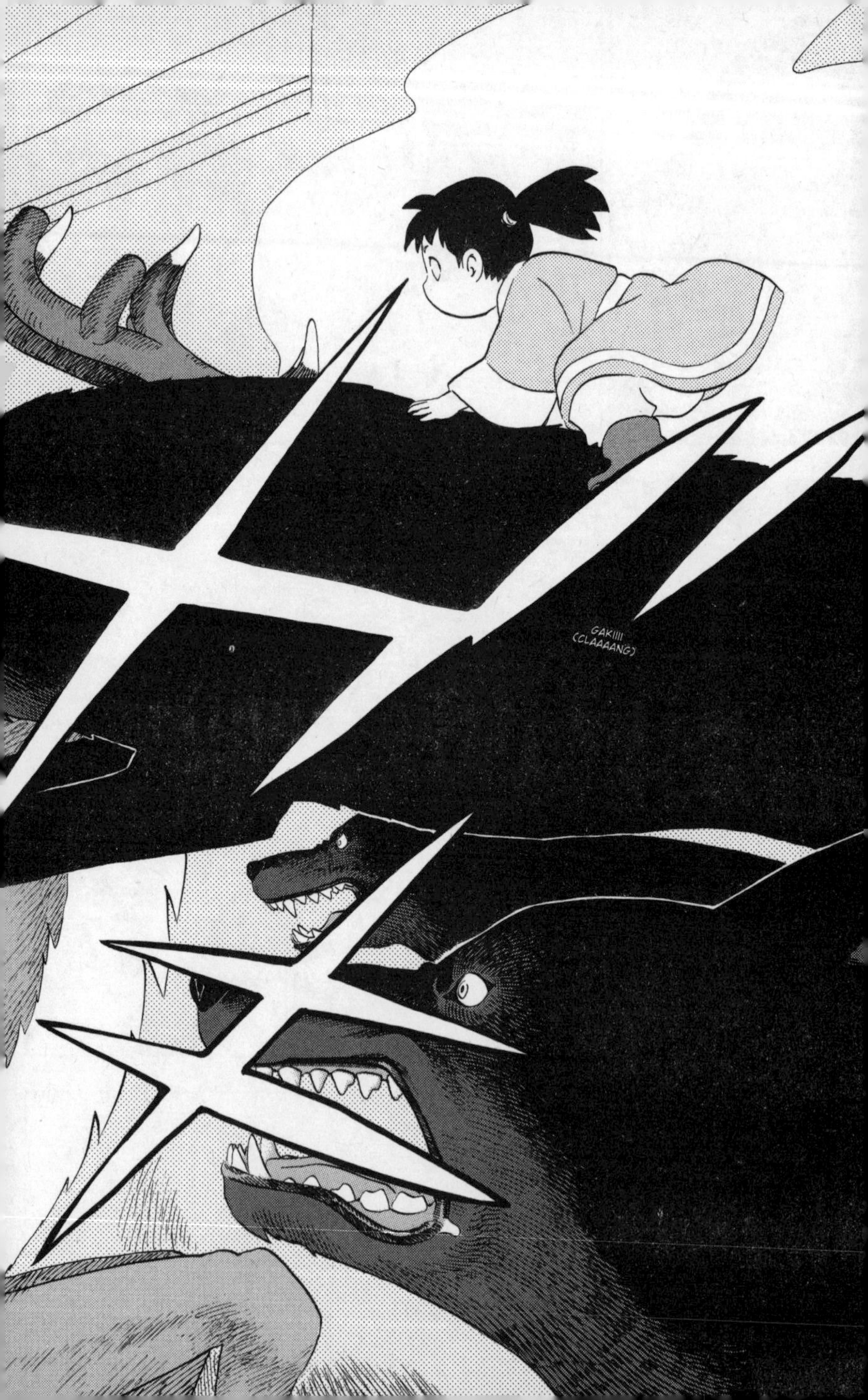
GAKIIII
(CLAAAANG)

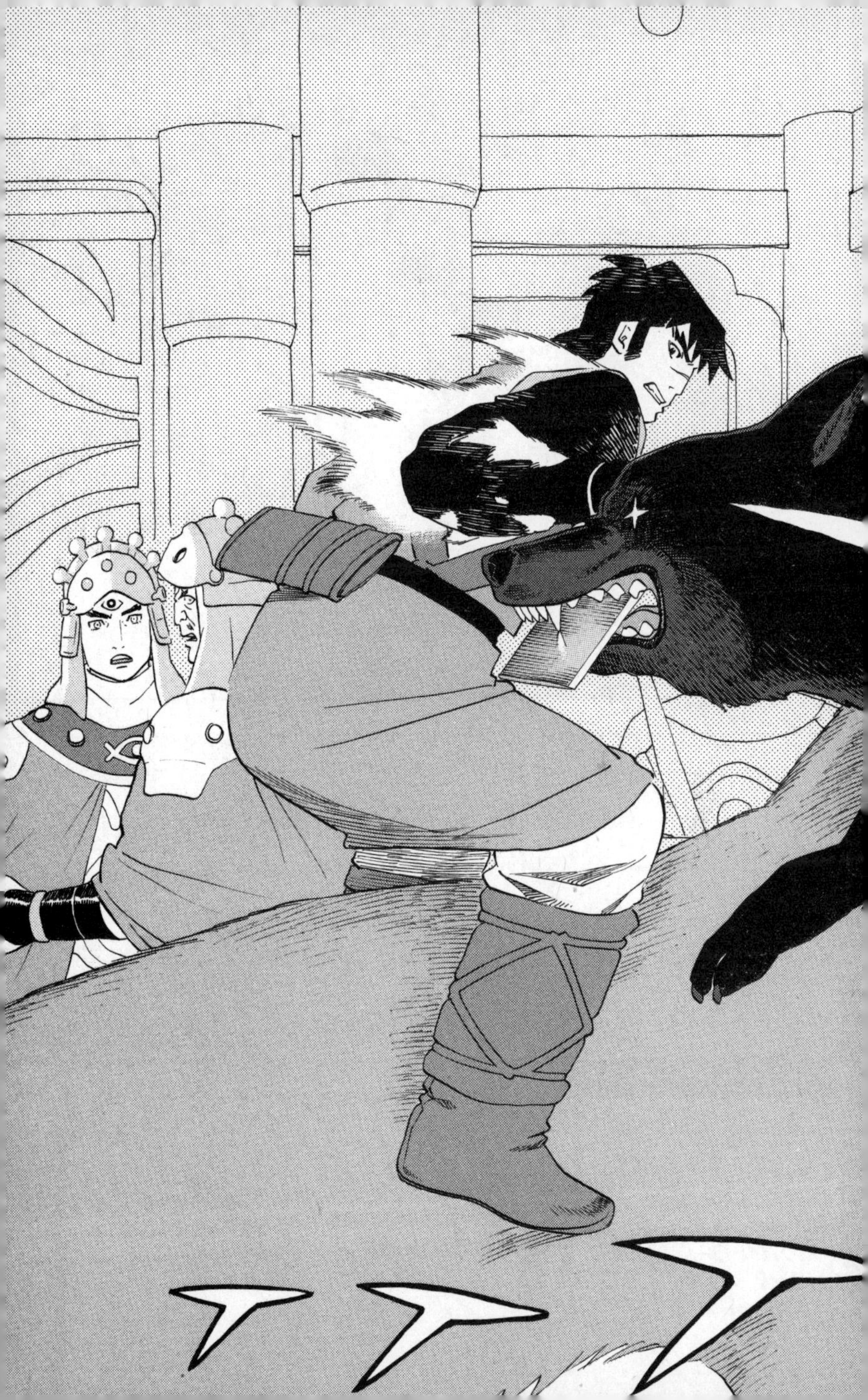

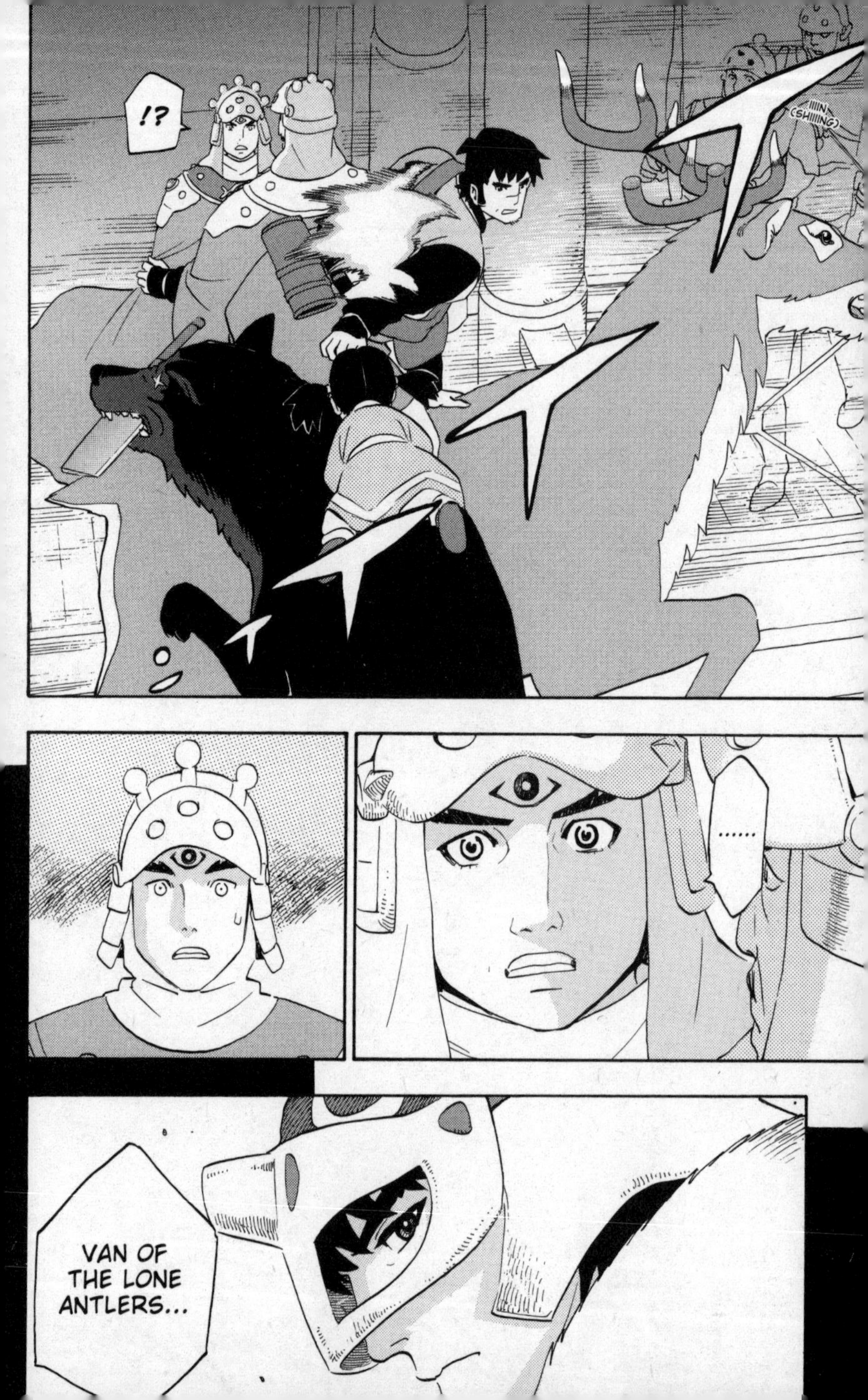

IIIIN (SHIIIING)
!?
......
VAN OF THE LONE ANTLERS...

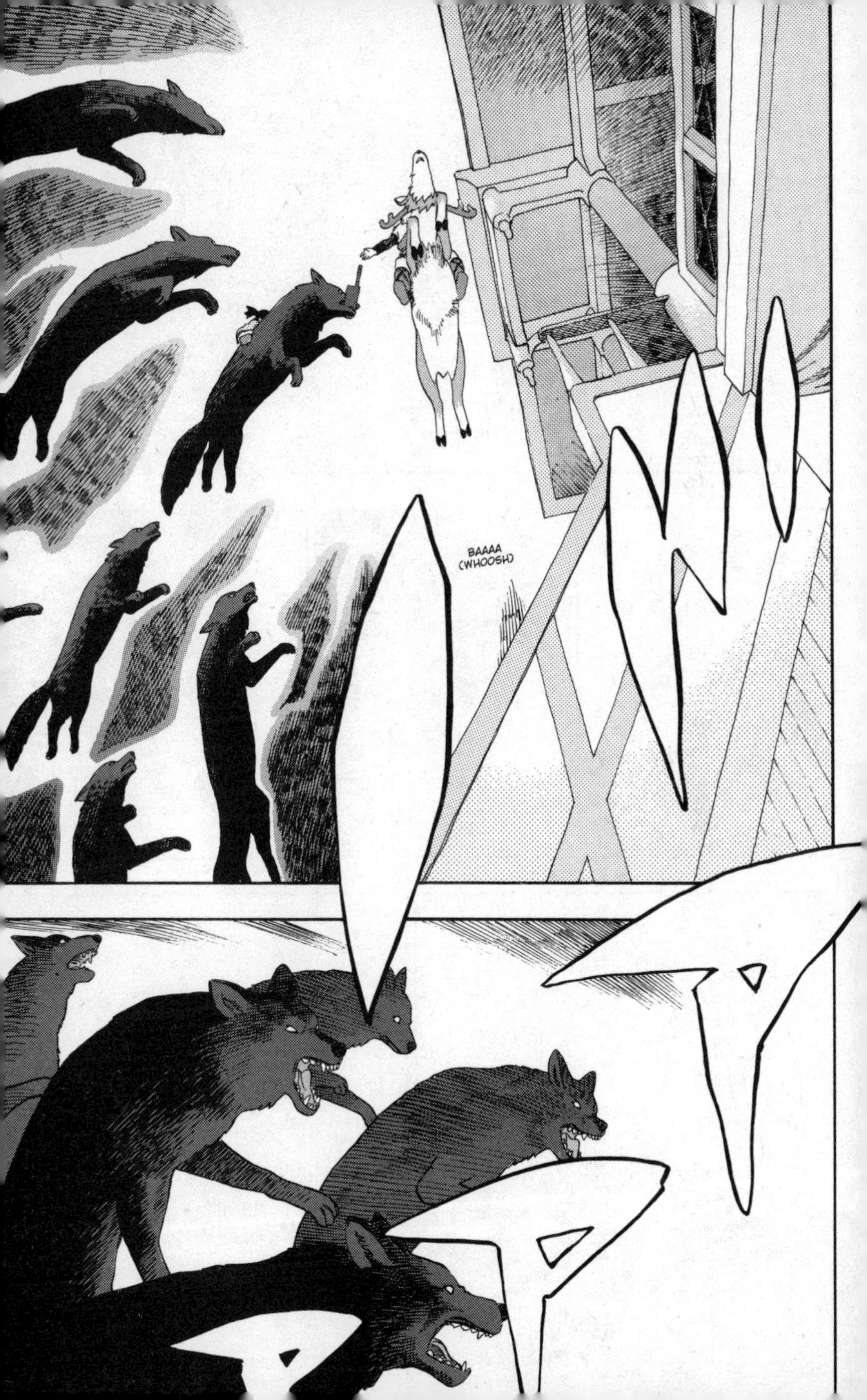
BAAAA
(WHOOSH)

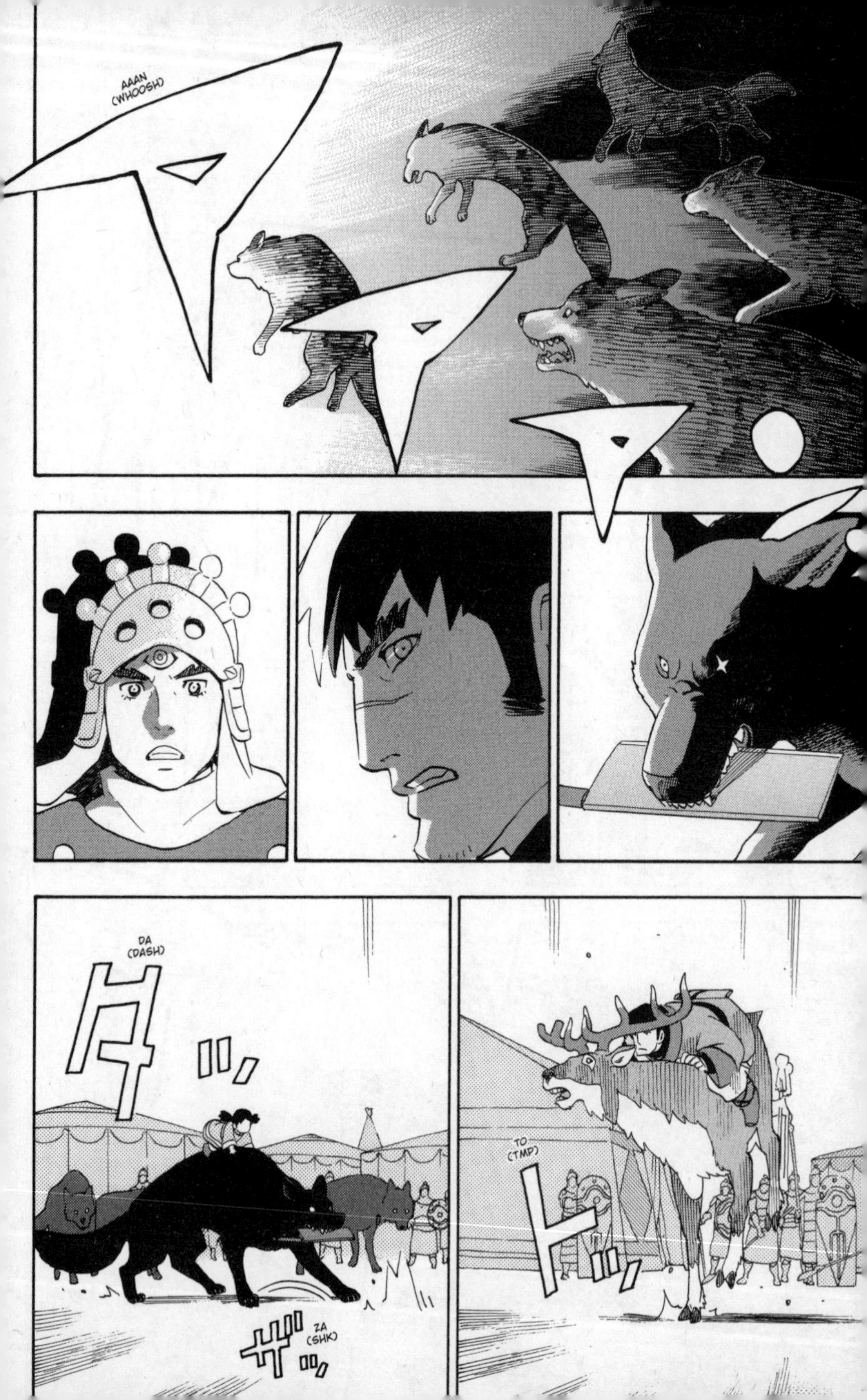
AAAN
(WHOOSH)
TO
(TMP)
DA
(DASH)
ZA
(SHK)

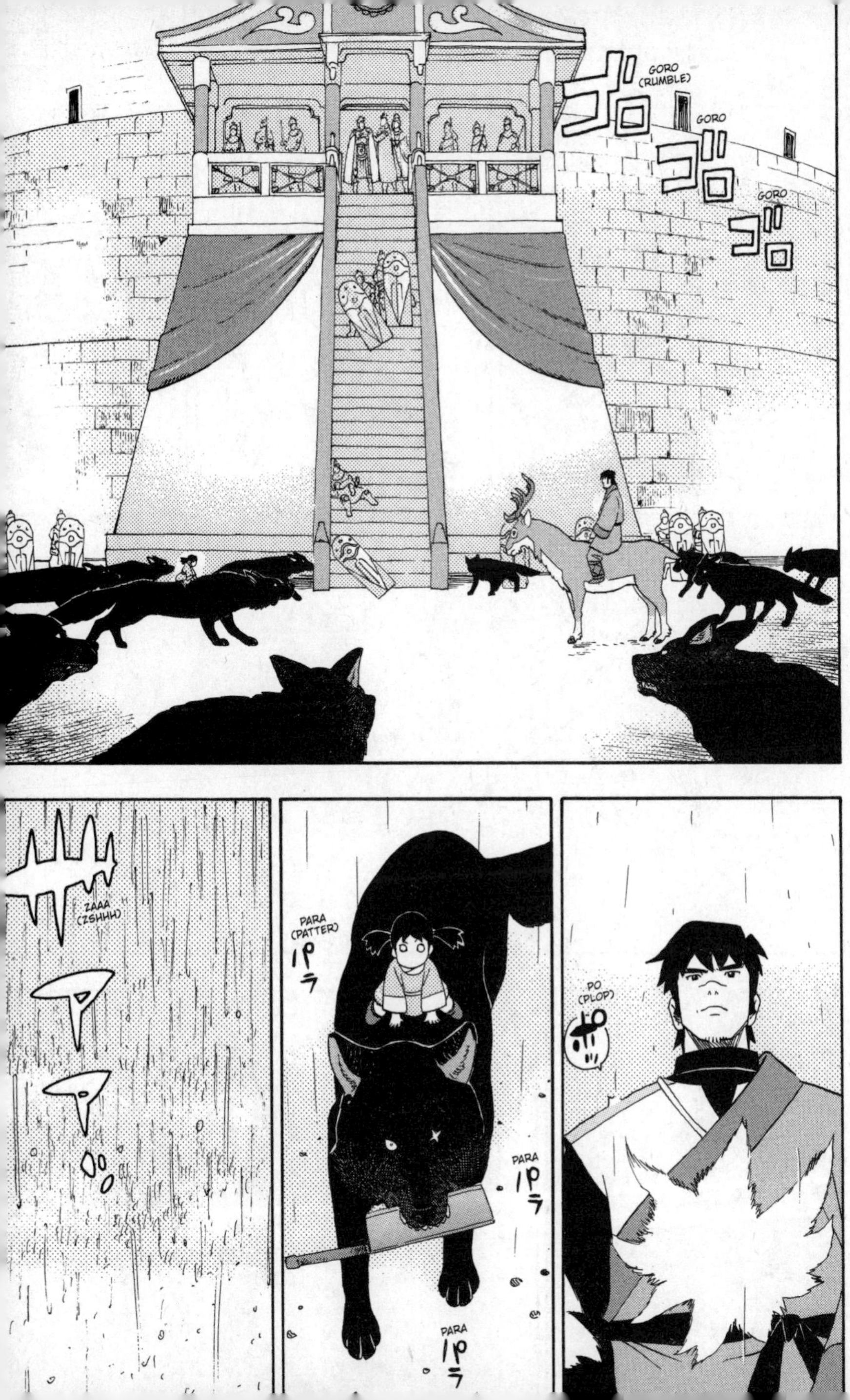GORO (RUMBLE)
GORO
GORO
PO (PLOP)
PARA (PATTER)
PARA
PARA
ZAAA (ZSHHH)

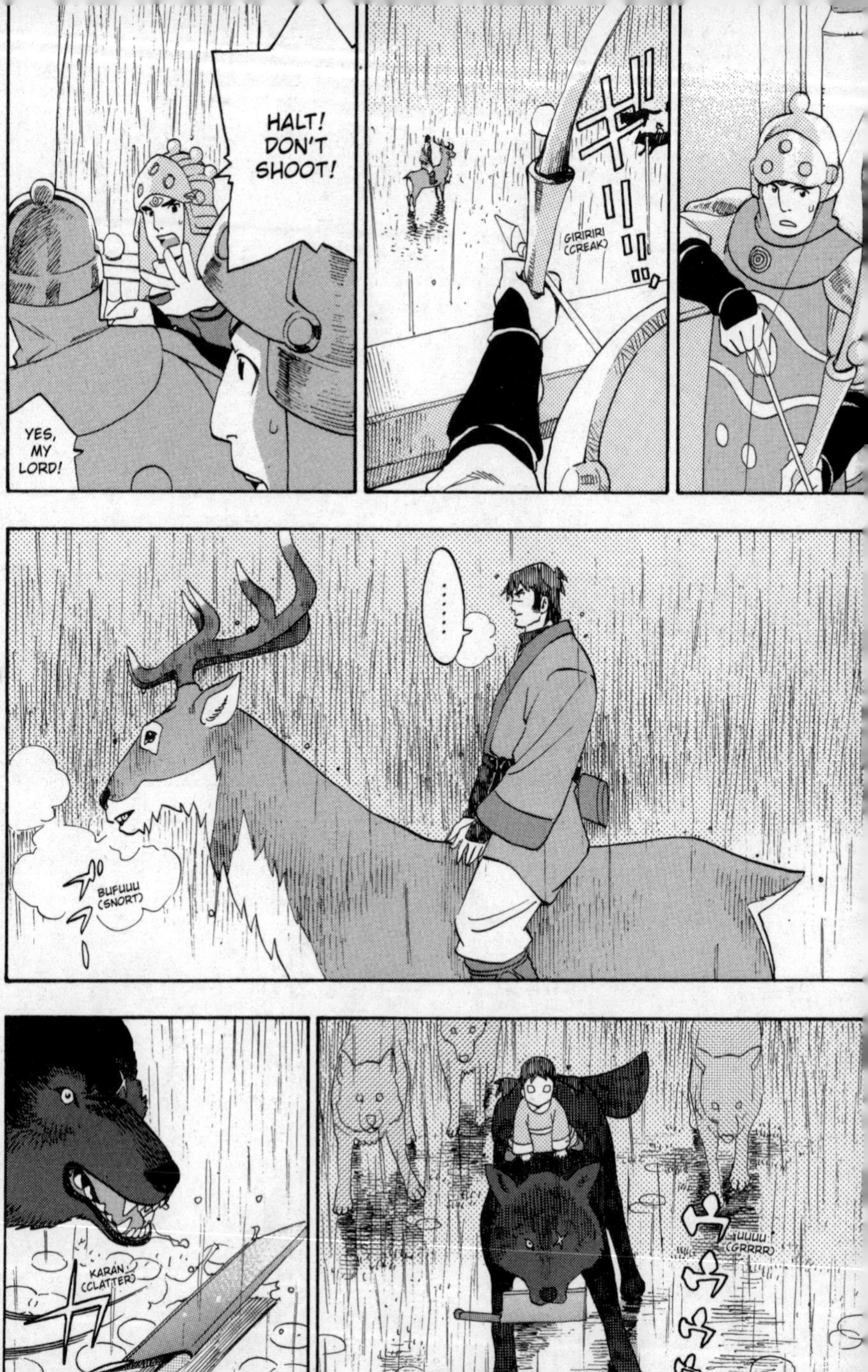
GIRIRIRI (CREAK)
HALT! DON'T SHOOT!
YES, MY LORD!
......
BUFUUU (SNORT)
UUUUU (GRRRR)
KARAN (CLATTER)

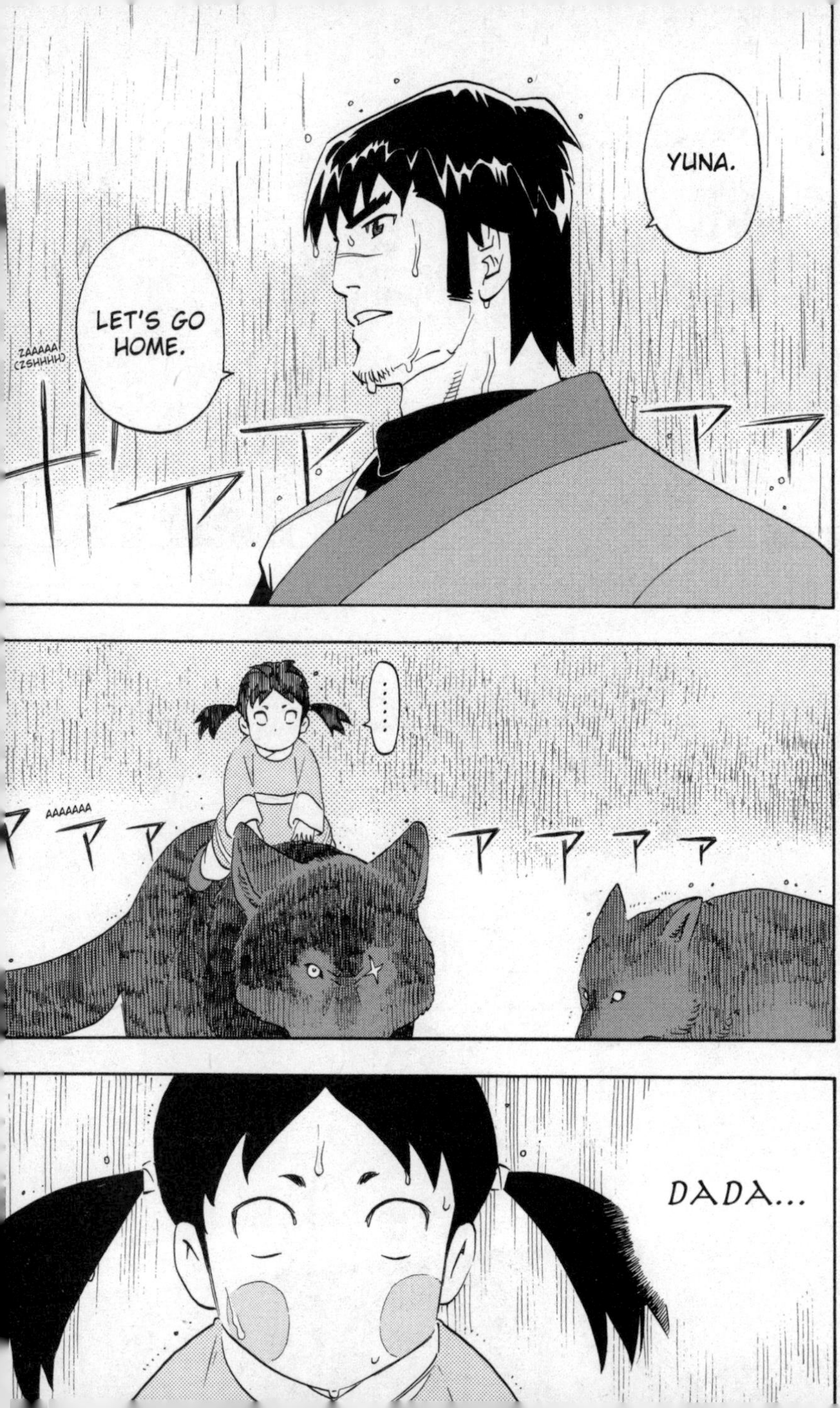
YUNA.
LET'S GO HOME.
ZAAAAA (ZSHHHH)
...
AAAAAAA
DADA...

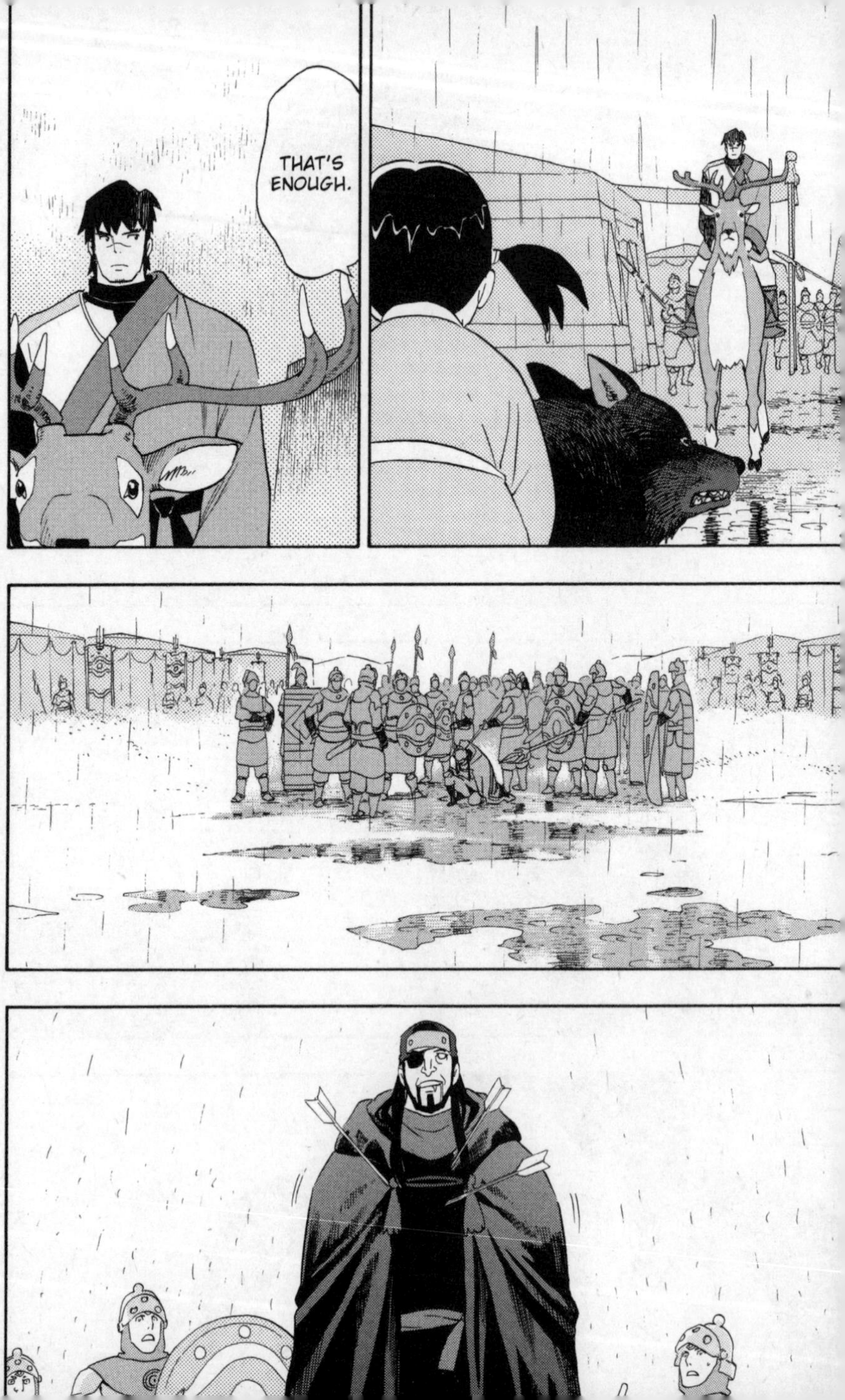
THAT'S ENOUGH.

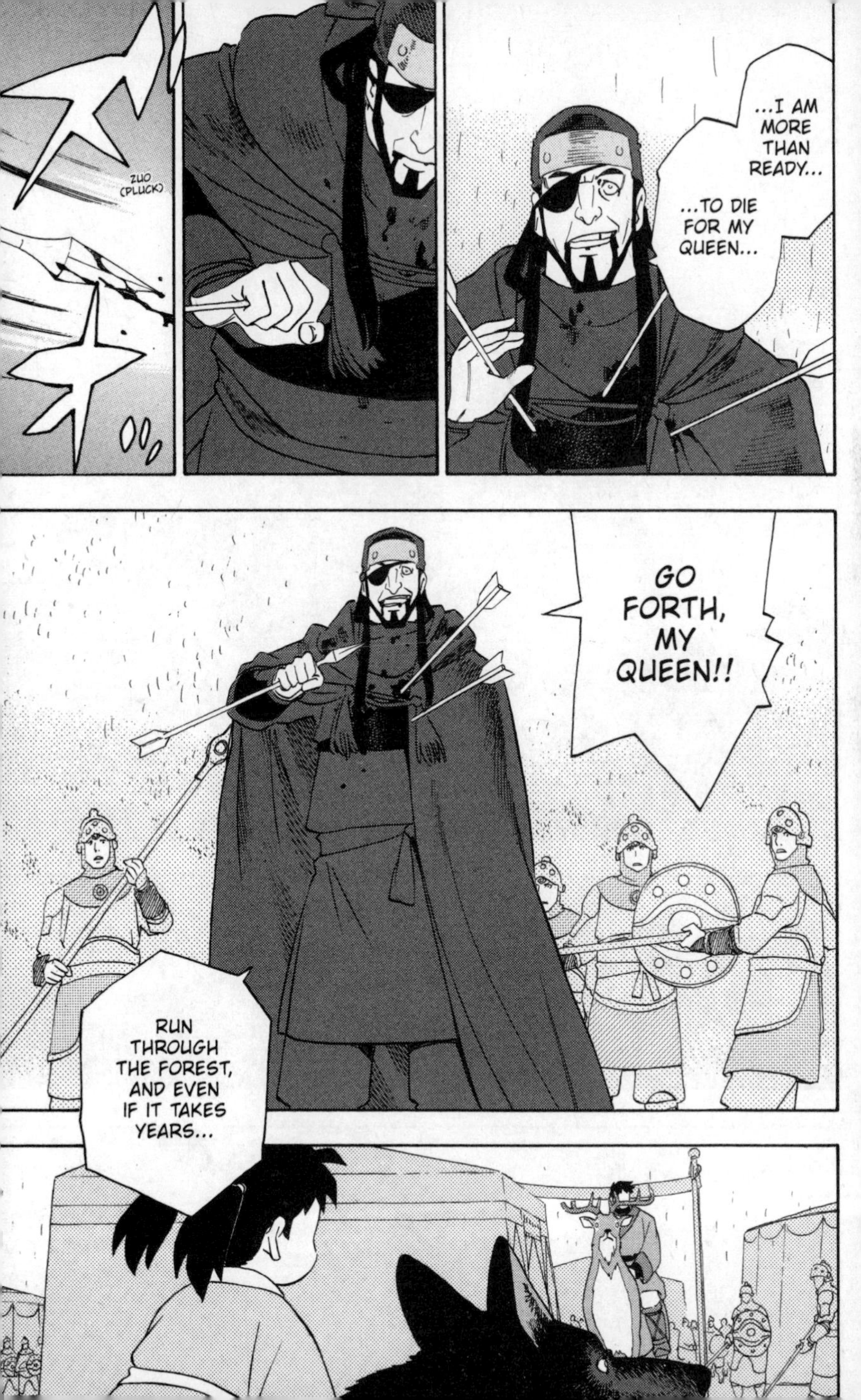
...I AM MORE THAN READY...
...TO DIE FOR MY QUEEN...
ZUO (PLUCK)
GO FORTH, MY QUEEN!!
RUN THROUGH THE FOREST, AND EVEN IF IT TAKES YEARS...

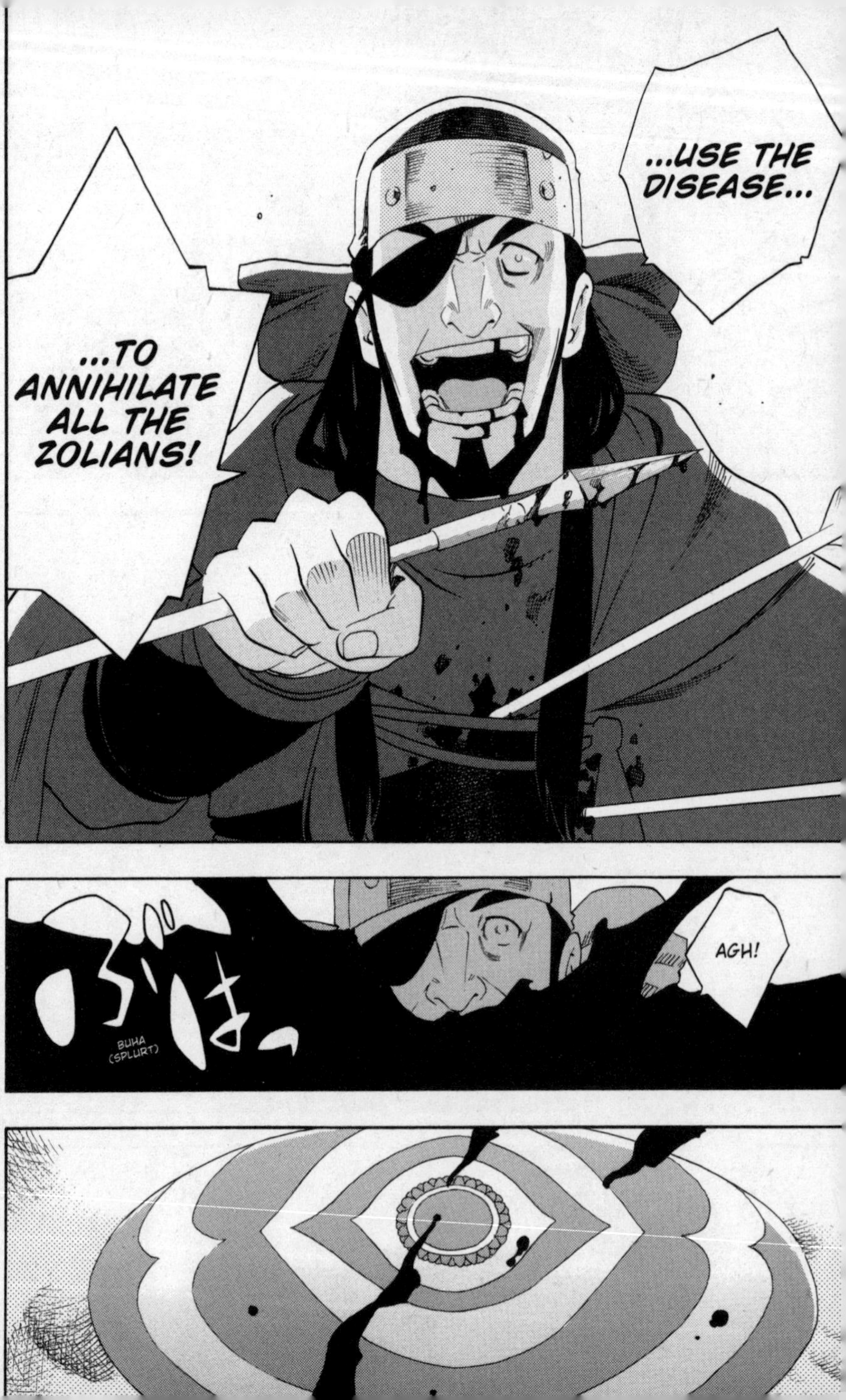
...USE THE DISEASE...
...TO ANNIHILATE ALL THE ZOLIANS!
AGH!
BUHA (SPLURT)

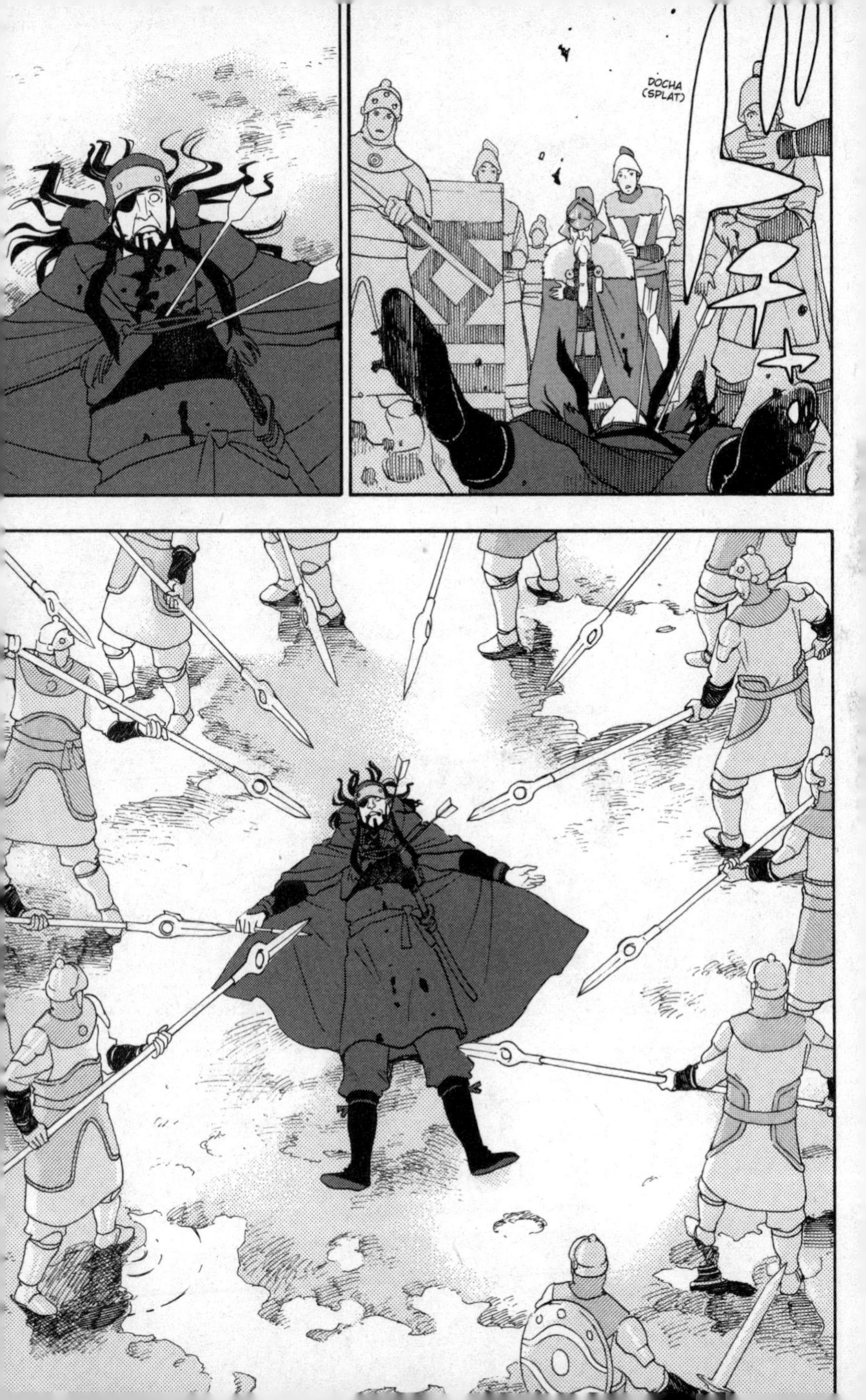
DOCHA
(SPLAT)

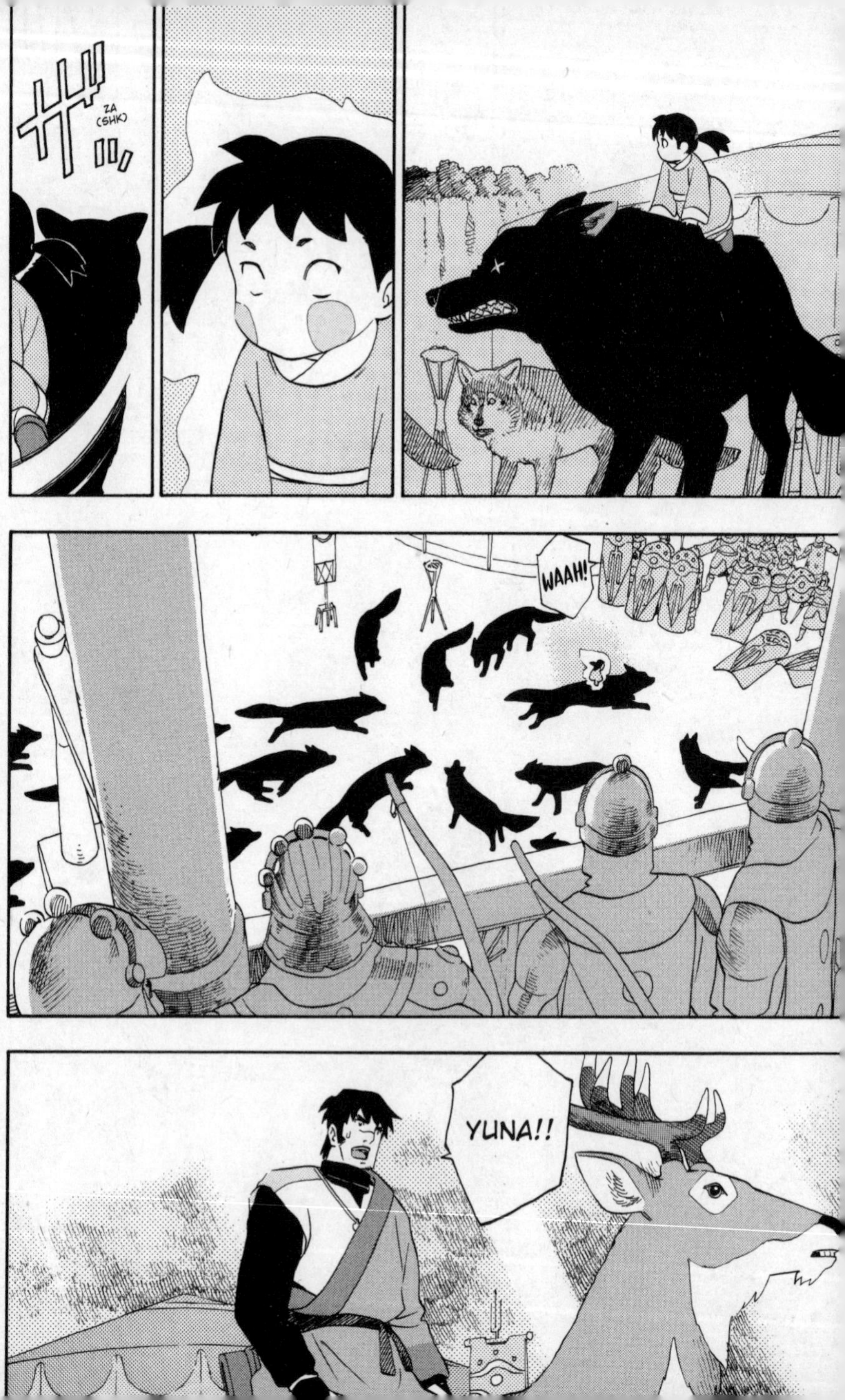
ZA
(SHK)
WAAH!
YUNA!!

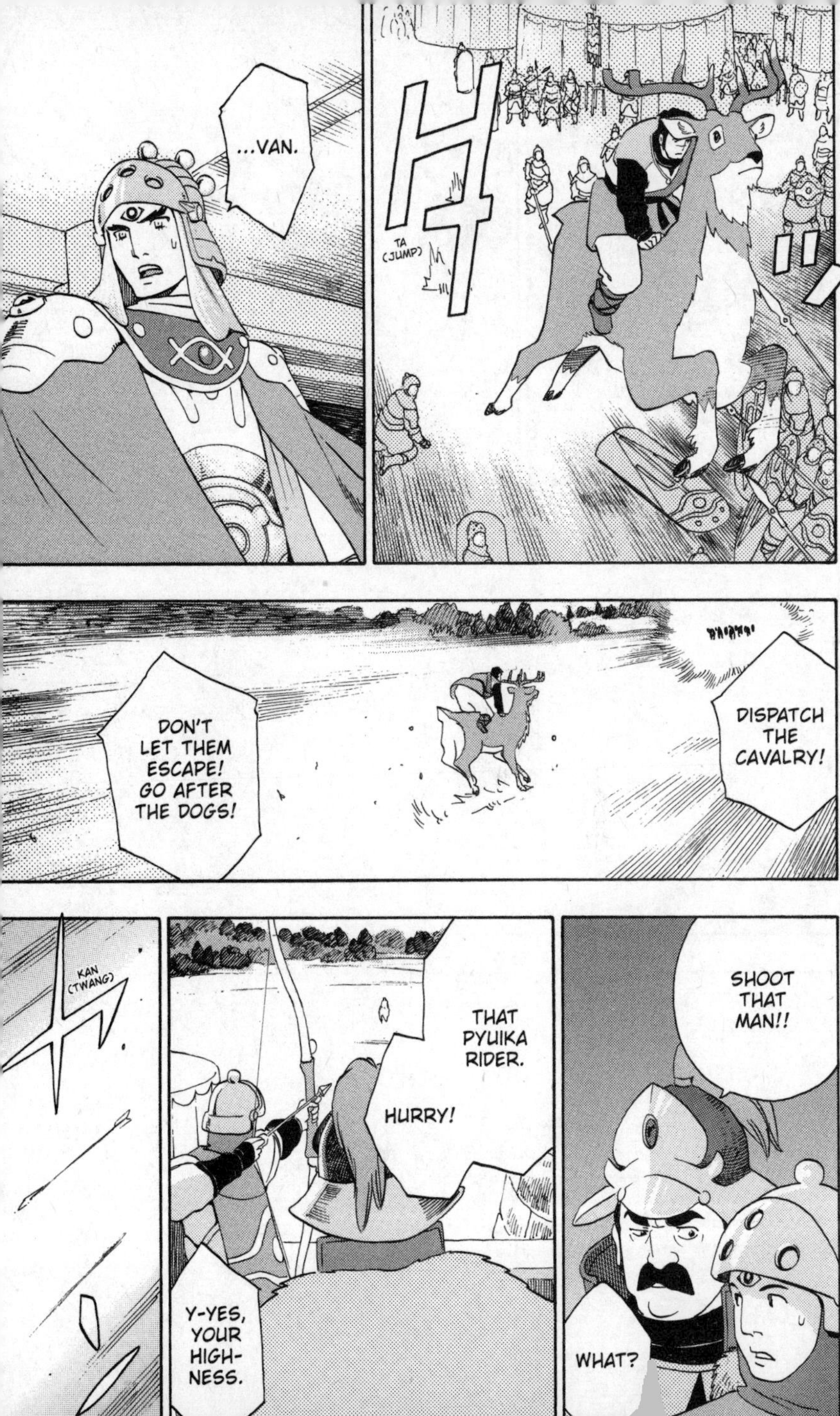
TA (JUMP)
...VAN.
DISPATCH THE CAVALRY!
DON'T LET THEM ESCAPE! GO AFTER THE DOGS!
SHOOT THAT MAN!!
WHAT?
THAT PYUIKA RIDER.
HURRY!
Y-YES, YOUR HIGHNESS.
KAN (TWANG)

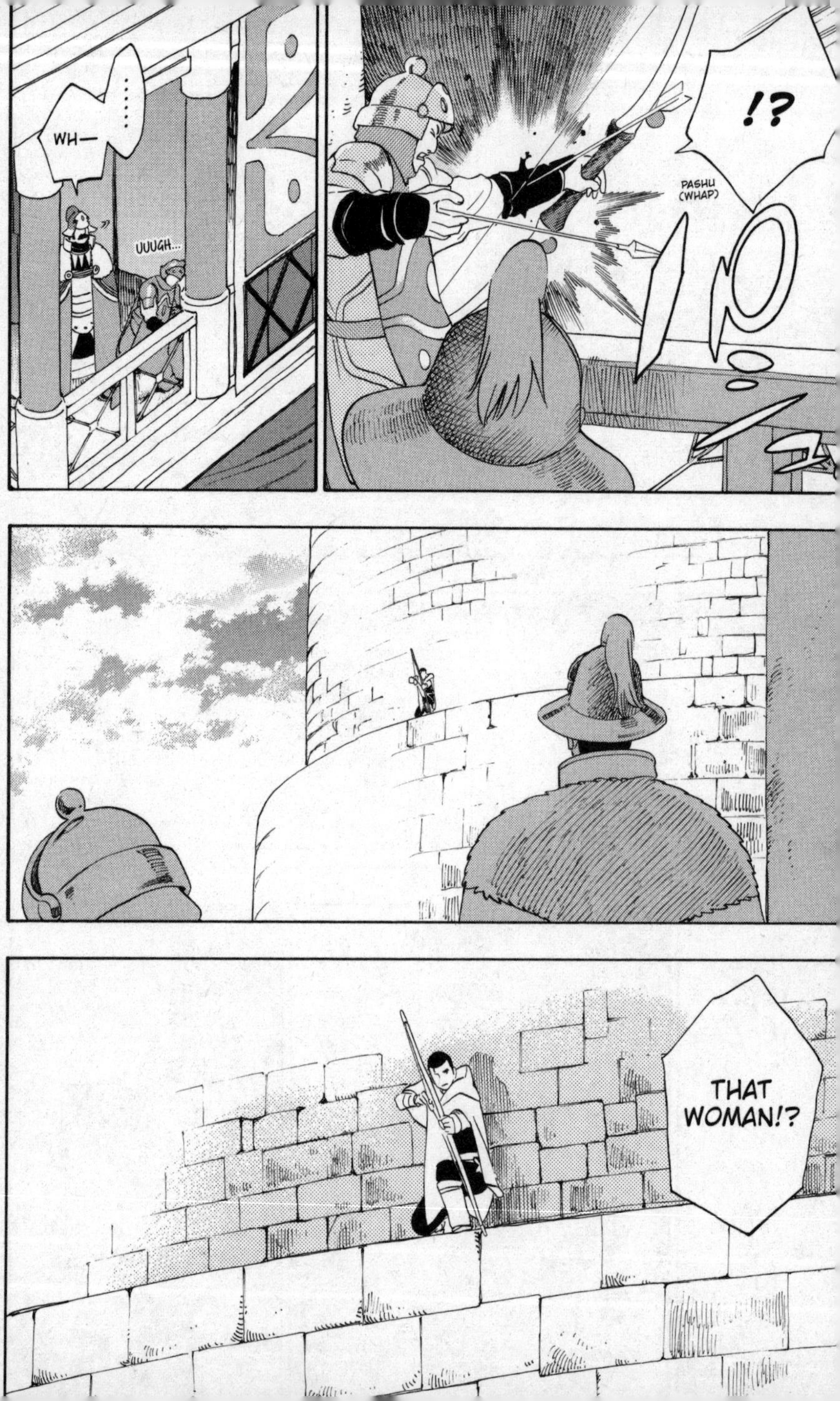
!?
PASHU (WHAP)
......
WH—
UUUGH...
THAT WOMAN!?

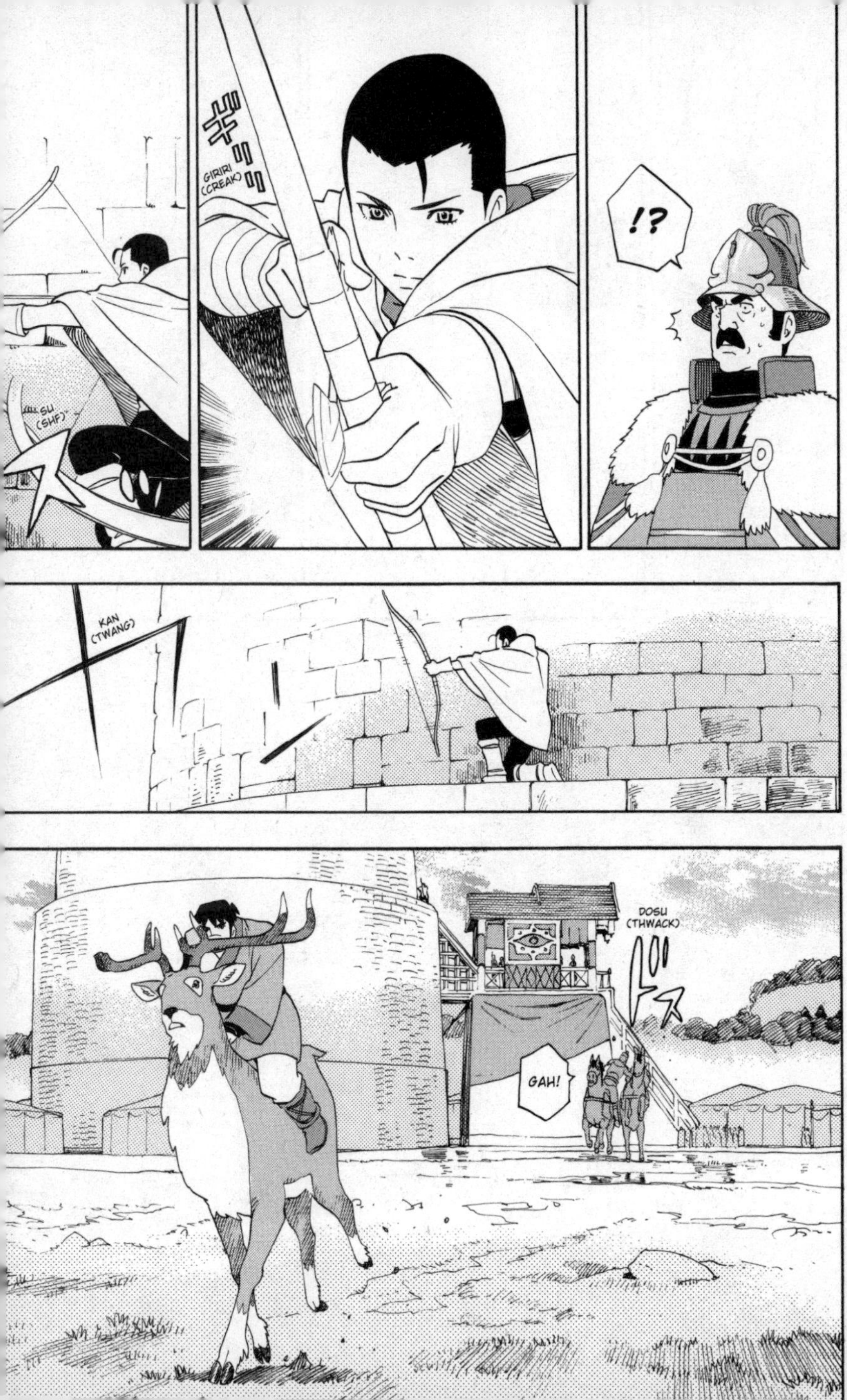
!?
GIRIRI (CREAK)
SU (SHF)
KAN (TWANG)
DOSU (THWACK)
GAH!

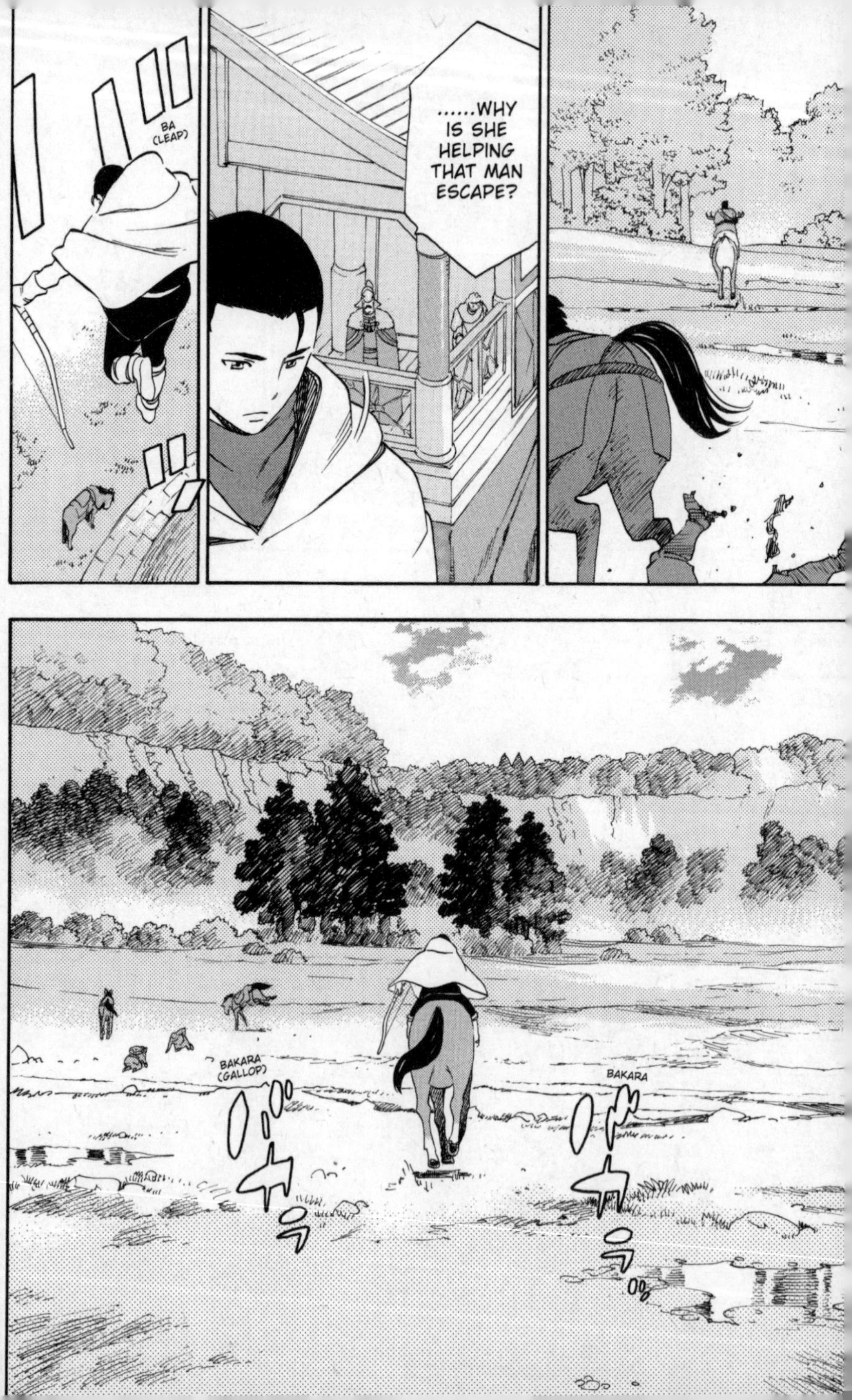
......WHY IS SHE HELPING THAT MAN ESCAPE?
BA (LEAP)
BAKARA
BAKARA (GALLOP)

YOU WANT US TO PROCEED AS PLANNED AND INVADE FIRE HORSE TOWN...

...AS SOON AS THE RANKS ARE DRESSED!?

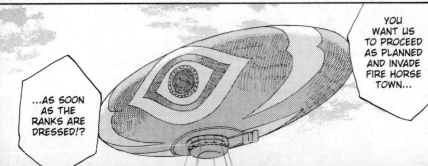

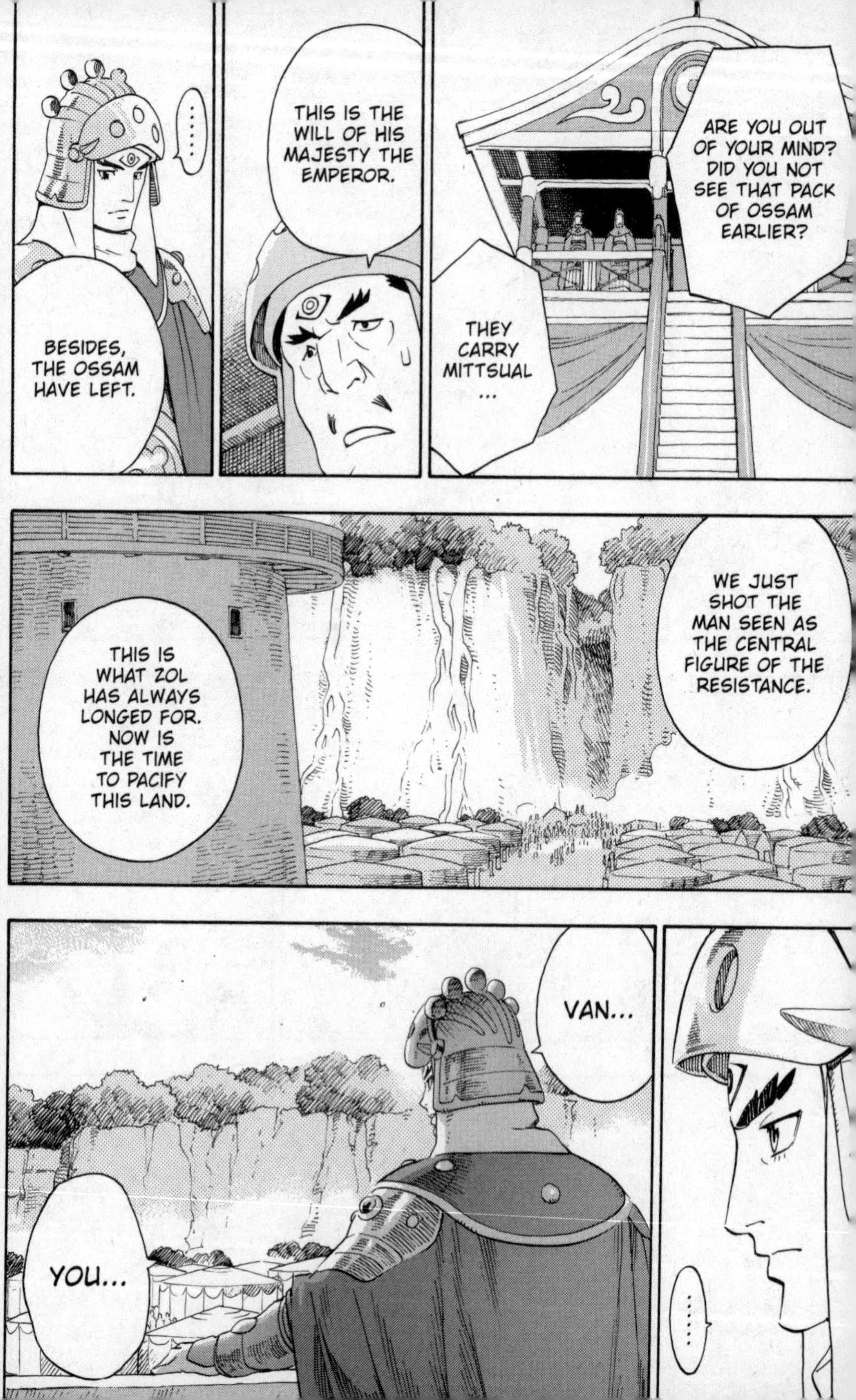
ARE YOU OUT OF YOUR MIND? DID YOU NOT SEE THAT PACK OF OSSAM EARLIER?
THEY CARRY MITTSUAL...
THIS IS THE WILL OF HIS MAJESTY THE EMPEROR.
......
BESIDES, THE OSSAM HAVE LEFT.
WE JUST SHOT THE MAN SEEN AS THE CENTRAL FIGURE OF THE RESISTANCE.
THIS IS WHAT ZOL HAS ALWAYS LONGED FOR. NOW IS THE TIME TO PACIFY THIS LAND.
......
VAN...
YOU...

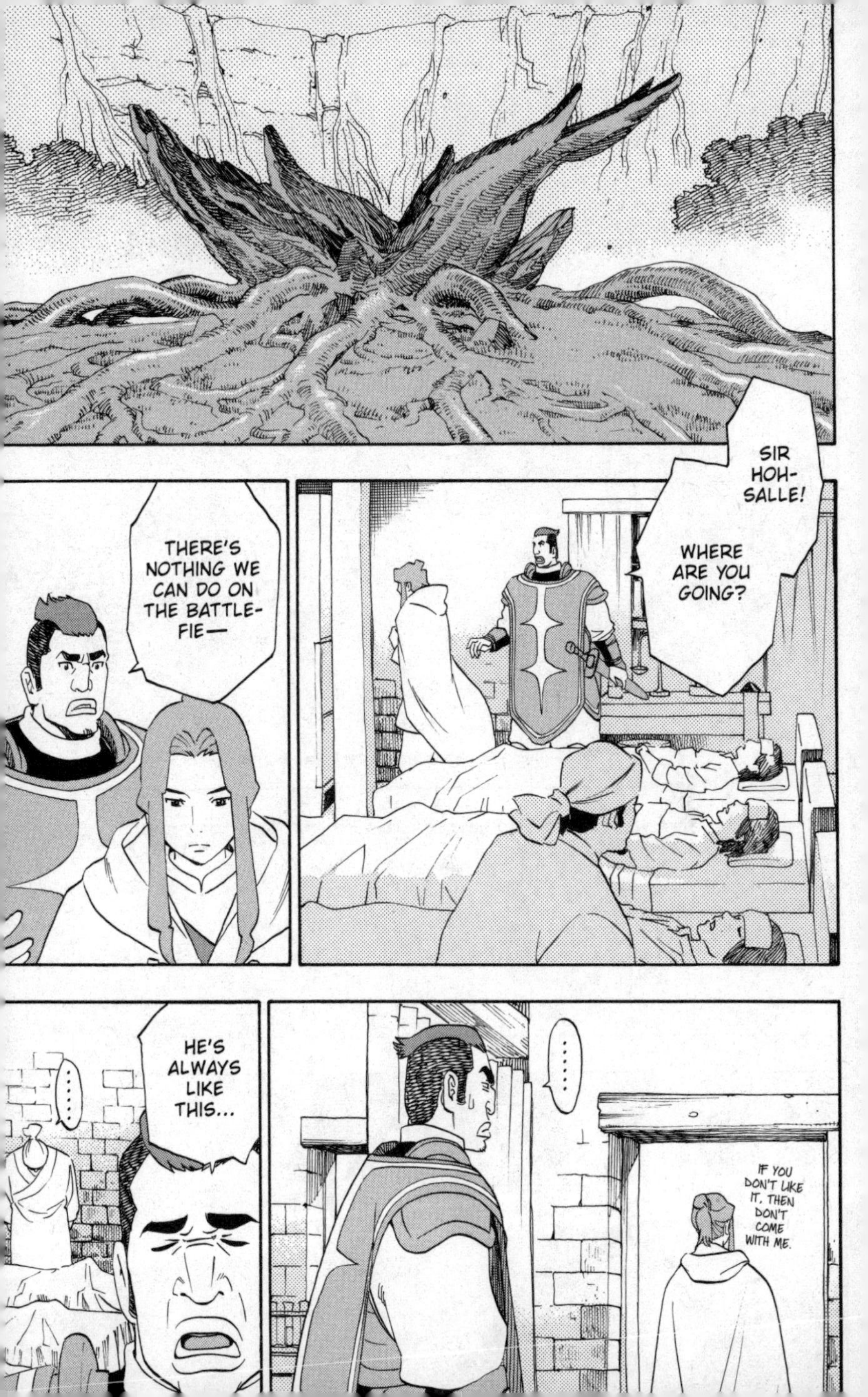

SIR HOH-SALLE!
WHERE ARE YOU GOING?
THERE'S NOTHING WE CAN DO ON THE BATTLE-FIE—
IF YOU DON'T LIKE IT, THEN DON'T COME WITH ME.
......
HE'S ALWAYS LIKE THIS...
......

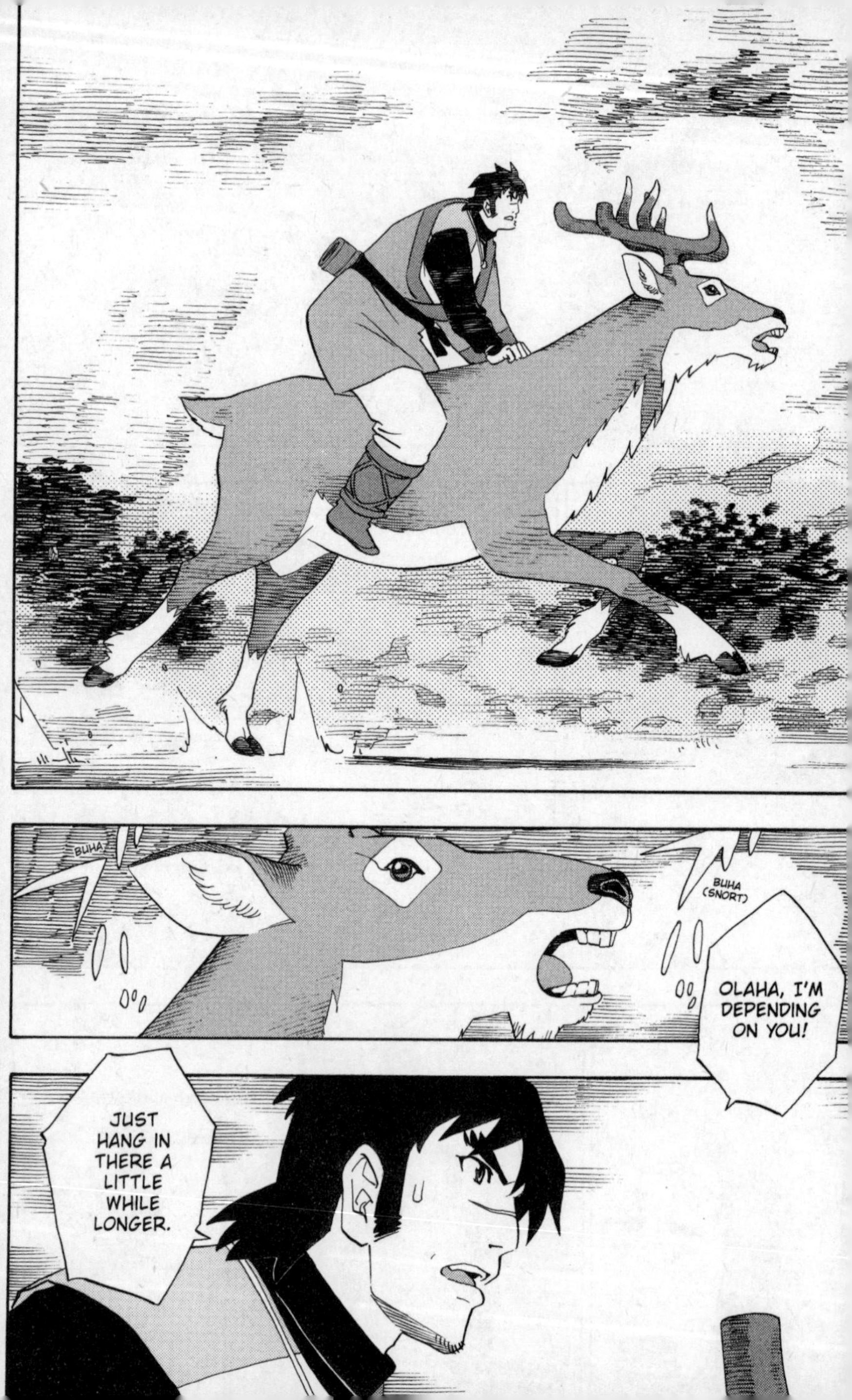
BUHA (SNORT)
OLAHA, I'M DEPENDING ON YOU!
BUHA
JUST HANG IN THERE A LITTLE WHILE LONGER.

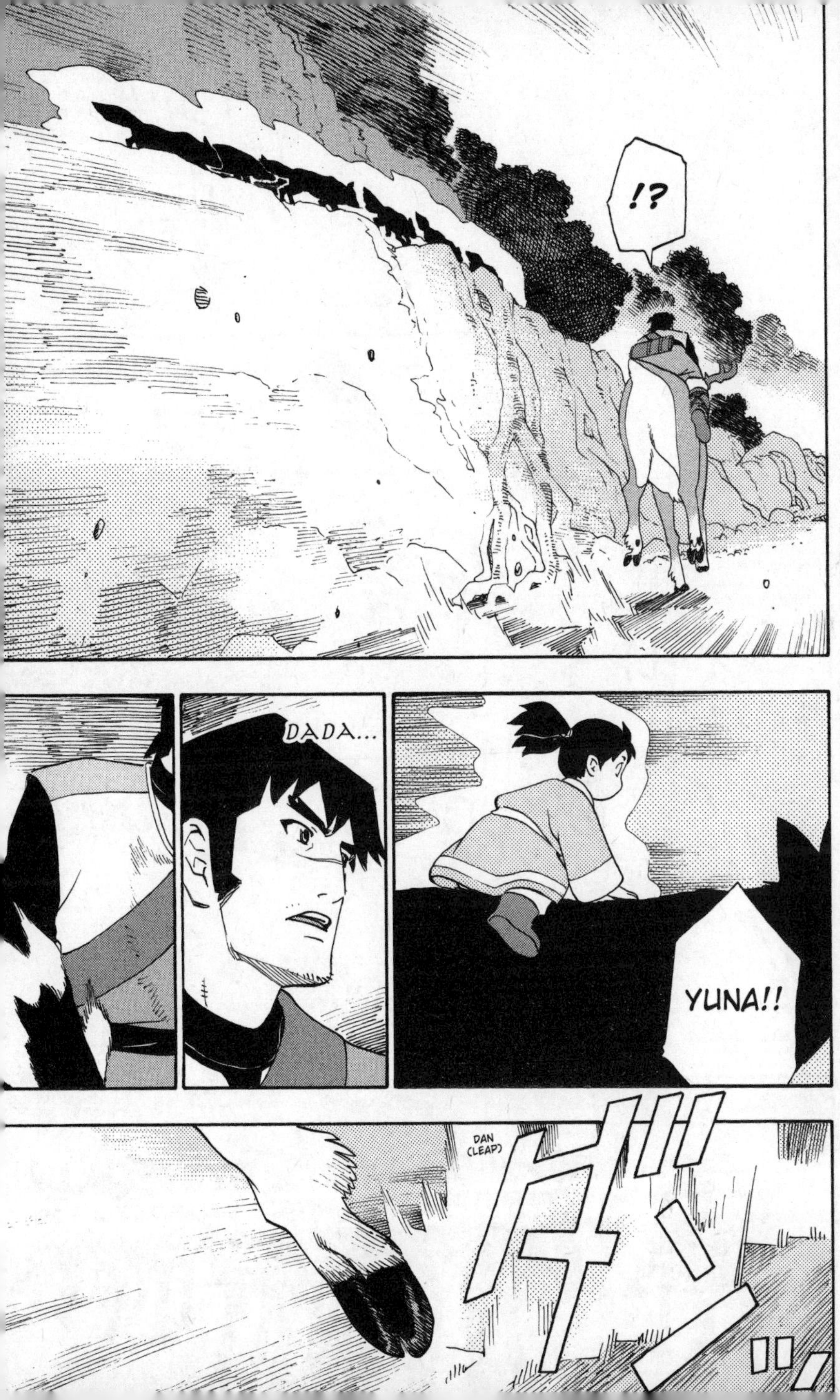
!?
YUNA!!
DADA...
DAN
(LEAP)

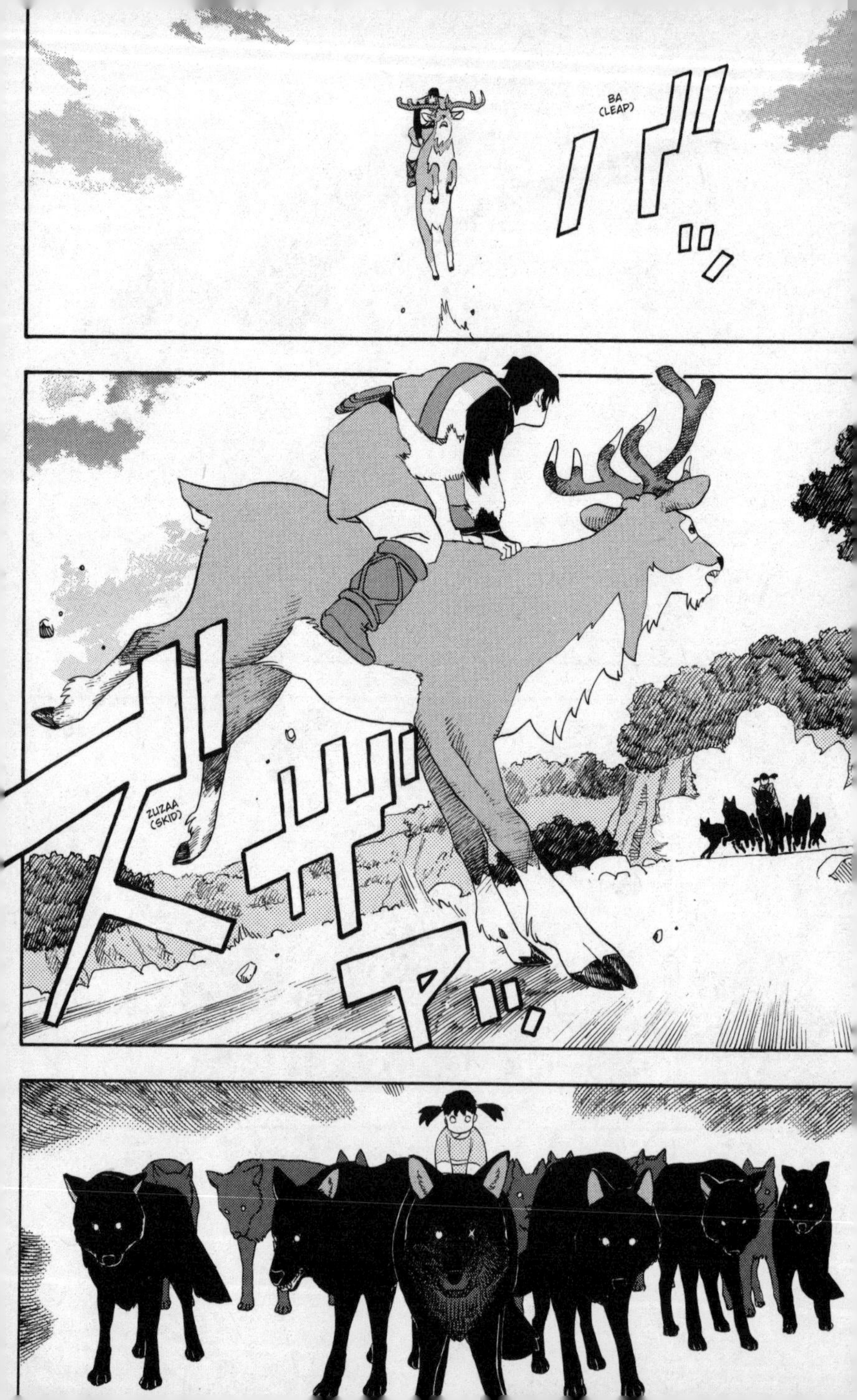
BA
(LEAP)
ZUZAA
(SKID)

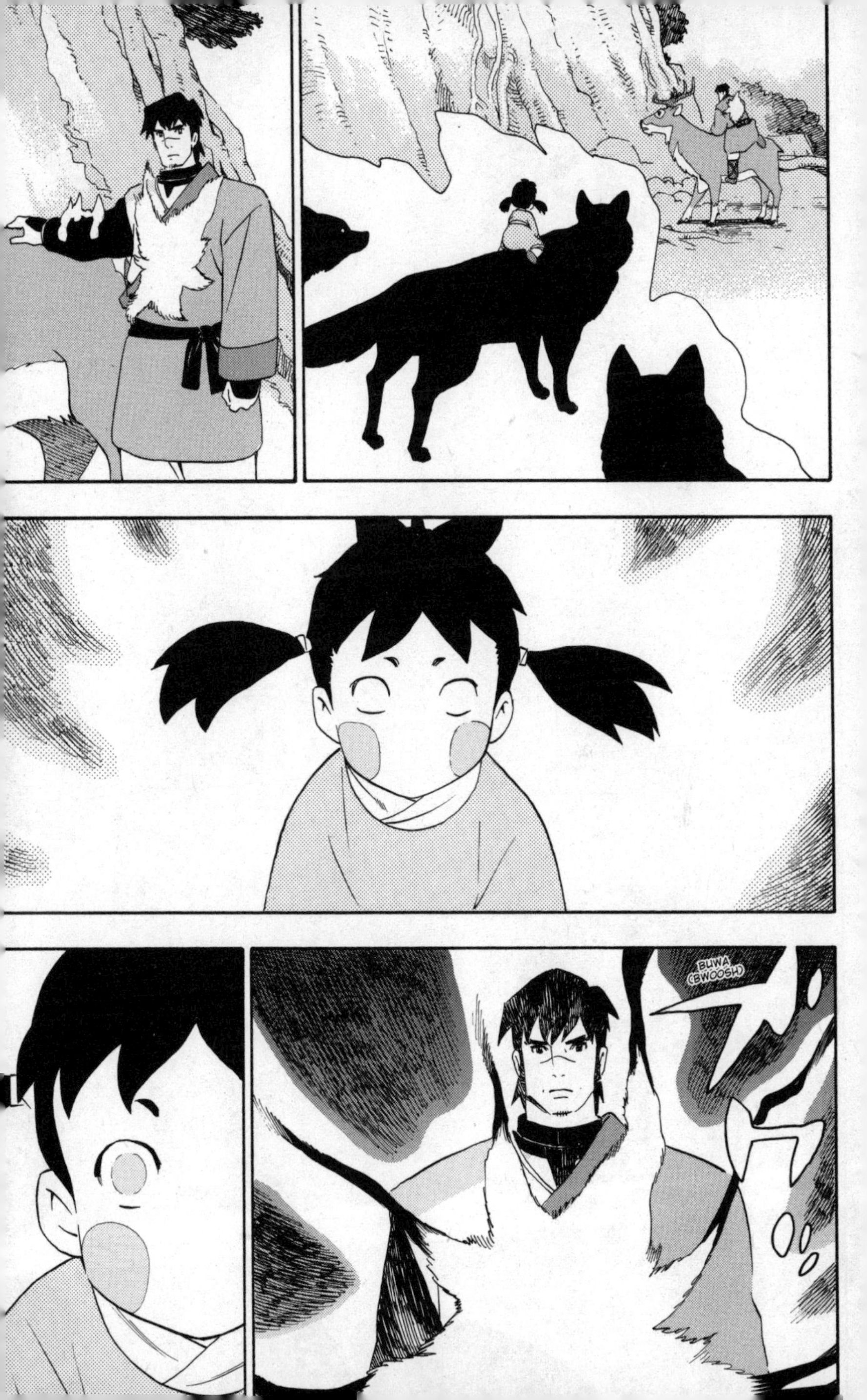
BUWA
(BWOOSH)

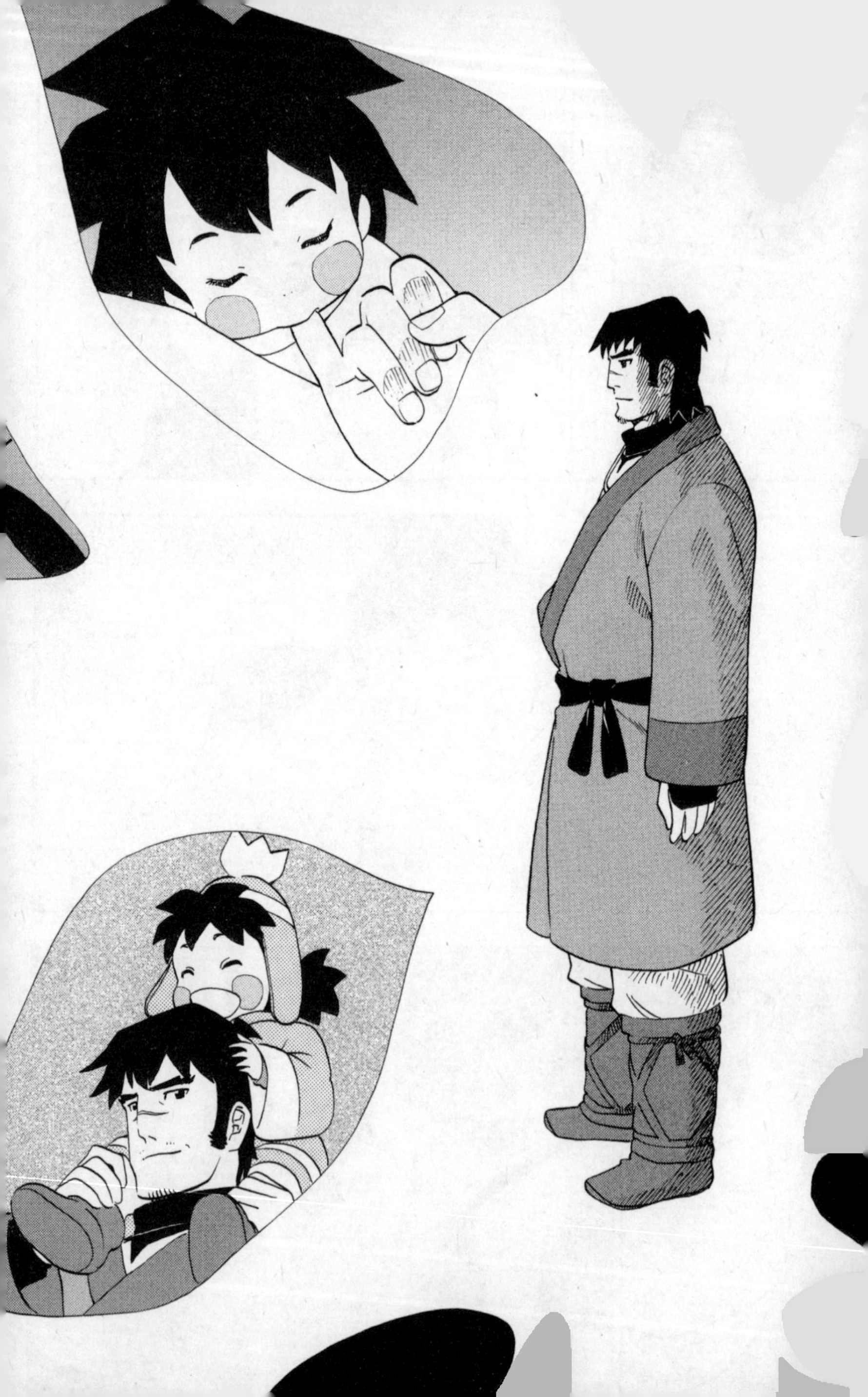

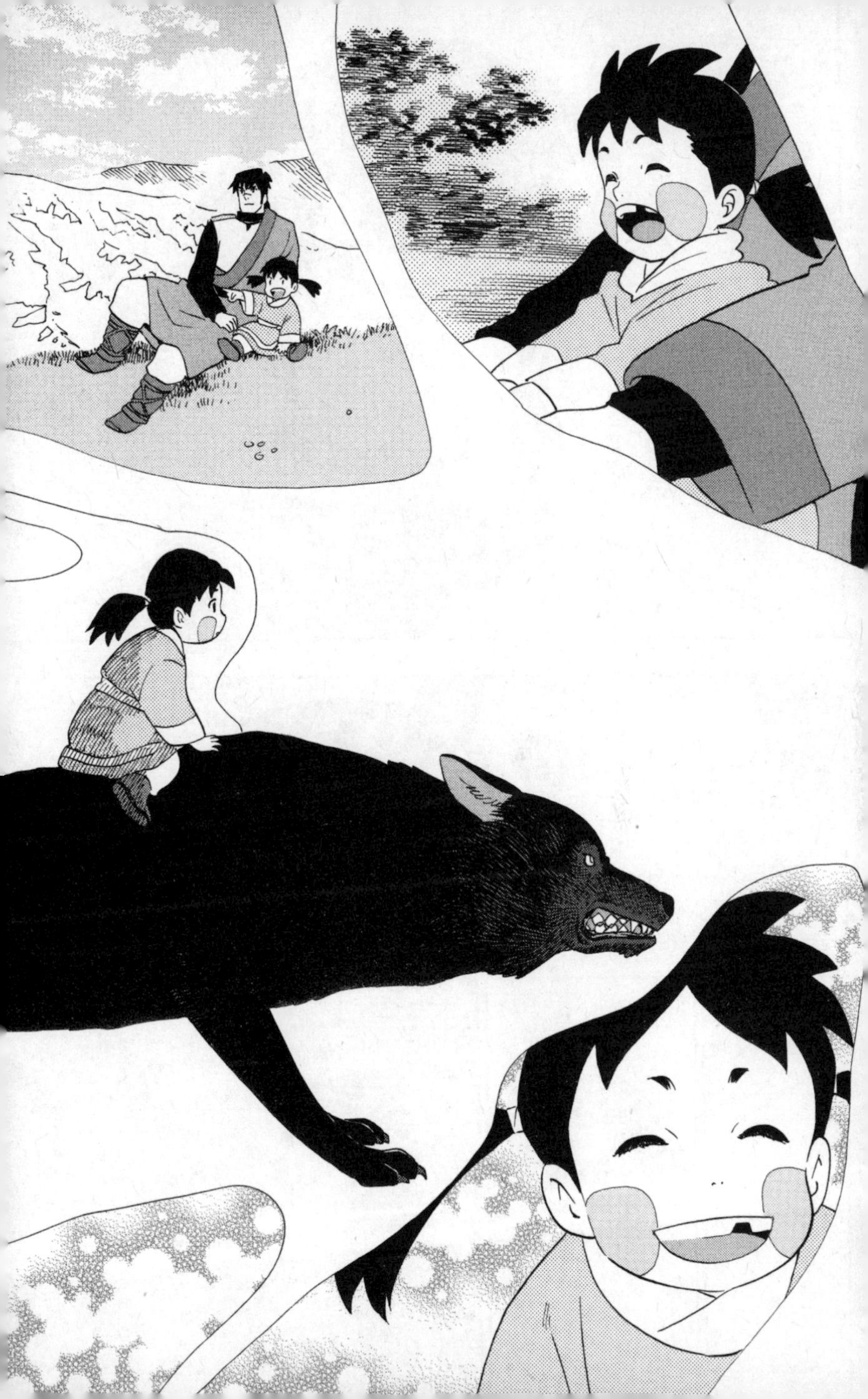

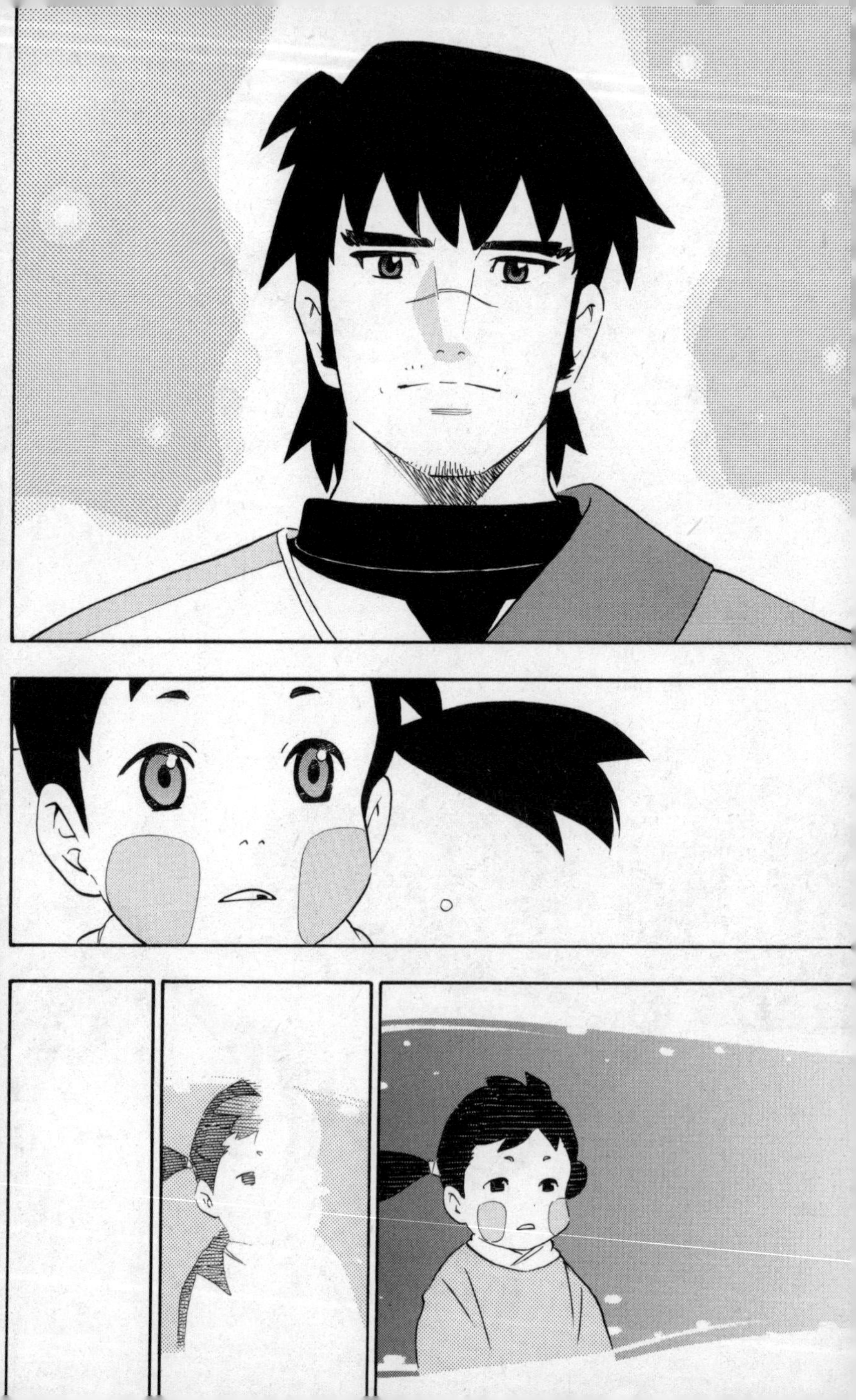

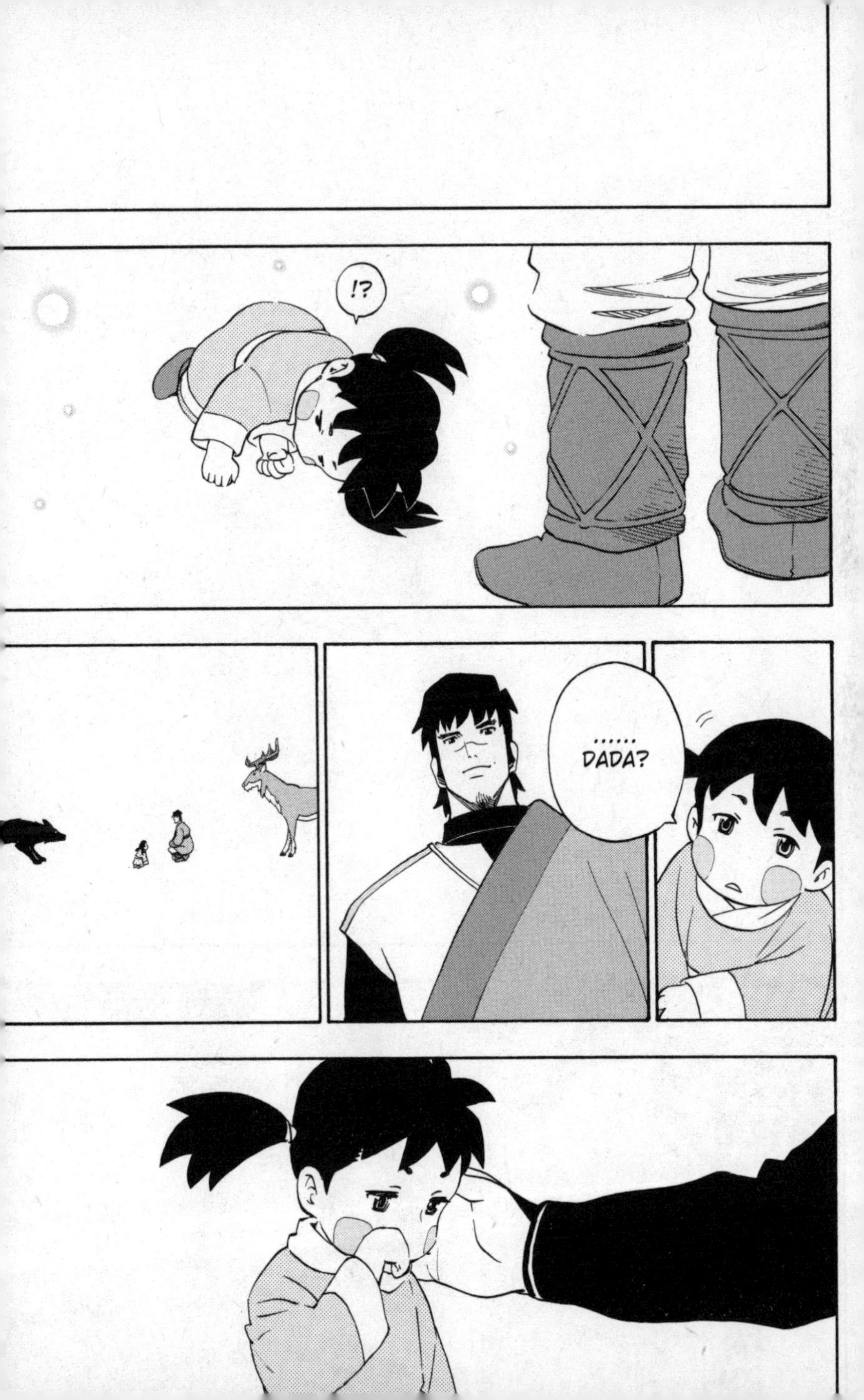
!?
......
DADA?

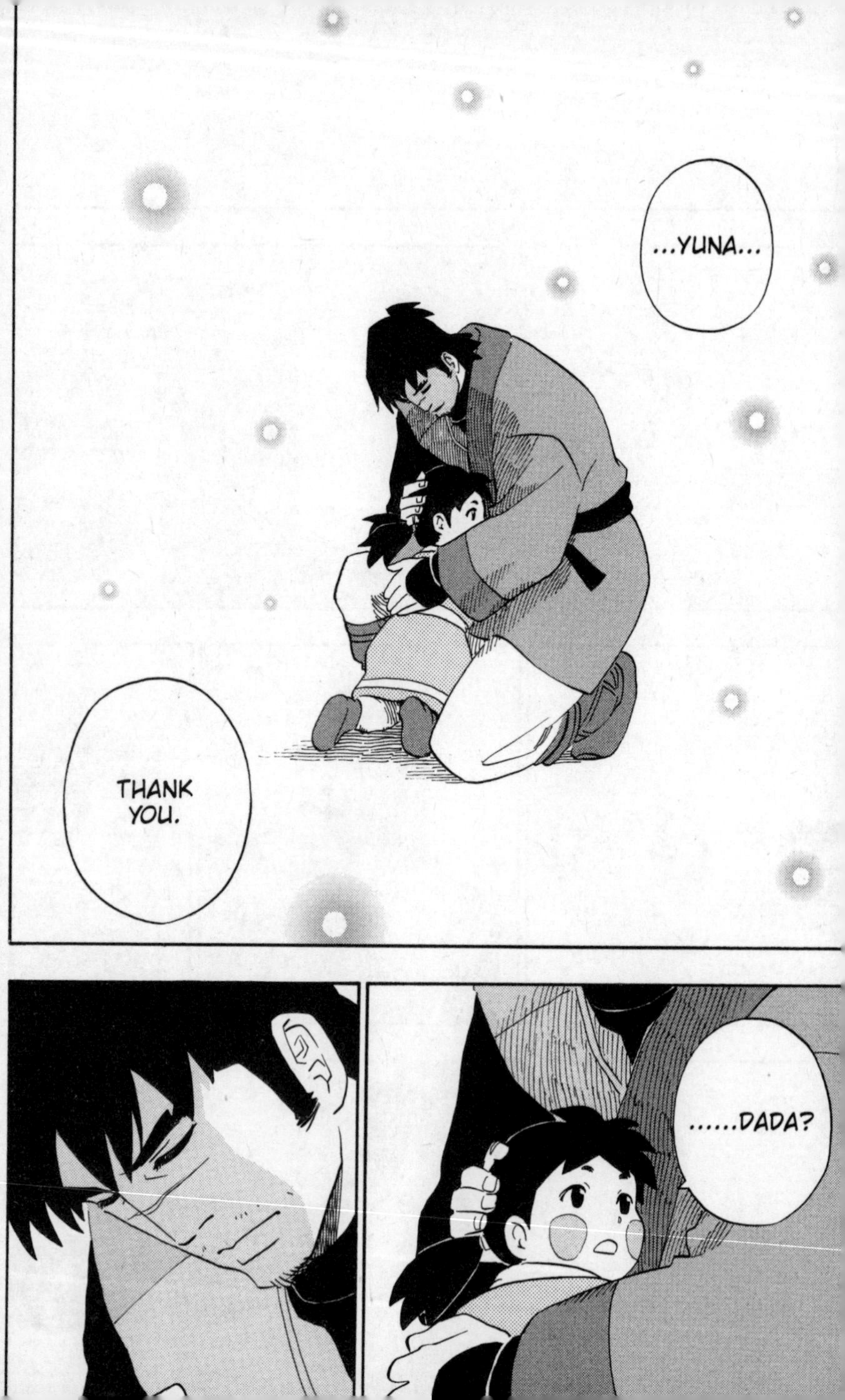
...YUNA...
THANK YOU.
......DADA?

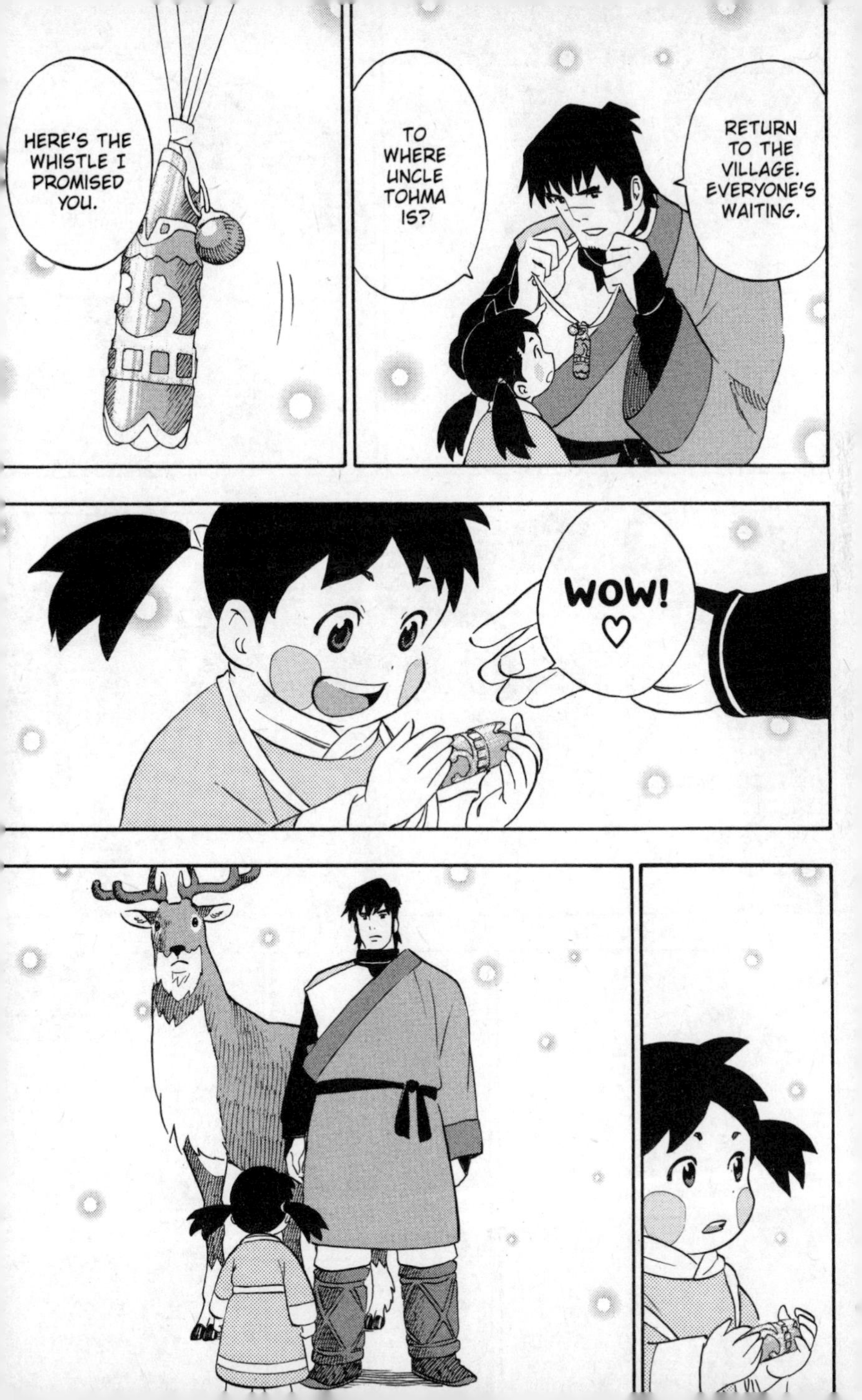
RETURN TO THE VILLAGE. EVERYONE'S WAITING.
TO WHERE UNCLE TOHMA IS?
HERE'S THE WHISTLE I PROMISED YOU.
WOW! ♡

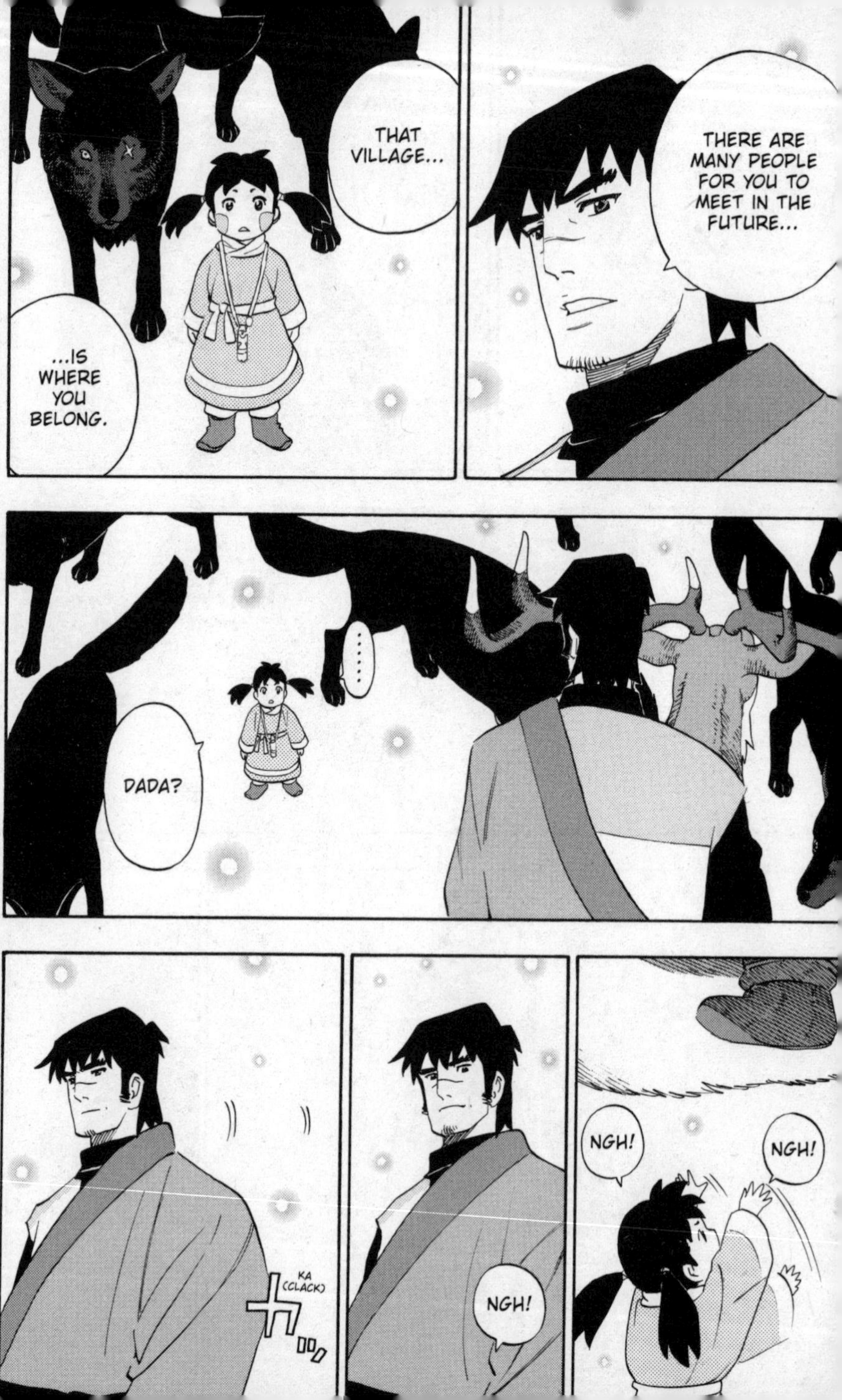
THERE ARE MANY PEOPLE FOR YOU TO MEET IN THE FUTURE...
THAT VILLAGE...
...IS WHERE YOU BELONG.
......
DADA?
NGH!
NGH!
NGH!
KA (CLACK)

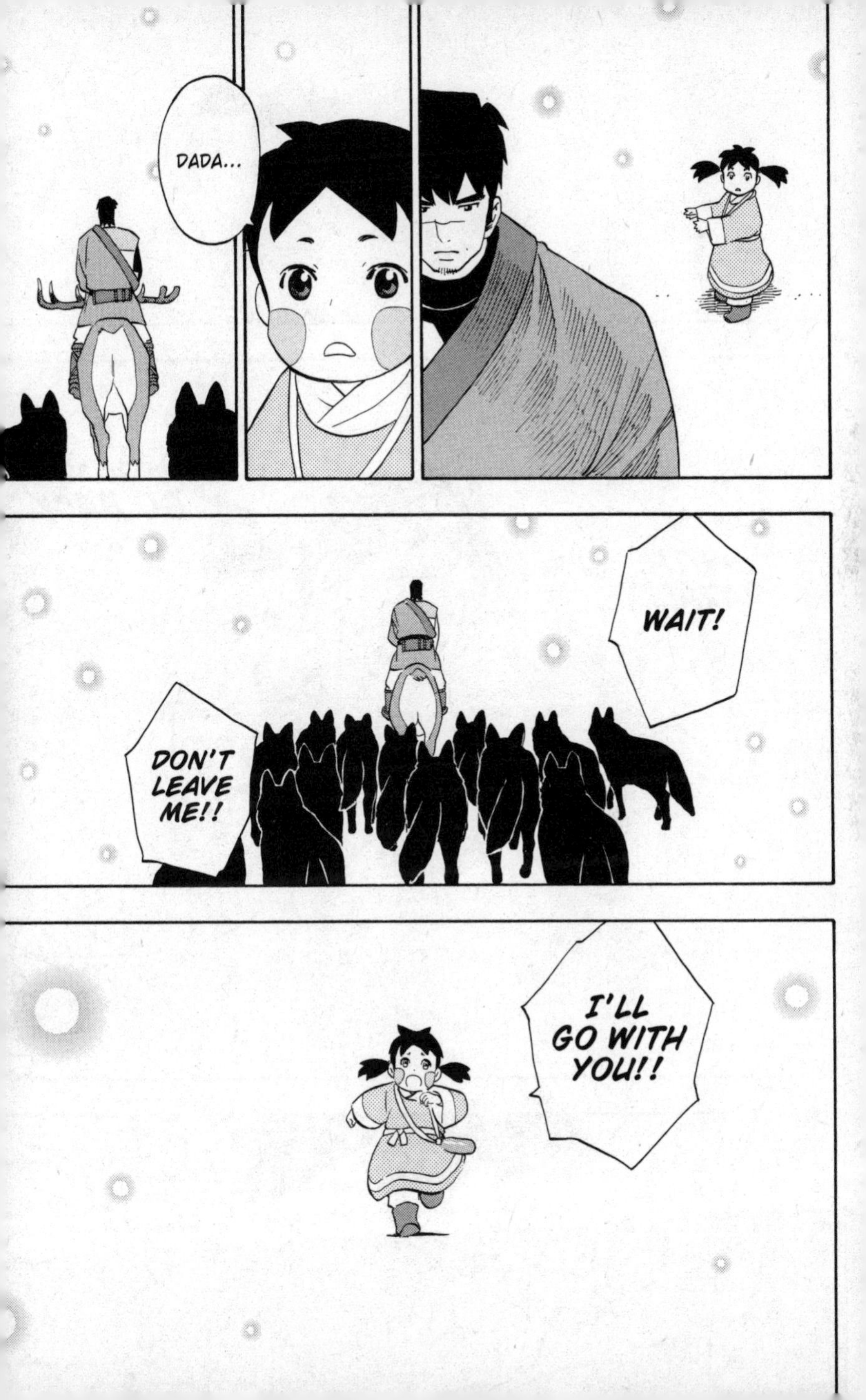
DADA...
WAIT!
DON'T LEAVE ME!!
I'LL GO WITH YOU!!

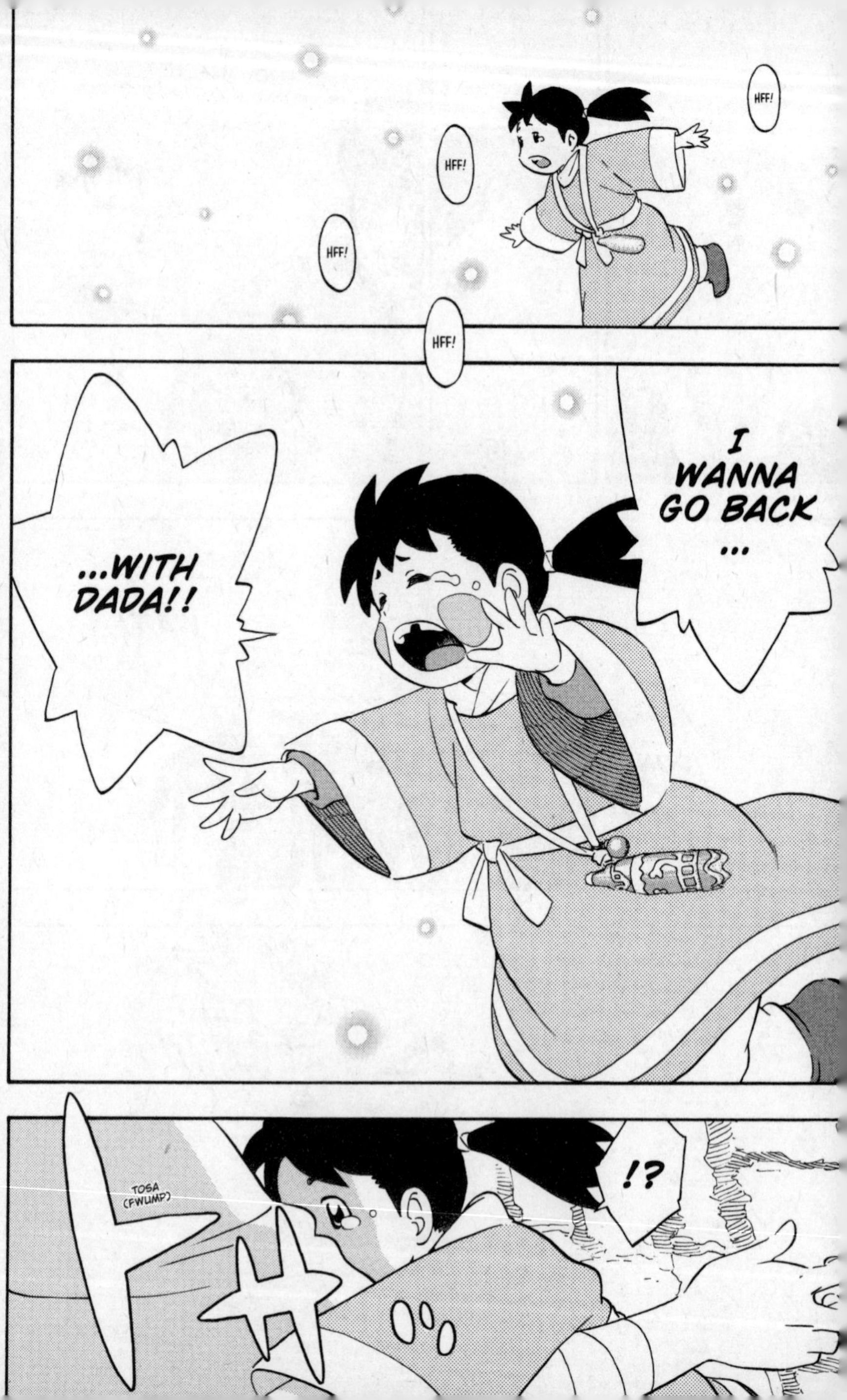
HFF!
HFF!
HFF!
HFF!
I WANNA GO BACK ...
...WITH DADA!!
!?
TOSA (FWUMP)

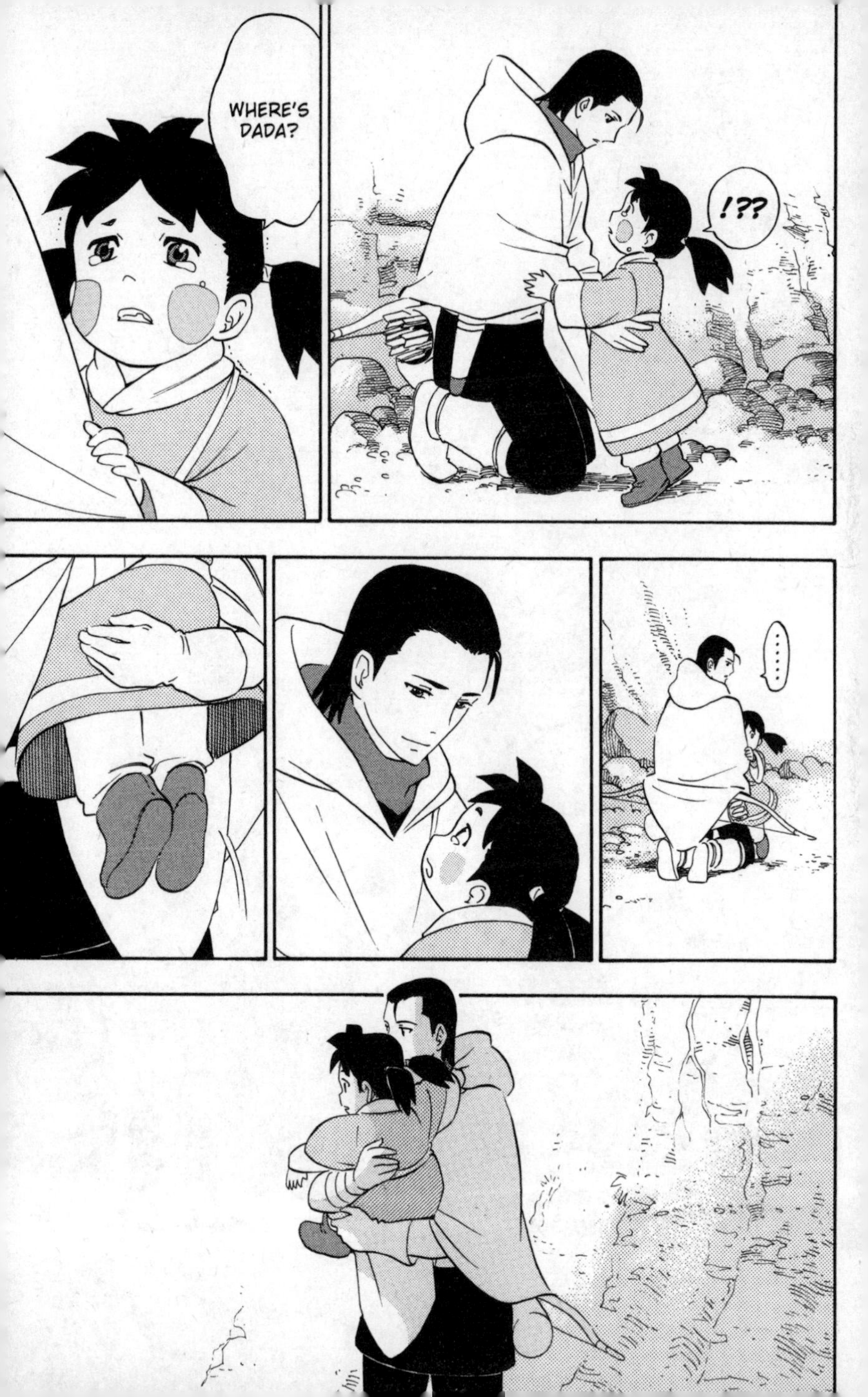
!??
WHERE'S DADA?
......

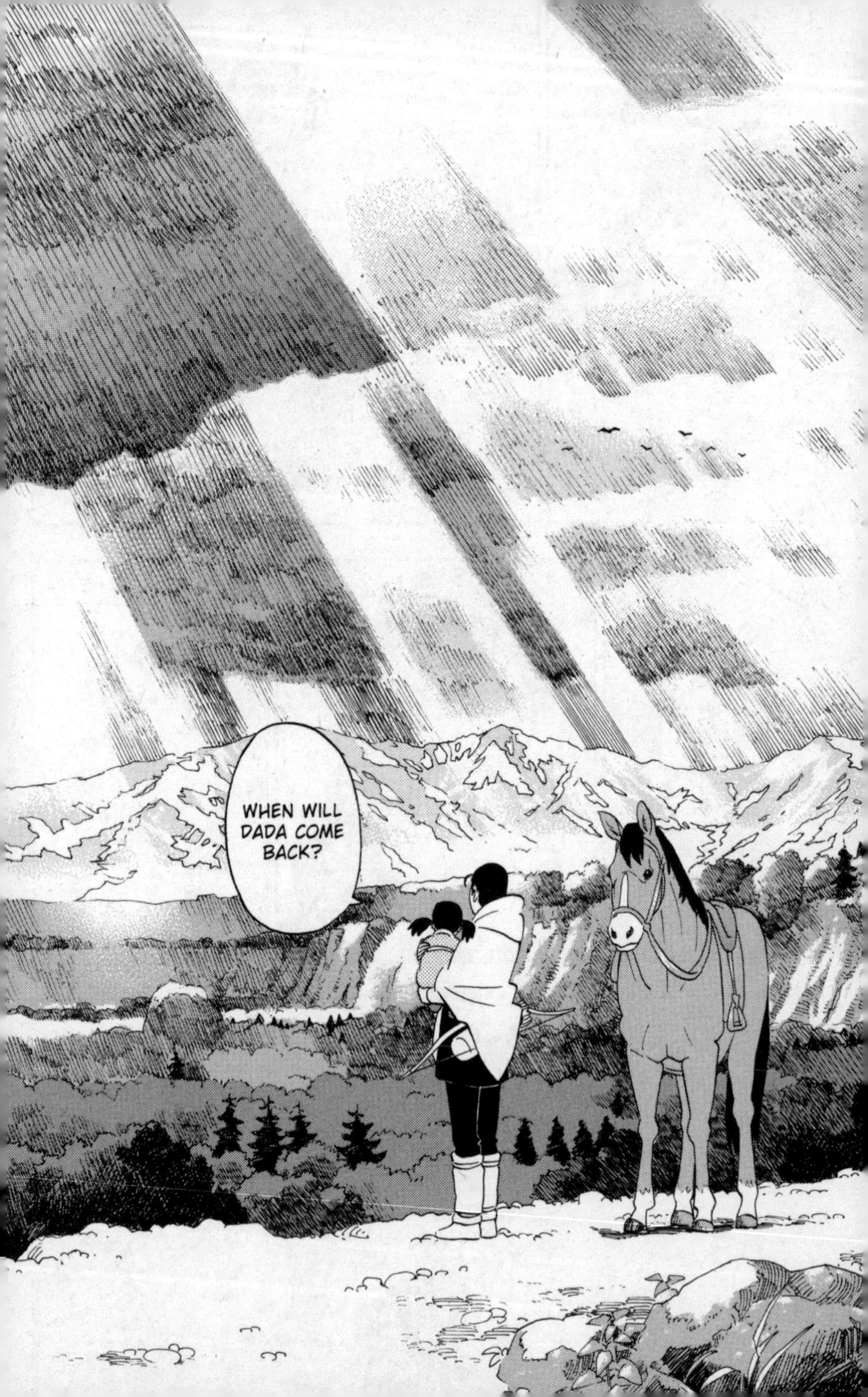
WHEN WILL DADA COME BACK?

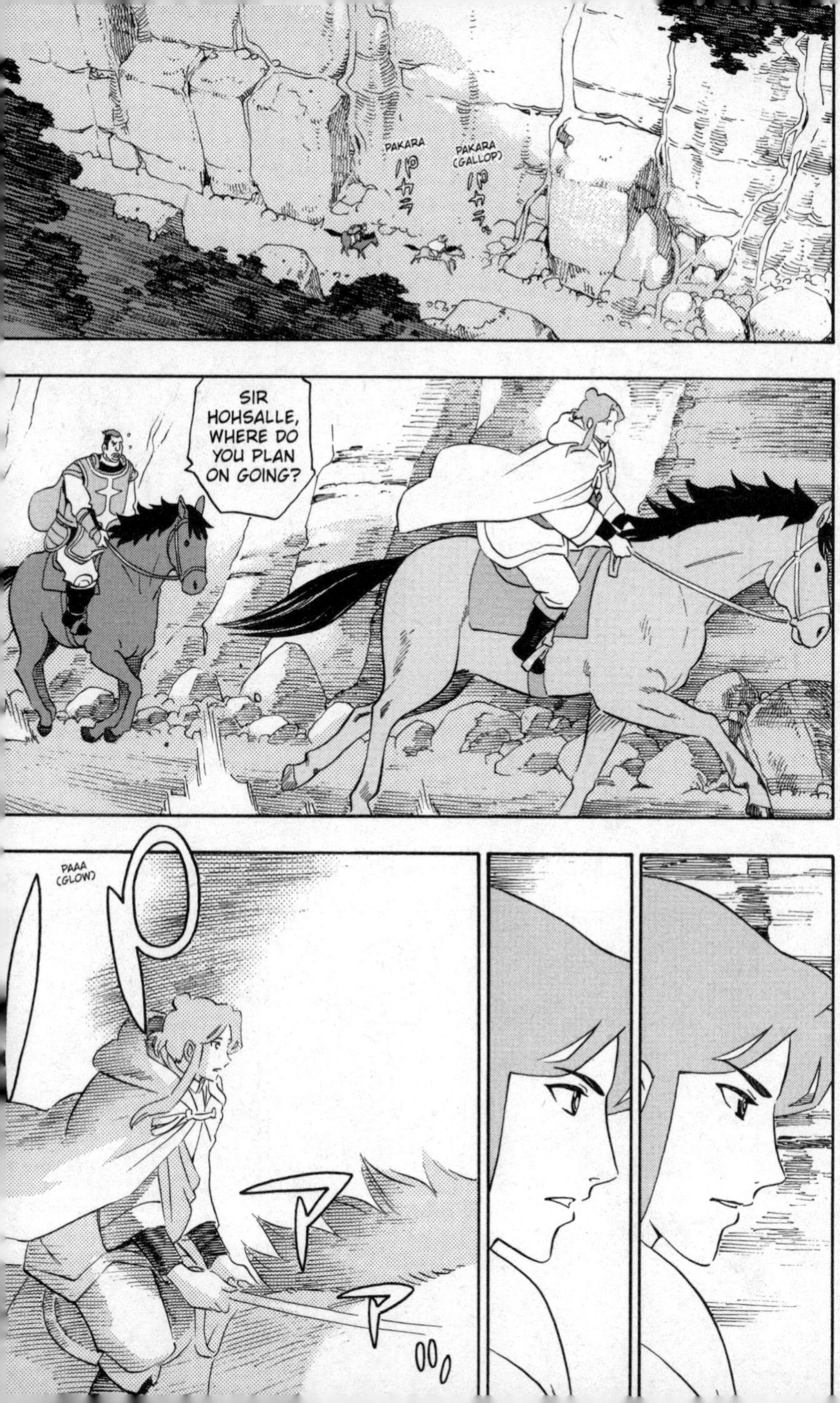
PAKARA (GALLOP)
PAKARA
SIR HOHSALLE, WHERE DO YOU PLAN ON GOING?
PAAA (GLOW)

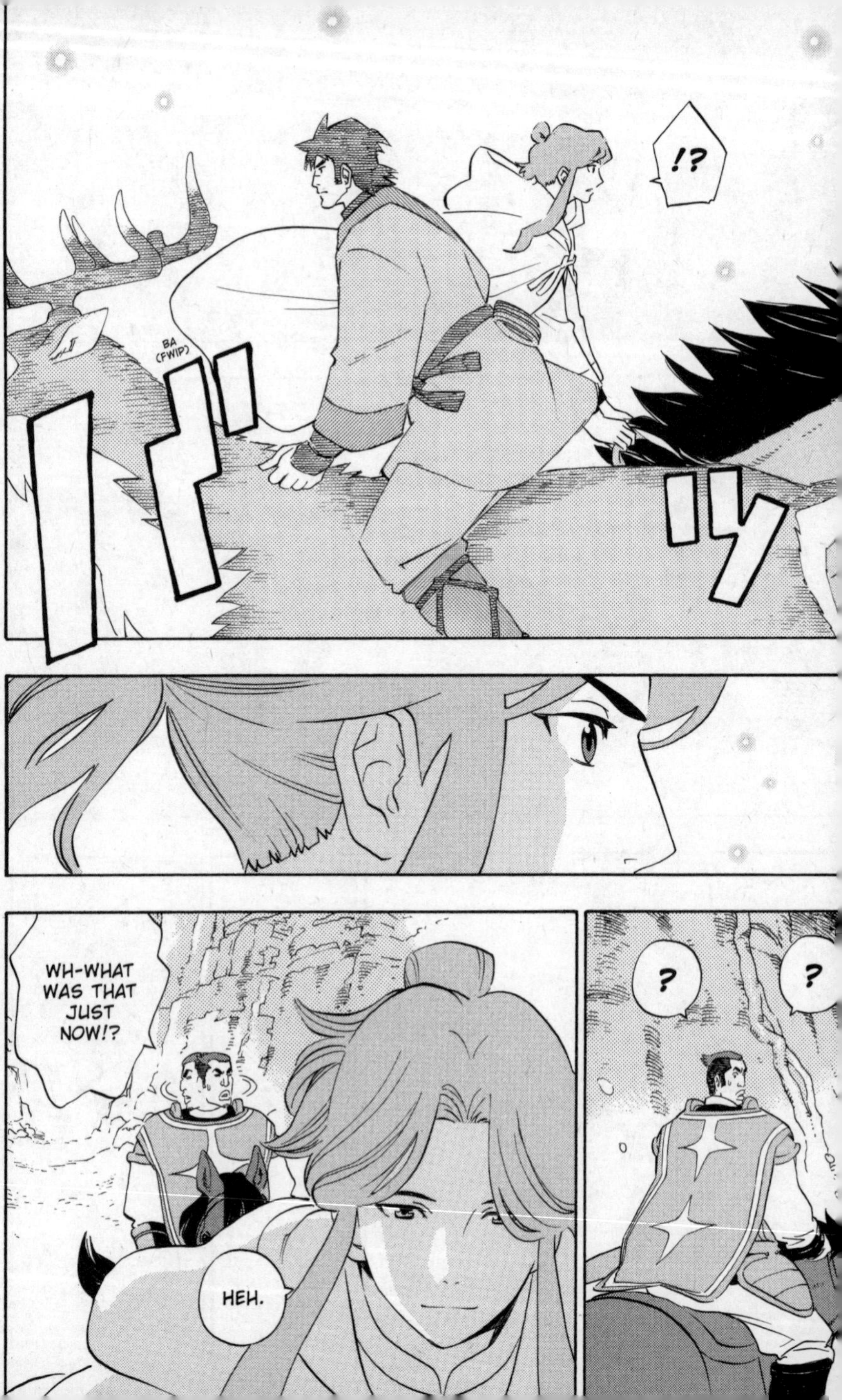
!?
BA (FWIP)
?
?
WH-WHAT WAS THAT JUST NOW!?
HEH.

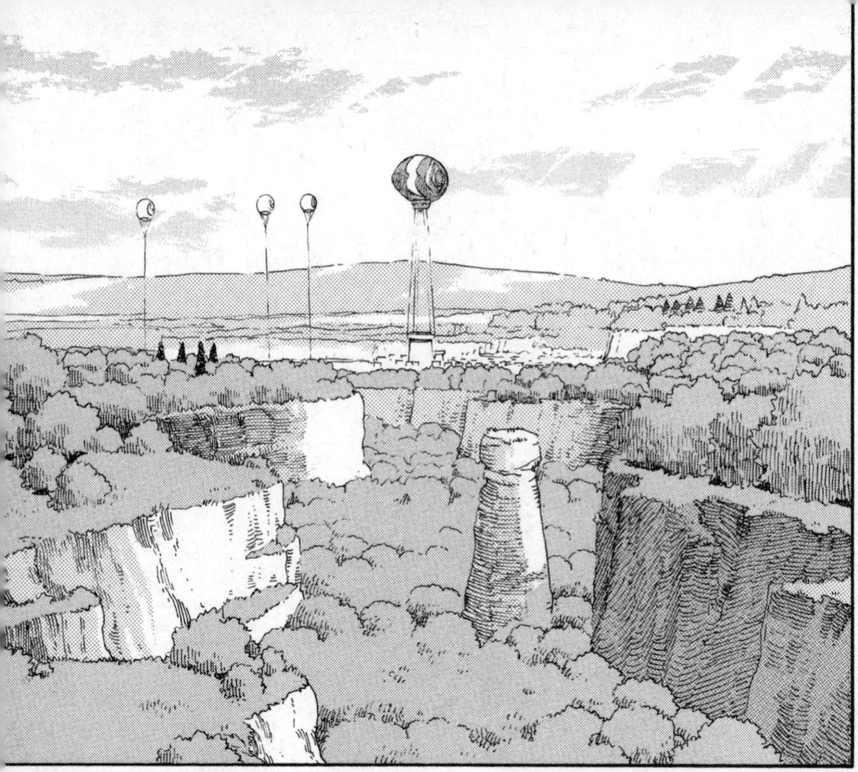
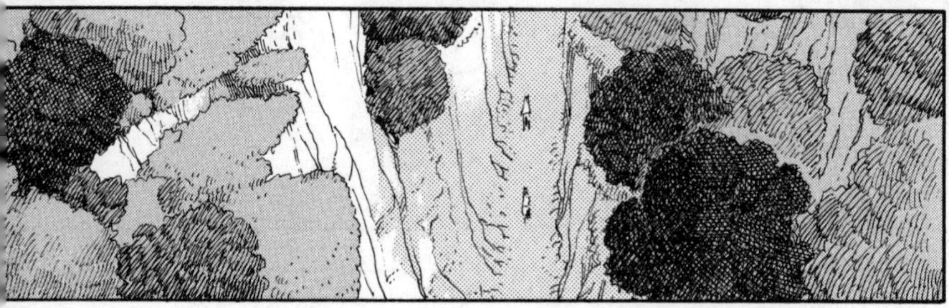
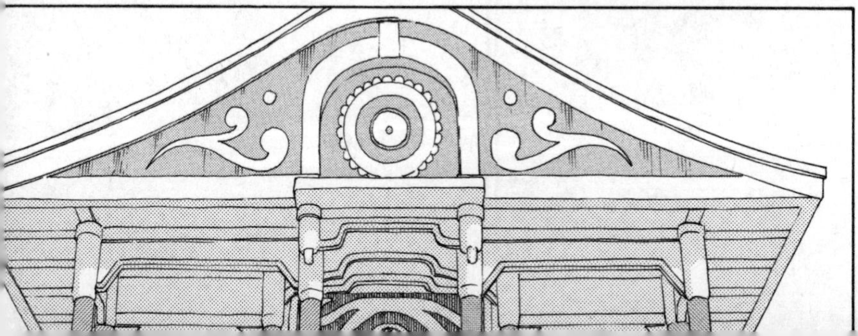

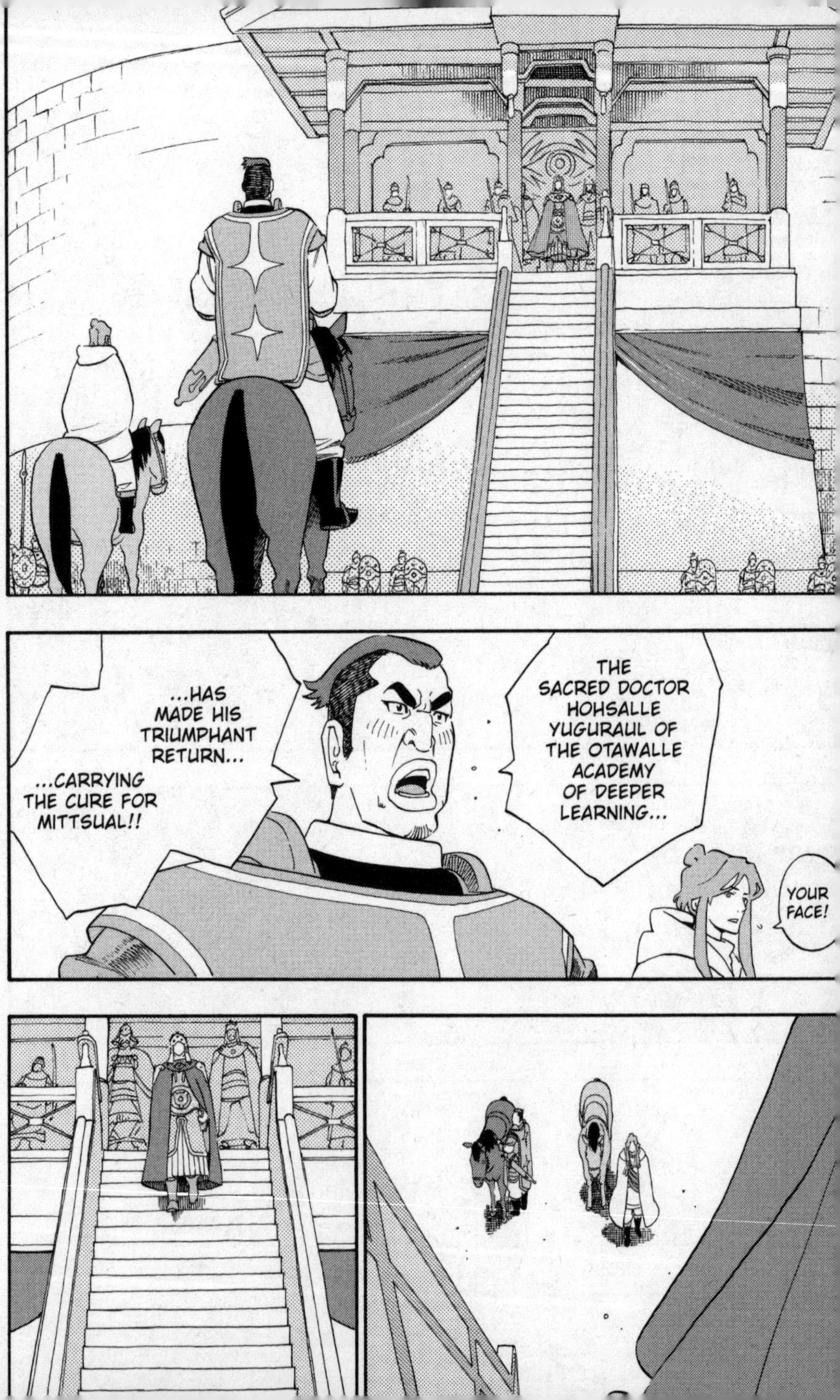
THE SACRED DOCTOR HOHSALLE YUGURAUL OF THE OTAWALLE ACADEMY OF DEEPER LEARNING...
...HAS MADE HIS TRIUMPHANT RETURN...
...CARRYING THE CURE FOR MITTSUAL!!
YOUR FACE!

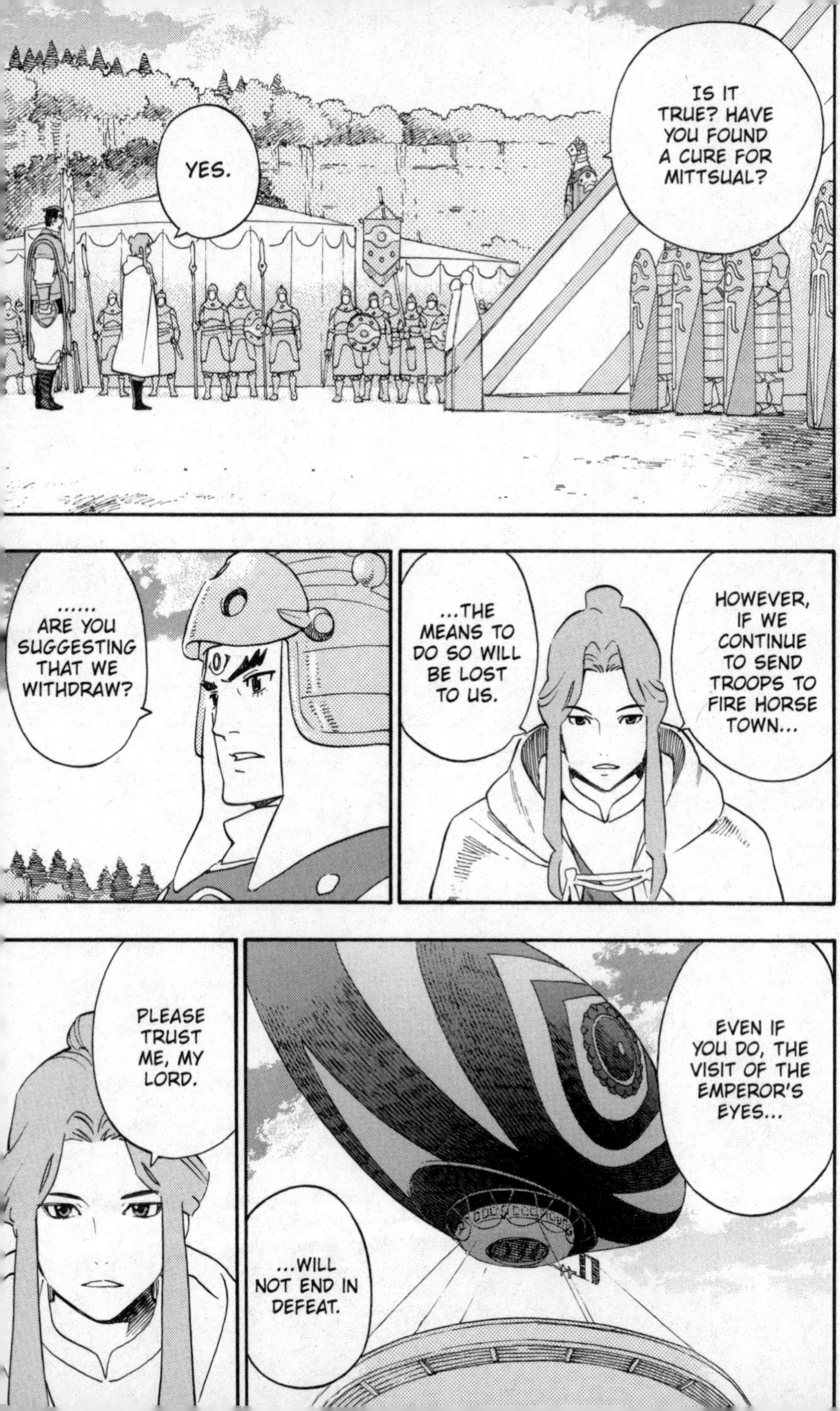
IS IT TRUE? HAVE YOU FOUND A CURE FOR MITTSUAL?
YES.
HOWEVER, IF WE CONTINUE TO SEND TROOPS TO FIRE HORSE TOWN...
...THE MEANS TO DO SO WILL BE LOST TO US.
...... ARE YOU SUGGESTING THAT WE WITHDRAW?
EVEN IF YOU DO, THE VISIT OF THE EMPEROR'S EYES...
...WILL NOT END IN DEFEAT.
PLEASE TRUST ME, MY LORD.

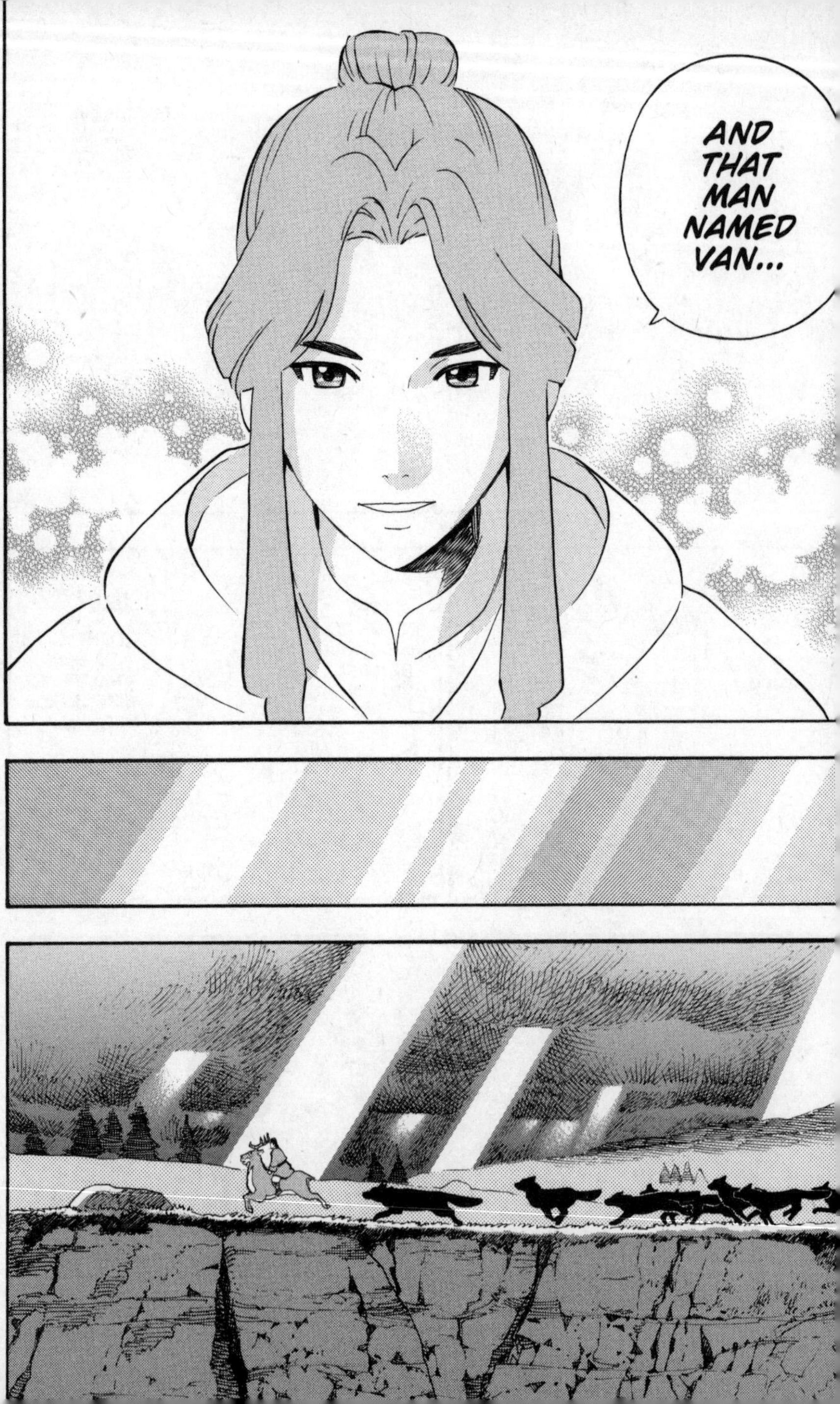
AND THAT MAN NAMED VAN...

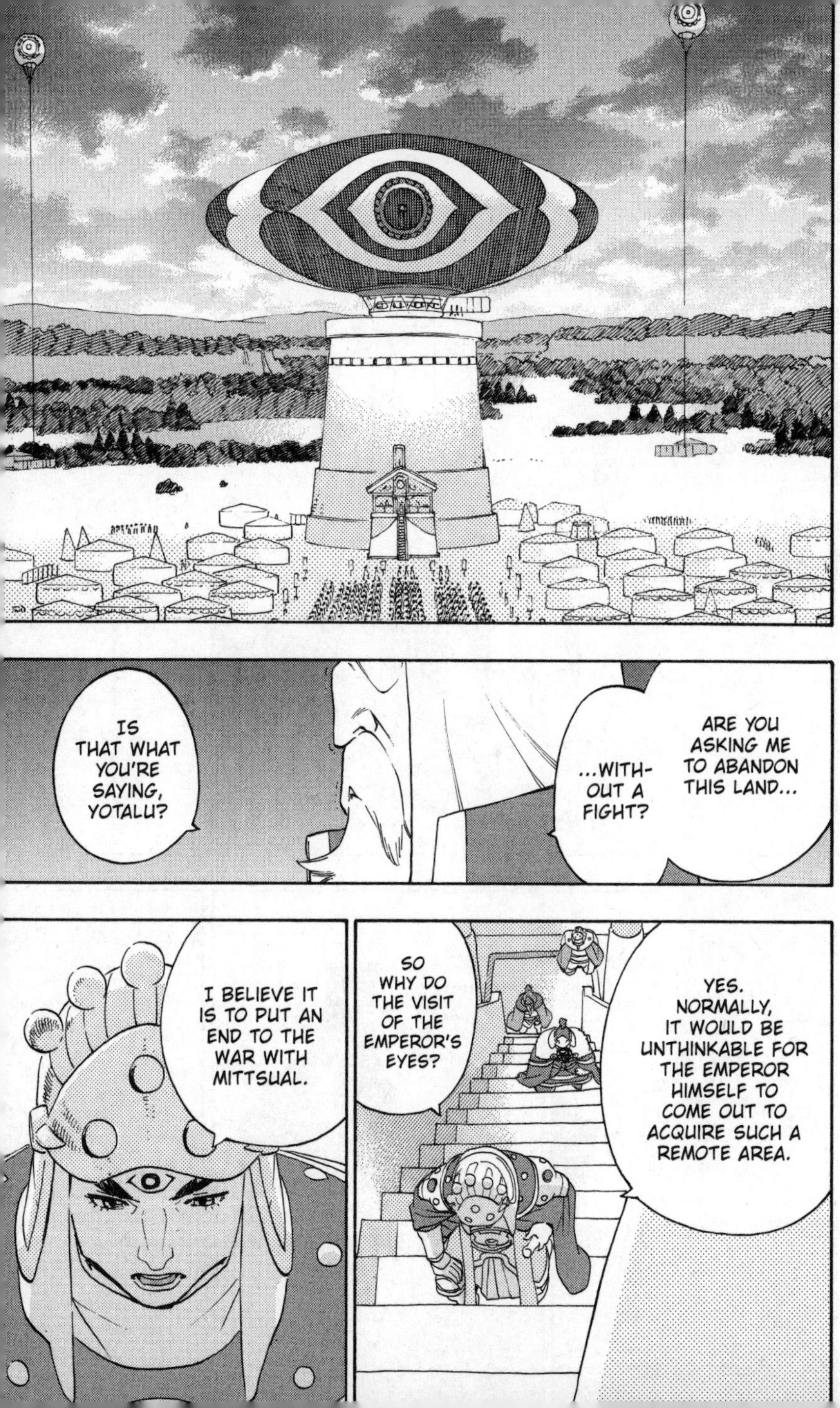
ARE YOU ASKING ME TO ABANDON THIS LAND...
...WITH-OUT A FIGHT?
IS THAT WHAT YOU'RE SAYING, YOTALU?
YES. NORMALLY, IT WOULD BE UNTHINKABLE FOR THE EMPEROR HIMSELF TO COME OUT TO ACQUIRE SUCH A REMOTE AREA.
SO WHY DO THE VISIT OF THE EMPEROR'S EYES?
I BELIEVE IT IS TO PUT AN END TO THE WAR WITH MITTSUAL.

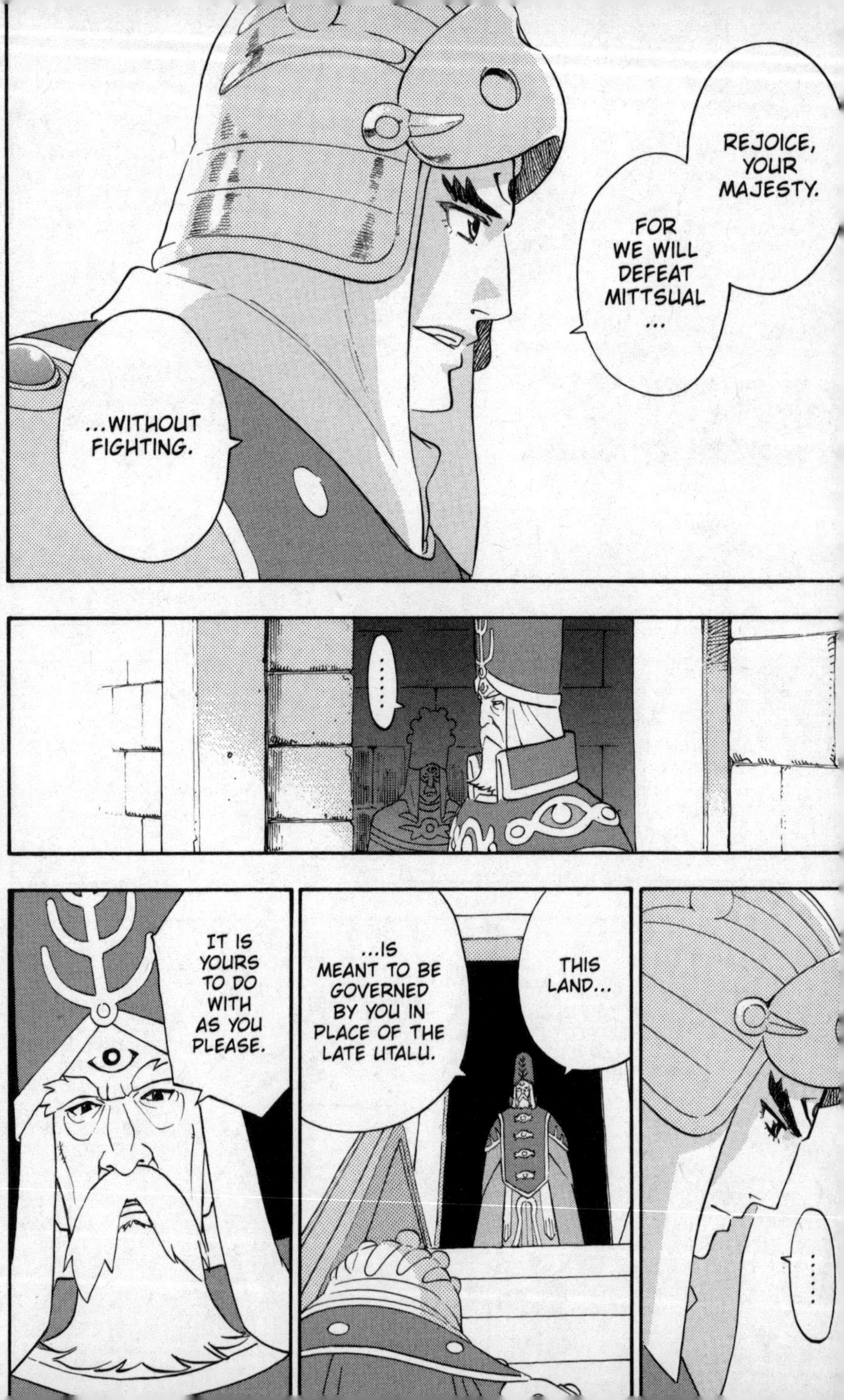
REJOICE, YOUR MAJESTY.
FOR WE WILL DEFEAT MITTSUAL ...
...WITHOUT FIGHTING.
......
......
THIS LAND...
...IS MEANT TO BE GOVERNED BY YOU IN PLACE OF THE LATE UTALU.
IT IS YOURS TO DO WITH AS YOU PLEASE.

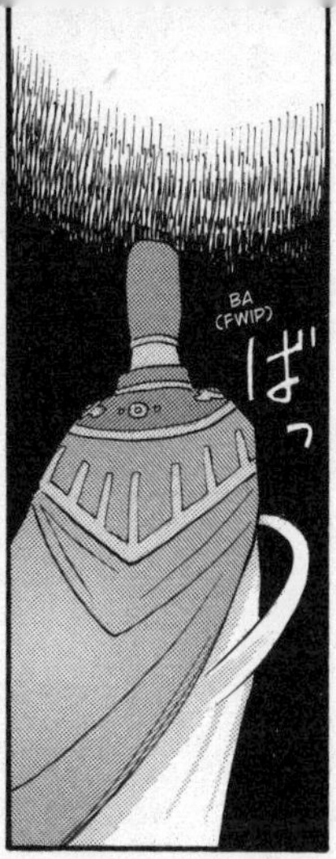
BA
(FWIP)
ばっ
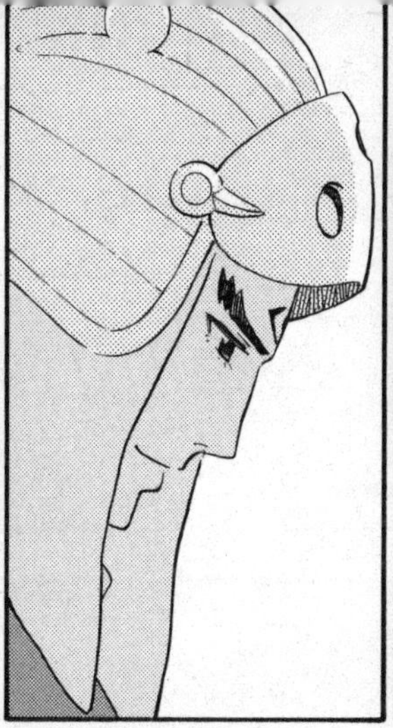
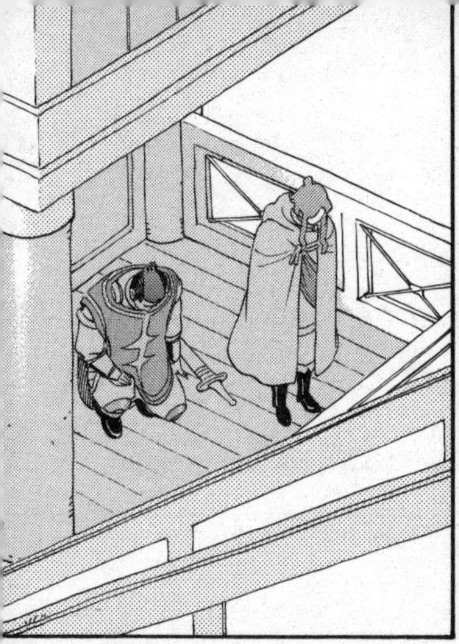
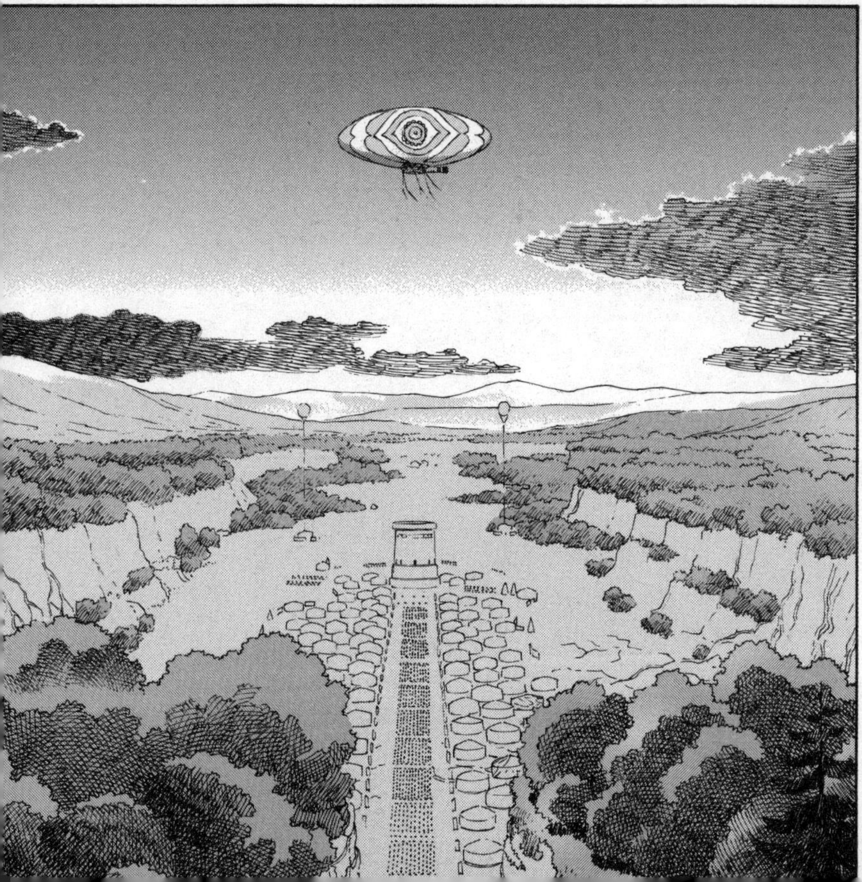

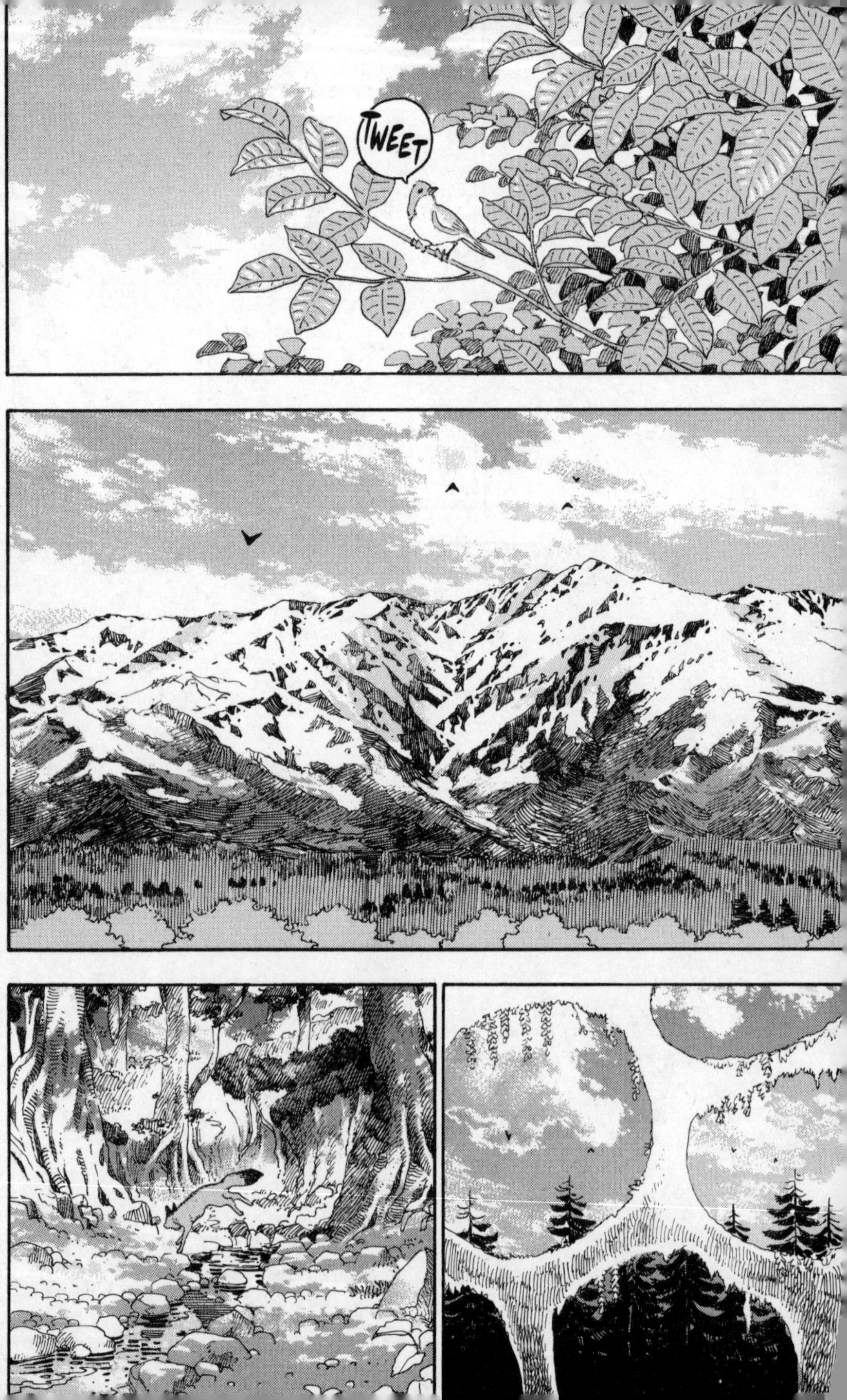
TWEET

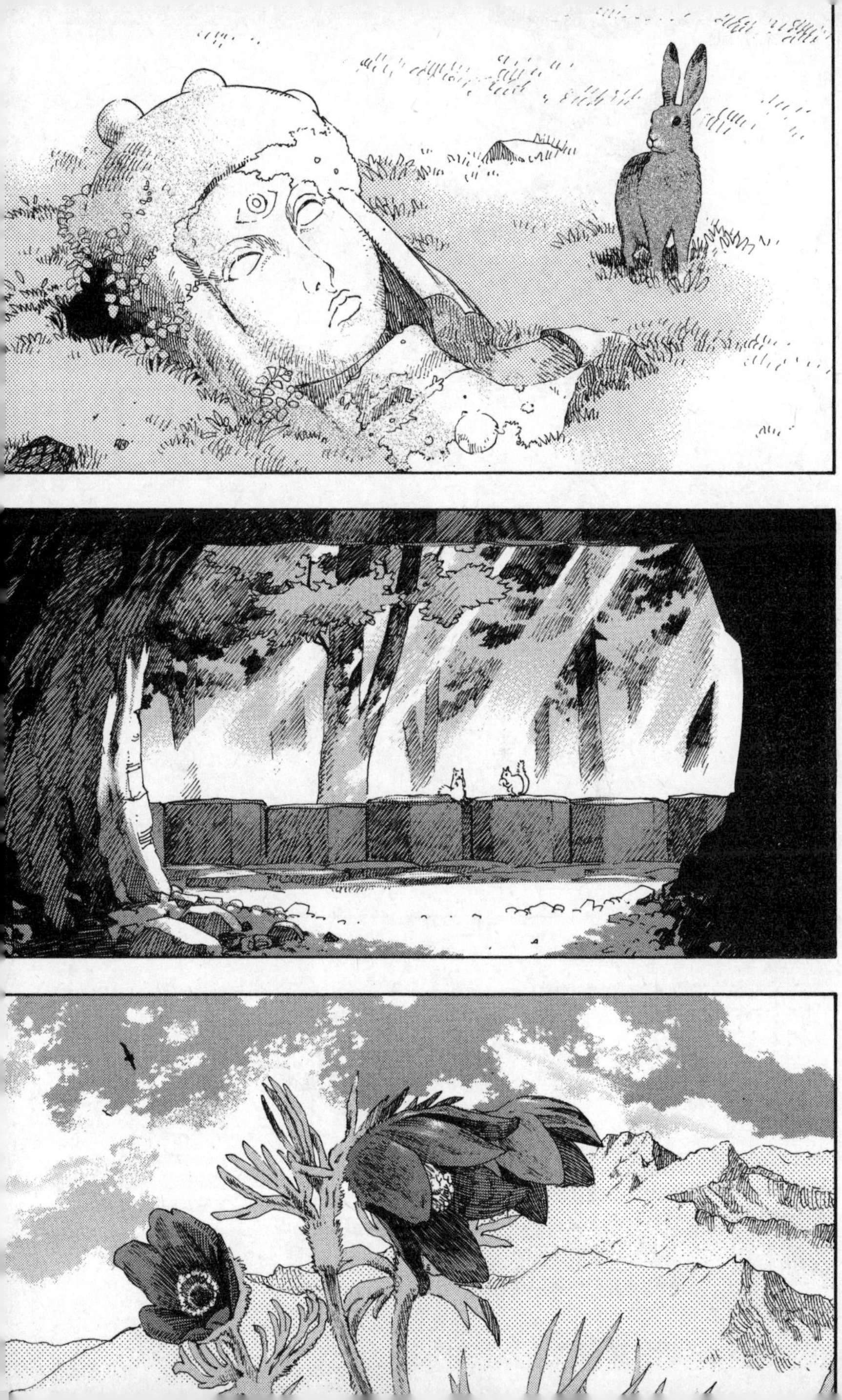

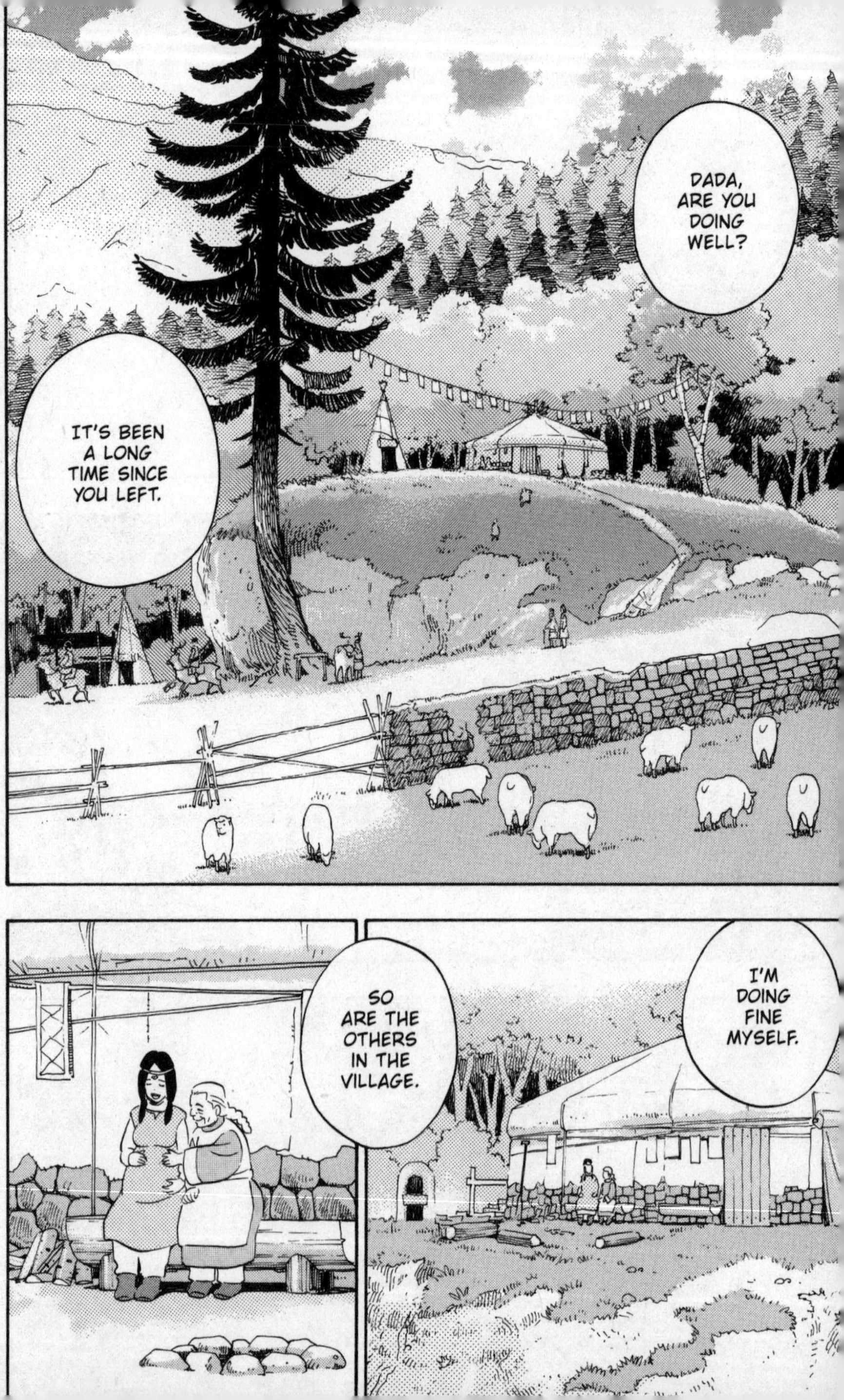
DADA, ARE YOU DOING WELL?
IT'S BEEN A LONG TIME SINCE YOU LEFT.
I'M DOING FINE MYSELF.
SO ARE THE OTHERS IN THE VILLAGE.

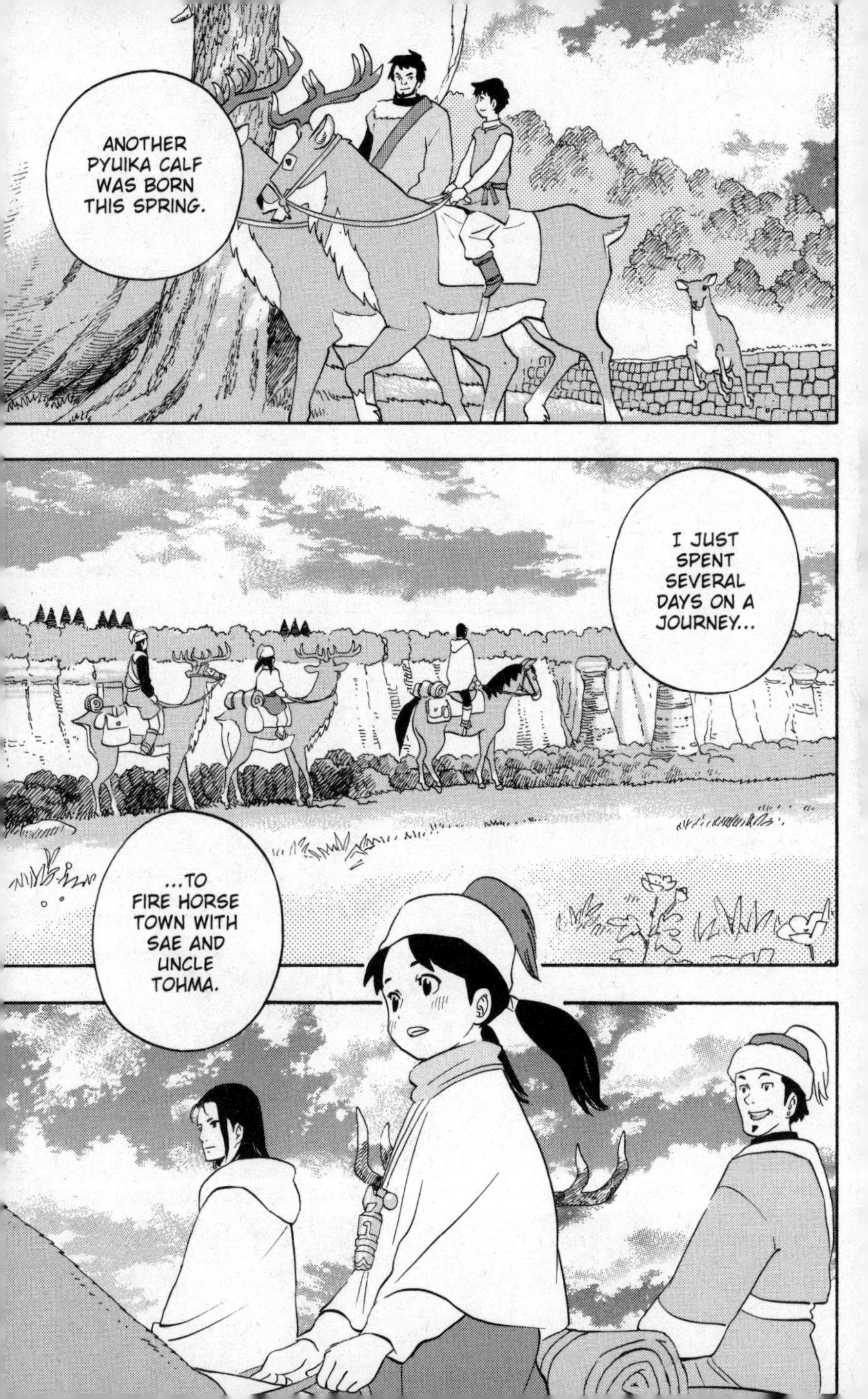
ANOTHER PYUIKA CALF WAS BORN THIS SPRING.
I JUST SPENT SEVERAL DAYS ON A JOURNEY...
...TO FIRE HORSE TOWN WITH SAE AND UNCLE TOHMA.

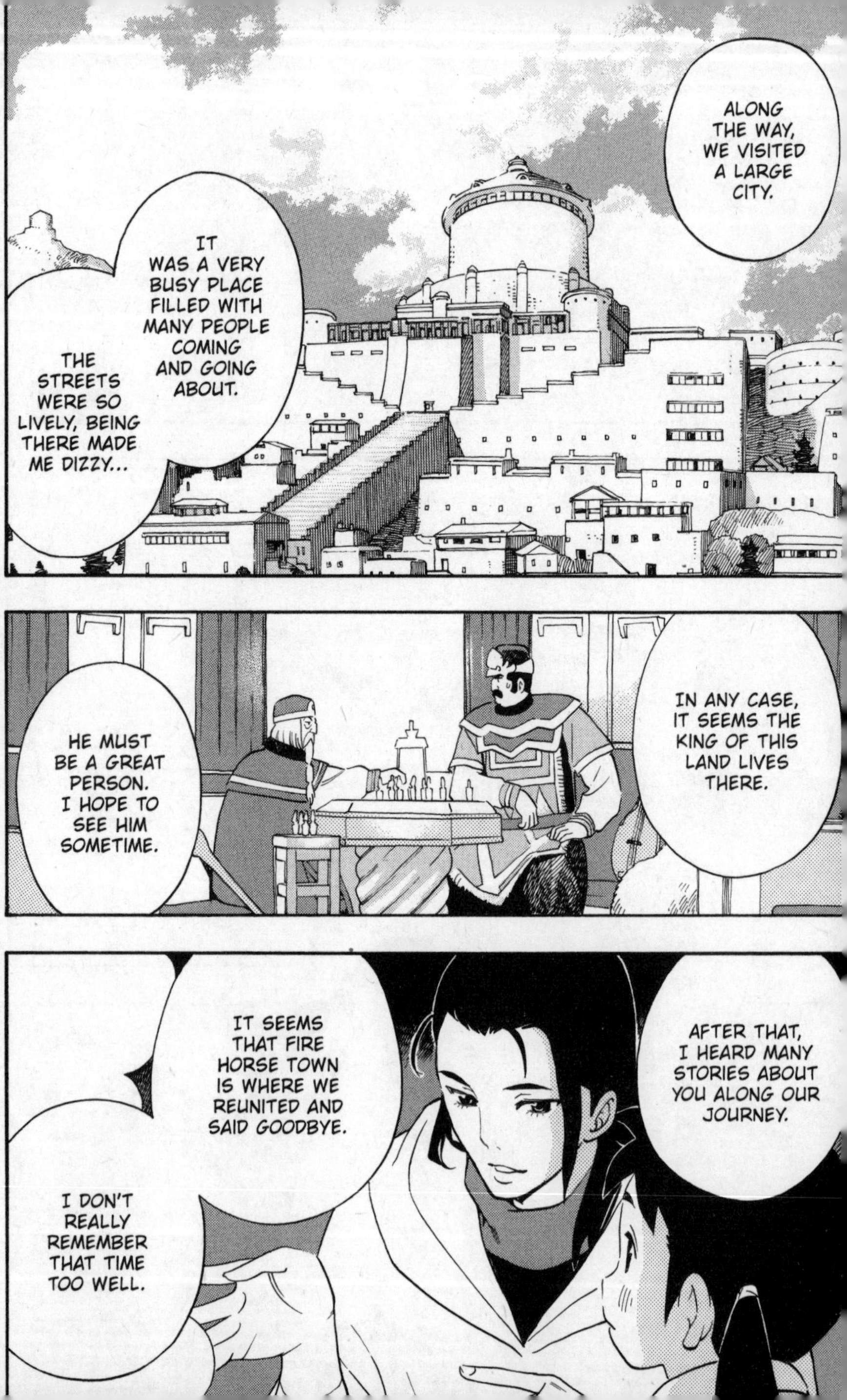
ALONG THE WAY, WE VISITED A LARGE CITY.
IT WAS A VERY BUSY PLACE FILLED WITH MANY PEOPLE COMING AND GOING ABOUT.
THE STREETS WERE SO LIVELY, BEING THERE MADE ME DIZZY...
IN ANY CASE, IT SEEMS THE KING OF THIS LAND LIVES THERE.
HE MUST BE A GREAT PERSON. I HOPE TO SEE HIM SOMETIME.
AFTER THAT, I HEARD MANY STORIES ABOUT YOU ALONG OUR JOURNEY.
IT SEEMS THAT FIRE HORSE TOWN IS WHERE WE REUNITED AND SAID GOODBYE.
I DON'T REALLY REMEMBER THAT TIME TOO WELL.

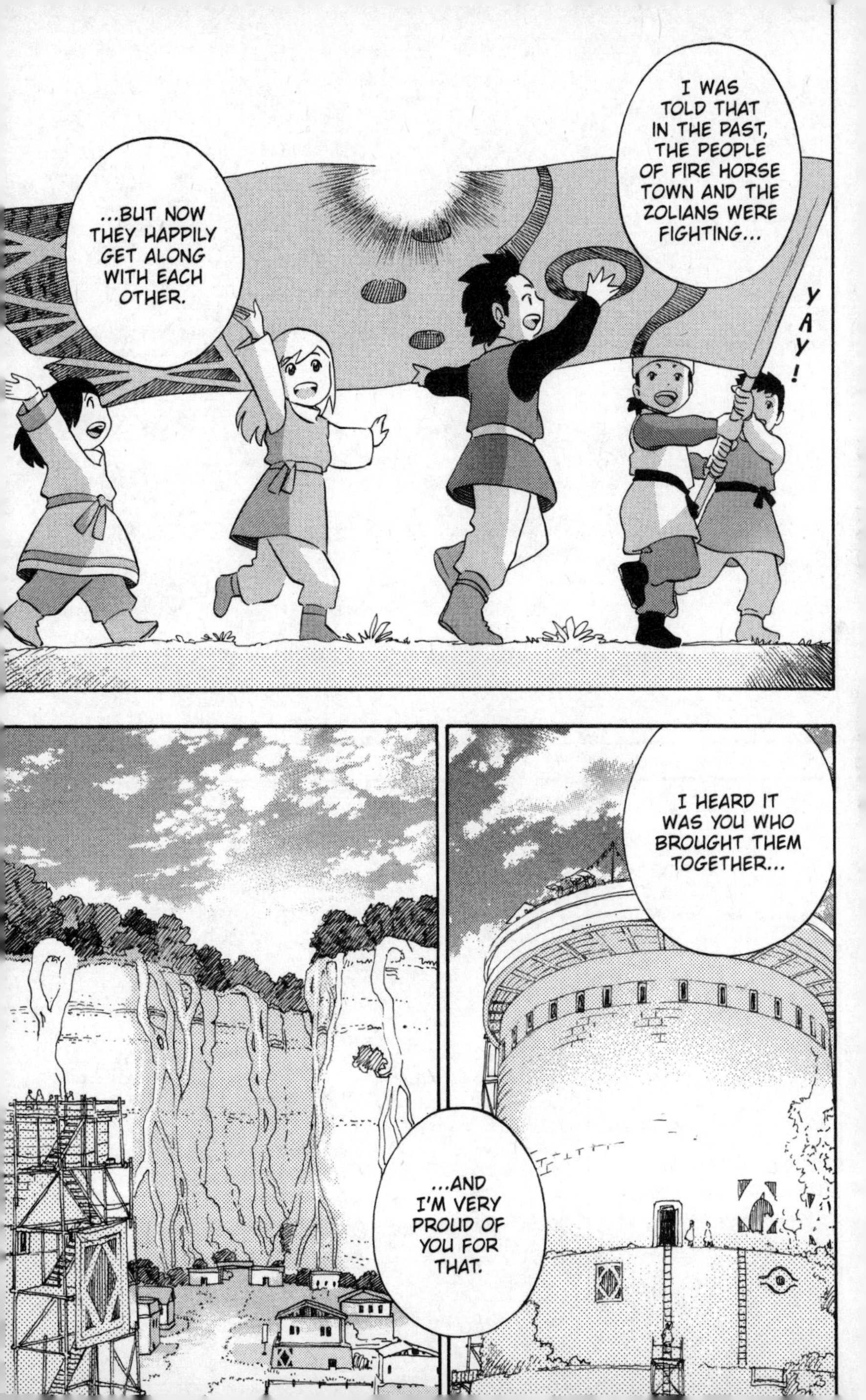
I WAS TOLD THAT IN THE PAST, THE PEOPLE OF FIRE HORSE TOWN AND THE ZOLIANS WERE FIGHTING...
YAY!
...BUT NOW THEY HAPPILY GET ALONG WITH EACH OTHER.
I HEARD IT WAS YOU WHO BROUGHT THEM TOGETHER...
...AND I'M VERY PROUD OF YOU FOR THAT.

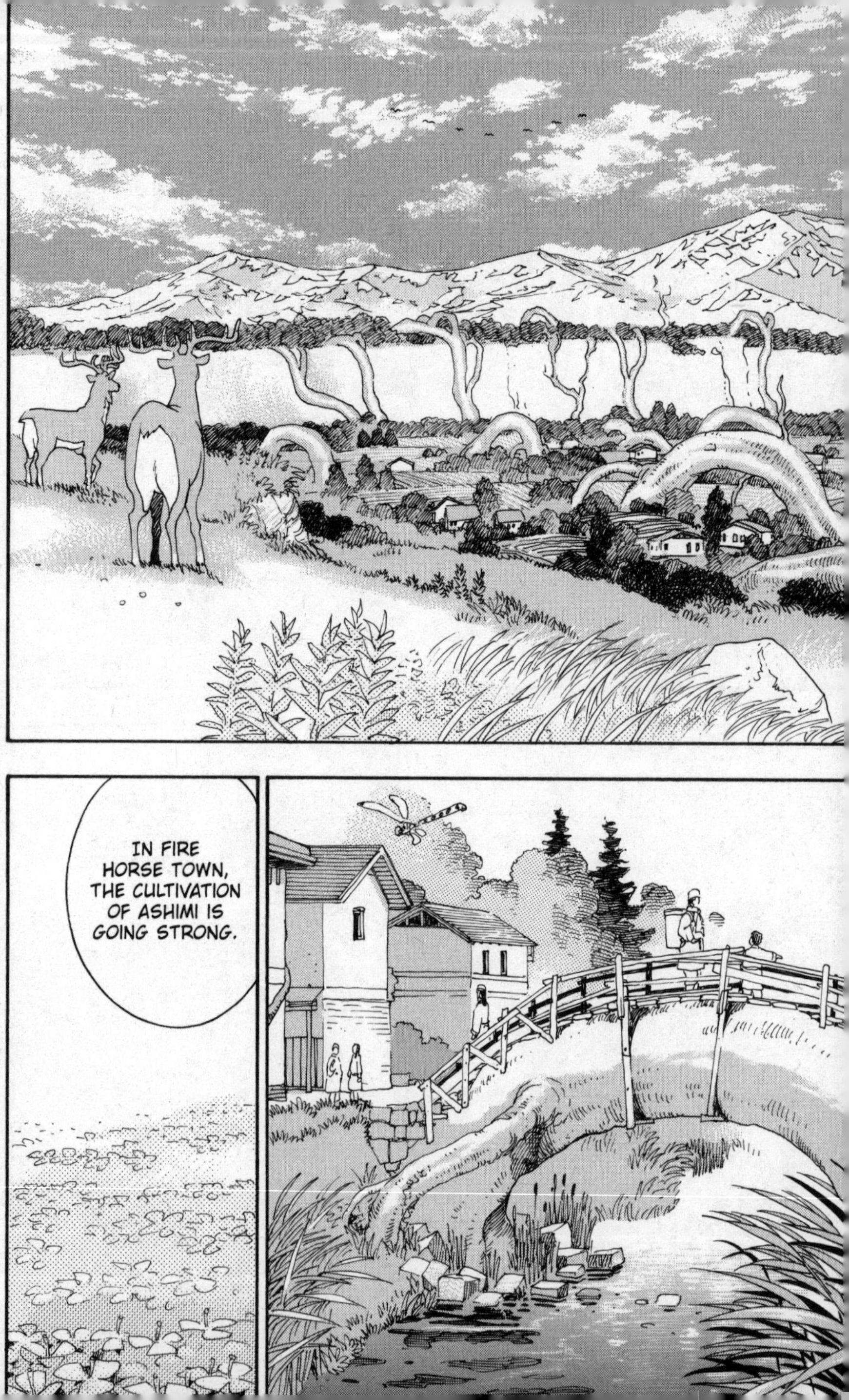
IN FIRE HORSE TOWN, THE CULTIVATION OF ASHIMI IS GOING STRONG.

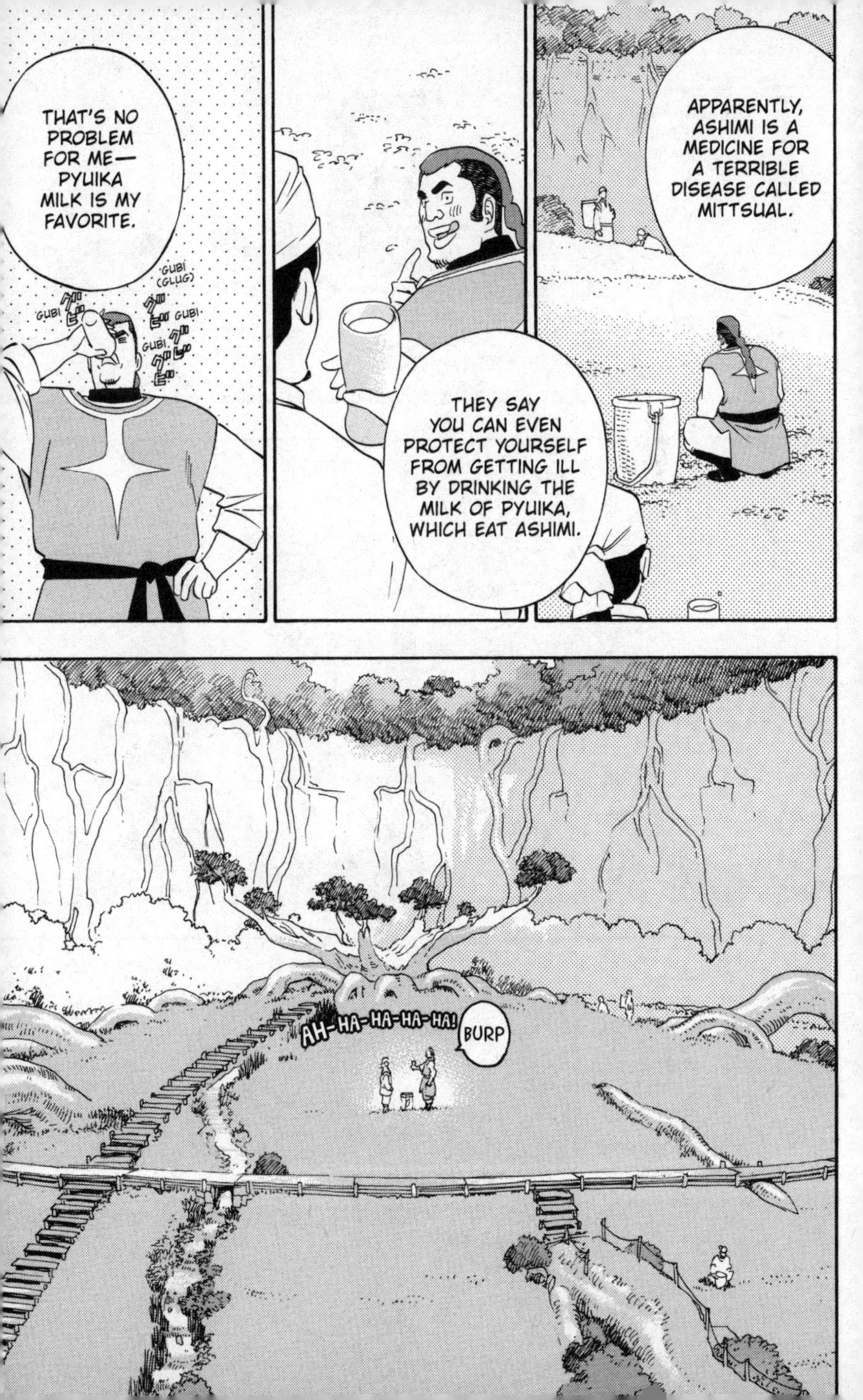
APPARENTLY, ASHIMI IS A MEDICINE FOR A TERRIBLE DISEASE CALLED MITTSUAL.
THEY SAY YOU CAN EVEN PROTECT YOURSELF FROM GETTING ILL BY DRINKING THE MILK OF PYUIKA, WHICH EAT ASHIMI.
THAT'S NO PROBLEM FOR ME—PYUIKA MILK IS MY FAVORITE.
GUBI (GLUG)
GUBI
GUBI
GUBI
AH-HA-HA-HA-HA!
BURP

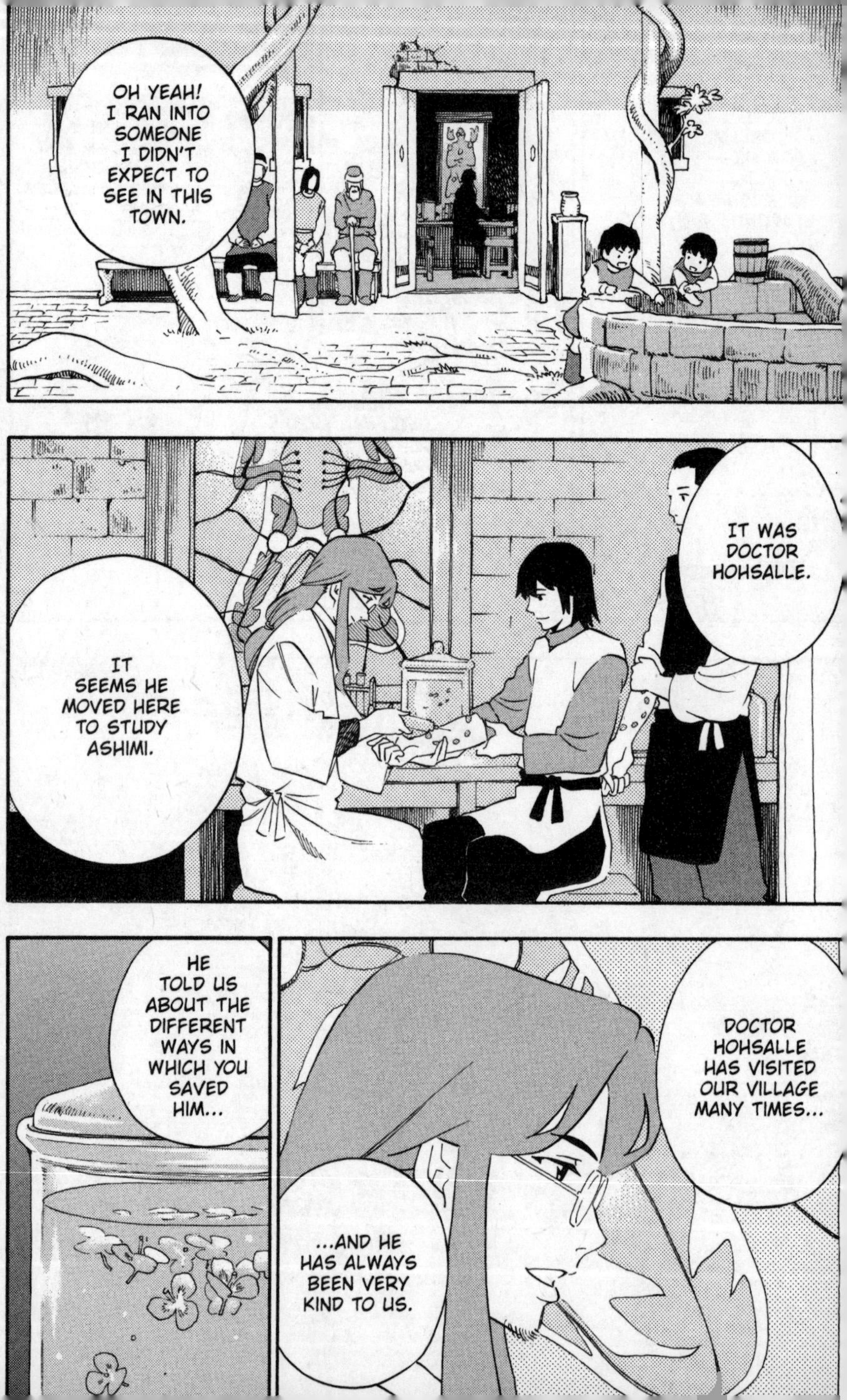
OH YEAH! I RAN INTO SOMEONE I DIDN'T EXPECT TO SEE IN THIS TOWN.
IT WAS DOCTOR HOHSALLE.
IT SEEMS HE MOVED HERE TO STUDY ASHIMI.
DOCTOR HOHSALLE HAS VISITED OUR VILLAGE MANY TIMES...
...AND HE HAS ALWAYS BEEN VERY KIND TO US.
HE TOLD US ABOUT THE DIFFERENT WAYS IN WHICH YOU SAVED HIM...

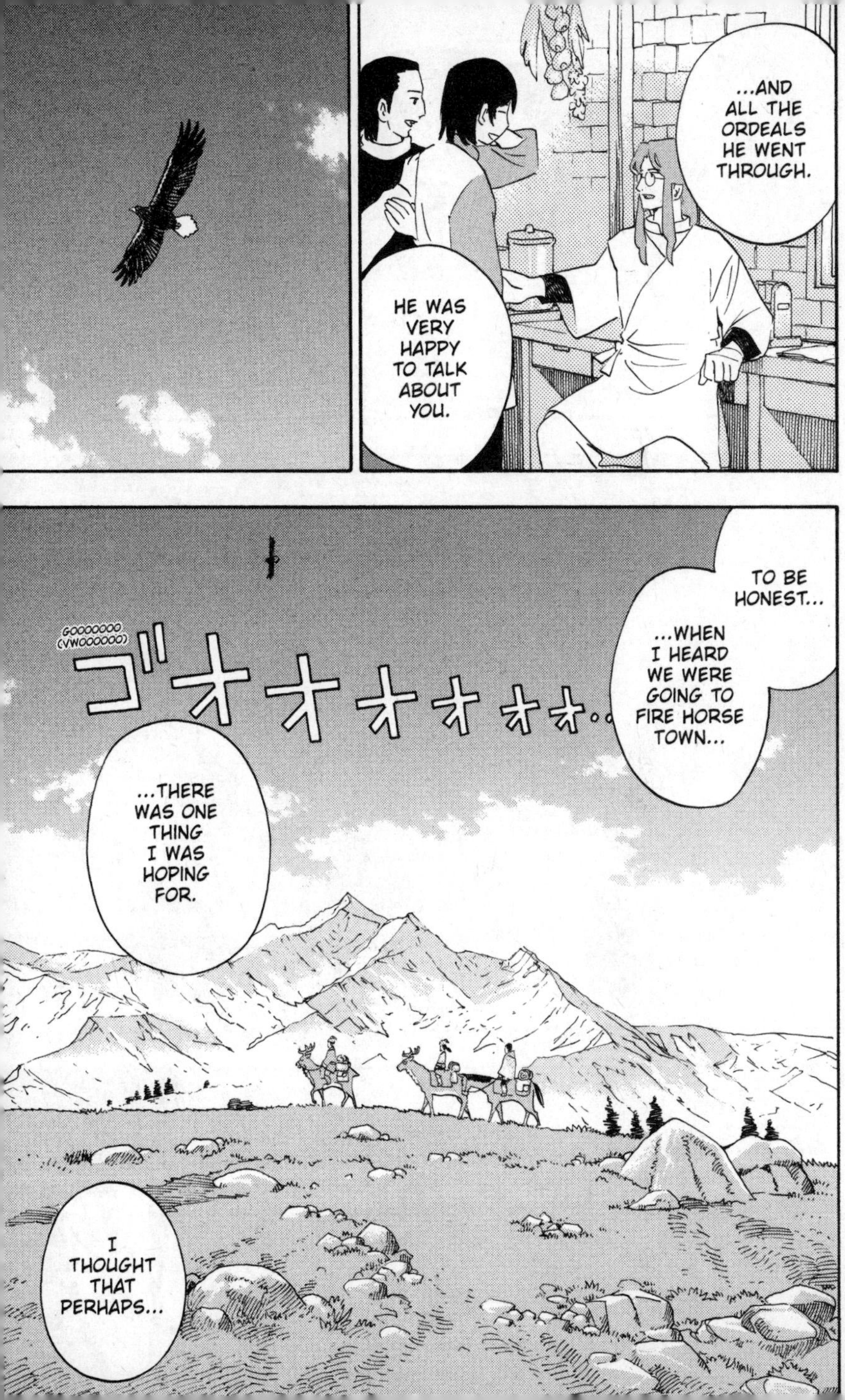
...AND ALL THE ORDEALS HE WENT THROUGH.
HE WAS VERY HAPPY TO TALK ABOUT YOU.
TO BE HONEST...
...WHEN I HEARD WE WERE GOING TO FIRE HORSE TOWN...
GOOOOOOO (VWOOOOOO)
ゴオオオオォォ..
...THERE WAS ONE THING I WAS HOPING FOR.
I THOUGHT THAT PERHAPS...

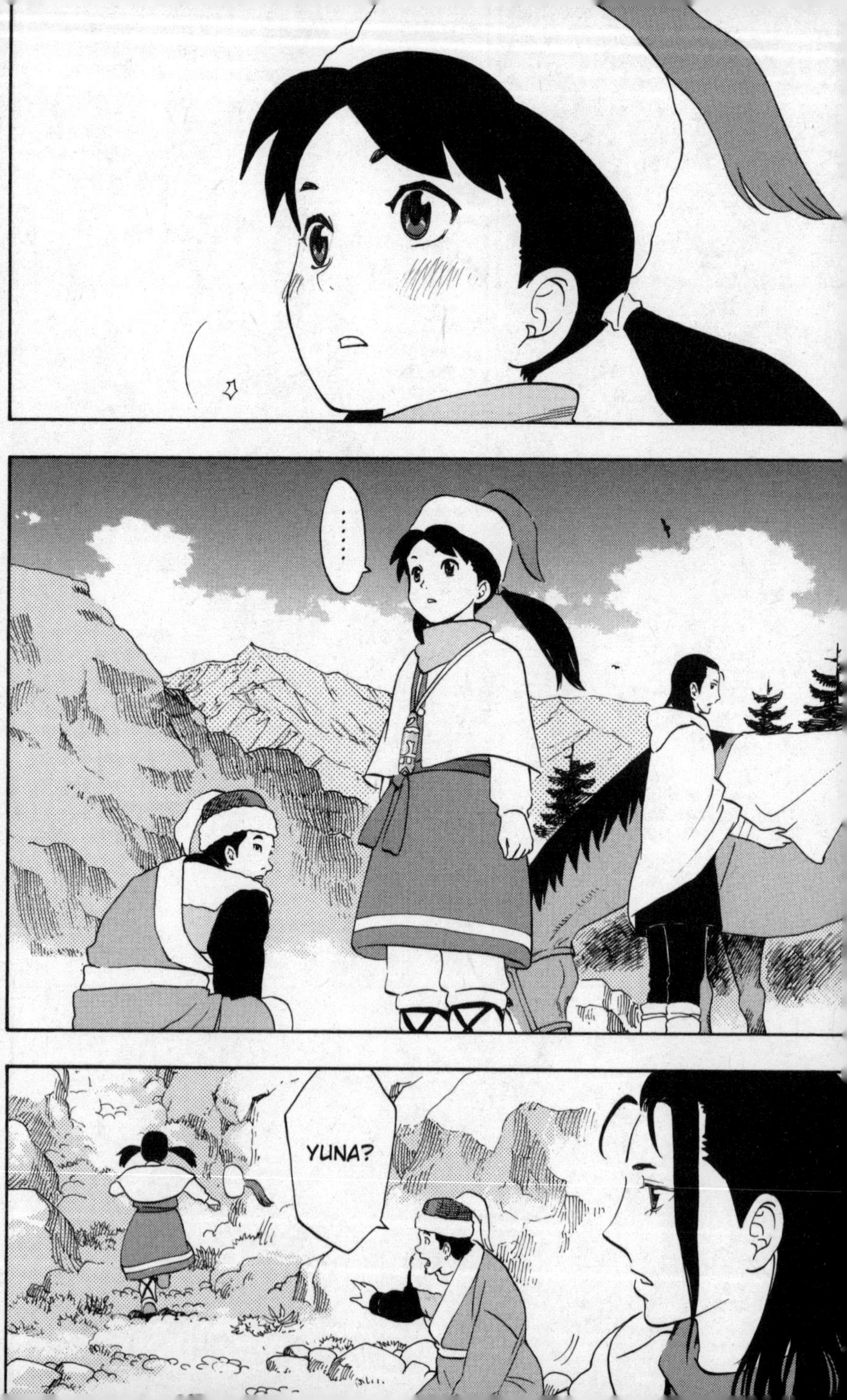
......
YUNA?

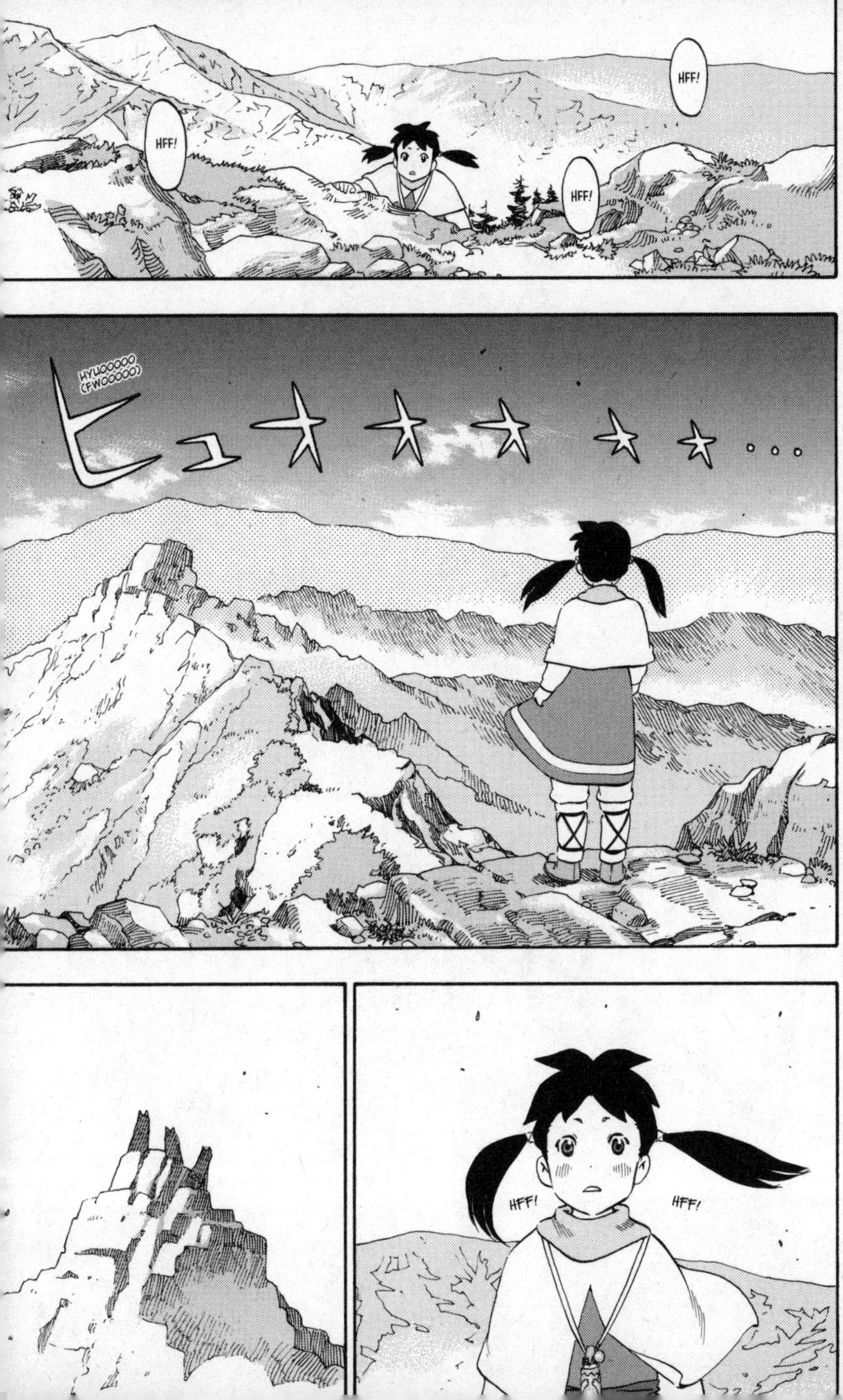
HFF!
HFF!
HFF!
HYUOOOOO (FWOOOOO)
ヒュオオオォォ…
HFF!
HFF!

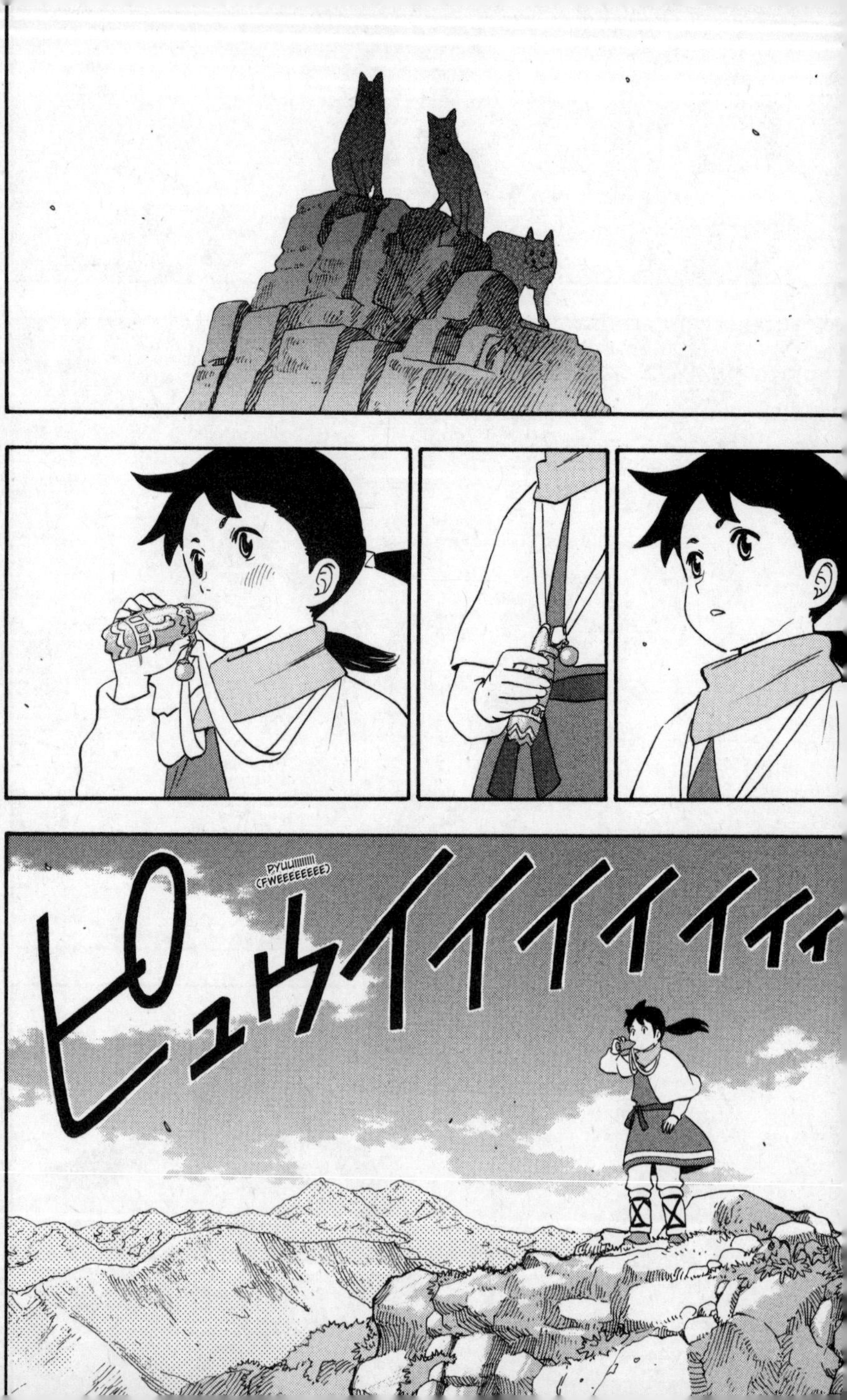
ピュウイイイイイ
PYUUIIIIIIIIIII
(FWEEEEEEEEE)

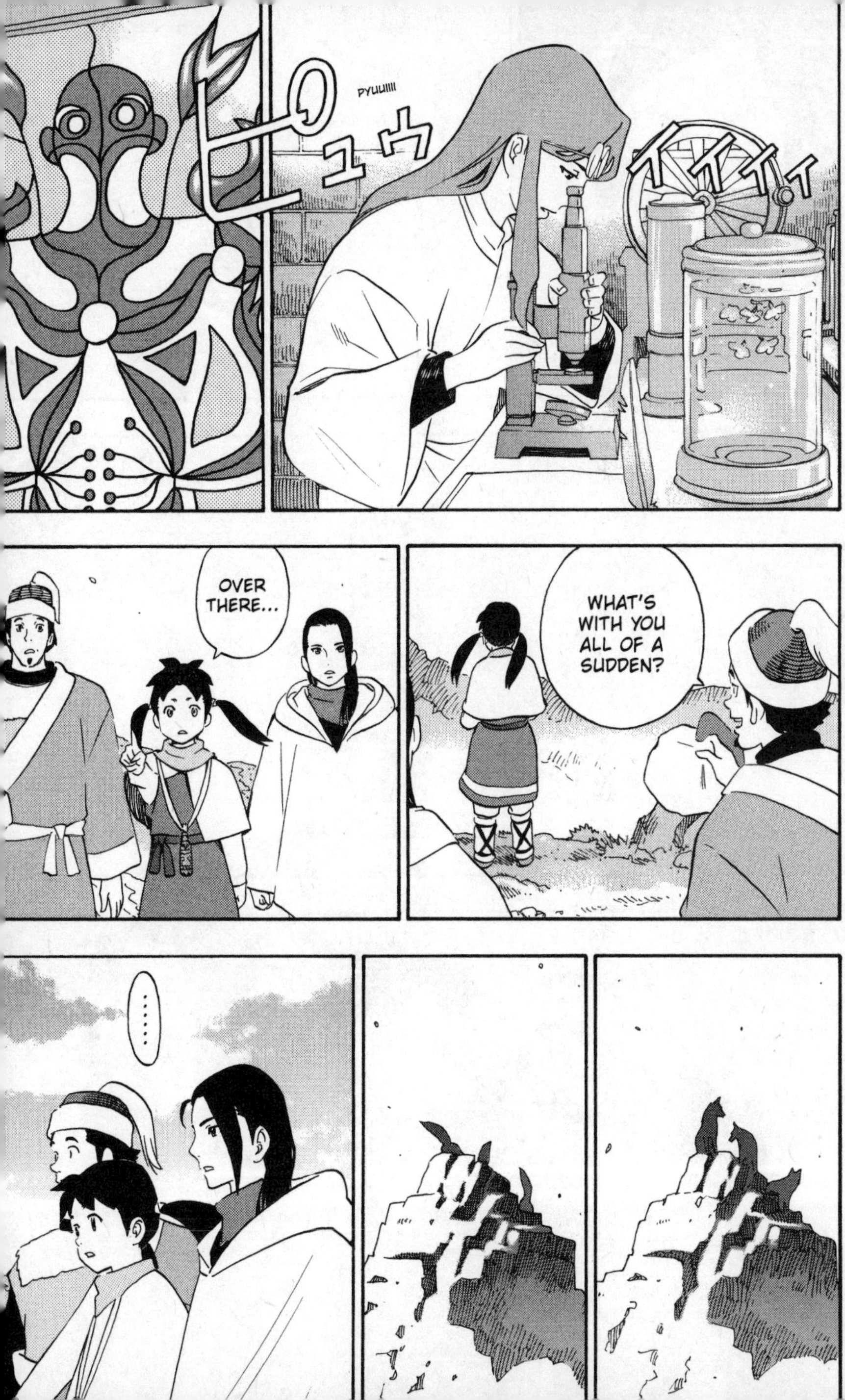
ピュウ
PYUUIIII
イイイィ
WHAT'S WITH YOU ALL OF A SUDDEN?
OVER THERE...
......

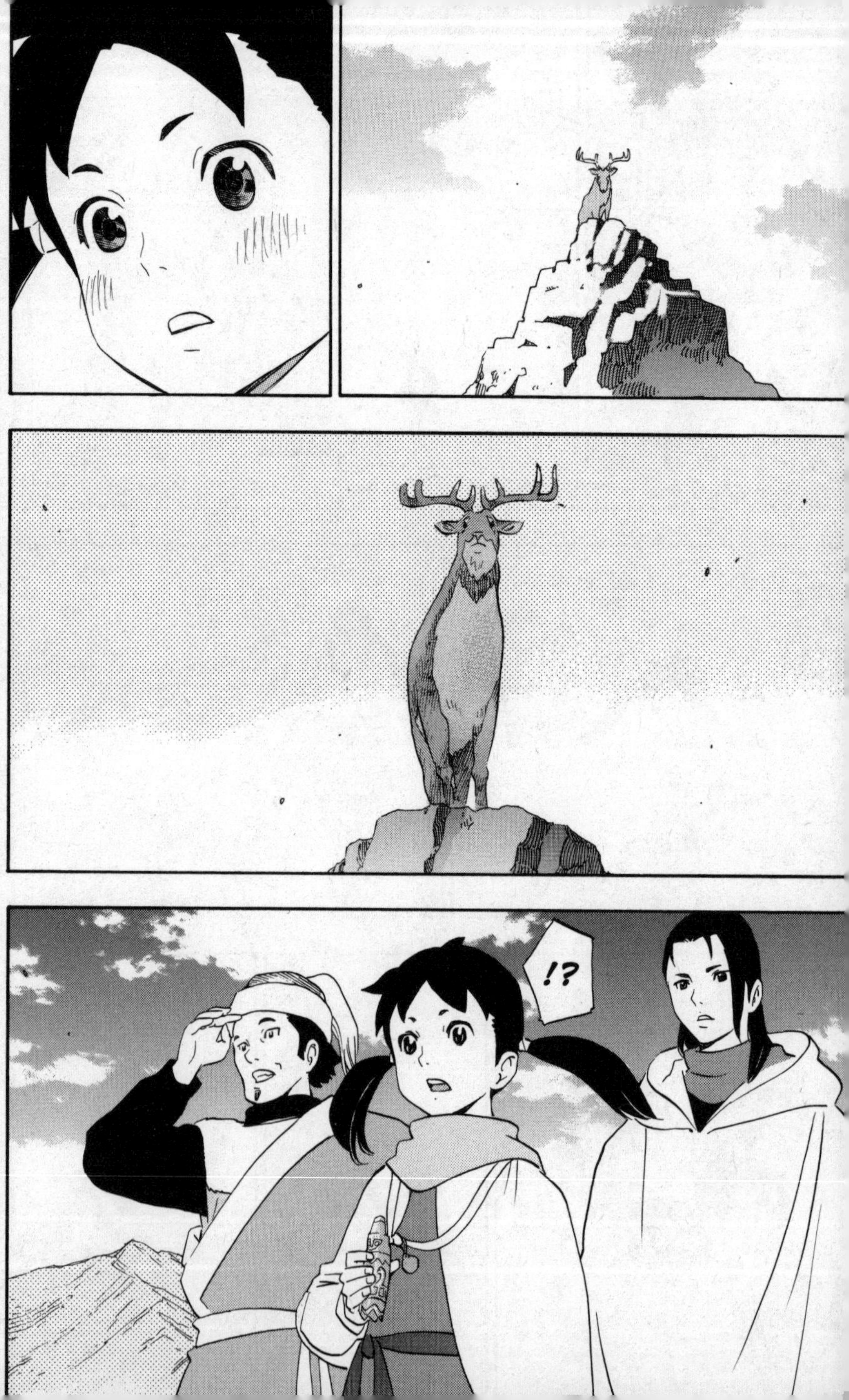
!?

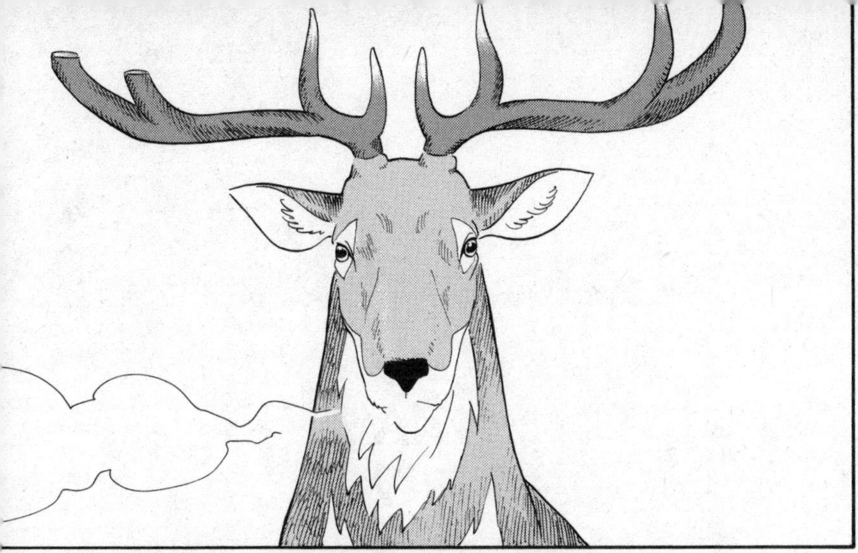

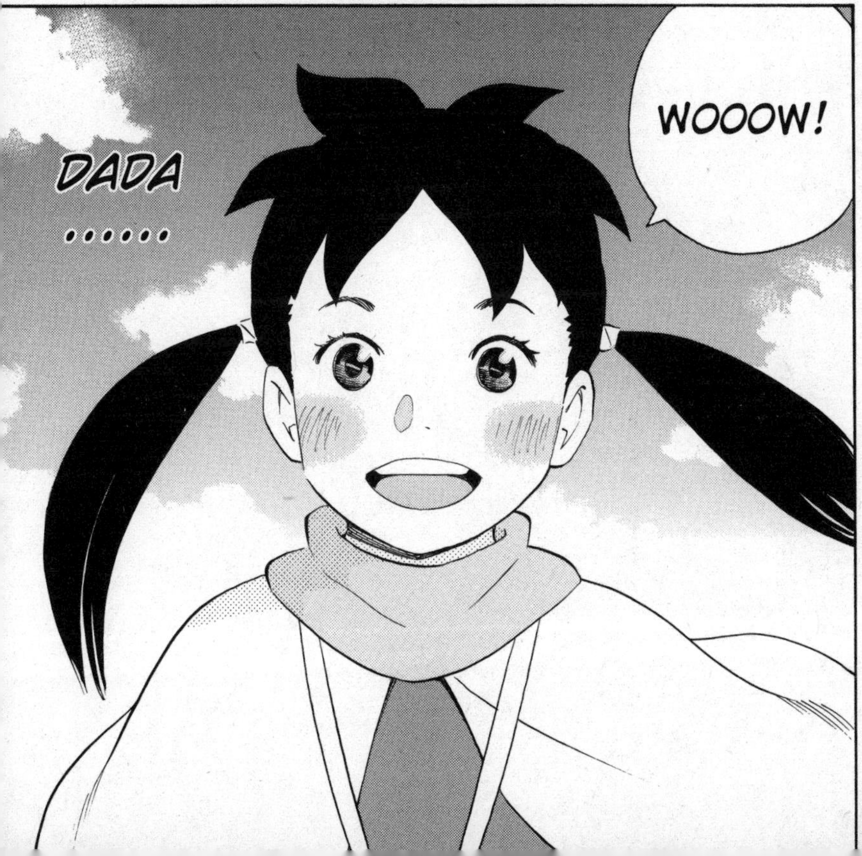
WOOOW!
DADA ......

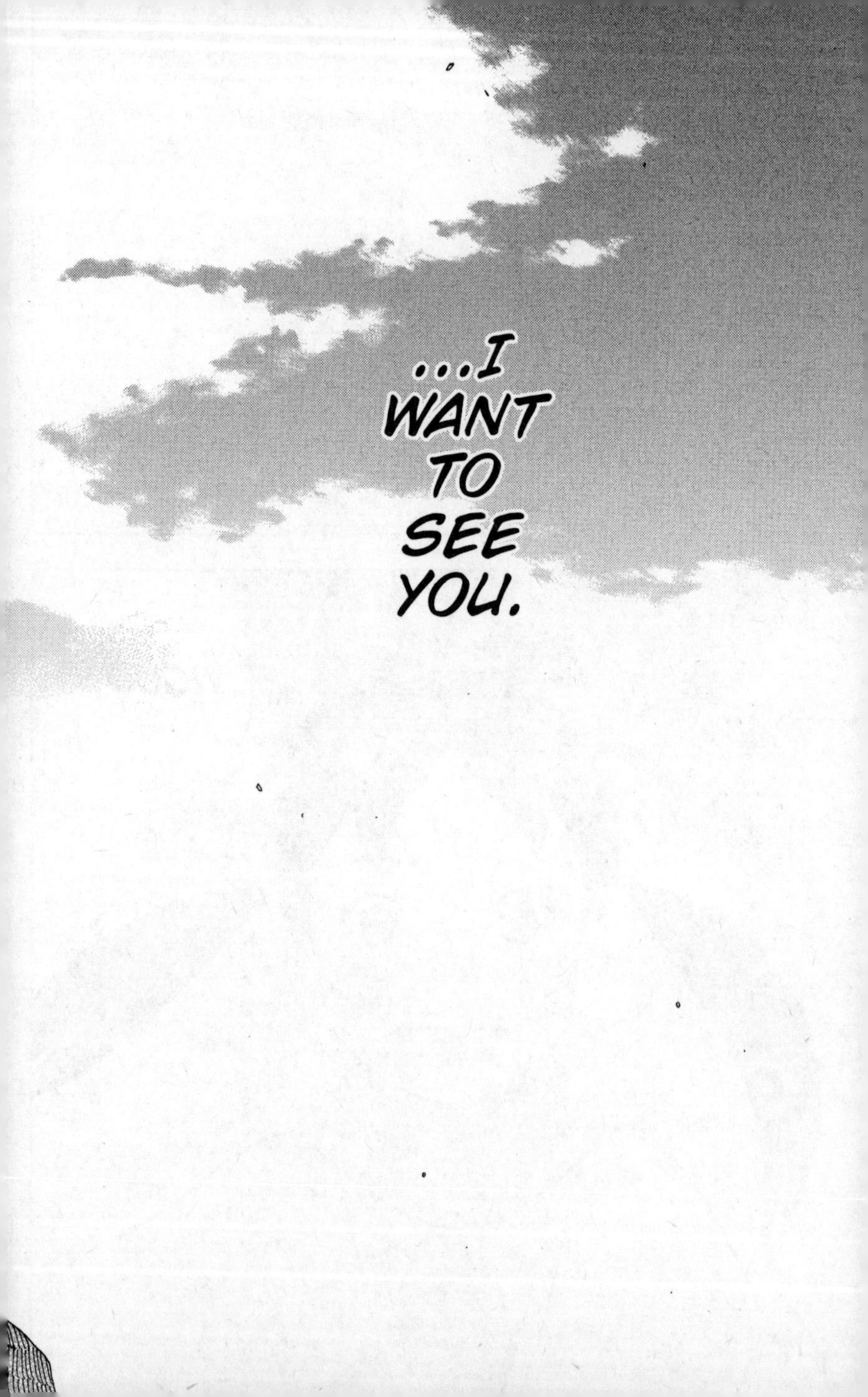
...I WANT TO SEE YOU.

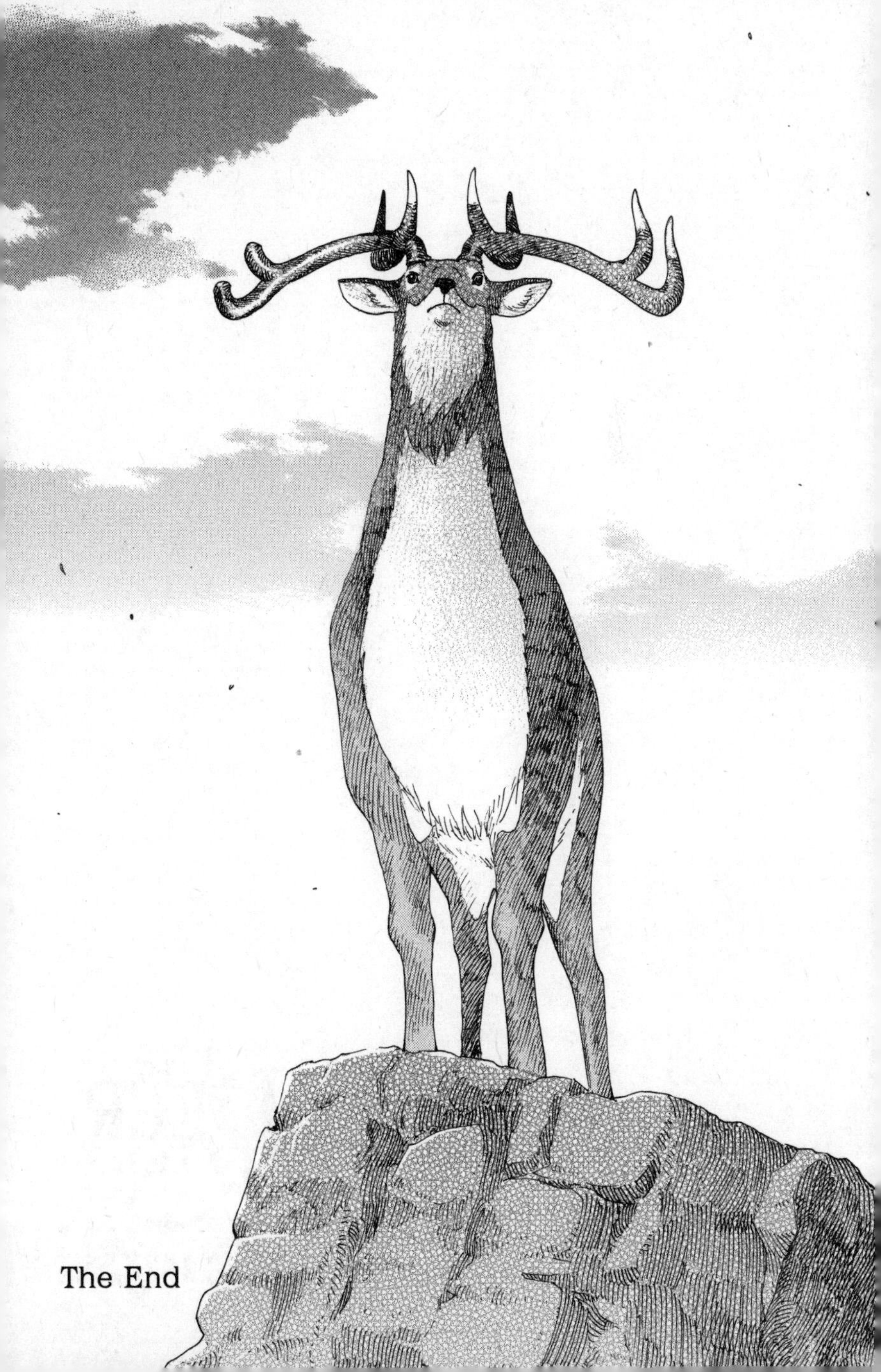
The End

THE
DEER
KING

YUNA AND THE
PROMISED JOURNEY

THIS IS MY FIRST
FULL-FLEDGED
FANTASY WORK.
I WANT TO EXPRESS MY
GRATITUDE TO NAHOKO
UEHASHI-SENSEI AND
EVERYONE ELSE INVOLVED.

ABOVE ALL,

THANK
YOU TO
ALL THE
READERS
FOR YOUR
LOVE AND
SUPPORT.

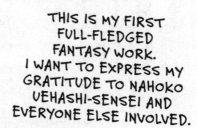

MAY THE
PLAGUE BE
VANQUISHED!

Special Thanks
to KAMI-SAN

Afterword    Taro Sekiguchi

# THE DEER KING 2

## YUNA AND THE PROMISED JOURNEY

Original Story:
**Nahoko Uehashi**
Art:
**Taro Sekiguchi**
Adaptation:
*The Deer King* Production Committee

Translation:
Ajani Oloye
Lettering:
Phil Christie

This book is a work of fiction. Names, characters, places, and incidents are the product of the author's imagination or are used fictitiously. Any resemblance to actual events, locales, or persons, living or dead, is coincidental.

SHIKA NO O YUNA TO YAKUSOKU NO TABI Vol. 2
©Nahoko Uehashi 2022
©Taro Sekiguchi 2022
©2021 "The Deer King" Production Committee
First published in Japan in 2022 by KADOKAWA CORPORATION, Tokyo.
English translation rights arranged with KADOKAWA CORPORATION, Tokyo
through TUTTLE-MORI AGENCY, INC., Tokyo.

English translation © 2024 by Yen Press, LLC

Yen Press
150 West 30th Street, 19th Floor
New York, NY 10001

Visit us!
yenpress.com • facebook.com/yenpress • twitter.com/yenpress
yenpress.tumblr.com • instagram.com/yenpress

First Yen Press Edition: January 2024
Edited by Yen Press Editorial: Ren Leon, Mark Gallucci
Designed by Yen Press Design: Andy Swist

Yen Press is an imprint of Yen Press, LLC.
The Yen Press name and logo are trademarks of Yen Press, LLC.

The publisher is not responsible for websites (or their content) that are not owned by the publisher.

Library of Congress Control Number: 2023941089

ISBNs: 978-1-9753-6299-7 (paperback)
       978-1-9753-6300-0 (ebook)

10 9 8 7 6 5 4 3 2 1

WOR

Printed in the United States of America